THE
GLAMORGANSHIRE
AND
ABERDARE
CANALS

Caeglas Lock. ILW photo 12 Feb 1944, neg 253

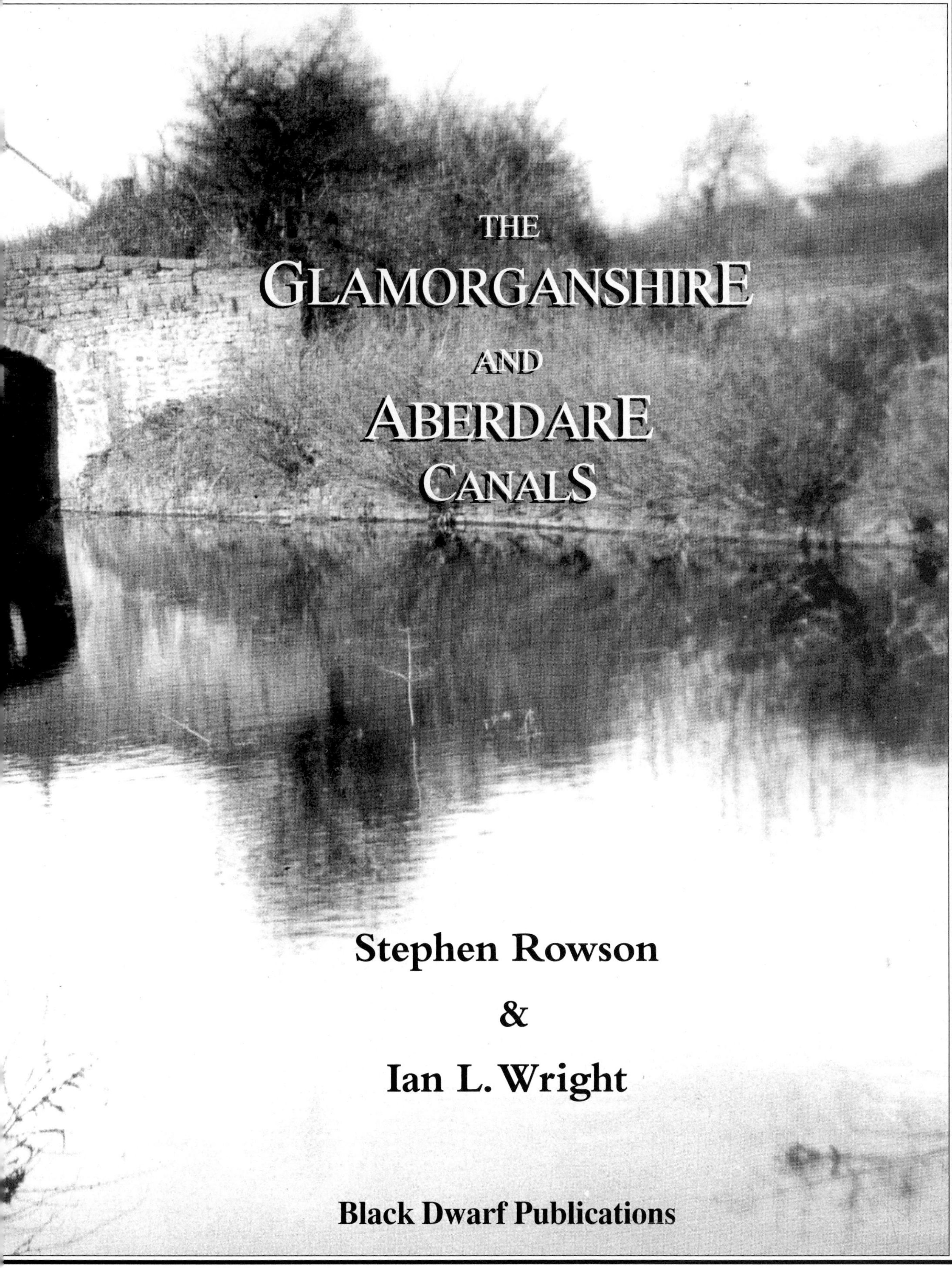

THE
GLAMORGANSHIRE
AND
ABERDARE
CANALS

Stephen Rowson

&

Ian L. Wright

Black Dwarf Publications

The watercolourist John Petherick responds to human activity in the Taff Valley; in this scene executed on 12 July 1854, looking south from Ynysangharad, Pontypridd. The acutely observed Glamorganshire Canal reveals Thomas Dadford's winding embankments, whilst the stone quarry on the Merthyr road is a reminder of Pentrebach's intensive exploitation of Pennant building stone. The quarry, probably associated with the canal trade, had connections with the Mantle family. Note the mooring posts on the approach to the locks and lower basin at Brown Lenox (out of picture) and, beyond them, the horse slip set into the towpath. Petherick has even included the waste stream making its way to the river below the canal's embankment. In the far distance are the chimneys of the Taff Vale ironworks.

Courtesy National Museums & Galleries of Wales

THE
GLAMORGANSHIRE
AND
ABERDARE
CANALS

TWO WELSH WATERWAYS AND THEIR INDUSTRIES

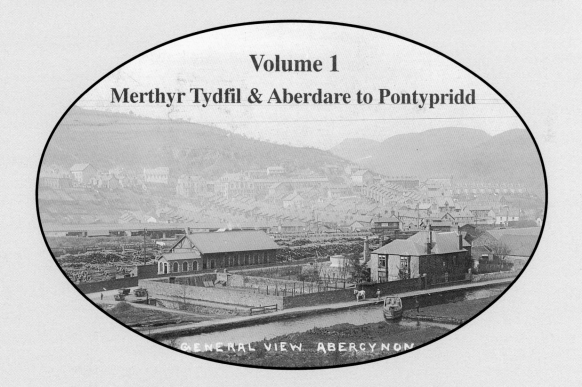

Volume 1
Merthyr Tydfil & Aberdare to Pontypridd

GENERAL VIEW ABERCYNON

Stephen Rowson & Ian L. Wright

Black Dwarf Publications

British Library Cataloguing-in-Publication Data. A catalogue
record for this book is available from the British Library
ISBN 0 9533028 9 X

Black Dwarf Publications
47 – 49 High Street, Lydney, Gloucestershire GL15 5DD

Printed by APB Process Print, Bristol

VOLUME 1
MERTHYR TYDFIL & ABERDARE to PONTYPRIDD

CONTENTS

PREFACE

In 1986 Harold Morgan approached me for a talk to the Welsh Railways Research Circle on the subject of the Glamorganshire Canal. It was to be one of a season of Saturday afternoon meetings to celebrate 150 years since the Taff Vale Railway got its Act. He had already been turned down by his first choice lecturer so he was ready to counter my reticence by thrusting his copy of John Lloyd's *The Early History of the Old South Wales Ironworks* into my hands and telling me to go away and prepare something special. It certainly was a daunting task as I knew how intense are the members of the WRRC and that they expect at least two hours of minutiae from a speaker. I agreed to the request not just out of personal flattery but (in some anthropomorphic sense) on behalf of the canal itself – that Harold should have acknowledged a place for the TVR's antecedent in his programme.

The task of preparing a lecture was to discipline me into getting my information on the canal into some semblance of order. I had plenty of photographs to put onto slide but I needed something to add coherence to what other documentary material I had been collecting over my years of interest in the canal. Nothing significant had been written on the canal since Charles Hadfield's *The Canals of South Wales and the Border* (Ian Wright's *Canals in Wales*, he will agree, was primarily a picture book) and I knew the WRRC would expect more. I had to go to primary sources so I sought Gordon Rattenbury's advice. Gordon's response was obvious –

"Read the minute books."

"But they're at the National Library at Aberystwyth."

"Yes, but there's a complete authenticated copy in the Bute deposits at Cardiff Central Library."

I felt stupid – how had this eluded me? I spent the following few Saturdays at the library and immersed myself in 150 years of canal company minutes. Preparing for that talk made me realise what rich material is available for a new history of the Glamorganshire Canal and from a slightly different viewpoint than Charles Hadfield's study. I did toy with the idea of an MA in Local History based on the minute books but concluded that, being a working man, I could not justify the time! A more manageable project on the water supply alone still came to nothing.

I was brought up in Llandaff North, which lies on the route of the canal. My fascination in the canal stems from its industrial archaeology and how it changed the landscape of the Taff Valley. From the late 1960s I was to walk the route several times from Merthyr Tydfil to Cardiff, searching out the lock sites, wharves, water intakes, weirs and the lines of connecting tramroads from ironworks and colliery. During that time much of the route has been systematically destroyed by road making. My favourite location was the section from Merthyr to Gethin, which I reconnoitred armed with the first edition 25 inch OS maps and a cherished copy of Pedler's *History of the Hamlet of Gellideg*. I am particularly saddened how much of the canal's hinterland there has been altered recently.

The idea of a book was suggested when in 1994 I published an article on the canal in the first edition of Lightmoor Press's *Archive* journal. By then I realised that, whilst the volume of material available for the first hundred years was huge but easily accessible, details of the sixty or so years of final decline were more difficult to come by. I had not known the canal in operation and had interviewed only a couple of surviving boatmen.

However, I was well aware that in the 1940s Ian Wright had sought out and interviewed several of the last canal employees and boatmen, and had been in regular correspondence with Bill Hamlin whose family had run a business at the Sea Lock in Cardiff. Ian also had himself photographed the canal in its final years and only some of these images had been published in his *Canals in Wales*. Whilst Bill prefers to keep his own material private, Ian and I agreed to pooling our resources and writing this book.

Our aims are really to add a more detailed dimension to what Charles Hadfield has already written so admirably. Another general history was not required, even if it were to accompany a book of previously unpublished photographs. A picture book would have been very easy to produce, and we have turned down that opportunity more than once. Because we have gone for detail, we acknowledge that the result is not uniform – it depends on what primary information survives and that we have uncovered. Not all the information we have included necessarily leads to an interpretation or conclusion. A quest for uniformity would have resulted in another general history based on secondary sources with all the mistakes that would inherit. Instead, what we offer is a sourcebook on the Glamorganshire Canal and the industries it served, which can be used for further research by school children, local historians, family historians and industrial archaeologists alike. For this last reason, and mindful that our approach has doubtless led us to creating errors of interpretation of our own, we have sought to include exhaustive references to the text.

Stephen A. Rowson
Cardiff, March 2001

I continue to be astonished – and awed – by the passage of time. My clearest memory of life on the Glamorganshire Canal is also my earliest: a GCC horse boat loaded with bagged flour for Pontypridd, making its way past the Castle estate of the Marquess of Bute bordering Cardiff's North Road and the Cathays Park. The year would have been around 1935. I was a schoolboy at the time, seeing it all from the top of a Kingsway - Rhiwbina bus. This image of the 1930s was already quite rare and was to disappear forever during the dark days of the Second World War.

Before starting war service in 1944, I had taken photographs on the canal and had explored the whole of the Cardiff-to-Merthyr towpath a number of times, a chapter in Edgar Chappell's *History of the Port of Cardiff* (1939) having stimulated further interest. After the war, much of the canal survived but it was in a mouldering state. Making a record of the canal was one thing but what about the people who had spent their working lives on the boats, on the locks and along the canal banks? Who was interested in them? Over 50 years ago I went on to record what boatmen and lockkeepers had to say and I have now come to regard this oral tradition as an important strand in the fabric of Welsh social history. The people of the boats have almost all gone. Even the streets and terraces they lived in have been flattened – *"systematically destroyed by road making"* as Stephen Rowson has described it.

Since 1965 my work on the Glamorganshire Canal has been confined to articles in magazines and journals. It has therefore been such a pleasure for me to work jointly with Stephen in writing this present book. He has already made clear our aims.

One of the aims of the book must be to throw light on the character and motives of powerful masters of industry and their interaction in the pursuit of trade and profit. But equally for both writers, it is the Glamorganshire Canal itself, as an example of 18th century engineering and working technology, that has captured our imagination. Here we have been especially fortunate in finding a publisher with similar enthusiasm to our own who has allowed us the space to reveal the canal in the detail it deserves; to move from the general and to look more closely at the particular. Perhaps also, between us, we may be able to convey an idea, not only of what the canal looked like but of what it felt like.

A word about Bill Hamlin who, indirectly, has contributed to this book. In 1969, Bill, a Cardiff schoolmaster, embarked on work towards his Glamorganshire Canal Source Pack for Cardiff schools. He contacted me and I was able to help with information and photographs, the pack being circulated in 1972. It is important that I put on record this impressive body of research work done by Bill in those years in Cardiff Central Library, Glamorgan Record Office and in Cardiff Corporation's Estate office – at a time when I could visit Cardiff only infrequently. Copies of all this material, including a number of key newspaper references and photographs from his collection, he has generously shared with me. Bill's behind-the-scenes assistance to me over many years is gratefully acknowledged.

Ian L. Wright
Whittlesford, March 2001

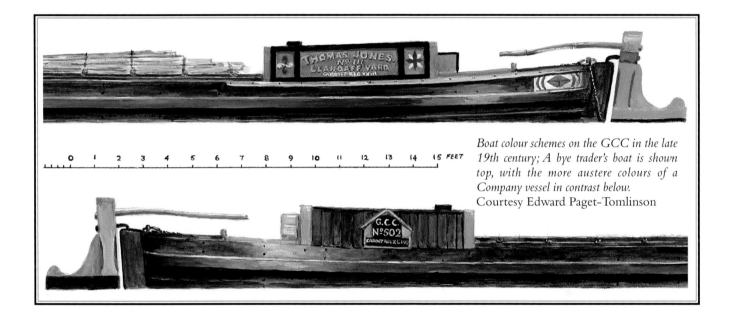

Boat colour schemes on the GCC in the late 19th century; A bye trader's boat is shown top, with the more austere colours of a Company vessel in contrast below.
Courtesy Edward Paget-Tomlinson

SPELLING

In many places the authors have found it difficult to standardise on spelling of place names and even of people's names. Spelling can fluctuate wildly. This is not necessarily through official anglicisation but simply through map-makers, letter-writers and copyists quite naturally placing their own interpretation on the spoken word. The spellings of many place names and family names have, indeed, evolved over two hundred years. For some, perhaps there is no accepted single spelling.

When quoting from primary hand-written documents we have tried to reproduce the original case and spelling. Elsewhere we have attempted to adopt a standard spelling. For example: Glyndyrus, Waun Wyllt, Coedpenmaen, Ynysangharad. Certain places seem to have their own spellings perpetuated on the canal, possibly because of the re-printing of its Table of Distances even when most of the mis-spellings seem to have been acknowledged. So we have Penydarran and Penydarren; Pontydderwen and Pontcaederwen, Perthyglyson and Perthygleision; Caerty Du and Cae Ty Du.

One ubiquitous place name is very difficult to spell consistently, and that is Dyffryn or is it Duffryn? Particularly in the Cynon valley we have tried our best to use the correct spelling for colliery names. The Powell Duffryn Company absorbed several of the Dyffryn collieries.

The most inconsistently spelt family name seems to be Llewellyn (Llewellin or Llewelyn) but there are also Davies (Davis) and Prichard (Pritchard). Even Copeland appears as Copland and Forrest as Fforest. If we adjust the spellings there is a danger that two people become one.

A final note on the alternatives for tramroad (dramroad) and waggon (wagon). Not just in South Wales but the West Country too, the word 'dramroad' slips off the tongue more easily than 'tramroad' and this seems to have been the case since the beginning of the period of our story. As far as we are concerned, the two words are interchangeable. As explained in the text, tramroads tend to be plate-ways (where the flange is on the tramplates and not on the waggon wheels), while railroads use edge rails (where the flange is on the wheel). We prefer to use 'tramway' for temporarily-laid lines and more recent light-railed lines from collieries and quarries. We have used 'waggon' for road and tramroad vehicles and 'wagon' for railways.

The reader will realise that the whole of the above is a disclaimer for any inconsistencies which remain in the text!

WEIGHTS & MEASURES

If the United Kingdom adopts the euro to replace the pound sterling, it will, no doubt, spawn a renewed fashion amongst history book authors of converting every historical monetary value in the text to its modern equivalent. This happened after decimalisation in February 1971, when the UK lost shillings and pence and gained New pence. The present authors have resisted what we feel is an unnecessary task, not only for monetary values but for weights and linear measurements too, where the metric system has now taken over. Here instead is a short explanation of what measures might be included in our text. It should be noted that for the whole period that the Glamorganshire Canal was in operation the weights and measures system remained constant.

Monetary Values

At the time of writing, the UK has not agreed to a common currency with other European states within the Economic and Monetary Union, and so there is not a fixed rate between the pound and the euro. In February 2000 £1 approximately equalled 61 euros.

Until 15 February 1971:
£1 = 20s (shillings)
1s = 12d (pence)
£1 = 240d

An amount of twelve shillings and sixpence might be written as 12s 6d or 12/6d and 12 shillings as 12s or 12/-.

A guinea was 21/- or £1 1s.

From February 1971, New pence were introduced and the UK abandoned the use of shillings and (old) pence. There are 100 New pence to the pound. Therefore, historical conversions are:
6d = $2^1/_2$p (New pence)
1s = 5p
1 guinea = £1.05

Weight

The UK's Avoirdupois system (dropped in 2000 in favour of the metric system) was:
1 pound = 16 ounces (1 lb = 16 oz)
1 stone = 14 lbs
1 quarter = 28 pounds
1 hundredweight = 112 pounds (1 cwt = 112 lbs)
1 ton = 20 cwt

On the canal they occasionally used the long ton (explained in the text) where
1 ton = 20 cwt – or even 21 cwt
but 1 cwt = 120 lbs (long weight)
The conversion to metric is:
1 ton = 1,016 kilogrammes
1 lb = 0.435 kilogrammes
[The metric tonne = 1,000 kilogrammes]

Linear Measure

1 foot = 12 inches (1 ft = 12 in, or 1' = 12")
1 yard = 3 feet
1 furlong = 220 yards
1 mile = 1,760 yards

In addition, surveyors' measures include:
1 rod (or pole, perch) = 25 links
1 chain = 4 rods = 22 yards

The conversion to metric is:
1 inch = 2.54 centimetres
1 foot = 30.48 centimetres
1 yard = 91.44 centimetres
1 chain = 20.12 metres
1 mile = 1.609 kilometres

Square Measure

1 acre = 4,840 square yards
The conversion to metric is:
1 acre = 40.47 ares = .4047 hectares

Capacity

The conversion to metric is:
1 gallon = 4.546 litres

ACKNOWLEDGEMENTS

The following, over the years have helped the authors in some way with information towards the writing of this book. To them we express our sincere thanks:

Colin Chapman, Brian Davies (Pontypridd), Chris Evans, John Evans (Blaenafon), Tom Evans (Aberdare), Bill Hamlin, Joseph Gross, Keith Harries, Tony Jukes, John Mear, Harold Morgan, John R. Norris, John Owen (Caerphilly), John Owen (Dowlais), Don Powell, Terry Powell, Gordon Rattenbury, Peter Tann, Dave Thomas (Ponthir), Richard Watson, Doug Williams, Robin Williams.

Members of Oxford House Industrial Archaeology Society, and staff at the following institutions: Aberdare Library, Aberdare Museum, Cardiff Central Library, Cyfarthfa Castle Museum, Glamorgan Record Office, House of Lords Records Office, Institute of Civil Engineers, Ironbridge Gorge Museum Trust, Merthyr Tydfil Library, National Library of Wales, National Museum of Wales, Pontypridd Historical Heritage Centre, Public Record Office, Welsh Folk Museum, Welsh Industrial and Maritime Museum, Worcestershire Record Office.

Those who have generously allowed photographs from their collections to be reproduced are acknowledged with the accompanying captions.

Introduction

THE STORY IN SUMMARY

The group of canals built in the South Wales valleys at the end of the 18th century had a common purpose – the improvement of communications between inland ironworks and the small ports on the Bristol Channel seaboard. The Glamorganshire was the first and greatest of these canals. It linked the ironworks of Merthyr Tydfil with the port of Cardiff, at that time a place of small importance with less than 2000 inhabitants. The engineer-contractors to the project were Thomas Dadford and son, assisted by Thomas Sheasby, and the principal promoters and shareholders were Richard Crawshay and Francis Homfray, ironmasters of Merthyr, who encouraged other industrialists, business interests and landowners to raise the necessary capital.

An Act of 1790 authorised a canal from Merthyr, down the valley of the Taff, to a shipping place on the river south of Cardiff. By 1792 the navigation was open to Treforest, near Pontypridd, and in 1794 it was completed to Cardiff. Meanwhile an extension had been opened from Merthyr to the ironworks at Cyfarthfa. In 1798 the canal was extended in Cardiff down to a sea lock, thus providing a mile long dock or floating harbour for shipping. The Glamorganshire was a valley-side canal, rising 543 feet in only $25^{1}/_{2}$ miles. Its 51 locks increased steeply in height towards the Merthyr end, where Dadford formed them in staircase pairs. At Nantgarw, uniquely on this canal, a three-rise lock staircase was built. A tunnel on the site of the medieval town moat took the canal under Queen Street in central Cardiff. Boats were horse drawn and measured 60 feet by 8 feet 9 inches, slightly shorter and wider than the English narrow boat.

From the beginning there were quarrels. In 1794 the canal was breached and the company was in dispute with Dadford, refusing money to repair the breach and alleging over-payments. Dadford walked off the site and took his construction men with him causing the GCC to opt for his arrest. The engineering expert of the day, Robert Whitworth, was called in for an opinion. He judged to the advantage of the Dadfords.

In 1798 there were acrimonious exchanges between dissident ironmasters and Richard Crawshay, who, as the most powerful and geographically advantaged shareholder, they accused of controlling the canal to his own personal gain. The dispute resulted in the building of the Merthyr Tramroad in 1802, which carried iron to a transshipment basin at Abercynon and brought back imported iron ore to the Dowlais, Penydarren and Plymouth works in Merthyr. Tramroads were important feeders to the Glamorganshire Canal and could be built under the 4 Mile Clause of the canal company's Act.

With increasing business and intensive use of locks, by far the most serious disputes were about water. The Hills of Plymouth works and Blakemore of Melingriffith both relied on water from the Taff for the operation of their works and complained for decades that the GCC was taking water from the river that was lawfully theirs. To help relieve the problem a waterwheel-operated beam pump was installed at Melingriffith and after 1806 a reservoir was constructed at Glyndyrus, near Merthyr, on the advice of John Rennie, whilst a steam pump was set up at Pontyrhun (Troedyrhiw) in 1809 to return water to the canal from Hill's works. Then, in 1821, water was stored in a reservoir built at Taffs Well to augment the Melingriffith supplies.

The Glamorganshire's Act of Parliament limited the company's dividend to 8% and so this very successful enterprise, now carrying increased tonnages of coal from the 1820s as well as iron, resorted to both reducing tolls and returning a percentage of tolls collected to the traders.

Success brought inevitable congestion along the line and at the Cardiff sea lock which had been lengthened in 1814. George Overton advised on a scheme for widening and deepening the Sea Lock pound but these improvements were opposed by Lord Bute on the grounds of encroachment. In 1828 James Green's plan for a Bute Ship Canal, separate from the Glamorganshire Canal, was recommended to Lord Bute and in 1830 the Marquess obtained an Act authorising the project, which became Cardiff's West Bute dock. The dock was opened in 1839 but the extended ship canal approach was omitted from the scheme. The Glamorganshire Canal's prosperity, kept buoyant on the iron trade and increasing steam coal exports, was not diminished by Lord Bute's dock. The canal was being worked around the clock, including Sundays, much extra business being generated by the Aberdare Canal, the Doctor's Canal and their tramroads. The heavy use of the locks produced a current which limited up-boats to a

Blast Furnaces Cyfarthfa, Merthyr.

The blast furnaces at Cyfarthfa steelworks, Merthyr, built on the site of the original Cyfarthfa ironworks. Cefn Coed can be seen on the distant hillside. It was the great ironworks of the Merthyr area – Plymouth, Penydarren, Dowlais and Cyfarthfa – and the need to be able to transport their produce to the port of Cardiff which led to the building of the Glamorganshire Canal, under the leadership of the forceful Richard Crawshay, owner of Cyfarthfa. By the time of this circa 1905 commercial postcard view, however, the iron trade in Merthyr was all but finished and the canal here had fallen out of use.
Bob Marrows collection

maximum loading of 15 tons. This in turn caused Merthyr-bound iron ore to be delayed on the wharves in Cardiff.

Frustrated by an overstretched canal with seasonal water shortages and periodic stoppages for repairs, the dissatisfied Hills of Plymouth works and Guests of Dowlais looked for a solution in a modern railway and joined others in promoting the Taff Vale Railway. Authorised in 1836, the TVR opened from Cardiff to Merthyr in 1841 but steam coal production, particularly in the Aberdare and Rhondda valleys, increased to such an extent that for two decades there was ample traffic for both canal and railway. Only in the 1860s, with new railway competition and a decaying iron industry, did canal tonnages fall dramatically.

A second Cardiff dock, the Bute East dock (like the West dock, served by a railway) came into full operation in 1859, and by now canalside works and collieries were being connected up to the railways. In 1865 and 1866 the canal company was proposing to build a dock of its own, which stimulated the Bute Trustees to reply with an offer to buy the canal. A sign of the canal's decline came in 1876 – the last year of the 8% dividend – whilst in 1882, when the company built a railway to serve the Sea Lock pound, the dividend had fallen to $1^1/_2$% and the canal's infrastructure was in poor condition. At this point the Marquess of Bute made an offer to buy all the canal's shares. It was accepted at the end of 1883 and his purchase of the Glamorganshire and the Aberdare Canals became effective from 1885, the Marquess becoming chairman of both companies. Some improvements to the canal now followed, including a new lock and timber floats in the Sea Lock pound, and the commencement of company canal-carrying between Cardiff and Merthyr and on the Aberdare Canal, with the provision of a steam tug for the Pontypridd service in 1893.

The decline of the canal continued. In 1886 Crawshay Brothers of Cyfarthfa left the Glamorganshire and sent their remaining output by rail. Serious damage from deep mining closed the canal to Merthyr in 1898, to Aberdare in 1900, and to Abercynon in 1915. The last boats carried a minimal traffic on the remaining Cardiff - Pontypridd section until 1942, when a breach in the bank destroyed the canal at Nantgarw. Cardiff Corporation purchased the canal under their Act of 1943 and the navigation was abandoned, although the Sea Lock pound continued in use for small shipping until 1951.

Except for a length of nature reserve at Melingriffith and at Nightingale's Bush, few traces of the Glamorganshire Canal remain in existence today. There are two major relics – the Melingriffith water driven

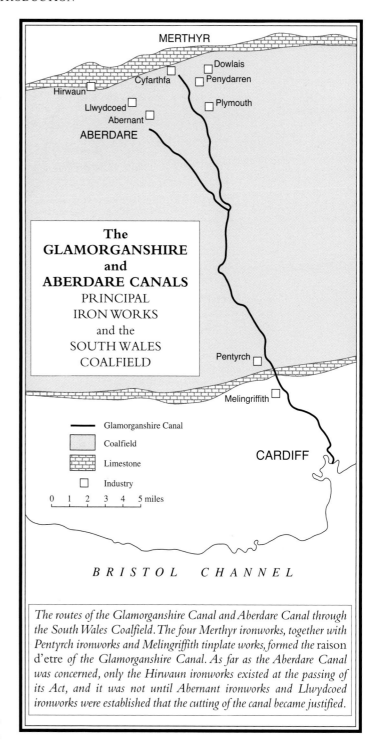

The routes of the Glamorganshire Canal and Aberdare Canal through the South Wales Coalfield. The four Merthyr ironworks, together with Pentyrch ironworks and Melingriffith tinplate works, formed the raison d'etre of the Glamorganshire Canal. As far as the Aberdare Canal was concerned, only the Hirwaun ironworks existed at the passing of its Act, and it was not until Abernant ironworks and Llwydcoed ironworks were established that the cutting of the canal became justified.

beam pump and the Brown Lenox boat-weighing machine. The former is still in situ after restoration by Oxford House Industrial Archaeology Society of Risca. The latter may be seen re-erected on the Grand Union Canal, at the Stoke Bruerne Canal Museum in Northamptonshire. The A470 trunk road has been built over much of the course of the canal between Cardiff and Aberfan.

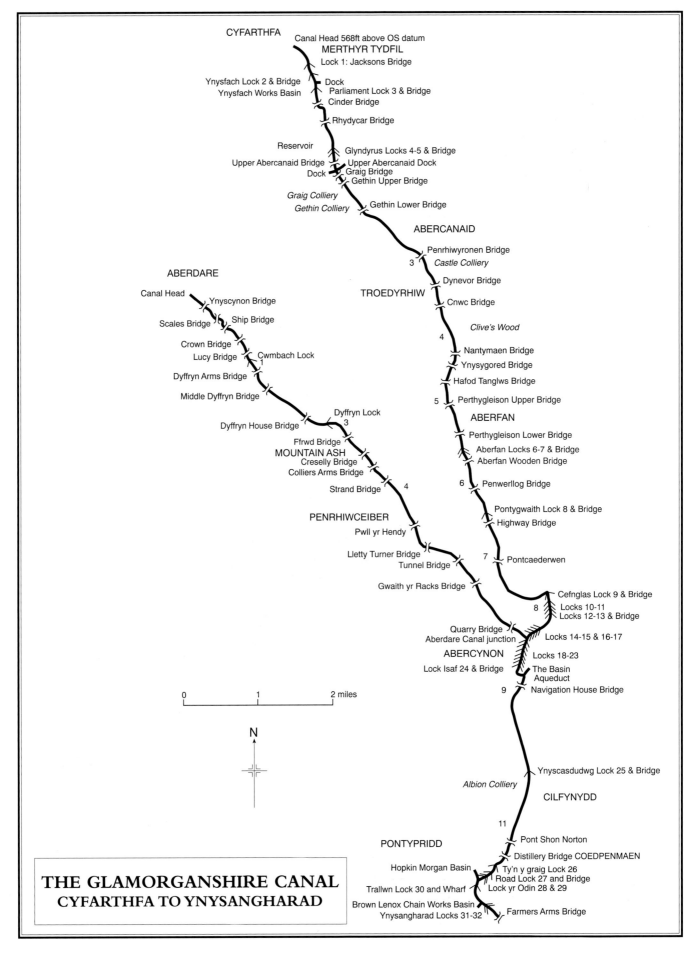

CYFARTHFA

Canal Head 568ft above OS datum

MERTHYR TYDFIL

Lock 1: Jacksons Bridge

Ynysfach Lock 2 & Bridge — Dock

Ynysfach Works Basin — Parliament Lock 3 & Bridge

Cinder Bridge

Rhydycar Bridge

Reservoir — Glyndyrus Locks 4-5 & Bridge

Upper Abercanaid Bridge — Upper Abercanaid Dock

Dock — Graig Bridge

Gethin Upper Bridge

Graig Colliery

Gethin Colliery — Gethin Lower Bridge

ABERCANAID

Penrhiwyronen Bridge

3 *Castle Colliery*

ABERDARE — Dynevor Bridge

Canal Head — Ynyscynon Bridge — TROEDYRHIW

Scales Bridge — Ship Bridge — Cnwc Bridge

Crown Bridge — *Clive's Wood*

Lucy Bridge — Cwmbach Lock — 4 — Nantymaen Bridge

Dyffryn Arms Bridge — 1 — Ynysygored Bridge

Middle Dyffryn Bridge — Hafod Tanglws Bridge

Dyffryn Lock — 5 — Perthygleison Upper Bridge

Dyffryn House Bridge — 3 — ABERFAN

Ffrwd Bridge — Perthygleison Lower Bridge

MOUNTAIN ASH — Aberfan Locks 6-7 & Bridge

Creselly Bridge — Aberfan Wooden Bridge

Colliers Arms Bridge — 6 — Penwerllog Bridge

Strand Bridge — 4

Pontygwaith Lock 8 & Bridge

PENRHIWCEIBER — Highway Bridge

Pwll yr Hendy

7 — Pontcaederwen

Lletty Turner Bridge

Tunnel Bridge

Cefnglas Lock 9 & Bridge

Gwaith yr Racks Bridge — 8 — Locks 10-11

Locks 12-13 & Bridge

Quarry Bridge — Locks 14-15 & 16-17

Aberdare Canal junction

ABERCYNON — Locks 18-23

Lock Isaf 24 & Bridge — The Basin

Aqueduct

9 — Navigation House Bridge

Ynyscasdudwg Lock 25 & Bridge

Albion Colliery — CILFYNYDD

11

PONTYPRIDD — Pont Shon Norton

Hopkin Morgan Basin — Distillery Bridge COEDPENMAEN

Ty'n y graig Lock 26

Trallwn Lock 30 and Wharf — Road Lock 27 and Bridge

Lock yr Odin 28 & 29

Brown Lenox Chain Works Basin

Ynysangharad Locks 31-32 — Farmers Arms Bridge

0   1   2 miles

N

THE GLAMORGANSHIRE CANAL
CYFARTHFA TO YNYSANGHARAD

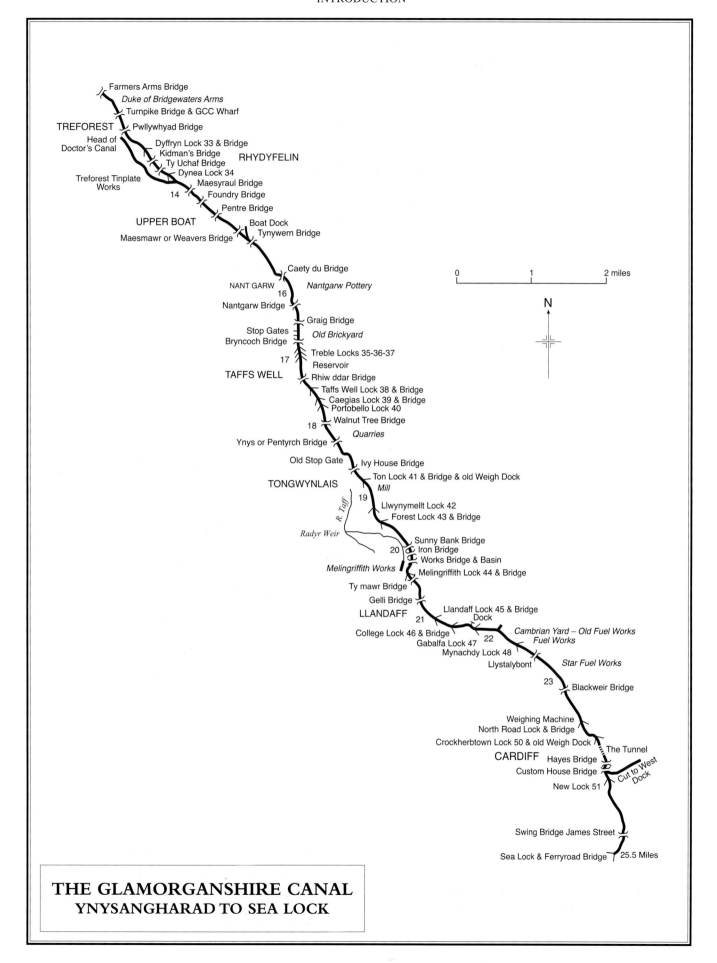

Farmers Arms Bridge
Duke of Bridgewaters Arms
Turnpike Bridge & GCC Wharf
TREFOREST
Pwllywhyad Bridge
Head of
Doctor's Canal
Dyffryn Lock 33 & Bridge
Kidman's Bridge
RHYDYFELIN
Ty Uchaf Bridge
Dynea Lock 34
Treforest Tinplate
Works
Maesyraul Bridge
14
Foundry Bridge
Pentre Bridge
UPPER BOAT
Boat Dock
Tynywern Bridge
Maesmawr or Weavers Bridge

Caety du Bridge
NANT GARW   *Nantgarw Pottery*
16
Nantgarw Bridge
Graig Bridge
Stop Gates   *Old Brickyard*
Bryncoch Bridge
Treble Locks 35-36-37
17   Reservoir
TAFFS WELL   Rhiw ddar Bridge
Taffs Well Lock 38 & Bridge
Caegias Lock 39 & Bridge
Portobello Lock 40
18   Walnut Tree Bridge
Quarries
Ynys or Pentyrch Bridge
Old Stop Gate   Ivy House Bridge
Ton Lock 41 & Bridge & old Weigh Dock
TONGWYNLAIS   *Mill*
19
Llwynymellt Lock 42
Forest Lock 43 & Bridge
R. Taff
Radyr Weir
Sunny Bank Bridge
20   Iron Bridge
Works Bridge & Basin
Melingriffith Works
Melingriffith Lock 44 & Bridge
Ty mawr Bridge
Gelli Bridge
LLANDAFF   Llandaff Lock 45 & Bridge
21   Dock
College Lock 46 & Bridge
22   *Cambrian Yard – Old Fuel Works*
Gabalfa Lock 47   *Fuel Works*
Mynachdy Lock 48
Llystalybont   *Star Fuel Works*
23   Blackweir Bridge

Weighing Machine
North Road Lock & Bridge
Crockherbtown Lock 50 & old Weigh Dock
The Tunnel
CARDIFF   Hayes Bridge
Custom House Bridge   Cut to West Dock
New Lock 51

Swing Bridge James Street

Sea Lock & Ferryroad Bridge   25.5 Miles

0   1   2 miles

N

THE GLAMORGANSHIRE CANAL
YNYSANGHARAD TO SEA LOCK

In 1789 the Yorkshire artist Julius Caesar Ibbetson visited South Wales as the guest of the third Earl of Bute, staying at Cardiff Castle. Ibbetson's work repeatedly portrays with sympathy the impact of industry on nature and the landscape. Here, in the very year that the Glamorganshire Canal was being promoted, is Richard Hill's Plymouth ironworks, which took its name from Hill's landlord the Earl of Plymouth. The single furnace is built against rising ground to facilitate charging it from the top with coke, ironstone and limestone. The furnace would be kept in blast by bellows on the hidden side of the furnace, the bellows being worked from a water wheel driven from a feeder taken off the River Taff near Merthyr bridge. In front of the furnace is the casting house, in which the molten metal would be made to run from the furnace into sand moulds and result in pig iron. In the distance, to the north, lies the village of Merthyr Tydfil and Cyfarthfa ironworks where the pig iron was sent to be refined.
Courtesy the Whitworth Art Gallery, the University of Manchester collection

Chapter 1

ORIGINS

Background

The heads of the Glamorganshire and Monmouthshire valleys form a region rich in the raw materials of iron making. During the latter half of the 18th century, a number of industrialists were attracted there to exploit these mineral resources – iron ore, coal and limestone – by setting up blast furnaces which also took advantage of the rivers for water power.

At Merthyr Tydfil four ironworks were so established – Dowlais (1759), Plymouth (1763), Cyfarthfa (1765) and Penydarren (1784). In 1766 Anthony Bacon, originally of Whitehaven in Cumberland and from 1763 MP for Aylesbury,[1] purchased Isaac Wilkinson and John Guest's Plymouth works to supply his newly built Cyfarthfa cannon-making foundry with pig iron. John Guest left Plymouth works to become manager of Dowlais – so beginning the long association of the Guest family with that ironworks. Cyfarthfa's ordnance business thrived but Clerke's Act of 1782 forbade sitting MPs from being Government contractors. Bacon's answer was to sub-let this part of Cyfarthfa's business to the West Midlands iron maker Francis Homfray, of Broadwaters and Stourton Castle, but to stipulate that Homfray was to buy his iron from Bacon. Homfray found the enforced supply relationship between the foundry and the Cyfarthfa and Plymouth furnaces too constricting, and he stayed at Cyfarthfa only a couple of years. In that time, however, he recognised the potential of the area and encouraged his two sons, Samuel and Jeremiah, to commence the ironworks at Penydarren. After another brief tenure by David Tanner of Monmouth, the Cyfarthfa foundry passed in 1786 to the partnership of Richard Crawshay, William Stevens and James Cockshutt. Crawshay was a Yorkshireman of great ambition, who already operated a lucrative ironware trade in London. His arrival at Cyfarthfa was to mark the beginning of over a century of Crawshay rule and influence.

In 1786 Anthony Bacon died, leaving as minors his three illegitimate sons and heirs. Richard Hill, Bacon's good friend (and effectively his brother-in-law, being married to his mistress's sister), took over the Plymouth lease as a going concern, while Richard Crawshay and partners were allowed to lease Cyfarthfa furnace in addition to the forge and foundry.[2]

Now that Crawshay and Co. were in complete control at Cyfarthfa, they turned to promoting the wrought iron trade using Henry Cort's puddling process. However, progress was hindered by a lack of adequate transport from Merthyr to the Bristol Channel seaboard, the finished iron having to be expensively hauled down the Taff Valley two tons at a time on road waggons and using 24 miles of indifferent turnpike road to Cardiff.[3] Crawshay, of all the ironmasters, felt himself held to ransom by road hauliers such as William Key. In 1788, anxious to be independent of these hauliers and meaning to take control of transport himself, Crawshay turned his thoughts to canals. Writing from the London office to Cockshutt, he informed his partner that he was hoping to promote a canal next spring, with the help of John Kemeys Tynte of Cefn Mably and Lord Cardiff. He instructed Cockshutt to prepare a list of landowners on both banks of the Taff between Cardiff and Merthyr Bridge.[4]

Crawshay now called on the services of the Midlands canal engineer and contractor Thomas Dadford, to make a field survey for the Merthyr - Cardiff waterway. He had already commanded the support of the other three Merthyr ironmasters who all contributed to the cost of the survey.[5] It was probably Francis Homfray who introduced Crawshay to Dadford, for Homfray had once worked a forge at Stewponey on the Staffordshire & Worcestershire Canal, a waterway on which Dadford had worked as resident engineer in the 1770s. It is likely that Francis Homfray knew Thomas Dadford and, in the light of his experience in manufacturing and distribution in this part of the West Midlands, Homfray could claim to be the one English industrialist at Merthyr who 'knew about canals.'[6]

It was late in the year 1789 when Thomas Dadford was out with an assistant along the hill slopes of the Taff Valley, taking sightings with levelling instrument, graduated staff and measuring chain for marking out the canal line. He calculated the number and the fall of the locks and made an assessment of the expense of the work. Armed with this information he was able to satisfy Crawshay of the practicability of the navigation. Although Dadford would not have realised it at the time, this assignment was to prove of great significance for him and for the future of canal building in South Wales. The success of the Glamorganshire

Michael Angelo Rooker's splendid 1795 view of William Edwards' bridge ('Pont-y-ty-pridd – Earth House Bridge'), at the place later to become Pontypridd, shows a train of packhorses crossing the River Taff. Before the coming of the canal, all merchandise was transported inland by either packhorse or road waggon.   Courtesy National Museums & Galleries of Wales

'A Party of Welsh Damsels on one Horse, Journeying', by Ibbetson, depicts the limestone mountains of the Taff gap beyond the southern edge of the coalfield. The ruins of Castell Coch add to the picturesque, while a limeburner rakes the fire of his kiln. A few years later the route of the Glamorganshire Canal was to pass parallel to this road and its builders were to use the produce of the limekilns. An oil painting of this same scene, by Ibbetson and entitled 'The Return from Market', is in the National Library of Wales collection. In the early 1870s Castell Coch was rebuilt and extravagantly furnished by its owner, the third Marquess of Bute, using the architect William Burges. Courtesy National Museums & Galleries of Wales

Canal Act of 1790 was to lead to the enthusiastic promotion of other canal projects in the region, and to the involvement of Thomas Dadford and Thomas Sheasby, and their sons, in the building of four major canals between 1794 and 1799. These were to run in neighbouring valleys of Glamorganshire, Monmouthshire and Brecknock, down to the sea at Swansea, Briton Ferry and Newport. In difficult terrain, unsuited to canal building, this was to prove no small achievement.

The Glamorganshire Canal Act of 1790

The contribution landowners could make to the success of canal bills was enormous, for in the early days of canal promotion they and their friends controlled Parliament.[7] Indeed, power to buy land compulsorily for canal building was not possible without the sanction of an Act. Accordingly, Crawshay's canal Bill was presented before the House of Commons where it was referred to the Commons Committee on 24 Feb 1790, being described as:

'*A Petition of the Earl of Plymouth and several Gentlemen and Freeholders of the County of Glamorgan . . . the making and maintaining such Canal will be of great Benefit to the Petitioners and to all other Persons having Lands and Estates within the said County as it will open communications with extensive Iron Works and Collieries, and will be of public Utility.*'[8]

Like other promoters of inland navigations before him, Richard Crawshay must have been pleased to have the approval of the region's most powerful and prestigious landowner. On 10 February he had written to Cockshutt to say he had spoken to Lord Cardiff '*who behaves nobly to our Navigation scheme.*'[9]

As part of the examination of the Bill before the Commons Committee, time was taken to look at Dadford's 'Plan of a Canal 1790' which had been prepared from his recent survey. Copies of the plan had been taken directly from an engraved copper plate and distributed to the Committee and, appearing in person before the assembly as a technical witness, Thomas Dadford answered questions and assured his examiners of the feasibility of the project. Samuel Homfray of Penydarren and William Taitt of Dowlais, both ironmasters and later to become shareholders, also gave evidence in support of the petition.[10] Their continued support during the framing of the Bill had not come easily and Crawshay had not had all his own way. Taitt and Homfray were well aware of his influence in attracting investment from his London associates and other non-freighters who, as subscribers to the Bill, were expecting a good rate of return. On the other hand, the ironmasters' main concern was as freighters and so to keep the tonnage rates as low as possible. In an early draft, rates were to be 6d per ton mile (compared to Taitt's much lower expectation of 3d) and Crawshay was forced to bow to their complaint, not just by lowering the rates but by fixing a ceiling on annual dividend to 8%. The maximum tonnage rate was set at 5d in order to give a 5% return on the initial capital of £60,000, based on estimated traffic. If the profits exceeded 8% and the canal company did not reduce the tonnage rates, then the justices at Quarter Sessions were empowered to reduce them.[11] These clauses seemed to satisfy Taitt and Homfray, while Richard Hill (Plymouth), William Lewis (Pentyrch) and Richard Blakemore (Melingriffith) were appeased by clauses protecting the water rights of their respective works.[12]

The Bill was safely through the Commons by 6 May 1790 and after Dadford, supported by James Cockshutt, had satisfied the Lords Committee as to the extent and cost of the canal, the Bill was reported without amendment.[13] It became an Act of Parliament (*30 Geo. III cap. 82*) on 9 June 1790, being entitled:

'*An Act for making and maintaining a Navigable Canal from*

An oil painting of Penydarren ironworks looking south-west, artist unknown. Apart from Wood's drawings in 1810, this is the only known image of the works in operation. It closed in 1859. The viewpoint is from the bank which carried the Morlais limestone quarry tramroad to the charging bank behind the furnaces. There were seven furnaces after 1843; six are depicted here and the artist has shown at least four in blast. Behind the flames issuing from them can be seen the long row of calcining kilns (for roasting the ironstone before loading it into the furnace). Lines of the works tramroad lead from in front of the casting sheds, past the blast engine houses, down to the rolling mills and forges in the middle distance. It was here that rails for the Liverpool & Manchester Railway were manufactured in 1830. The Dowlais Brook passes into a culvert in the middle foreground and runs to where

it joined the Morlais brook at the rolling mills. The line of the Dowlais railroad is shown coming in from the lower right and losing height behind the solitary figure, on its way down to the Glamorganshire Canal in the Taff Valley below. The quarry tramroad is shown appearing from between the workers houses and snaking its way across the line of the Dowlais railroad. The busy road in front of the terrace of houses between the two tramroads is Penydarren High Street. Penydarren House, seat of the ironworks' founder Samuel Homfray, peeps from among the trees in the right background. From here, Homfray and his successors could survey their enterprise and the growing town of Merthyr Tydfil. This picture gives a graphic impression of the height the canal would have had to reach if the projected Dowlais branch had been built. Courtesy National Museums & Galleries of Wales

Merthyr Tidvile, to and through a Place called The Bank, near the Town of Cardiff, in the County of Glamorgan.'

The Act allowed a capital of £60,000 to build the canal, with power to raise a further £30,000. Each share had a face value of £100. Richard Crawshay became the largest shareholder, he and his family between them subscribing £13,100. Other large subscriptions came from the Harfords of Melingriffith tinplate works (£6,000), John Kemeys Tynte of Cefn Mably (£5,000) and William Stevens of Cyfarthfa (£5,000), with smaller holdings being taken up by the Homfrays and Richard Foreman of Penydarren ironworks, the Hills of Plymouth ironworks, and William Taitt and Thomas Guest, both of Dowlais. The canal contractors, the Thomas Dadfords, father and son, described as then residing at Redland in the county of Gloucester, each took £500 worth of shares.[14]

The canal company was given powers to fix its own bye laws and also to regulate its charges to the freighters. The rate for Stone, Iron, Timber, Goods, Wares and Merchandise was not to exceed 5d per ton per mile. For Ironstone, Iron Ore, Coal, Limestone, Lime and Manure the maximum rate was 2d. Navigation was to be free i.e. any trader could operate a boat on the canal freely, provided he paid the rate per mile on the goods he carried. Ships passing through the Sea Lock would be charged 1d per ton of burden. At North Road in Cardiff no canal buildings were to be erected and the towpath was to be built on the opposite side of the canal where it passed Lord Cardiff's castle grounds, presumably to keep away reminders of industry and the perils of predatory boatmen. A clause authorised the laying of feeder railways to the canal from works within four miles of the canal i.e. land and wayleaves could be compulsorily purchased for the building of these railways as if part of the canal itself. Another clause authorised the building of branch canals.

The canal company was owned by its shareholders, or proprietors, who were entitled to one vote for each share at annual General Assemblies (to be held the first Wednesday in June) and at extraordinary Special Assemblies. When five years had passed, the maximum number of votes a shareholder would be entitled to was twenty, even if he owned more shares than twenty. This stipulation did not prevent the Crawshay family dominating canal proceedings for years to come. A proprietors' meeting was deemed to be quorate if members (or their proxies) present held a total of at least 300 shares.

Valuation of land and compensation for damage to property was placed in the hands of independently sworn-in Commissioners, for whom there was a land-owning and income qualification. There was an escalation procedure for disputes to be resolved in front of a jury. The Clerk to the Commissioners had to be elected from names recommended by the canal company's committee. The members of the canal committee for the coming year were elected at the General Assembly.

The first meeting of the Company of Proprietors of the Glamorganshire Canal Navigation took place in Cardiff at the Cardiff Arms Inn on 30 June 1790, where a committee was formed to manage the canal's affairs. James Harford of Melingrffith was appointed Treasurer and John Wood of Cardiff became Clerk at a salary of £40 per annum.[15] That day Richard Crawshay, as Chairman, was authorised to enter into final agreement with the Dadfords and Sheasbys for making the canal for £48,288, the work of cutting the canal to be started from the Merthyr end. The first meeting of the committee, held on 19 July 1790, ratified and confirmed the agreement with the contractors and a bond of £10,000 was taken from them as security for the performance of the contract. At this meeting also, William Llewellyn (Tynte's agent at Cefn Mably) was appointed to value the lands of the Proprietors that would be required for the canal line. In May 1791 the Commissioners proper had their first meeting and Charles Brown of Cardiff became their first Clerk.

Thus was the scene set to oversee the building and operation of the Glamorganshire Canal.

NOTES TO CHAPTER 1

1 For Anthony Bacon and his earlier involvement in the slave trade see L.B. Namier *Anthony Bacon MP an Eighteenth Century Merchant,* Journal of Economic and Business History II, 1929.

2 Lawrence Ince *The South Wales Iron Industry 1750-1885,* Merton 1993; Chris Evans *The Labyrinth of Flames,* Cardiff 1993; John Lloyd *The Early History of the Old South Wales Iron Works, 1760-1840,* London 1906.

3 W.H. Smyth *Nautical Observations of the Port of Cardiff,* Cardiff 1840.

4 Letter 10 Sept 1788 calendared in Chris Evans *The Letterbook of Richard Crawshay 1788-1797,* Cardiff 1990. This book includes much of interest on the promotion and building of the canal but also provides an insight into Crawshay's promotion of Cort's process at Cyfarthfa. The letterbook itself is held at Gwent Record Office, ref. D2.162.

5 R. Hill to T. Key 19 Feb 1790. Letterbook of Richard Hill 1786 – 1792, NLW MS 15334E.

6 Charles Hadfield *The Canals of South Wales and the Border,* Cardiff 1960, p17.

7 Charles Hadfield *The Canal Age,* Newton Abbot 1968, p22.

8 House of Commons Journal 24 Feb 1790.

9 Evans *Letterbook.*

10 House of Commons Journal 26 March, 15 April and 6 May 1790.

11 Letters 2 April, 7 April, 9 April and 13 April calendared in Evans *Letterbook*; see also William Taitt's published *Address to the Landowners….,* Cardiff Jan 28 1799.

12 See the several chapters on water supply.

13 House of Lords Committee Book 14 May 1790.

14 Glamorganshire Canal list of subscribers, bound at the front of the canal company's minute book. CCL ms 5170 and NLW Deposit 91B.

15 For John Wood see T. Mansel Hodges *Early Banking in Cardiff,* Economic History Review XVIII 1948.

Chapter 2
BUILDING THE CANAL

Richard Crawshay and the new canal committee were in a mood of expectancy in the summer of 1790, as Thomas Dadford and his men were eagerly awaited in Wales. No doubt the observer on the windy slopes of Cefnglas, near Quaker's Yard, would have noticed the posts marking out the line that the navigation would follow, high above the River Taff between Merthyr Tydfil and Abercynon. For nine miles the markers of Dadford's survey followed the hill slopes on the west side of the Taff. At what is now called Abercynon, the canal line changed sides in the valley and continued on the east bank of the river for a further 15 miles to Cardiff. William Llewellyn and William Morris had been busy that summer valuing and bargaining for land for the canal; they had been told not to agree a price more than thirty times the annual rental value of the land between Merthyr and Newbridge (Pontypridd). Annual rentals of the hill land that might be wanted at Pontygwaith were quoted by the surveyors: '*4s per acre for the Common, 8s for Inclosed Lands and 10s for Woodlands.*'[1] By comparison, in Gloucestershire, on the line of the Thames & Severn Canal in the mid-1780s, the valuers were discovering common average rentals of 30 shillings per acre.[2]

From the letterbook of Richard Crawshay, it is clear that Thomas Dadford senior arrived on the canal site with his workmen in the August of 1790. Only recently, Dadford had abandoned a contract for building the Cromford Canal, in Derbyshire.[3] He brought with him Thomas Sheasby, who had worked with him there, and soon he was joined by his son, Thomas Dadford junior, an engineer like his father. Richard Crawshay had personally made sure that food and supplies were on hand for the workforce. In a letter to James Harford of Melingriffith, Treasurer to the canal company, he wrote of his confidence in Dadford, and that a cargo of flour and Truman Harford & Co's porter ale was ready at Cardiff for their consumption. On 25 August Dadford was wished speedy success with the canal work. Money and supplies were available and '*Beds, Porter, Bacon (at 4 1/2 d a lb, good Yorkshire stuff), Timber and Wheat is coming from the Baltic.*' On 27 August Crawshay wrote to Dadford again, saying he had ordered '*50 Cots [beds] . . . . By the Bristol Waggon . . . . Directed to you Cardiffe to the Care of Harford Partridge & Co Bristol.*'[4]

Who were these men arriving with Dadford and how were they organised? We gather almost nothing about them from the canal company's minutes, since they were entirely answerable to the Dadfords and Sheasby, acting as engineers and contractors. They are almost certain to have been a skilled workforce of journeymen masons, quarrymen, carpenters, sawyers, limeburners and smiths, some of whom were foremen-gangleaders taking on responsibility for the management and payment of groups of men cutting the canal in open country, digging out lock pits, building lock walls and laying down the oak frames of lock gates or making and fitting the ironwork.[5] Some would bring to South Wales the specialist skills of canal boat building. Whilst some of the labourers were itinerant 'navigators', migrating to the region in search of work, it does seem that Dadford also relied on local organisers of labour. Edward David of Black Brook, near Quaker's Yard, was probably one of them. In August 1792 he successfully brought an action against Thomas Dadford for the recovery of £42 13s 8d '*for work and labour on the Merthyr Canal.*'[6]

The gangleader-piecework system of organising labour was well established in 18th century manufacturing industry and was common in the mining of coal. A local example was the Harford Partridge works at Melingriffith, where the complex processes of tinplate production were managed in this way.[7] As contractor-employers following accepted procedures in the building of canals, the Dadfords and Sheasby probably let out jobs to gangleaders on piecework rates for measured amounts of work. Before the inflationary conditions of the war with France in 1793, the price paid the gangmasters for digging was about 3d a cubic yard.[8] The price could rise to 3 1/2 d in lockpits, 5d or 7d in deep cutting and 9d for blasting rock. Leaders of groups of masons could get 5d a square foot for quoining and 21s for a hundred square feet of general masonry. For clay puddling the bed of the canal, the men were paid 6d a square yard and there were allowances for felling trees and for moving soil beyond a measured distance.[9] Extra payments went to men on unpleasant jobs working in water, where sometimes there were rewards of allowances of gin or beer.[10]

As engineer-contractor to the canal company, Dadford estimated his costs at so much a mile and calculated the lockage in vertical feet. John Bird of Cardiff was well

John Petherick's topographical watercolour of November 1855 depicts the Trallwn district of Pontypridd, looking south and dominated by the quarries on Coedpenmaen (Pontypridd Common). The straight line through the quarries is the old Cardiff-Merthyr turnpike. Below that is the line of the canal and then the rows of cottages (Smithfield Row) mark the line of the Berw feeder, as it makes its way to the chain works at Ynysangharad in the far distance. In the extreme lower right hand corner, the artist has cleverly positioned a portion of William Edwards' river bridge from which Llanover Street approaches Trallwn wharf. The quarry, which was worked by Thomas Edwards in the 19th century and Charles Ash in the 20th, is presumably the source of the stones seen lying along the canal bank. The steep lane on the left is identified as Cornstores Hill.

Courtesy National Museums & Galleries of Wales

The sites of the various processes involved in ironmaking at Dowlais ironworks were strung out along the valley of the Dowlais Brook, upstream from Penydarren. This watercolour is one of three which survive by George Childs, painted in 1840. Looking north-east towards the rolling mills and the furnaces beyond, it depicts in the foreground the claymill and brick kilns. Here tens of thousands of bricks were manufactured, not just for surface buildings and company housing but for arching the pit shafts and many of the main underground roadways of Dowlais's collieries. Here also were made the silica bricks for lining the furnaces, using ganister obtained with the limestone from the quarries in the far distance. Courtesy National Museums & Galleries of Wales

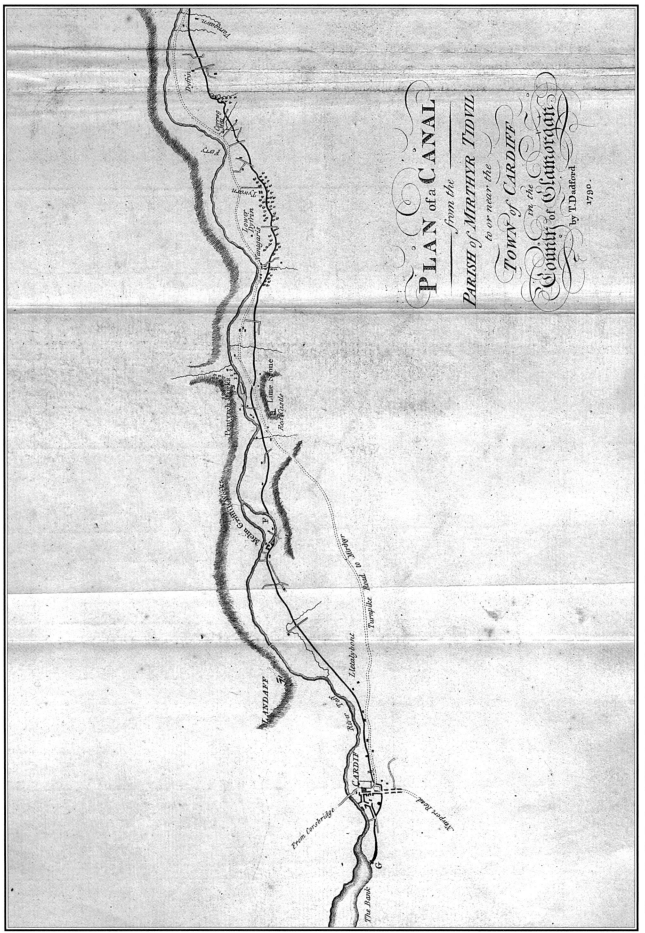

Thomas Dadford's plan of 1790 for the canal Act. This is the section from The Bank, Cardiff to Pentrebach (Treforest).

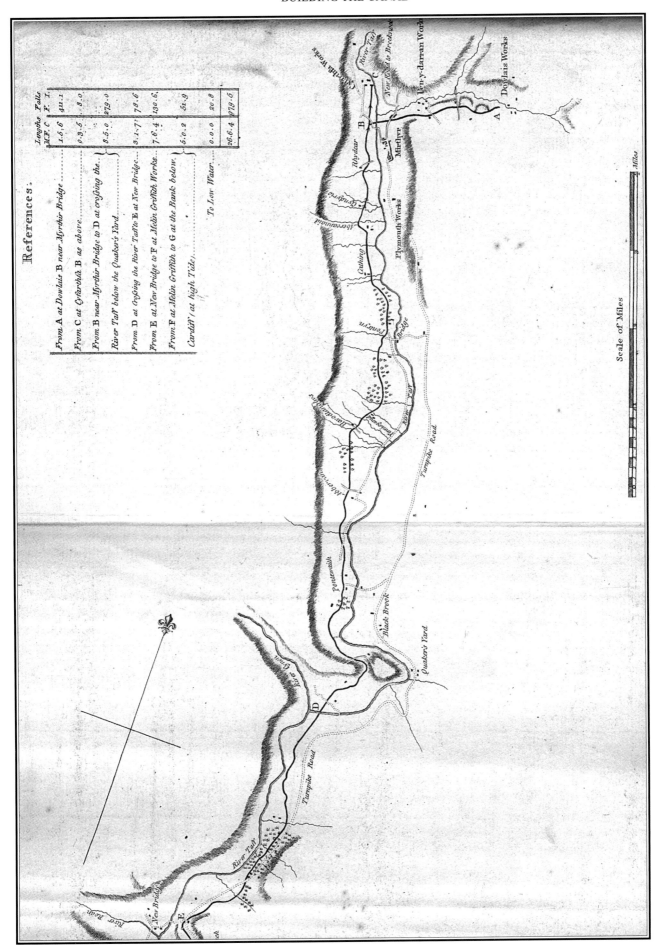

The second section shows the canal from Pentrebach to Merthyr. Note the branch to Dowlais which was abandoned after the Bill became enacted.

informed about the canal for he wrote in his diary:

'The elevation [on the Glamorganshire Canal] from Cardiff to Merthyr is said to be 537 feet, which will cost £40 per foot exclusive of £800 per mile for cutting.'[11]

Under their contract, in July the Dadfords and Sheasby agreed to make the canal for £48,288, not including the cost of the land, and a bond of £10,000 was taken from them for its completion. A clause in the contract outlined the canal's dimensions:

'The canal to be made 30 feet wide at the surface of the water and four feet deep. The bridges to be 18 feet span with a Haling path under them. The locks to be 65 feet in length from Gate to Gate and nine feet six inches wide.'[12]

In the last days of August 1790, unparalleled scenes of bustle and activity were being played out in Merthyr, on the banks of the Taff on the western side of the Plymouth weir, as around a hundred labourers fell to the task of hollowing out sections of the canal line with picks and shovels. Interminable loads of earth were hand barrowed up the uneasy barrow runs, where it was tipped to form the raised outer bank of the towing path. Round about were the barrows, planks, scoops and buckets of the navigators and the tall timber tripod of Dadford's hand-worked pile driver. The horse-drawn carts of the hauliers brought casks of building lime on site, took away earth to form embankments, carried in the stone needed by the masons and clay for the puddle which, when worked with water and compacted by treading under foot, formed an impervious seal to keep the sides and bottom of the canal watertight.

It was typical of Richard Crawshay's thrusting style that he should put pressure on the canal committee to insert into the contract that work should start at the Merthyr end. In this way, even if only partly completed, the canal would be serving his ironworks from the earliest moment. Crawshay was also clearly behind the company's decision in 1791 to extend the canal upwards, through Merthyr, for half a mile to his works at Cyfarthfa.[13] The extension was to involve Dadford in extra work and cause a dispute over payments which had to be painfully sorted out by arbitration.

The original Plan of 1790 also envisaged the building of a branch canal from Merthyr Bridge to Dowlais, intended to serve both the Penydarren and Dowlais ironworks. Apart from its doubtful water supply, this was a visionary project by any British canal engineering standards, Dadford calculating that in $1^3/_4$ miles the lockage to Dowlais would be no less than 411 feet. Wisely, the plan for this stairway to heaven was dropped, so the aggrieved ironmasters, William Taitt and Samuel Homfray, were obliged to build a railroad from their works to the canal in Merthyr, under the Canal Act's four mile clause. Crawshay's committee decided that the canal company should not build the railroad itself but would make a contribution towards the cost of the section from Dowlais to Penydarren and would also build the necessary river bridge at Merthyr, to be shared with the canal company's access road to the new Brecon to Merthyr turnpike.[14]

Crawshay was not the only ironmaster at Merthyr who could be bloody-minded and the tension that existed between all rival parties in this frontier town is well illustrated by the ensuing events. Homfray had passively left Taitt to have the railroad surveyed and built from the Dowlais end but had a shock when the route arrived at Penydarren. Assuming this to be a joint undertaking, he had, of course, expected the Dowlais railroad to carry Penydarren traffic to the canal but he found that the railroad clung to the side of the valley and passed Penydarren on the opposite side of the Morlais Brook, at too high a level to allow him to make a connection from his works. Taitt laid the costs in front of the canal company committee and was awarded £1,000 of the £1,766 expended on the route to Penydarren, the total cost of the Dowlais railroad

With so many locks between Merthyr and Cardiff it seems a paradox to describe the Glamorganshire Canal as a 'contour canal'. Yet what Dadford did was to follow the contours as far as possible and then concentrate the drops in height by providing double lock staircases at a minimal number of locations. From the double locks at Glyndyrus to Aberfan the boatmen enjoyed an uninterrupted four miles of water. This photograph of the derelict canal in 1962 gives a good indication of the 28 feet drop in height from Aberfan Locks, as the canal then clings to its new contour round the bend at Aberfan Rocks, on its way to the next lock at Pontygwaith. The upper of the Aberfan Locks is thought to be the deepest canal lock built in the British Isles.   ILW photo 1962

'Nothing appears more extraordinary than, from a boat navigating the canal, to look down on the river Taaf [sic], dashing among the rocks 100 yards below.' *This early description must surely refer to the landscape at this dramatic spot south of Pontygwaith. The canal, seen disused on its hillside ledge high above the river in 1955, may be traced from right to left across the slopes of Cefn Glas. The quarry on the canal level (extreme right of photograph) bears all the signs of use by the canal builder, Thomas Dadford. Three rail formations threaded the narrowing valley here in 1955, where the rural pre-industrial landscape has, remarkably, escaped destruction. Dominating the left of the picture is the winding course of the Taff Vale Railway, with a passenger train from Cardiff to Merthyr which has just left Quaker's Yard station. The train is hauled by a BR Class 3 locomotive of the 82000 series. Immediately below the train is the course of the Merthyr Tramroad, hidden by trees. On the opposite side of the river the formation of the GW & Rhymney Joint Railway may be observed below the canal. This portion of the line was closed in 1951 and its course taken later for the A470 Cardiff - Merthyr Trunk road.* ILW photo 10 Aug 1955, neg 1438

to the canal being £3,000. Even then, Crawshay's committee contrived to not pay Dowlais the £1,000 outright but to set it against tonnage due and so it took almost three years before the Dowlais company was recompensed for its capital outlay.[15]

Dowlais consistently referred to its line as a 'railroad' and it is thought the track consisted of edge rails, spiked to longitudinal supporting rails of timber, similar to the waggonways which served their coal and ironstone pits. The waggons would have had flanged wheels. A letter from Taitt to a prospective customer, an iron-founder in Newcastle upon Tyne and dated 17 March 1791, states:

'We are now making Rails for our new Waggon way which weigh 44Li or 45Li per yard. The Rails are 6 feet long, 3 pin holes in them, mitred at the ends, 3 inches broad at Bottom, 2½ inches top & near 2 inches thick.'[16]

The gauge of the railroad is not known but since Thomas Dadford senior was the engineer it is likely that he chose 3 feet 4 inches, as used by his sons Thomas and John on the Monmouthshire Canal railroads, and the Clydach Railroad

of the Brecknock & Abergavenny Canal.[17]

Penydarren ended up having to lay its own tramroad to the canal, parallel to the Dowlais line. It too shared Jackson's bridge (Jackson was the Ledbury mason to whom Dadford sub-contracted the masonry work), before terminating at its own canal wharf at Merthyr. The canal company made no contribution to the cost of the Penydarren tramroad, citing the original joint agreement with Taitt and Homfray. Crawshay must have known full well what was going on when Dadford's survey of the Dowlais railroad was accepted. The canal company's commissioners were even called upon to value the land.[18] But Crawshay kept his distance and acted the mediator. At this time he wanted harmony because he was attempting to found a joint bank at Merthyr with the other ironmasters.[19] Samuel Homfray's fury with Dowlais was returned by a terse letter from Taitt:

'Your Several letters to Mr Guest about the direction of our Rail Road from Dowlais to the canal Surprizes me exceedingly as I know not what pretence you can possibly have to interfere in that more than in the Conduct and Management of our Furnaces . . . . If you want an

Looking up the Taff Valley in 1955, the canal bed can be seen sweeping round to the left beneath the hill-side waste tips from Penrhiwceiber colliery, situated in the Aberdare Valley. In the far distance are the Aberfan tips from Merthyr Vale colliery. The River Taff is hidden by trees but its line can be traced northward beneath the two railway viaducts. The lower track passing beneath a line of trees on the eastern side of the valley is that of the former Merthyr Tramroad.
ILW photo 10 Aug 1955, neg 1441

Accommodation from us, ask it as a favour, but do not think of demanding it as a right . . . . Mr Dadford . . . . recommended the opposite side of the Brook to your Works as the most Eligible way to take the road . . . .'[20]

The Penydarren line was almost definitely a plateway (i.e. where the flanges are not on the waggon wheels but on the rails), built to Penydarren's standard 3 foot gauge over the guiding face of the plates (2 feet 10 inches back to back).[21]

Progress on cutting the canal through late 1790 and into 1791 seems to have been good and Richard Crawshay was euphoric when, on 5 November 1790, he wrote to his continental friend Frederick Wilhelm von Reden in Berlin: *'the Canal goes beyond expectation – you will certainly lose your wager.'* Reden had visited Crawshay the previous year. They were undertaking similar projects, the difference being that Reden was not the owner of capital but a mining engineer, appointed by King Frederick the Great of Prussia to oversee the state coal mining, iron making and lead mining activities in Silesia.[22] Reden was building a canal which was to enter the coal workings directly, just like the Cyfarthfa Canal and the Duke of Bridgewater's canals at Worsley, near Manchester. Crawshay playfully suggested that Reden's own canal engineer be placed under the instruction of Dadford. Their correspondence also covered the subject of boat-carrying inclined planes as an alternative to locks – a device which Reden did employ on his canal from Gliwice to the River Oder.[23]

Crawshay was keen that Dadford should want for nothing and he was very impatient with the circumspection with which James Harford provided him with money. Referring to Harford, the treasurer, Crawshay wrote to Dadford on 9 December 1790: *'You must be supplied as wanted . . . . If he's tired of the Office we must elect another.'* Harford and John Wood had to manage the bank balance and know when to make calls for money from the subscribers. The Glamorganshire Canal was not unusual among 18th century canal projects – when the time came to come up with the money subscribers were slow to pay and often dropped out. Crawshay overcame this to his advantage, by himself making loans, with interest, to the canal company, to pay the calls on the subscriptions of his London associates who had backed the enterprise.[24] In his single-minded efforts to get his own way, his contempt for Harford's over-carefulness came to a head. In letters to his partner Cockshutt (of whom Crawshay also held a low opinion which resulted in his sacking in September 1791), Crawshay described Harford, in his typical inflammatory way, as insolent and *'a rude selfish Jew Quaker'*, and again that *'Harford is a mercenary Fellow & must be treated as Circumstances require.'*[25] Although Harford remained official treasurer to the canal company until June 1793, from July 1791 Crawshay addressed most of his letters relating to canal finance to Harford's manager at Melingriffith and a canal committee man, Joseph Vaughan.

Work along the Merthyr to Quaker's Yard portion of the line was going on in several places so that the whole of the workforce could be usefully employed. Two sets of staircase pairs of locks were in course of construction along the way, one pair at Glyndyrus and the other by the farm of Aberfan Fawr. Stone was being dressed in the masons' shelter, set up as near as possible to the originating quarry where, from time to time, the ear was deafened by explosions dislodging the rock. Dadford's own reports to the canal company tell us that stone was being moved out of the quarries by 'rail ways' and it would be interesting to know if this mode of transport was in more general use along the canal line.[26] At the lock sites, carpenters and masons laboured to the rhythm of mallet and chisel and saw. The most senior among the craftsmen checked the accuracy of the work against the engineer's plans spread out in front of them. Gates made of oak had to be measured to fit and mitre together exactly. The masons had to maintain the correct angle of the lock walls by the accurate use of bevels. On site was a large iron-strapped tool chest and a grindstone, whilst close by were the temporary yards laid out for carpenters to fit together the frames of lock gates, to make the centring for forming bridge arches and to make and repair the sheerlegs, pulleys and derrick cranes used for lifting blocks of masonry into position. Cutting of timber into baulks and planks was done the hard way – from the solid tree by men working in the thick dust of sawpits. Hot water was needed during the day and was kept boiling in giant kettles set over a fire. Next to the anvils of the smiths were the coal hearths for heating the ironwork. Fires were also required by the masons, for preparing a hot hydraulic lime mortar. This was used for jointing the underwater masonry of lock walls and floors. Somewhere along the line of the canal was temporary hutted accommodation for the labourers and makeshift stables for the many horses. Nothing was built to be permanent and when work was completed in one place the whole organisation moved on to set up camp again

A boat horse with decorated nose can, recorded at Stewponey, near Stourbridge, on the Staffordshire & Worcestershire Canal in 1948. Francis Homfray had owned a forge at Stewponey and knew this canal well before coming to Wales to set up the Penydarren ironworks in the 1780s. Thomas Dadford was even more familiar with the Staffordshire & Worcestershire Canal. In the 1770s he had been the resident engineer.
ILW photo 26 March 1948 neg 631

The earliest depiction of the Glamorganshire Canal is this fine sketch by Rooker of Pontypridd Locks (probably Locks 28 and 29), drawn in 1795. In the background, Graig yr Esk rises menacingly from across the valley. Courtesy National Museums & Galleries of Wales

further down the valley.[27]

No contemporary account has been found on the impact Thomas Dadford's army of navigators had on the village of Merthyr Tydfil and on the rural tranquillity of the valley. Traditionally a hard-working and hard-drinking breed, the tough gangs of cutters must have looked for relaxation in local beer houses, where noisy and aggressive behaviour could well have erupted. However, there seems to be no evidence that these men were '*a constant nuisance to the neighbourhood and the terror of all other descriptions of people.*'[28] If this had been so the news of it would have reached John Bird of Cardiff, whose diary is full of contemporary events and gossip. Control of the Glamorganshire's cutters was probably good because Thomas Dadford was resident engineer for almost the whole period of construction. In the valley of the Taff there is little to suggest '*that turbulence and riot with which foreign workmen are inspired.*'[29]

For different reasons one of the four original promoters of the canal, Richard Hill of Plymouth ironworks, was not pleased. In the summer of 1791 he was complaining:

'*Since the canal has begun in this country workers have been extremely scarce, that has obliged me to pay all my workmen weekly which makes me poorer.*'

and

'*My stock of iron is unavoidably increasing, which I cannot prevent without any security to myself being materially injured in the winter by a scarcity of carriers and hands, occasioned by the great demand of both to the canal.*'[30]

By June 1791 Thomas Dadford could present to the canal company his first progress report over the 10³/₄ miles

between Merthyr and the lower end of Cilfynydd. Cutting had been done for 7³/₄ miles '*through the most difficult parts consisting of Hillsides and rocks.*' In hand was '*about 1000 yards in length through Aberfan Rocks*' and there was work still to do '*above the road at Rhydycar.*' Only two locks were reported finished by the masons and seven others partly done but '*twenty lock pitts dug out.*' This is an indication that work had started on the 'Abercynon Sixteen', where Richard Crawshay had tried unsuccessfully to persuade Dadford to build an inclined plane similar to William Reynolds' one at Ketley.[31] It seems that Dadford had decided to increase the depth of many of the locks from an earlier agreed maximum of nine feet and so reduce the numbers of locks required.[32] Six bridges had been built over the canal and the aqueduct over the Taff was '*in great forwardness, the arch now turning.*' Some sea banking had been done on Cardiff Moors, near the site of the proposed canal basin, by Lord Cardiff's men by agreement with Crawshay, although Dadford had disapproved.[33] Dadford concludes his report:

'*We presume to promise the proprietors a Navigable Canal from Merthyr to Bridwaynath [Cilfynydd] by the end of the present year which is more than half of the Undertaking, there being 276 feet of lockage and the Aqueduct across the River Taff.*'[34]

On 1 September, Richard Crawshay wrote to his son William and William Stevens, urging them to enquire whether the Dadfords '*will fill the upper part of the Canal down to the Aqueduct.*' With the massive task of the Sixteen Locks and the aqueduct still incomplete, there seemed no possible way Dadford could earn himself Crawshay's promised Gold Medal for '*floating boats from the summit to the Road near New Bridge before Michaelmas 1791 and another*

William Pamplin was Richard Crawshay's gardener, yet he is best remembered for two exquisite pencil drawings which he executed about 1800. This first is a view looking across the Taff to the Cyfarthfa ironworks. Beyond the four furnaces, on the hillside, are piles of ironstone collected by scouring and also coal, which is being coked before being taken to the charging houses. Beside the furnaces is the famous 50ft water wheel, brainchild of Watkin George, Cyfarthfa's renowned engineer. The tail races from the several water wheels combined to enter the canal at canal head, off to the left. In the foreground the tramroads allowed pig iron to be moved easily from casting house to forge and cinders to be moved to the waste tips.
Courtesy Cyfarthfa Castle Museum

Pamplin's second view, a little south from the first, is the earliest depiction of a Glamorganshire Canal boat – complete with cabin and towing mast. The boat is ready to leave canal head and piles of iron rails lie awaiting shipment on the Cyfarthfa wharf. Behind the wharf is Richard Crawshay's house (formerly Anthony Bacon's) alongside one of the Cyfarthfa forges. The tramroad bridge on the right carries the rails from the rolling mills to the wharf.
Courtesy Cyfarthfa Castle Museum

on *Completing the whole in 3 years.'*[35] An additional burden for Dadford at this time was the building of Navigation House, on Craig Evan Leyshon, near the aqueduct. Authorised by the canal committee on 25 Sept 1790, this administrative building of the company was to cost no more than £100. Dadford's estimate in January was £270 and it was arranged that he would live there as resident engineer at a rent of £18 p.a. In November 1791 it seems that it was still not complete as the builder, William Prichard of Cardiff, was advanced a further £80. Dadford and Prichard were ordered to attend the January 1792 meeting to explain themselves.[36]

An interesting postscript to a letter from Crawshay to Lord Cardiff, on 4 April 1791, underlines the importance of lime to the builders of locks, houses, bridges, walls and weirs on the canals at this time:

'In Dadford's great distress for Lime I have undertaken to indemnify Mr Lewis from your Lordship's Resentment for permitting the Kiln at Castle Coch to be worked.'

In much the same way a landowner of substance could

Until recent times Dowlais and Merthyr were well used to tramroads and railways running through their streets. In this picture, taken on 3 August 1948, Guest Keen & Nettlefolds loco No. 11 Gower propels wagons across the High Street in Dowlais on its way between the Ivor works and the yard at Dowlais Cae Harris on the former Cwmbargoed Joint line of the GW and Rhymney Railways. The engine and wagons were working on one of the surviving railways built by the Dowlais Iron Company who had introduced steam locomotives on its tramroads from the late 1820s. ILW photo neg 667

help the contractors with the produce of his woodlands and we learn from Crawshay that timber from the estate of John Kemeys Tynte would be made available for Dadford's work on the canal.[37]

Among the factors causing delay and frustration to Thomas Dadford was the bitter weather leading up to mid January 1792. It was the contractor's slack season, when work in mid-winter came to a stop through ice and frost. Later came a thaw and the danger of flood, and at Dowlais in February the iron company had to postpone work on the railroad.[38] In Cardiff, on 1 April, it rained all day in the town and the following day a pier of Cardiff bridge fell into the flooded Taff.[39] We can perhaps imagine the misery fifteen miles up the Taff Valley, on a rain-soaked hillside, as men swathed in sacking attacked the ground with pick and spade, keeping an uneasy foothold in the mud and clay. They must have welcomed the sounding of the horn along the banks to signal the end of labour for the day.

With the return of the longer days and good weather, Dadford and Co completed the great flight of locks at Abercynon, finished the aqueduct and carried the canal along the steep and unstable ledge under Bodwenarth Wood, at Cilfynydd. In June 1792 Dadford presented his second report to the committee, who must have been relieved to be told that the navigation was open and working for traffic over the 12 miles between Merthyr and Newbridge.[40] Dadford was now supervising the day

to day running of the canal and providing some lock keepers. At Newbridge, arrangements had to be made to transfer Cardiff-bound iron from boat to road waggon, for the rest of the journey to the port. The 1792 report states that 22 locks were navigable on the line, to a height of 278 feet, and that side pond reservoirs had been constructed for the locks at Keven Glace (Goetre Coed). Three more were nearly complete on the Cyfarthfa extension and the canal company's boat maintenance yard, dock and workshops at Navigation were almost finished. No doubt for some time Dadford had been able to bring building materials directly on site using boats.

In January 1793 it was becoming increasingly clear to the canal committee and to Dadford that the canal was going to cost more than the contracted amount. Richard Crawshay's original timescale of three years to build the canal now looked optimistic and the concerned committee determined to examine progress more closely. From the spring of 1792, Richard Crawshay's son William took over management of Cyfarthfa's London yard, allowing the father to become permanently based at Merthyr and so be able to oversee the final stages of canal building at first-hand. In January 1793 the canal was open for traffic only as far as Pwllywhyad (Treforest). By June they reported that the cut was still not in a state to be taken off Dadford's hands. Gone was the generous and conciliatory tone towards Dadford. Authorising another £3,000 to be paid the engineer in April, Crawshay wrote '*but what he is drawing so much money for I cannot conceive.*'[41] The General Assembly must have been worried by the June report, not just because the canal was only navigable to Taffs Well but also there was a bill from Dadford for £17,221 for extra work and a notice that £5,000 more needed to be spent. The whole of the unfinished canal, including the collection of tonnage charges, was still under Dadford's management and his son James was providing the boats. Tonnage receipts to 25 March amounted to £1,231 7s 1d and for the further period to 18 May were £279 8s 5¼d.[42] Dadford pressed on with the canal through Melingriffith, through the moat of Cardiff Castle and a tunnel to the Town Ditch at Crockherbtown. The navigation ended to the south of the town at a point on the River Taff called the Bank. It was complete enough to be opened for traffic from Merthyr to Cardiff on 10 February 1794 and there was much excitement in Cardiff. John Bird had his account published in *The Gentleman's Magazine*:

'*The canal from Cardiff to Merthir-Tidvil is completed and a fleet of canal boats have arrived at Cardiff laden with the products of the iron-works there, to the great joy of the whole town .... The first barge that arrived at Cardiff was finely decorated with colours and was navigated from the Mollingriffield works by Mr Bird, senior water-bailiff of Cardiff.*'[43]

Dr Richard Griffiths, a committee man and landowner who was to gain much from the canal's existence, put on a celebratory entertainment at John Bradley's Angel Hotel in Cardiff, for which the company paid £14 11s 9d.[44]

It was a leaking and ill-formed navigation which had been hastily put together between Melingriffith and Cardiff. Dadford had cut corners in his efforts to economise and complete the canal quickly. There were numerous stoppages for repairs throughout 1794 and Dadford struggled on with the extra burden of traffic management. Crisis point was reached in December, when a major breach in the bank brought traffic to a standstill. There was now also the damaging effect of ice and frost. The canal company ordered the engineer to repair the breach but he would not agree to do the work without payment. This the company would not allow and the committee referred him to the terms of

his contract. Dadford replied by dismissing his workforce and quitting the canal, leaving the company to manage the navigation themselves and to attend to repairs as best they could without their own engineer.[45] The committee promptly sued the Dadfords for the bond sum of £10,000, which was part of the alleged overpayment of £17,000 and they were arrested. Two independent surveyors, Charles Hassall and William Pitt, were brought in to examine the extra work on behalf of the arbitrating engineer, Robert Whitworth[46] but it was adjudged that only £1,512 of the £17,000 claimed should be refunded by the contractors.[47]

January 1795 saw severe frosts followed by a sudden thaw which, at Cardiff, caused the temporary road bridge over the Taff to be swept away by flood and floating ice.[48] Merthyr Bridge also suffered the same fate. The floods of February brought devastation on rivers in Wales and to bridges in almost every county in England.[49] The unfinished works on the Glamorganshire Canal would not have escaped such universal damage. With the Dadfords gone, Crawshay's engineer at Cyfarthfa, Watkin George, took control of the work. Some degree of normality was eventually restored and, in June 1796, Patrick Copeland was appointed as the first Clerk to the company to take on sole management of the canal. Under a new Act of 1796, the canal was extended for a further half mile from the Bank to a pill on the River Taff at the Lower Layer.[50] Here a Sea Lock was built and opened in June 1798; the sloop *Cardiff Castle*, arrived from Bristol, was the first vessel to enter the lock and the mile long floating basin.

With its valley-side mode of construction, sometimes on critical slopes, and its remarkable fall of 200 feet at Abercynon, the Glamorganshire Canal was a notable engineering achievement of its time, reflecting great credit on its designer and builder. As completed throughout to the Sea Lock in 1798 it cost £103,600, including land, for a '*Canal in a Mountainous Country under very great risk and difficulties.*'[51] Thomas Dadford senior set his costs too low and left the Taff Valley under a cloud. Yet the engineer, Robert Whitworth fully vindicated him. A writer of 1796 could not have summarised Thomas Dadford's achievement more simply:

'*The canal is brought through a mountainous country with wonderful ingenuity.*'[52]

NOTES TO CHAPTER 2

1 GCC minute book 28 Aug 1790.

2 Humphrey Household *The Thames and Severn Canal,* Newton Abbot 1987, p.54. The Thames & Severn was completed one year before Dadford commenced the Glamorganshire.

3 Charles Hadfield *Canals of South Wales and the Border,* Cardiff 1960 p.17.

4 All calendared in Chris Evans *The Letterbook of Richard Crawshay 1788-1797,* Cardiff 1990.

5 Household *T&S,* p.56.

6 Entry in John Bird's diary 23 Aug 1792; see Hilary Thomas *The Diaries of John Bird 1790-1803,* Cardiff. The original diaries are in CCL ms2.716.

7 Edgar L. Chappell *Historic Melingriffith,* Cardiff 1940, p.33, 37 and 40-41.

8 Hadfield *The Canal Age,* Newton Abbot 1968 p.42.

9 Household *T&S,* p.56.

10 Paul Vine *London's Lost Route to Midhurst,* Newton Abbot 1995, p.40.

11 Entry 6 March 1790 in Thomas *Diaries of John Bird*.

12 GCC agreement with Thomas Dadford, GRO QAW 2/119.

13 GCC minute book 18 June 1791.

14 GCC minute book 9 Oct 1790.

15 GCC minute book 1 June 1791, GCC balance of accounts 1798 and William Taitt's '*Address to Landowners*', 1799.

16 GRO Dowlais Iron Company letters William Taitt to William Hawks 17 March 1791 printed in Madelaine Elsas *Iron in the Making. Dowlais Iron Company Letters 1782-1860*, Cardiff 1960, also cited by Rattenbury and Lewis in Michael J.T. Lewis *Steam on the Penydarren, Industrial Railway Record No.59*, April 1975, where Taitt's diagram from the letter is reproduced.

17 Gordon Rattenbury *Tramroads of the Brecknock and Abergavenny Canal*, Railway & Canal Historical Society 1980.

18 GCC minute book 7 May 1791.

19 Richard Crawshay to James Cockshutt 30 April 1791, to William Lewis 3 May and to Samuel Homfray 3 May 1791, calendared in Evans *Letterbook*.

20 GRO Dowlais Iron Company letters, William Taitt to Samuel Homfray March 1791, printed in Elsas *Dowlais Letters 1782-1860*, p.148.

21 Per Gordon Rattenbury. See also C.F. Dendy-Marshall *A History of Railway Locomotives down to the end of the Year 1831*, London 1953 and Lewis *Steam on the Penydarren*.

22 For Reden see W.O. Henderson *The State and the Industrial Revolution in Prussia 1740-1870*, Liverpool 1958, p1-20. Reden purchased cast iron cylinders for steam pumps from Homfray at Penydarren and employed William Wilkinson (brother of John) to advise on technical matters including coke-fired smelting.

23 Letters 10 Feb and 14 April 1791. See also Mike Clarke *British Canal History in Perspective*, in *Waterways Journal*, the Boat Museum Society May 1999 p 31-3.

24 Richard Crawshay to James Harford 15 Dec 1790 calendared in Evans *Letterbook*. Also, J.R. Ward *The Finance of Canal Building in Eighteenth-Century England*, Oxford 1974.

25 RC letters 22, 23, 24 Dec 1790, 4 Jan and 10 Feb 1791. All in Evans *Letterbook*.

26 Dadford's first report, dated 1 June 1791 GRO QAW 2/118.

27 There is almost no information surviving on how the Glamorganshire Canal was built, largely because the canal company took no direct part in the work. The authors have relied on the following sources: Abraham Rees *Cyclopedia*, 1819; Humphrey Household *Thames and Severn Canal*; Paul Vine *Midhurst*; R.W. Passfield *Building the Rideau Canal*, Canada 1982, which includes illustrations made on site by the officers of the Royal Engineers who built the Rideau between 1826 and 1832. Passfield describes the building of a lock chamber (p.121) '*A masonry floor was usually built in the form of an inverted arch. The 2-foot deep floor stones conformed to voussoir stones in a conventional masonry arch. They were laid on a foundation of macadamised stone built up in compacted layers of small chipped stone. Hot lime mortar was poured over each layer as it was shaped to match the shape of the arch.*'

28 As the navvies who built Lord Egremont's Canal were described in Arthur Young *General View of Agriculture of Sussex*, 1808.

29 Ibid.

30 Richard Hill to Anthony Harrison 18 July and 10 August 1791 in Richard Hill's letterbook NLW ms 15334E.

31 Richard Crawshay to William Reynolds 9 April and 9 Aug 1790 and to Count de Reden 10 Feb 1791, calendared in Evans *Letterbook*.

32 Richard Crawshay to James Cockshutt 24 Feb 1791 calendared in Evans *Letterbook*.

33 Richard Crawshay to James Cockshutt 22, 23 Dec 1790 and 1 Feb 1791 calendared in Evans *Letterbook*.

34 Dadford's first report, dated 1 June 1791 GRO QAW 2/118.

35 Richard Crawshay to James Cockshutt 16 July 1790 and to Count de Reden 14 April 1791 calendared in Evans *Letterbook*. In the latter letter, Crawshay was full of confidence that Dadford will win both medals and a bonus of £10,000.

36 GCC minute book. Prichard was also working for John Dadford, building a bridge across the Usk for the Brecknock & Abergavenny Canal tramroad to Llangrwyne Forge. When Prichard was declared bankrupt in January 1794, the Canal Company minuted that they were in debt to his assignees for £132 15s 7d for work not only on Navigation House but on the company's warehouse and bridge over the Taff.

37 Richard Crawshay to James Cockshutt 24 Aug 1791 calendared in Evans *Letterbook*.

38 Robert Thompson to William Taitt 24 Feb 1792 calendared in Elsas *Dowlais Letters*.

39 Entries 1 and 2 April 1792 in Thomas *Diaries of John Bird*.

40 Dadford's second report, dated 6 June 1792 GRO QAW 2/118.

41 Letter Robert Crawshay to Joseph Vaughan 8 April 1793 private collection ex Melingriffith papers (not in the Crawshay letterbook).

42 Dadford's third report, dated 5 June 1793 GRO QAW 2/118; GCC minute book 13 July 1793.

43 Reprinted in J. Phillips *A General History of Inland Navigation*, 4th ed. 1803 p.585.

44 GCC minute book 15 March and 5 June 1794.

45 GCC minute book 13 and 16 Dec 1794.

46 At that time Whitworth was working on the Wilts & Berks Canal and Hassall had just published his brilliant *General View of the Agriculture of Pembroke*, in which he included a reference to the short canal of Lord Milford, running from his Kilgetty collieries to Wiseman's Bridge. In the following ten years or so, both Hassall and Pitt went on to write several similar Government reports on English counties, including Monmouth, all of which include information of industrial interest.

47 Case GCN v T. Dadford GRO QAW 1/118; award of Robert Whitworth of Burnley 17 Oct 1745 GRO B/C GCa 4/10.

48 Entries 27 Jan 1795 in Thomas *Diaries of John Bird*.

49 Letter Richard Crawshay to Winter and Kaye 13 Feb 1795 in GCC minute book; E. Jervoise *Ancient Bridges of Mid and Eastern England*, London 1932, has eight references to the Feb 1795 floods.

50 Glamorganshire Canal Act 36 Geo III c.69.

51 GCC case against the Tramroad 1799, GRO QAW 2/44 p.2.

52 John Bird *Cardiff Directory and Guide*, Cardiff 1796.

Chapter 3

MERTHYR TYDFIL – CANAL TOWN
1792 – 1898

To the generation living in Merthyr Tydfil today, the concept of canal boats loading and unloading at busy wharves and yards in the town must be difficult to grasp. Almost nothing now remains of the pattern of canal settlement in Georgetown and Ynysfach. Yet Merthyr, once the iron metropolis of the world, was for over a hundred years an inland port. Not only was the Glamorganshire Canal loading and sending down to Cardiff prodigious tonnages of wrought and cast iron products, demanded by the wars with France and, later, rails for the world's railways, but in the return direction the waterway was the major means of supplying shop goods and building materials for Merthyr's expanding working population. Shop goods were imported from London, Bristol, the West Country and Ireland, while timber was imported from the Baltic. Locally obtained produce and materials, such as timber, stone, bricks, tiles, slate, lime and limestone, also reached Merthyr by water. The waterway kept the growing town supplied with domestic fuel and, when the iron industry needed to augment its local deposits of iron ore, it was the Glamorganshire Canal which brought imported ore up the valley to Merthyr.

Until the arrival of the Taff Vale Railway (TVR) in Merthyr in 1841, the Glamorganshire Canal was the sole means of moving heavy consignments over the 25 miles from Merthyr to Cardiff and for another twenty years the canal company's tonnages were scarcely diminished by the railway. A decline in traffic accelerated through the 1870s as the ironworks closed or went over to steel making – Dowlais even relocating its works nearer to the coast. Coal mining had become the dominant industry south of Merthyr by the 1880s, with almost every coal consignment leaving the pits by rail. By 1886 the lines of six railway companies were competing for traffic in Merthyr. Small wonder, then, in the face of such acute competition, that there was almost no business left for the boats at the company's wharves. The year 1898 saw the end of canal trading in Merthyr, though the closure was an engineering decision taken to safeguard the mining community of Aberfan. On 6 December 1898, after over a century of association with waterborne trade, Merthyr Tydfil ceased to be a canal town.

The Canal Corridor

Compressed within the space of only half a mile between Cyfarthfa and Parliament Lock, the narrow ribbon of the Glamorganshire Canal ran down the western bank of the River Taff, protected from the river floods by masonry walls. Three canal locks conveniently divided this commercial artery into three sectors:
1. The Cyfarthfa Pound, largely serving the yards, wharves and rail finishing shops of the Crawshays, extending from below Cyfarthfa ironworks to Lock 1 and Jackson's bridge.
2. The Penydarren or Middle Pound, extending from Jackson's Bridge to Lock 2 at Penry Street, near Canal Square and the river crossings at Iron Bridge (1800) and Ynysgau (1879). In this pound the Dowlais and Penydarren ironworks had their yards.
3. The Ynysfach or Parliament Pound, between Lock 2 at Penry Street and Lock 3, the Parliament lock. The west bank of this stretch of canal served the Crawshays' Ynysfach ironworks, established in 1801 as a subsidiary to Cyfarthfa. On the east bank were the timber yards, a boat dock, the canal company's toll office and the lock keeper's house dating from the very beginning of the canal and where, in 1807, the company ordered '. . . . the Clerk at Merthyr to live in the Lock keeper's house at Parliament Lock and do the lock keeper's work at 16s a week and to keep a daily account in a book of what every boat brings up and grant permits to every boat going down.'[1]

The Early Years 1792-1830

From Cyfarthfa House by the Canal Head, Richard Crawshay could literally step out onto the canal bank. As canal promoter, principal shareholder and dominant proprietor, he wrote in 1797:

'My canal commences at my Door down to Cardiff River. Our boats . . . . go up and down in 3 days when Active but oftener 4 and are attended by a little welch horse & 2 Men.'[2]

Few images of the Glamorganshire Canal in Merthyr exist and it is very fortunate that William Pamplin,

Crawshay's gardener, produced a drawing of the Canal Head about 1800 showing Crawshay's house (built originally for Anthony Bacon), a canal boat and one of the Cyfarthfa forges (see page 33).

Some idea of the traffic in iron passing to the canal from the four ironworks, two years after the canal was fully opened to Cardiff, can be seen in the following table for production at the four Merthyr Ironworks in 1796.[3]

WORKS	NUMBER OF FURNACES	PRODUCTION (TONS)
CYFARTHFA	3	7,204
PLYMOUTH	1	2,200
PENYDARREN	2	4,100
DOWLAIS	3	2,800

It must be appreciated that Merthyr was then living through momentous times. Britain was involved in the Napoleonic Wars, and food shortages and high prices affected most parts of the country, bringing the threat of social unrest to the volatile working population of Merthyr. The Corn Act of 1791, formulated to protect domestic farmers, was preventing cheap foreign cereals from reaching vulnerable industrial settlements like Merthyr. Dreading rebellion, Richard Crawshay successfully appealed to Lord Hawkesbury in May 1793, who then allowed the importation of 1,200 tons of American flour and wheat for his workers. On the assumption that it arrived by sea at Cardiff, Crawshay would have consigned this food by road waggon as far as Pontypridd, transferring there into boats for onward shipment on the completed part of the canal to Merthyr. He urged all speed on Philip Sansom, writing *'we are in Danger of being Starved.'*[4]

The canal company's warehouse at Merthyr is on the list of additional works in Thomas Dadford's June 1793 report. In a letter on 25 November 1794 to A. Hellicar & Sons (Bristol), Crawshay ordered two hogsheads of the best Taunton ale and a whole sloop's cargo of malt, oats, beans and beer, stating that a warehouse is ready built to receive it, *'to be conducted by one of the canal people.'* It is hoped that this consignment reached Merthyr before the breach in the canal bank put the navigation out of action in December 1794. Perhaps it went by road, which is what may have happened to the Dowlais order for potatoes and blacking dust:

'. . . . the breach in the Canal has put out of our power to send you either the Potatoes, or the blacking Dust, unless it is by land, and I cannot find with any degree of certainty when the Canal will be navigable again to Merthyr. When it is you may depend on both, or the dust sooner if you want it may be sent by Thomas Lewis Hughes Wagon . . . .'[5]

Whilst the Merthyr terminal for the Dowlais boats was at a yard to the south of Jackson's Bridge, the canal company's warehouse stood next to Lock No 1. The canal bridge here soon acquired the name Pont Storehouse and

as Merthyr grew from a collection of hamlets into a town, the district close to this important river crossing became the focus of considerable commercial activity. It was not long before the whole area around the Bethesda Street canal bridge became known as Pont Storehouse and the name remained in common use into the 20th century.[6]

Though the waters of the Glamorganshire Canal would have presented an outward appearance of calm, it was obvious that bitter grievances and dissatisfaction were boiling over among the east bank ironmasters, who looked across the river to see Richard Crawshay controlling the canal and running it to his exclusive advantage. Plymouth works had its own special problem in that the canal was taking its water supply. Richard Hill also had his personal grievances with Crawshay, who was charging him excessively for limestone from the Gurnos quarry. Dowlais and Penydarren encountered a succession of problems. Having actively supported the Canal Bill in Parliament, they saw the canal branch to their works immediately dropped from the scheme and were forced to build their own tramroads to their canal wharves at Merthyr. Next the tonnage rates were set higher than had been at first promised, which, they argued, made it only marginally cheaper for them to use the tramroads and canal instead of the former method of horse-back and road waggon to Cardiff. This was not the end of their problems, for as soon as the canal was opened through to Cardiff, Crawshay's canal committee squeezed the profits at Dowlais and Penydarren further by declaring that, from 1 July 1794, all tonnages were to be charged at the statute ton instead of the long ton. The long ton of 21 cwt of 120lbs (2,520lbs) was a traditional measure for freight which, by allowing for loss or breakage, attempted to ensure that the correct weight in the statute ton was delivered, the statute ton being 20cwt of 112lbs (2,240lbs). The original agreement was that shipments would be charged per long ton. At first they refused to pay the excess by continuing to return their tonnages to the toll clerk on the long ton basis. In 1798 the canal company decided to enforce the byelaw and ordered John Wood to take proceedings against Dowlais and Penydarren immediately.[7]

The response by the dissident Dowlais, Penydarren and Plymouth ironmasters to Crawshay's uncompromising attitude was their promotion in 1798 of a Bill in Parliament to build a Merthyr to Cardiff Dramroad, to rival the canal. The main route was to be joined by a branch to Carno Mill, to serve the embryonic Rhymney ironworks, and by another branch from Quaker's Yard to the Cynon Valley and Hirwaun ironworks. In an attempt to reconcile the differences between the parties, a special assembly (an extraordinary general meeting) of the canal company was called by Sir Robert Salusbury, Sir Benjamin Hammel and Colonel Wood, to propose a new canal Bill to repeal the clause which limited dividends to 8%, to revert to charging by the long ton and also to reduce the tolls by two fifths. The proposals were endorsed by Homfray, Taitt and John Wilkinson but were rejected by the Crawshay majority in favour of simply reducing tonnage rates to 4d for iron, $1\frac{1}{2}$d

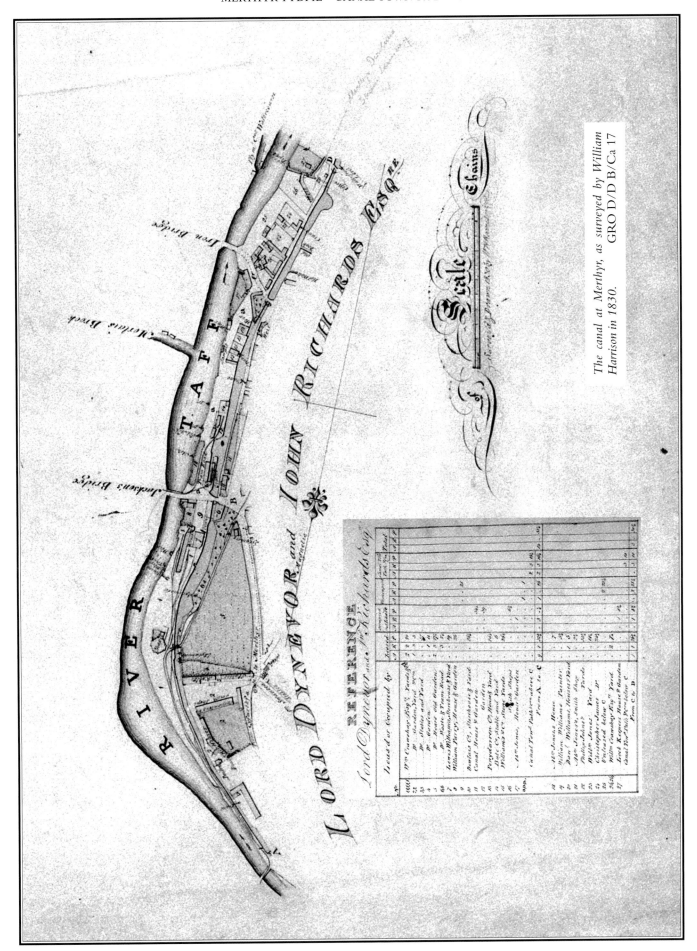

The canal at Merthyr, as surveyed by William Harrison in 1830.   GRO D/D B/Ca 17

The site of the Canal Head at Cyfarthfa as it was in 1947. This location, where water entered the canal from the mill races of Crawshays' Cyfarthfa ironworks, was 568 feet above sea level and the highest level reached by a major canal in Wales. Remains of the iron and steel works are seen behind the bridge arch, which spanned the lines of the Cyfarthfa works tramroad and later railway. ILW photo 28 June 1947 neg 474

for coal and 1d for stone, with the additional benefit that coal, stone and limestone should attract a maximum charge of 1/6d even if it were carried the whole length of the canal.[8] The tramroad project, described by the canal company as a '*barbarous horse road*', was successfully opposed by the Cyfarthfa party and they celebrated by awarding a pipe of wine to Edmund Escort, solicitor of the Beaufort estate and representative of the Monmouthshire Canal Company, who had spoken in opposition to the Dramroad Bill. In victory, the canal company resolved that all tonnage accounts should, after all, be in long weight, backdated to 1 April 1799.[9]

Unbeknown to Crawshay at that time, the tramroad scheme was far from dead but was soon replaced by a less grand plan, removing the branch to Hirwaun and finally by one which removed the Carno Mill branch and, by extending only part-way to Cardiff, did not require an Act of Parliament. The resultant Merthyr Tramroad ran through Penydarren, down the eastern side of the Taff Valley past the Plymouth works, to a basin on the canal just a stone's throw from the canal's river aqueduct at Navigation. For the majority of its length the Merthyr Tramroad ran on land owned by the sympathetic Lord Plymouth but it was also laid legally under the canal Act's four-mile clause. The tramroad opened to traffic in 1802. At Navigation, iron was transferred to the canal for onward carriage to Cardiff.

The engineer was George Overton and the gauge he chose was 4 feet 2 inches between the backs of the plates or 4 feet 4 inches over them. From Penydarren the Dowlais railroad was relaid to Dowlais as a plateway, to the new gauge, and northward to the Plymouth estate's Morlais limestone quarries. Thus the Hills of Plymouth were finally able to transfer their limestone account away from the Crawshay-controlled Gurnos quarry. This extension to Morlais was laid on the same line as the 3 foot gauge Penydarren tramroad to their own part of the quarry, both plateways becoming a mixed-gauge road by sharing one of the lines of tramplates.[10] Despite these developments, and the new exchange basin at Navigation, the Dowlais and Penydarren proprietors still maintained their canal yards at Merthyr. It seems that the Dowlais railroad was abandoned and lifted from Penydarren End to the wharf but that the 3 foot gauge Penydarren plateway remained. In 1815, when a bridge on the Merthyr Tramroad collapsed, the Dowlais Company was forced to temporarily divert its traffic to the Penydarren tramroad and use its wharf at Merthyr instead of Navigation. Clearly a lot of water had flowed under the bridge since Samuel Homfray's and William Taitt's arguments in 1791! Penydarren and Dowlais were now partners in the Merthyr Tramroad but it is possible that Penydarren was also obliged to allow public use of its tramroad to the Merthyr yards because it had

A rare view of the canal at Merthyr at the time of its closure, in the 1890s, taken from a glass lantern slide. Abandoned Cyfarthfa boats lie sunken against the towpath where the canal turns to the left, past the site of the tramroad bridge from the red ore wharf to Ynysfach ironworks. Across the canal, Cyfarthfa chapel is still roofed and serving as a warehouse. Note the wall and door giving secure access to the canal company's property at Lock 1 alongside the company warehouse.   W. Hamlin collection

been built under the four mile clause.[11]

Whilst the ironmasters were sorting out their differences, or at least seeking a basis by which they could all continue in business within an atmosphere of guarded respect, unrest of a different kind surfaced at Merthyr in 1800. Low prices in the iron trade brought severe reductions in wages among the ironworkers who were already hit hard by the inflationary wartime cost of food. As would be repeated in 1816 and again in 1831, violence and riot hit the town. In the September of 1800 there was anxiety for the safety of boats arriving in Merthyr with food for Dowlais. William Pritchard, agent at Cardiff, wrote to Thomas Guest:

> *'I await your Answer tomorrow before I will load the Boat with Shop goods, flour &c lest the tumult may not have subsided, & that the Mob may take it into their Heads to destroy the Cargo . . . .'[12]*

From the opening of the Merthyr Tramroad, the Cyfarthfa and Ynysfach ironworks now provided most of the finished iron loaded in boats for shipping through Merthyr to Cardiff. Both works were close to the canal

and labour at the furnaces went on day and night. A contemporary traveller wrote:

> *'In proceeding towards the new colony of Merthyr Tydvil, the valley becomes sprinkled with numerous edifices, and, on advancing, the ear is assailed by the strokes of massive hammers and the roar of furnaces.'[13]*

Many turned from these haunts of Vulcan but those who stayed observed the night sky glowing with fire, and witnessed the excitement of the pyrotechnics at the casting houses and the flowing disposals from the slag ladles on the engulfing cinder tips.

Evidence of the canal company's prosperity at this time emerged in an unusual form. Dividends were still limited to 8% on the major part of the capital. Once paid to the shareholders there remained the problem of disposing of the rest of the surplus revenue. Between the years 1804 and 1828, with a few gaps only, the company chose to return large sums to the traders, allowing the freighters free carriage over specified periods and reducing the tolls by up to 75% below the rates fixed by Parliament.[14] It

The remains of Cyfarthfa chapel and part of Chapel Row in August 1951. The Chapel of Ease was erected at Richard Crawshay's expense, perhaps even before the canal was built. It ceased to be a chapel not many years later and was in use as a storehouse and carpenters shop by 1850.
ILW photo neg 1129

Below: *In the 1970s and again in 1982 the canal was excavated from Chapel Row to the site of Lock 1. The remains of several boats were unearthed but then left to rot away. Note the heavy keelson running the length of the flat-bottomed boat (the design of the Glamorganshire Canal boats will be discussed in volume 2). In the background is the cast iron bridge from Rhydycar, re-sited here by the Merthyr Tydfil Heritage Trust.*

might be thought that the canal workers would have shared in the bounty. This was not so. The canal proprietors were also the ironmasters, who jealously controlled the employment of their Merthyr ironworkers and colliers – they did not wish to sow discontent within these sensitive workplaces and made sure that wages were kept in line. So in 1822, at a time of slump in the iron industry but continuing prosperity for the canal, the unfortunate canal workers suffered not a rise but a cut in wages. At the same meeting the canal committee ordered '*in future no man be taken into employ under the age of thirty and that no tools or beer*

be allowed the men.'[15] Men in the prime of life were expected to sacrifice their vitality to the demands of iron making or working at the coal face.

It has been stated elsewhere that, until 1845, British canal freighters who were also canal proprietors were not authorised to engage in canal carrying.[16] Certainly the Glamorganshire Canal Company did not carry at this time, but the ironworks and collieries of which their principals were on the canal committee did possess and operate their own boats. At Merthyr, apart from the trade in Crawshay iron, there was a steady number of boats arriving with

Lock 1 and the canal company's warehouse near Jackson's bridge. Boats unloaded behind the warehouse, from the navigable canal feeder which entered the canal below the lock. The Cyfarthfa wagon shed, rail sheds and boat repair yard are seen beyond, with Cyfarthfa Castle, the Merthyr home of the Crawshays from 1825, on the hillside in the distance.
ILW photo 28 June 1947, neg 479

market provisions and hay for the many hundreds of horses on which the industrial town relied. In the early years, William Taitt managed Dowlais traffic from his base at Cardiff and the Dowlais letterbooks give a fascinating account of these pioneering days. Initially, James Dadford carried for them on his several waggons and boats. The hasty departure of his father Thomas from the canal contract seems to have forced James to sell up and retire gracefully from the district. Taitt bought several of the Dadford boats and horses on behalf of the Dowlais company.[17] Taitt also entered into a partnership with John Key (brother of Thomas and William). Key was to provide their yard at Merthyr with flour and barley from his and neighbouring farms at Ely and St Fagans near Cardiff, the boats being loaded at Llandaff Yard.[18] While John Key provided Merthyr with flour, Thomas Key provided it with house coal and the other brother, William, sold pitwood from his land at Gwaun y Geryn. For many shop goods, Merthyr relied on places farther afield and these were

imported to Cardiff invariably via Bristol. In 1801 William Taitt further extended Dowlais's control over its supplies by purchasing Captain Walters' sloops in the Bristol trade for £1,500.[19]

As has been already mentioned, the canal company's public warehouse was situated above Lock 1. In September 1818 it was resolved to enlarge the lower end of the partially culverted branch of the Cyfarthfa tailrace which supplied the Penydarren pond:

'. . . . a Cut no less than 10 feet wide be made to admit the Canal Boats as far as the Chapel Gate passing as near to the Canal Company's warehouse as to unload the same. The Cut to be arched from the Penydarren pond . . . .'[20]

This arrangement meant that the boats could use the lower part of the underground feeder as a branch canal, to reach a wharf alongside the warehouse basement and so obviate the need to use Lock 1. From the 1820s (and probably a decade before that) market boats were running daily from Cardiff to Merthyr. John and Matthew Pride carried on a trade from Bristol to Merthyr, owning both sea-going ships and canal boats.[21] In 1828 their Bristol trader *Amity* was advertised as connecting with Merthyr-bound boats at the Sea Lock.[22] They also advertised regularly in *The Cambrian* newspaper.

By the late 1820s increasing imports of iron ore were being handled at Merthyr. Cargoes of ore were entering Cardiff from the Cumbrian and Lancashire ports of Whitehaven, Ulverston, Ravenglass and Barrow.[23] A certain amount of iron ore was already being imported when the canal was being built and the company gave orders for work to be halted on making an ore wharf at Cardiff during its dispute with Dadford in 1795. A proportion of the incoming iron ore was transshipped from boats to the Merthyr Tramroad at the basin at Navigation and hauled up to the works at Dowlais, Penydarren and Plymouth

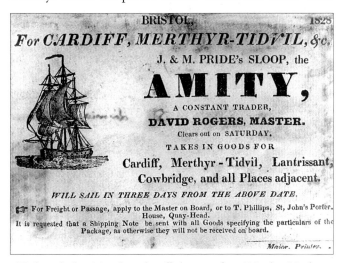

Trade card advertising through traffic by water from Bristol to Merthyr.
Courtesy Welsh Industrial & Maritime Museum

Merthyr circa 1830, in an engraving by Henry Gastineau, dominated by the newly-built Cyfarthfa castle. Spanning the River Taff is Jackson's bridge, carrying the tramroads to the Dowlais and Penydarren canalside wharves, whose buildings can be seen on the left. Smoke rises from a chimney on the canal company's warehouse (let at that time to Lewis Williams) and beyond is the octagonal Cyfarthfa chapel. On the right, Gastineau shows clearly the extent of waste tipping on the river bank by the Penydarren ironworks. The houses in the right foreground hide where the Morlais Brook empties its polluted waters into the River Taff. If the canal branch to Dowlais had been built, it would have crossed the river here on an aqueduct. From *South Wales Illustrated*, London 1830

but, as the imports grew, significant tonnages stayed with the canal the whole way to Merthyr, usually only 15 tons per boat because of the heavy down current produced by the continual use of locks. Crawshay imports were taken up to the Red Mine tramroad just above Lock 1, where they were loaded into drams and hauled to the Ynysfach works. Dowlais ore, on the other hand, was transferred to drams at the Jackson's Bridge wharf and taken through Bethesda Street, on the tramroad past Penydarren, to Dowlais. In preparation for locomotive haulage in 1827, the land of the long-disused Dowlais railroad from Penydarren to the canal wharf was conveyed to the Penydarren company, who realigned their route to by-pass the Bethesda Street tunnel under Penydarren's plateway to its waste tips at Abermorlais. In doing so, they also added a third rail to the 3 foot gauge plateway, to take the 4 foot 4 inch gauge Dowlais traffic. The mixed gauge line is shown on the 1851 Public Health Act map of Merthyr. The section of tramroad from Penydarren to Dowlais was fitted with rack rails to provide adhesion for the Dowlais steam locomotives.[24]

Some interesting facts emerge from a study of the Dowlais figures for iron ore forwarded to Merthyr by boat in 1827. A particular boatman was invariably in charge of the same boat. A named boatman, M. Morgan, with boat number 52, left Cardiff for Merthyr with iron ore on 14 April. He was back in Cardiff and leaving again for Merthyr

seven days later on 20 April. From 14 April to 21 April inclusive, seven different boatmen moved 116 tons of ore from Cardiff to the Dowlais wharf at Merthyr. All but one carried the full 15 tons. Morgan, as already noted, completed two round trips in that period.[25] Boating hours from Cardiff to Merthyr were subject to a number of variables – hours of daylight between summer and winter, duration of the overnight stop, congestion of traffic, ice and shortage of water. From 1822 conditions were eased as the canal was opened for traffic on Sundays.

Reference is made elsewhere to the sale of coal from the canal at Merthyr but, to conclude this survey of the canal town's business pre-1830, it is noted that land above Parliament lock and lying between the River Taff and the canal had already become the traditional centre of Merthyr's timber trade. In March 1825 the canal company leased yards here to Christopher James, at £22 10s per annum, and to William Rugg, Philip Jones and John James at 15s each per annum. Christopher James was authorised to spend £150, and William Rugg and Philip Jones £100 each on their respective premises.[26] No doubt a proportion of the timber imported to these yards was the commonly used St. Petersburg and Memel woods coming in from the Baltic. Next to the timber yard site was an Old Dock (probably Dadford's original, established for the repair of boats). By the 1850s, at the top end of the canal near Canal Head, the Crawshays maintained a private timber yard and a large

J.G. Wood's Rivers of Wales *was published in 1811. A large proportion of his original drawings and watercolours, on which the book's engavings are based, are in the collection of Cardiff City Library. This view of Merthyr from the north shows the two furnaces, casting house and blowing engine house of Ynysfach ironworks on the right, behind which are its cinder tips running along both sides of the canal, bridged by a high arch. In the foreground is Jackson's bridge, leading to buildings clustered around Lock 1 and the Dowlais and Penydarren wharves. Wood has also included Middle Lock bridge on the canal and Ynysgau iron bridge on the river.*
Wash drawing by J.G. Wood 1810, CCL collection

The iron bridge over the Taff, with the canal company's Jackson's bridge beyond. The iron bridge, designed by the Cyfarthfa engineer Watkin George, replaced the ancient stone Merthyr bridge which collapsed in the winter of 1795. Jackson's bridge was built by the canal company and was probably named after its stonemason, who came from Ledbury.
Original wash drawing by J.G. Wood 1810, CCL collection

The Ynysgau iron bridge was dismantled in an official act of vandalism in 1963, even though it had been replaced as long ago as 1880 as the Swansea road bridge. Although the bridge was not directly connected with the canal, this photograph is included to show some of the detail of its 1799-1800 construction. The stonework was made by David Edwards.
Courtesy WIMM, 84.784

This view of David Williams & Co's Taff Vale brewery was published in Wilkins' Merthyr Illustrated *after the canal was closed. The brewery was on the bank of the second pound just above Middle Lock (Lock 2). Between Locks 1 and 2 the towpath was on the canal's west bank.*

graving dock, where boat building and repair work were in the hands of a group of craftsmen dedicated to keeping the wooden boats of Cyfarthfa and Ynysfach works in sound condition. It is likely that the majority of Merthyr boat-owning freighters relied on the shipwrights at Cardiff to supply their boats. William Rugg, himself, had a yard at Cardiff.

Prosperity and Decline 1830 – 1898

The 1830s mark the start of a steady rise in steam coal exports from the collieries of Merthyr. The census of 1841 shows that Merthyr was easily the largest town in Wales, having a population greater than that of Swansea, Cardiff and Newport combined. At this time of increasing business at the canal wharves of the town, the canal company stepped up its organisation to deal with the trade. From 1833, William Edwards' wages were increased from 13s to 15s per week for granting coal permits, including night working, and in 1839 Edwards was appointed to superintend the upper part of the canal at 21s per week and a house. Lock 2 at Penry Street, then called Teague's Lock, was found to be in bad shape that year and the carpenters, masons and work gangs were brought up from Navigation yard to rebuild it.[27] In 1841, the company's respected clerk at Merthyr, William Harrison, was given £30 for '*extra services*' to add to his salary of £120 a year.

He died in 1848 having been clerk at Merthyr since 1827. Posterity owes a good deal to Harrison, for in 1829-30 he surveyed and mapped the whole of the Glamorganshire Canal from Cyfarthfa to the sea and the book of maps survives at Glamorganshire Record Office.[28]

Newspapers and trade directories provide a useful picture of how the public canal carriers were serving Merthyr. Pigot & Co's Commercial Directory of 1830 lists under Merthyr Tydfil:

> *Conveyance by water:*
> *By Canal to Cardiff*
> *James & Thomas and Lewis Williams, every day*
> *Pride & Co and Daniel Llewellin, weekly.*

Hunt & Co's Directory of 1848 informs the Merthyr public:

> *Canal Offices George Town. Agent James Lewis.*
> *Canal conveyances to Cardiff from Jackson's Bridge*
> *Thomas Williams and Woodman & Co boats three times a week.*

In fact, by the beginning of 1848, the firm of Woodman & Co was dissolved and their fly boats were advertised for sale by auction at Cardiff. They comprised one oak covered boat with tarpaulins, two red pine covered boats with tarpaulins and another open red pine boat.[29]

In 1858-9 we find William Harris's boats running to Cardiff from the Merthyr Canal Wharf and Williams & Co's boats from Jackson's Bridge daily.[30] A '*water conveyance*' to Cardiff was still being advertised by William Harris in 1878, with boats from the Canal Wharf daily.[31] The canal company did not guarantee permanence of tenure at the yards but rather granted tenancies at will. Old leases were ended and new ones granted, and in 1843 Lewis Lewis took a lease of Philip Jones' old timber yard and warehouse at Merthyr, as a yearly tenant at £20 per annum. Previously, these had been leased to Watson & Co, who had a corresponding yard on the Sea Lock pound in Cardiff and a yard on the Aberdare Canal.[32] In 1849, when Thomas Williams was ordered '*to quit the warehouse and yards at Merthyr Tydfil*', the canal company's boats he had been renting were required to be given up.[33] No doubt these would have been the four good boats sold to Edward Roach in 1850 when Roach took a yearly lease on the Merthyr warehouse for £50.[34]

In the absence of much contemporary description of what life was like on Merthyr's canal, we have to build a picture from the newspapers of the time, from a variety of archive material including census returns and maps, and from our predecessors' attempts to paint the picture. Gwyn Alf Williams has done this admirably in his 1978 study of the 1831 Merthyr Rising and the story of Dic Penderyn. F.J. Pedler, looking back from the 1930s, gives useful insights into the canal environment of Georgetown, of local industry between Cyfarthfa and Gethin, and something of the atmosphere around the Iron bridge, with its peripheral characters and trades. Well before 1840 a good deal of industrial housing had been built near to the canal, largely to house the ironworkers and colliers of Cyfarthfa, and those working in the town's canalside trades – farriers, ostlers, hauliers, warehousemen, clerks, boatmen, boatboys, labourers and platelayers – the last whose trade was essential

for maintaining the permanent way of tramroads (the tramplates being laid and spiked into holes in stone block sleepers and kept in gauge by cast-iron tie bars). Pedler records the public houses, many of them in and around the canal at Dynevor Street, and all of these favourite haunts of the boatmen – the Corner House, the Canal House and Y Briwhouse Bach – where there was beer, lively conversation, music and song, and perhaps the chance of

By 1910, the canal had begun to be filled in at Merthyr. Here, children play beneath Penry Street bridge, below Middle Lock. Penry Street took the main road from Swansea across the river at Ynysgau. It also took the towpath from the canal's west bank back to the east bank. Behind, to the right, is the Taff Vale brewery.

Courtesy Merthyr Tydfil Library

Three men haul a boat from the bank opposite Ynysfach ironworks, in an oil painting executed by Penry Williams, c1815-20. Crawshay family collection

G.F. Harris's magnificent 1877 multi-print panorama of Merthyr Tydfil now hangs fittingly in the Ynysfach off-station of Cyfarthfa Castle Museum, the site from which the image was composed when the building was the blowing engine house of Ynysfach ironworks. It takes in a vista from the distant Cyfarthfa Castle in the north to St Tydfil's church in the south but, due to its size, only the leftmost third of the panorama is reproduced here. In the foreground the upper gate of Lock 3 (Parliament Lock) lies open and the single storied white-washed building, with the tall chimney, at the lock is the canal clerk's office, at which boat permits were granted for all canal traffic leaving Merthyr. In the garden behind is the lock keeper's house, whilst further to the right (off picture) is the River Taff and the Plymouth Weir, from which the feeder supplied water power successively to Plymouth, Pentrebach and Duffryn ironworks. Just upstream from the lock, a gap in the towpath wall and a door in the

wall marks the entrance to the boat dock. Beyond that are the timber yards and out-buildings, Canal Square and finally the coal yard below the canal bridge at Middle Lock. From Middle Lock, Penry Street runs behind the coal yard to Watkin George's iron bridge across the Taff, whilst Ynysgau chapel is beyond, again off picture. Above Middle Lock can be seen the Taff Vale brewery on the canal's east bank and across the river to the right of the brewery is the massive Bethesda cinder tip (christened 'Newfoundland'), crowned by Abermorlais school. The tip was formed of waste from the Penydarren ironworks. The waste was brought down by a tramroad, which parted from the main line to the canal wharf and, after maintaining the high ground, swung south to then cross it before reaching the tipping area alongside the northern bank of the Morlais Brook.

G.F. Harris photo 1877, Cyfarthfa Castle Museum collection

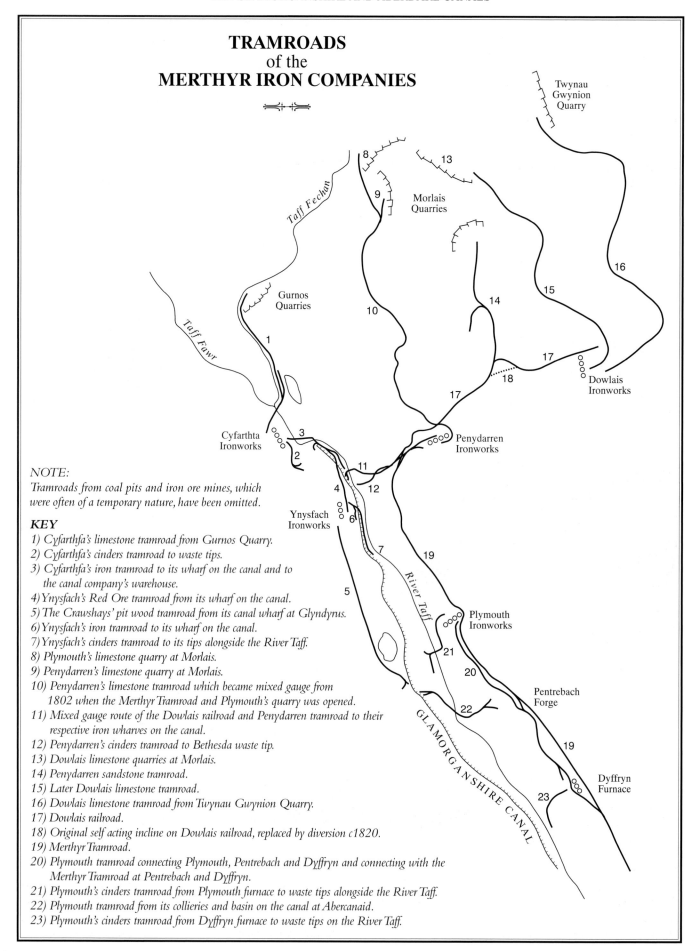

TRAMROADS
of the
MERTHYR IRON COMPANIES

NOTE:

Tramroads from coal pits and iron ore mines, which were often of a temporary nature, have been omitted.

KEY

1) *Cyfarthfa's limestone tramroad from Gurnos Quarry.*
2) *Cyfarthfa's cinders tramroad to waste tips.*
3) *Cyfarthfa's iron tramroad to its wharf on the canal and to the canal company's warehouse.*
4) *Ynysfach's Red Ore tramroad from its wharf on the canal.*
5) *The Crawshays' pit wood tramroad from its canal wharf at Glyndyrus.*
6) *Ynysfach's iron tramroad to its wharf on the canal.*
7) *Ynysfach's cinders tramroad to its tips alongside the River Taff.*
8) *Plymouth's limestone quarry at Morlais.*
9) *Penydarren's limestone quarry at Morlais.*
10) *Penydarren's limestone tramroad which became mixed gauge from 1802 when the Merthyr Tramroad and Plymouth's quarry was opened.*
11) *Mixed gauge route of the Dowlais railroad and Penydarren tramroad to their respective iron wharves on the canal.*
12) *Penydarren's cinders tramroad to Bethesda waste tip.*
13) *Dowlais limestone quarries at Morlais.*
14) *Penydarren sandstone tramroad.*
15) *Later Dowlais limestone tramroad.*
16) *Dowlais limestone tramroad from Twynau Gwynion Quarry.*
17) *Dowlais railroad.*
18) *Original self acting incline on Dowlais railroad, replaced by diversion c1820.*
19) *Merthyr Tramroad.*
20) *Plymouth tramroad connecting Plymouth, Pentrebach and Dyffryn and connecting with the Merthyr Tramroad at Pentrebach and Dyffryn.*
21) *Plymouth's cinders tramroad from Plymouth furnace to waste tips alongside the River Taff.*
22) *Plymouth tramroad from its collieries and basin on the canal at Abercanaid.*
23) *Plymouth's cinders tramroad from Dyffryn furnace to waste tips on the River Taff.*

Twynau
Gwynion
Quarry

Morlais
Quarries

Gurnos
Quarries

Taff Fechan

Taff Fawr

Cyfarthta
Ironworks

Dowlais
Ironworks

Penydarren
Ironworks

Ynysfach
Ironworks

River Taff

Plymouth
Ironworks

Pentrebach
Forge

GLAMORGANSHIRE CANAL

Dyffryn
Furnace

some business for a boatman anxious to pick up a cargo for Cardiff. As an accompaniment to the shouts of men on the towpath, urging on their boathorses, there was the tainted air drifting from John Bryant's tanyard and the thick and pungeant smoke from the brick kilns by his limepits.[35] We can imagine the din and clatter of the unsprung drams on the tramplates at Jackson's bridge, and the hiss of steam and billowing smoke from the Dowlais Co's tram locomotive, as it waited for the last iron ore boat to be unloaded into the drams in the

was hard to believe, as the 1860s drew to a close, that life on their busy canal was slackening its pace.

No photographer, amateur or professional, seems to have ventured on to the Merthyr towpath to record canal activity during the working days, even though there was a sixty year opportunity from the birth of photography in 1839 to the demise of this section of the canal. The earliest photograph we know is Harris's magnificent panorama of 1877 Merthyr which takes in the Ynysfach pond. But activity there is none, perhaps due to

The Cyfarthfa company's limestone quarry at Gurnos, photographed in the 1870s by Robert Thompson Crawshay. From this point (just beyond the quarrymens' bridge) the Cyfarthfa water supply was taken from the Taff Fechan. In the far distance the ruins of Morlais Castle indicate the source of limestone for the Crawshays' rivals.
Courtesy Welsh Industrial & Maritime Museum, 86.187/60

Dowlais yard.[36]

For those who worked on the boats, life on the canal to Merthyr was harsh, exhausting and often brutal. Boatmen worked long hours to earn a living, loading and unloading their own craft, leading the horse along miles of towpath, as well as steering the boat, working locks and waiting turns through the fifty locks to Cardiff. Despite this, for the men of Merthyr engaged in this job it

the long exposure which Harris would have used but, even so, depicting not one boat.

The second half of the 19th century was a period of increasing competition and decline for the ironworks of Merthyr. The boom years of British and foreign railway expansion through the 1830s and 1840s were now passing, and the decline of the works was rapid. Unlike the newer iron-producing centres of Cleveland and

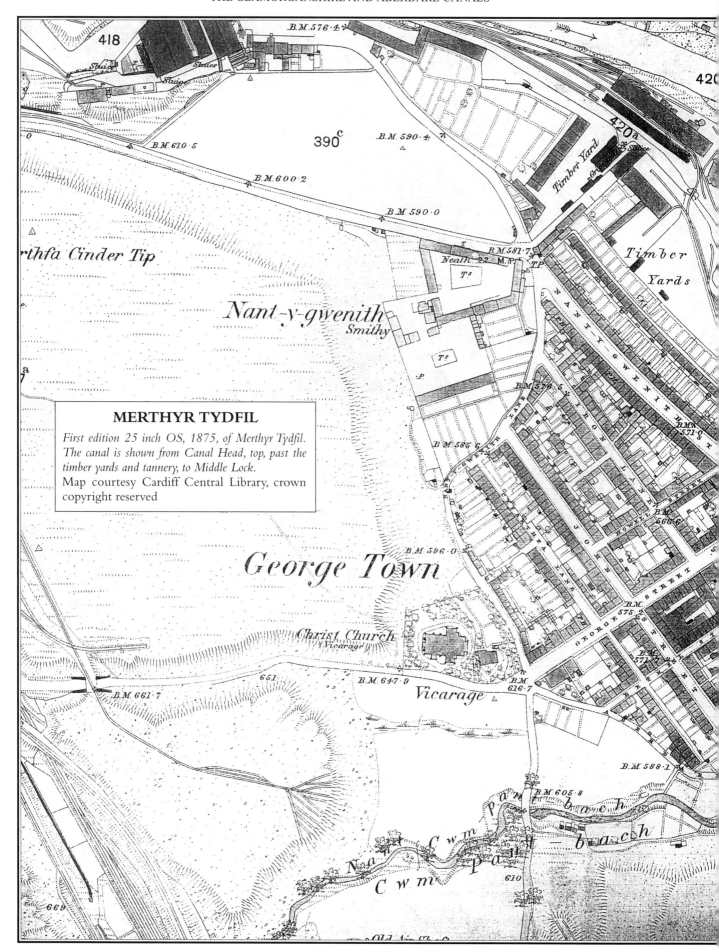

MERTHYR TYDFIL

First edition 25 inch OS, 1875, of Merthyr Tydfil. The canal is shown from Canal Head, top, past the timber yards and tannery, to Middle Lock.

Map courtesy Cardiff Central Library, crown copyright reserved

the Cumbrian coast, the Merthyr ironworks were now too far from their sources of iron ore and production was becoming uneconomic. In 1859, the Penydarren works ceased production, never to reopen. Always the handmaid of the iron industry and now under threat from the railways, the Glamorganshire Canal was in decline and losing heavily the fight for coal traffic. In Merthyr, the Dowlais company opened its own branch railway direct to the Taff Vale Railway in 1851[37] and in May 1853 Crawshay was reported to be bridging the River Taff, for a low level branch to connect his Ynysfach works with the TVR.[38] In 1874, Robert Thompson Crawshay, nephew and successor to William Crawshay II at Cyfarthfa, shut down the Cyfarthfa furnaces in a spiteful reaction to long-running disputes with his labour force. His sons, trading under the name of Crawshay Brothers (Cyfarthfa) Limited, took over the idle

works after his death and converted them to steel making in 1884.[39] In spite of the fall in its fortunes, the Glamorganshire Canal was still being used by the Crawshays in 1884-5 when they were reported to be the owners of 35-36 boats.[40] It was a hard blow to the canal company when, in 1886, the Crawshay company transferred the whole of its traffic from the canal to the newly completed Great Western & Rhymney Joint Railway. The new railway had incorporated the Crawshays' private line from their collieries at Gethin and Squirrels Castle (Troedyrhiw), and had been built parallel to the canal over the seven miles between Merthyr and Quaker's Yard, where it had a junction with the GWR line to Pontypool.[41] In the meantime, shortly after 1882, a second Ynysfach branch railway had been opened from the works, to connect across the River Taff to the TVR near Plymouth Street goods station.[42]

A general view of Cyfarthfa steelworks taken from the Cyfarthfa cinder tip, a decade or so before the canal's closure at Merthyr. Canal Head is off picture centre-right. The bridge shown in the photograph on page 40 can be seen as it continues across the River Taff towards Williamstown and Cyfarthfa Castle. The steel furnaces are on the left of the photograph, built in front of the original stone-built iron furnaces. Centre picture are the rolling mills. The River Taff separates them from the furnaces and then turns behind the engine house and continues its hidden course in front of the rolling mills. In the foreground is the Swansea road, whilst in the background, right, is Cyfarthfa Castle, built by William Crawshay and positioned so that he could look out over his industrial empire.

Courtesy Cyfarthfa Castle Museum

This TVR branch crossed the canal below Parliament Lock, using the line of the former Plymouth cinders tramroad and adding to the network of railways that now encircled the Glamorganshire Canal at Merthyr.

A date of 1865 has many times been quoted as the date of disuse of the canal pound between Jackson's bridge and Canal Head at Cyfarthfa.[43] The more likely date would seem to be 1885 since, even if there were no trade, Crawshay Brothers would have needed to bring boats up through Lock 1 until that time for repair and maintenance at their Cyfarthfa dry dock (although there was another dry dock above Parliament Lock, where the overflow to the river had once been). The top pound must have been still usable for some years after this, for a Rhydyfelin boatman claims to have loaded light tramrails into his boat in the Cyfarthfa pound in the 1890s and to have delivered the consignment to the Albion colliery at Cilfynydd.[44] The year 1865 could have been a simple misprint in Bradshaw's for 1885 because it was in the latter year that the canal company exchanged land at canal head for Crawshay land at Cardiff, to enable them to build the Cardiff timber pond.

The Glamorganshire Canal was now in serious trouble. Since 1876 the company had been unable to pay the maximum 8% dividend to its shareholders and by 1882 the payment had fallen to a mere $1\frac{1}{2}$%. Five years later there was no dividend at all. From 1885 the canal was sold to the third Marquess of Bute and control for the first time passed out of the Crawshay family's hands. The move was not without irony, for here was the fifth generation of the once-powerful Crawshay family finally relinquishing the controlling interest to the canal company's traditional landowning enemy, the Bute family. Bute undertook certain improvements, chiefly at the Cardiff end and the company itself now started carrying on the canal.[45] New boats were built, old ones were purchased and well-known traders such as William Harris Stores sold their boats to the company. From 1887 a regular service of market boats was put on between Cardiff and Pontypridd, Aberdare and Merthyr. Later, Abercynon also became a destination. The steam boat *Bute*, introduced experimentally between Cardiff and Pontypridd in 1893, aroused much interest at the time but it was considered neither safe nor practicable to allow the steamer into the upper part of the valley to Merthyr.

The Bute initiatives, originating from the enthusiasm of Lewis Llewelyn, the canal company's traffic manager, were ultimately to be unsuccessful. The GCC had been worried for some years over subsidence to the canal on the hill slopes at Aberfan, caused by the Nixon colliery's deep mining operation in the valley at Merthyr Vale. In a GCC report of 1885, the canal manager, Percy Harwood, wrote in some alarm:

'. . . . the bridge at Ynysygorred is fast sinking and the arch is now touched by the stove pipes of boats when water is high in the pond.'[46]

He might have added that in places the water under the boats, normally four feet in depth, was now increased to 12 or 15 feet because of mining activity.

A daily boat arrived at Jackson's bridge throughout the 1880s and early 1890s,[47] bringing up such commodities as flour, meal, oil, groceries and square Irish hay, and casks of stout from Dublin. In 1893 Lewis Llewelyn told the *Western Mail* that the canal company was storing 4,000 to 5,000 sacks of flour at Merthyr. Boats were horse-drawn and fitted with cabins to provide overnight sleeping accommodation on the long haul up from Cardiff. In the final years of the canal in Merthyr, a dwindling number of bye traders (independent owner boatmen) were looking for what business they could pick up but were finding the trading insufficient to make a living from their boats. The Merthyr Tydfil census return for the canal on 6 April 1891 is a revealing record of the low level of activity on the waterway, suggested by the one boatman in the area who slept aboard

In the mid-1890s, when this photograph was taken, the track of the Gurnos tramroad was still in situ as it followed the left bank of the Taff Fechan beneath Cefn Bridge to Cyfarthfa. Here the river and tramroad have lost so much height that the feeder from Gurnos to Cyfarthfa castle pond is above the level of the road behind the buildings on the right.

SR collection

The Penydarren company's limestone quarry at Morlais. The tramroad extension on the left continues northward and around the corner to the Plymouth company's quarry. The Dowlais quarry was to the east on the other side of the mountain. On the very summit lie the remains of Morlais Castle. SR collection

his boat. John Lewis, single, aged about 40 and born at Nantgarw, was in charge of the GCC boat *Castell Caerdydd*, moored at Jackson's bridge. The census officer, recording only those boats with cabin accommodation, found two boats in Merthyr in the general trade, one in the stone trade and one in the coal trade at Aberfan. Two others were moored empty at Abercanaid. In these last years from 1890, we know that some shipments of coal were leaving Perthygleision level for Merthyr's Taff Vale Brewery in Georgetown and small coal loaded at Abercanaid dock and at Gethin was being boated to Cardiff, chiefly for the use of the patent fuel works at Maindy and Blackweir.[48]

With the iron and steel trade of Cyfarthfa now gone to the railways, the decrease in traffic on the Merthyr section of the canal was dramatic. From 284,041 tons in 1871, traffic was reduced to 31,113 tons in 1897 (made up of 11,368 tons carried by the canal company and 19,745 tons carried by bye traders). The cost of maintenance of the Abercynon to Merthyr section was escalating because of worsening mining subsidence – from £38 per mile in 1891 to £122 per mile in 1897.[49] The end was now imminent for Merthyr's canal. Seriously concerned about the mounting danger from colliery subsidence at several places along the Four Mile Pond at Aberfan, where rows of houses lay below the canal banks, the GCC in 1898 made an on-site inspection by boat, with its engineer W. T. Watkin Lewis

Penyard Road marks the entrance to Penydarren ironworks from the Dowlais road. At this spot there is a fitting memorial to Richard Trevithick and Samuel Homfray of the Penydarren ironworks who, in 1804, built the first steam locomotive to run on rails. What this photograph also shows is the source of Samuel Homfray's frustration with William Taitt, of the Dowlais ironworks. The Dowlais company's railroad to the canal wharf passed this point on a high level course behind the railings. It was impossible for Penydarren to form a junction here so they were forced to build their own tramroad to the canal at Merthyr, instead of being able to share the grant the canal company had made towards building the Dowlais railroad.

SR photo 7 May 1995

and Sir Leader Williams, accompanied by Sir Douglas Fox.[50] The inspection confirmed that the sinking canal now posed a real threat to the mining settlement below it and the decision was taken to close the canal between Abercynon and Merthyr for the public safety. We can recognise here another irony. Coal mining, which had contributed so much to the prosperity of the Glamorganshire Canal, was now an agent of its ruin. It is not possible to remain unmoved by the terrible event overwhelming this same community in October 1966 but, perhaps, there is cause to be grateful that, by closure of the upper canal to Merthyr on 6 December 1898, an earlier disaster at Aberfan was avoided.

By 1898 virtually no economic impact would have been felt in the town of Merthyr by the canal's closure. There may have been some regret at the social level. There would be no more chapel Sunday school outings in swept-out coal boats from Merthyr down to the green fields of the Four Mile Pond, with accompanying music, games and picnics. Boatman Thomas Jones, of Llandaff, in 1948 remembered being in charge of such a party one summer in the 1880s. "*We took 600 that day*," he recalled "*and there were four boats under the Parliament.*" It was Jones, too, who took charge of the final inspection boat in 1898.[51]

We leave the Merthyr canal bank with a memory of John Lloyd, the solicitor, who, when compiling his *History of the Old South Wales Ironworks* from the Maybery papers in 1906, made a special point of visiting the canal head:

'I found to my surprise it had fallen into complete disuse: not a vestige of a canal boat was to be seen, and the water supply turned off into the river! Very little more than one hundred years have been long enough to bring about this marvellous change from high dividends and great prosperity to absolute ruin. A hundred years, I thought, can do much!'

GCC masons boat No 4 lay forlorn and decaying just north of James' boat yard at Gabalfa, when photographed by S.C. Fox in the 1920s. According to Thomas Jones, this was the boat in which he took the final inspection party on the Merthyr and Aberdare sections. The boat was fitted with a canvas canopy for the occasion. Masons boats carried only ten tons as opposed to the usual 22 tonners for normal carrying.
Courtesy Cardiff City Library

The ruins of Penydarren ironworks photographed by Robert Thompson Crawshay in 1876, looking towards Merthyr.

Courtesy Welsh Industrial & Maritime Museum

NOTES TO CHAPTER 3

1 GCC minute book 3 July 1807.

2 RC to Thomson Bonar 24 Oct 1797, Richard Crawshay's Letterbook 1788-97, Gwent Record Office D2162.

3 H. Scrivenor *History of the Iron Trade*, 1854 p.96.

4 RC to Lord Hawkesbury 6 and 13 May 1793 and RC to Philip Sansom 13 May 1793 calendared in Chris Evans *The Letterbook of Richard Crawshay 1788-1797*, Cardiff 1990.

5 Thomas Vaughan, Pentyrch ironworks to Robert Thomson, Dowlais ironworks 8 Dec 1794, calendared in Madelaine Elsas *Iron in the Making. Dowlais Iron Company Letters 1782-1860*, Cardiff 1960.

6 F.J. Pedler *History of the Hamlet of Gellideg*, Merthyr 1930 p.104.

7 GCC minute book 4 June, 15 Nov 1794, 6 June, 27 June 1798; William Taitt's *Address to Landowners* 1799.

8 GCC minute book 26 March 1799.

9 GCC minute book 26 June 1799.

10 A quarter of a century later, the Dowlais company was to lease limestone quarries from Lord Plymouth at Morlais after the Marquess of Bute had evicted Dowlais from Twynau Gwynion in 1825 in favour of his lessees, the Rhymney and Bute ironworks. Dowlais built a tramroad (later to be converted to a railway) from its quarry at Morlais to its furnaces in 1833.

11 Josiah John Guest to William Taitt 16 and 18 Feb 1815, quoted in Madeleine Elsas *Dowlais Letters*. Much of this analysis of the tramroads of Merthyr results from conversations between SR and the late Gordon Rattenbury. See also Michael J.T. Lewis *Steam on the Penydarren, Industrial Railway Record No.59* April 1975 and Stanley Mercer *Trevithick and the Merthyr Tramroad*, presented to the Newcomen Society 11 Feb 1948.

12 Wm Pritchard to Thos Guest 23 September 1800, calendared in Elsas *Dowlais Letters*.

13 J.T Barber's 1803 tour, cited in Nicholson's *Cambrian Traveller's Guide*, 1840.

14 GCC minute book cited in Charles Hadfield, *Canals of South Wales and the Border*, Cardiff 1960 p.105.

15 GCC minute book 7 Mar 1822.

16 Charles Hadfield *The Canal Age*, Newton Abbot 1968 p.146.

17 GRO Dowlais letterbooks 1794-5.

18 CCL Deeds II 2584 articles of co-partnership 8 Jan 1795.

19 Entry 18 Feb 1801 in Hilary Thomas *The Diaries of John Bird 1790-1803*, Cardiff.

20 GCC minute book 11 Sept 1818.

21 Thomas Ridd's Cardiff Directory of 1813 and Pigot & Co's Cardiff Directories from 1822.

22 Trade card in the WIMM collection.

23 Madelaine Elsas *Dowlais Letters*, pp.95, 163 and 164.

24 F.J. Pedler *Gellideg*, p.104; NLW Maybery 155.

25 Elsas *Dowlais Letters*, p.90.

26 GCC minute book 3 March and 7 April 1825; the yards are shown on Harrison's map of 1830.

27 GCC minute book 13 Dec 1833, 26 June 1839.

28 GCC minute book 3 June 1829; Harrison's map is GRO D/D B/Ca 17.

29 *Cardiff & Merthyr Guardian* 22 Jan 1848.

30 Slater's Commercial Directory 1858-9.

31 Wales Register & Guide 1878, p.187.

32 GCC minute book 7 June 1843.

33 GCC minute book 6 June 1849.

34 GCC minute book 5 June 1850.

35 On 2 June 1841 Bryant was granted leave to pipe water from the canal to his skin yard for twenty shillings per annum. GCC minute book.

36 From 1829 steam locomotives were used on the Dowlais, Penydarren and Merthyr tramroads. (The experimental Trevithick locomotive of 1804 was a one-off). See Lewis *Steam on the Penydarren*.

37 *Railway Magazine*, October 1937 p.291.

38 *Cardiff & Merthyr Guardian*, 28 May 1853. The railway later became part of the Brecon & Merthyr Railway by Act of 1868. Thanks to Colin Chapman for this information.

39 For the Crawshays see John P. Addis *The Crawshay Dynasty*, Cardiff 1957; Margaret Stewart Taylor *The Crawshays of Cyfarthfa Castle*, London 1967.

40 Royal Commission on Canals 1906. Evidence of Lewis Llewelyn para.10804.

41 See Edward A. Evans *The Quaker's Yard & Merthyr Joint Railway*, in *Archive*, the Quarterly Journal for British Industrial and Transport History, issue 11 and follow up correspondence in issue 12, Lydney 1996.

42 Built under the provisions of the TVR Act 1882.

43 R. de Salis *Bradshaw's Canals*, 1918 p.113.

44 William Gomer in conversation with ILW 6 Sept 1950.

45 *Western Mail*, 7 April 1893.

46 Copied in the GCC minute book 12 Aug 1885.

47 John Ballinger (ed) *Cardiff Handbook*, Cardiff 1896 p.56.

48 William Gomer in conversation with ILW 13 Sept 1950.

49 Royal Commission on Canals 1906, paras 10807-9.

50 W.T. Watkin Lewis *Recollections* (W. Hamlin collection), privately published c.1943, p.147. Sir Leader Williams was creator of the Manchester Ship Canal and Sir Douglas Fox was president of the Institute of Civil Engineers.

51 Thomas Jones, aged 85, of Llandaff North in conversation with ILW 1948.

Chapter 4

THE WATER SUPPLY TO THE CANAL AT MERTHYR

Cyfarthfa and Plymouth

'You will be surprised perhaps when you consider that I was one of those 4 that joined in the Expence of taking the Level from Merthyr to Cardiff and to know the probability of carrying & extending a Canal from the former place to the latter, I say you will no doubt be surprised at my saying or you hearing from me a word in opposition to it – but when I am informed from the great Stickelers and promoters of this business that it is intended to take the Water for the Supply of the Canal out of the River Taff above the Wear of Merthyr Mill, I think you will not be surprised, but say that I have just cause to be alarmed for my property, when it will be so very detrimental to me in the Season of Scarcity of Water – It is a well known Fact our being so near the Spring Head that the Water in Summer is so short that it is with difficulty I can go on at my works at all. In what Situation must I be in if such a Supply is taken from me as will be required for ye Canal. Perhaps Lord Plymouth might not consider Merthyr Mill in that point of Value as to give it a Consideration when such a Matter is in Agitation but come hastily under a promise to give it his Hearty Support – notwithstanding I think it is a matter that will deserve from you a representation of the Predicament that Mill will be under as early as possible. I most certainly shall write to his Lordship upon it . . .
Mr Taitt & Mr Homfray is gone to London and I dare say will wait upon Lord Plymouth as soon as they arrive in town therefore no delay ought to take place.' [1]

So Richard Hill wrote on 19 February 1790 to his landlord's steward, Thomas Key. Hill owned the most southerly of Merthyr's four ironworks, which lay on the Earl of Plymouth's land east of the River Taff. Hill had contributed to the cost of the canal survey, along with the main promoters, Richard Crawshay of Cyfarthfa, William Taitt of Dowlais and Samuel Homfray of Penydarren ironworks. Publication of Thomas Dadford's survey and of the draft Parliamentary Bill caused Hill to realise that the canal would have to extract its water from the Taff above the extraction point for his own Plymouth works (which he refers to as Merthyr Mill in his letter). There was a real danger that the canal would starve Hill's works of its very

life blood. With no water, on which it totally relied for power, the furnace could not continue in production.

Lord Plymouth had agreed to Richard Crawshay's request to be the Bill's sponsor to guide its passage through Parliament. Hill's protestations had the desired effect and Lord Plymouth's consequent threat to oppose the Bill became the talking point in Cardiff society.[2] Crawshay had quickly to assent to inserting a clause to Hill's satisfaction, although characteristically in his attitude to his neighbour and rival in trade, he told him that he could not see what all the fuss was about.[3]

In supporting his tenant, Lord Plymouth could not have chosen any more experienced and able an engineer than the great John Smeaton.[4] Although aged 65, Smeaton was still hard at work on canal and harbour projects, and was preparing for publication his account of the building of the Eddystone lighthouse. Smeaton was to meet Dadford and agree both a method of safeguarding the supply to Plymouth works and a form of wording by which it would be described in the Bill.[5]

From its head the canal would be supplied with water by the tailraces of Cyfarthfa ironworks, which formerly had emptied into the Taff for the convenient re-use by Plymouth ironworks, downstream of Cyfarthfa. The canal was to run close to the river at the Plymouth weir. Here the third lock on the canal was to be sited and the agreement's intention was to redirect water out of the canal, into the river above the weir, so that it could then enter the Plymouth watercourse. To ensure this happened, the lower lock gates at Lock 3 were to have no draw gates or paddles; the lock could be emptied only through a special draw gate in its side, from which the water would be channelled into the river. This arrangement was described in Clause IV of the final version of the canal Bill which went to the printers in April. By 17 May the Bill was passed by the House of Lords and so became enacted.[6]

Richard Hill attended the first General Assembly of the canal company on 30 June 1790 and was appointed to the committee. However, he attended only two meetings and, by the following year's general assembly, the disillusioned ironmaster was conducting his cautious opposition to the canal company as an outsider. Distrustful of Crawshay, he kept a watchful eye on the canal's progress and continued

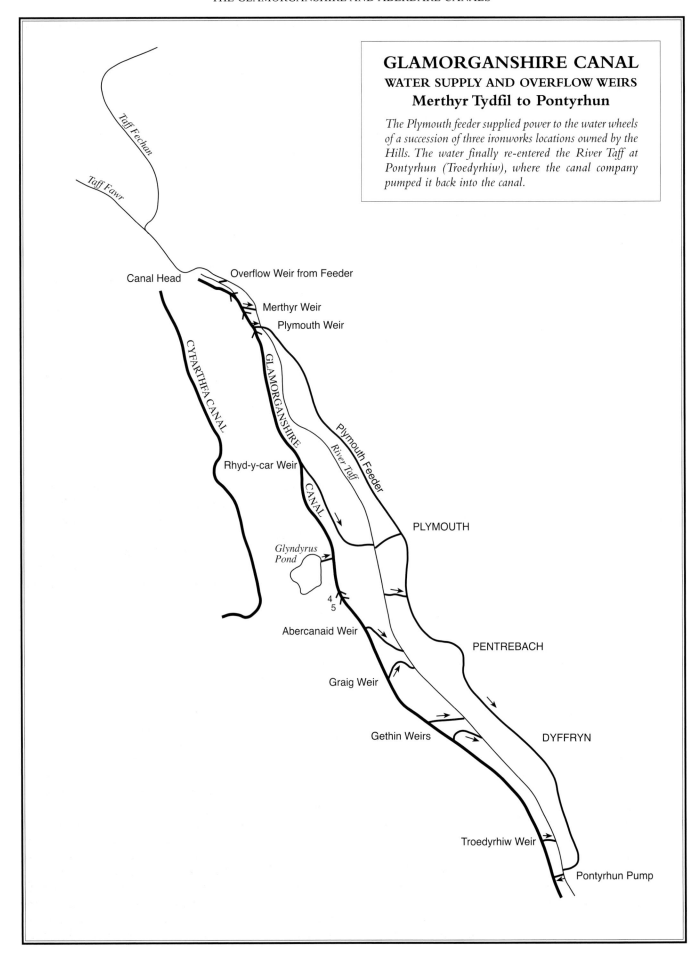

GLAMORGANSHIRE CANAL
WATER SUPPLY AND OVERFLOW WEIRS
Merthyr Tydfil to Pontyrhun

The Plymouth feeder supplied power to the water wheels of a succession of three ironworks locations owned by the Hills. The water finally re-entered the River Taff at Pontyrhun (Troedyrhiw), where the canal company pumped it back into the canal.

Taff Fechan

Taff Fawr

Canal Head

Overflow Weir from Feeder

Merthyr Weir

Plymouth Weir

CYFARTHFA CANAL

GLAMORGANSHIRE

Plymouth Feeder

River Taff

CANAL

Rhyd-y-car Weir

PLYMOUTH

Glyndyrus Pond

4
5

Abercanaid Weir

PENTREBACH

Graig Weir

Gethin Weirs

DYFFRYN

Troedyrhiw Weir

Pontyrhun Pump

to report his concerns to Lord Plymouth's steward. By the summer of 1792 there was water in the upper pounds and, already, the canal committee found themselves having to appease Hill.[7]

A year later Crawshay was formalising an agreement for water from Cyfarthfa works to supply the canal head and Hill immediately issued a complaint.[8] Crawshay continued and allowed the canal company use of water from both Cyfarthfa's upper and lower feeders. In return, however, the company granted Crawshay's ironworks prime land between the canal and river at Cyfarthfa.[9] Cyfarthfa emptied its waters not only into the canal head but also via a separate watercourse, partly culverted, which was made to run between river and canal and enter the latter below Lock 2, where Dadford had originally planned the junction with the Dowlais branch.[10] Years later, this feeder was enlarged to over ten feet in width to admit canal boats to the back of the canal company's warehouses and as far as Chapel Gate.[11]

Hill's works had suffered from droughts even before the coming of the canal but now Crawshay was retaining water for the canal and diverting it away from the river weir. Even in winter things were now bad for the Plymouth supply and on 10 January 1794 Hill wrote to Crawshay at Cyfarthfa:

'My works stood all last Night, and now in the same state, for want of water, the same being turned into the Canal. I have before Complained to you, the Committee and Proprietors of the Canal: But without Effect. I find I now have no other Recourse than the Law to remedy the Complaint and to Compell a Compliance of the Act of Parliament, which I am determined to do, unless effectually remedied, and immediately.'[12]

Sending copies of his correspondence with Crawshay to his solicitors, Hill wrote:

'I might as well have no ffurnace, to be in every time of short Water Harrassed in the manner I am and have been now at times near Two Years. It is really Cruel that I am obliged to fight a Body of such Magnitude.'

Crawshay's evasive answers had made Hill decide to fight. Hill instructed his solicitors to lose no time in commencing an action then, before the Quarter Sessions, since it would make a good plea before Parliament and could assist him in getting his clause in the Act strengthened.[13]

Crawshay and Thomas Dadford responded by meeting Hill but there was no way they could convince him of their innocence. They had not only built the lock gates with paddles but had also built a bypass weir to take water around Lock 3. So, even if every lock-full was released into the river, there was a steady stream of water passing round the lock and feeding the canal pounds below. That this arrangement was contrary to the Act was confirmed in an independent statement by James Birch, the Engineer at Penydarren works.[14] Hill sought an injunction to have the sluice gate on this bypass weir stopped up immediately.

The seriousness of the situation did not prevent Hill from remarking wryly:

'While the Shuttle is in the Gate contrary to the Act, it is liable to be applied to my prejudice; I will therefore if Possible shut the door.'[15]

Instructing his own solicitors, William and John Powell of Brecon, and Lord Plymouth's solicitor, John Inge, he hoped the injunction would be in place before the summer drought:

'I am as well satisfied under the presumption of obtaining the Injunction in May, as the present time, because there is a probability they will not get over it before Nov. In that Case I may get the Summer over under the Injunction. This you will say perhaps – an Ironmaster's manoeuvre, but I wish it to be so, if possible as they are now making the evasion more flagrant if Possible – and I am determined to get an Able Engineer's report thereon if Possible.'[16]

Unfortunately for Hill, by March the deadline had lapsed for presenting private petitions to the House of Commons that session. Inge provided the encouraging information that several noblemen were willing to assist Lord Plymouth in fighting Hill's cause but not until the next Parliamentary session.[17] By accepting the situation, Hill's profits were suffering.[18] He had to maintain production at his works and so he felt forced to resort to physical methods which might also bring forward a legal ruling in his favour.

The first recorded incident was when Hill's head carpenter, James Davies, broke the lock on the head gates of Lock 3, to allow water into the lock and so through the special draw gate to the river.[19] Richard Hill himself was caught doing the same on 16 June and again on 21 June. So successful were his efforts that he ran the whole pound dry above Lock 3.[20] These incidents prompted the canal company to decide to protect the gates by a building. Watkin George (the Cyfarthfa engineer and present partner of Richard Crawshay, who was beginning to take over engineering responsibilities on the canal as Dadford struggled to complete his contract on the lower section) also proposed an idea of installing indexes 'showing the state of the Water . . . [which] will tend in a great measure to settle the dispute.'[21] A new lock keeper with some notoriety was installed by the canal company to replace the ageing John Morgan and prevent further attacks on the lock. In August, before the protective building work could be completed, the most violent encounter took place when Hill's eldest son, Richard Hill junior, came out the better after a fierce fight with the new lock keeper, William Williams. Williams (and the canal company's pride) was seriously hurt. With Richard Crawshay's support, Williams took an action for assault on Hill, claiming substantial surgeon's fees and a £5 annuity to prevent it coming to court.[22] Thus Hill's solicitors were kept busy preparing for several cases in the autumn and winter of 1794. The assault case took a couple of years to settle and shook Hill enough to deter him from supporting further physical action. Court action was slow and the Plymouth workforce, when the works were on stand and they were laid off, must have been only too willing to help restore the water supply but Hill decided to remain on the right side of the law.

The Court of Chancery, hearing Hill's plea for an injunction against the canal company, recommended arbitration and, on 6 September 1794, the canal company authorised the appointment of Hugh Henshall, of Longport, Staffs. This pioneering English canal engineer and pupil of James Brindley was then in his early sixties.[23] At the time of his appointment to the Glamorganshire Canal, he was working on the Brecon & Abergavenny Canal with Thomas Dadford junior (who had left the Glamorganshire Canal contract to be completed by his father).[24] In accepting Henshall's appointment, the Glamorganshire Canal Company must have thought they were in with a fighting chance of beating Hill. The official appointment by the Court of Chancery was made on 22 November[25] but Henshall took his time and was not ready to report until the following summer.[26] Hill too was optimistic but by August was asking impatiently for the award to be published as he prepared to put his refurbished furnace back in blast.[27]

When it arrived, Henshall's award was a bitter defeat for the canal company. He made plain that they had not adhered to Clause IV of their Act at Parliament Lock. Not only was the bypass weir, or circular cut, deemed illegal but the canal company had even made a draw gate in the tail gate of the lock, which was in blatant contravention of the Act.

The award ordered that:

'. . . the drawgate that is now in one of the lower or tail gates shall be immediately taken away and the aperture or opening in such tail gate shall be effectually closed up and always remain so'

and that the circular cut should

'be completely and effectually stopped up and that no water shall be conveyed round the said lock from or out of the said canal above the said lock into the canal below the said lock. But that all the

The culverted tail races from Cyfarthfa meeting to form the canal feeder, photographed in 1995.
Courtesy Ironbridge Gorge Museum Trust Archaeology Unit

water brought into the said canal above the lock No 3 shall be discharged into the aqueduct or trench made for conveying the water out of the said lock chamber into the river Taff above Plymouth Weir.'

Henshall's award was so unambiguous that it was quoted for many years to come in the continuing struggle for a regular and sufficient water supply at the expanding Plymouth works.[28]

The canal committee met on 25 August 1795 and authorised payment of Henshall's fee of £36 15s. On 2 September, they were informed by Watkin George that, in implementing the award, the draw gate in the tail gate had been closed and a weir was to be made, to direct the excess water from the upper pound into the aqueduct from the lock to the river above the weir. Only when this was complete could the circular cut and screw gate be stopped up also. Watkin George was instructed to direct the work.[29]

The canal company were now in a difficult situation with regard to keeping water in the pound between Parliament Lock and the double Locks 4 and 5 at Glyndyrus. It is not surprising, therefore, that they took their time stopping up the circular cut. In October an angry Richard Hill wrote to John Powell, '*Mr Crawshay continues – Obstinate – nothing done at the Locks but as usual depredations – and he at the head of them giving directions to run the Water round the Lock.*'[30] Powell charged the canal company with contempt of court, while Hill sought to drum up support to oppose the second Glamorganshire Canal Bill which was then being framed. At the canal's committee meeting on 7 November, Watkin George reported that the weir and paddle at Lock 3 were finished, and sworn affidavits were drawn up to that effect and signed by William Williams and by David Edwards, the contractor for the work.[31] These seem to have placated Hill for the remainder of the winter as the canal, still in only its second full year of operation, struggled to manage.

The following summer, in May 1796, the canal company themselves found reason for complaint. Hill, they claimed, must repair his weir because too much water was being lost on the river by leakage through the weir.[32] This affected the canal because their channel from the lock to the weir was built with a swing sluice, or valve, which at times when the river was in flood would direct water in the opposite direction, down a branch cut to the pound below Parliament Lock. Such an arrangement was necessary to empty the lock at such times when the level of the river was higher than the canal level.[33] Hill maintained it would cost him as much as £3,000 to make the weir watertight.

In September 1797, the canal company were making almost the opposite accusation, as they claimed that Hill's encroachment on the bed of the River Taff above and below the river was causing its waters to damage their aqueduct.[34] The Taff was a natural dumping ground for all the ironworks as they sought to dispose of cinders and slag waste from their furnaces. The aqueduct constantly became choked up by the volume of this material entering the river. Why should the canal company clear it? This became the stock answer to Hill's annual reminders of their responsibilities

The high level water course from the Taff Fawr was originally carried on the left bank of the river on this stone-piered wooden aqueduct, as depicted here in an oil painting of 1817/20 by Penry Williams. On its way south it crossed the Taff Fechan, whose waters joined with the Taff Fawr just beyond where the cows are depicted. The aqueduct then turned right and crossed the River Taff on the aptly-named Pontycafnau (bridge of troughs). The bridge also carried the Gurnos limestone tramroad and the lower water course from the Taff Fechan. The chimneys of Cyfarthfa's forges can be seen through the wooden uprights of Pontycafnau. By 1850 the aqueduct had gone (although the stone piers remained) and the feeder had been re-sited on the right bank of the Taff Fawr, where it can be traced today. Until Pontycafnau was renovated in 1994-5, the remnants of the wooden uprights were still attached to the cast iron bridge members. It was this high level water course which worked Watkin George's fifty feet diameter water wheel, to supply the blast to the Cyfarthfa furnace. The aqueduct and wheel (given the name Aeolus *in recognition of its purpose) were quite an attraction to Cyfarthfa visitors and several contemporary descriptions and illustrations survive.*

Courtesy Crawshay family collection

under Henshall's award,[35] so that by 1799 Hill again felt his only recourse was to the courts.

A case was prepared for the spring assizes at Hereford[36] but was not tried until the autumn great sessions at Cardiff.[37] Hill's brief[38] explained that his furnace output was frequently reduced from 40 tons per week to 25 tons, since the canal company had been depriving him of water. To avoid litigation he claimed he had actually offered to sell them his interest in the water to allow him to work his furnace in another way (presumably by steam). Alternatively, he had suggested that the canal company should partially restore the water supply above Plymouth weir but install a fire engine and pump at the tail of the Plymouth works. This would then be used to pump the water back to the head of the water wheels at Plymouth works for their re-use. This is a restatement of a 1794 suggestion of Watkin George's:

'*that an Engine shall be erected on the Tail of Mr Hill's Works to obtain a Quantity of Water into Mr Hill's pound. Mr H on his*

part agreeing to give to the Canal Co a like quantity into Lock No 3.'[39]

Hill claimed this would cost a mere £200 per annum, which was miniscule compared to the canal company's revenues of some £10,000 per annum. Henshall's award may not have imposed on the canal company the duty of repair and maintenance of the aqueduct from Lock 3 but it still laid on them the obligation to return the water into the river above Plymouth weir and this could not be done without a properly functioning aqueduct.

The day before the trial, six of the jury, with the deputy Sheriff, visited the site of the aqueduct at Merthyr. John Bird's diary records that the case was tried on 8 August and took up 8 hours:

'*Mr Crawshay was in Court the greatest part of the time and could hardly be restrained from speaking, At one time he got up and asked the Witness then under examination "Do we choak the River, or do the River Choak us?",*

which threw the Court into a burst of laughter. He was Cautioned not to speak but by his Council, and which with difficulty he complied with.' [40]

Hill won the case and was awarded £300 damages.[41] For Crawshay and the canal company this was a paltry sum but for Hill his continuing legal costs in fighting for the rights of Plymouth works were a constant drain. His letter of 6 November 1798 to his solicitors, Messrs W. & J. Powell, is telling as he asked them to keep the law expenses relating to the canal dispute separate from their other charges, whilst he also asked for assistance in securing a

loan of £1,000 for six months.[42]

The courts on their own could not change the situation on the ground and only a couple of months after the judgement, in response to complaints from Hill, the canal company were still requesting that his company clean up the river at the weir.[43] Next summer the weary Hill commenced a suit in Chancery. The canal committee met Richard Hill and his sons to discuss making an outlet from the canal upstream at Lock 2 and into the river above the houses at Penybont. This would be more practicable than the aqueduct at Lock 3, since the river bed had risen so much due to the continual dumping of waste.[44] They also then resolved to

Cyfarthfa ironworks in 1811, looking north. The aqueduct comes in from the distant right and passes behind the forge whose hammers relied on water power. The Aeolus wheel is hidden behind the blast house beside the far furnace. In the middle distance a train of drams is being hauled from the rolling mills on the other side of the river.
J.G. Wood lithograph from *The Principal Rivers of Wales Illustrated*, London, 1813

replace the aqueduct at Lock 3 with an iron pipe, which would be less likely to become choked. Watkin George was to install the pipes, in payment for which the canal company allowed the Cyfarthfa company the abandoned Merthyr properties of Thomas Key and the storehouse of Sutton & Co, rent free.[45] Watkin George also took up the suggestion made the previous year, by proposing to pump water back into the canal from where the Plymouth works tail race returned water to the river. For this to be effective, a shaft would be sunk near Glyndyrus Locks (Locks 4 and 5) to which a culvert would be made from the Plymouth tail race.[46] It was not until January 1801 that a formal proposal

was made to Hill to test his reaction to a pump at Glyndyrus. At the same time, a way of supplying the river with water below Lock 2 was finalised, because the idea of iron pipes at Parliament Lock had proved ineffectual.[47] The legal manoeuvrings to claim damages to date continued, though slowly. In March the canal company saw fit to minute:

'in last Summer he had all the water during a dry season of near three months & our present watercourse to his feeder is the best that can be devised.'[48]

As they prepared their answer to Hill's lastest bill of

THE PLAN REFERRED TO IN THE INDENTURE HEREUNTO ANNEXED.

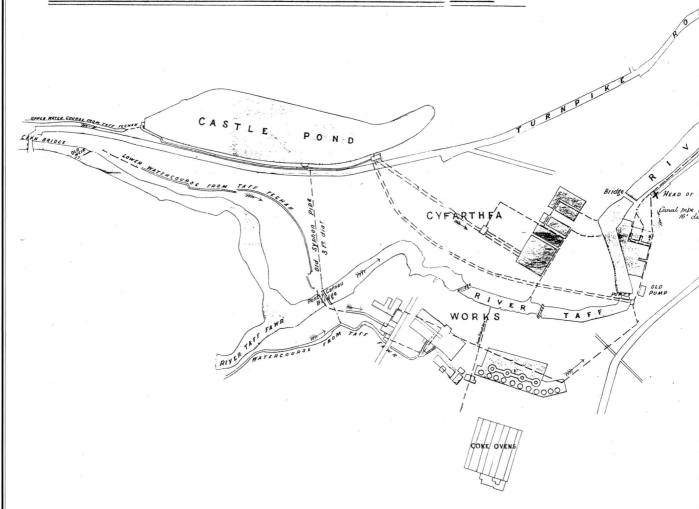

complaint, they were able to postpone the case coming to court until late summer 1801.[49] Once again they lost the case despite the building of the new watercourse from Lock 2 and their defence that Hill's works were requiring much more water from the river than when the canal Act was passed, eleven years previously. By July 1801, Hill was building his third furnace and was expanding his ancillary water powered mills.[50] Hill's extant water lease of 1765, from Lord Plymouth, made no mention of limiting his usage, much to the canal committee's consternation.

In June, Richard Crawshay and Dr Benjamin Hall had met Richard Hill junior in London and offered him £250 if the Hills would stop their latest action. When this was put to the father he refused but by September 1802 a compromise was being reached.[51] The reason they were all in London was to follow the Bill for the Merthyr Tramroad.

This was a scheme by the three Merthyr ironmasters, Taitt, Homfray and Hill, to provide a railway alternative to the Glamorganshire Canal, which Crawshay had always operated as his own. Their initial grand plan to build a tramroad to Cardiff, with branches from Rhymney and Aberdare, was being successfully opposed by the canal company. However, with the support of Lord Plymouth, on whose land most of the route lay, they managed to acquire all the necessary land outside of Parliament to build the tramroad as far as Navigation under the four mile clause. They were therefore able to withdraw the Bill. The resultant Merthyr Tramroad opened in 1802 and ran on the east of the Taff Valley from Dowlais and Penydarren ironworks, passing Plymouth works, to Navigation, where a transshipment basin was provided with the canal. The tramroad not only allowed the three ironworks to bypass

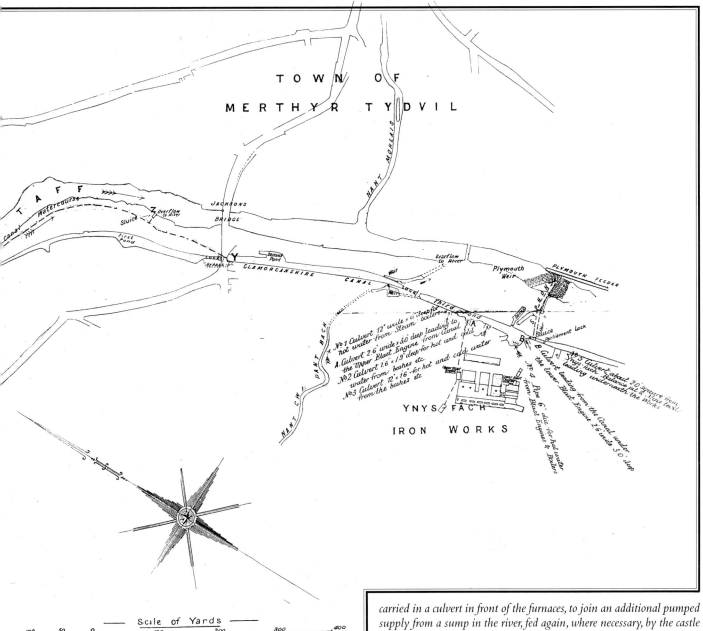

TOWN OF MERTHYR TYDVIL

Scale of Yards

The water supply to the canal at Merthyr in its final form. From the north (on the left of this 1893 plan) the upper water course from the Taff Fechan at Gurnos quarry is seen to feed the Cyfarthfa Castle pond, which was not just an ornamental feature in the Crawshays' garden but also served as a reservoir for the Cyfarthfa works' water supply. Water from the pond was fed to the rolling mill complex on the left bank of the river. A siphon pipe also carried water from the pond, down its dam and across the river alongside Pontycafnau, then up to join the high level water course from the Taff Fawr. Together they worked the water wheels at the forges and in earlier years had worked the large water wheels operating the blast to the furnaces (the four furnaces shown on this plan are the steel furnaces which stand in front of the disused stone iron-making furnaces). A lower water course from the weir below Cefn bridge on the Taff Fechan flowed in parallel with the Gurnos limestone tramroad and crossed Pontycafnau in a trough beneath the track of the tramroad. This supplied water to Cyfarthfa's brick works, before the waste water (joined by the tail water from the forges) was carried in a culvert in front of the furnaces, to join an additional pumped supply from a sump in the river, fed again, where necessary, by the castle pond. This combined water supply finally worked more forge wheels at the mills on the right bank of the River Taff, before then forming the feeders to the Glamorganshire Canal at Canal Head (marked X on the plan) and below Lock 1 (marked Y on the plan).

Further south, the plan shows the weirs above Lock 2 which took the waters from the Nant Cwm Pant Bach and allowed the second pond to be drained into the river. In the third pond, the plan shows how the canal supplied water to the boilers of upper and lower blast engines at Ynysfach ironworks and received the condensed hot water in return, together with water from the boshes. Next the arrangement for the canal to supply water to the Plymouth feeder at Lock 3 (Parliament Lock) is shown (although this had been long out of use). The canal overflow alongside the dry dock joins the siphon pipe from the side of the lock chamber and together they carry water across the river, between the two weirs, to the start of the Plymouth feeder. Finally, below Lock 3 is shown a water intake from the drainage adits of the Ynysfach balance pit and mine levels. This plan was attached to a lease held in the Cardiff City archive. The original is assumed lost as the whole archive was destroyed senselessly when the new Cardiff County authority was created in the mid 1990s.

Cardiff City Blue Box 2141

Taken from a Cyfarthfa slag tip and overlooking Pontycafnau, this photograph shows the line of the siphon pipe. It starts on the extreme right at the castle pond then reappears above ground to cross the river (hidden in a small ravine) and rise to empty into the Taff Fawr water course coming in from the left foreground. In the left distance can be seen the road-side limekilns on the Gurnos tramroad where, in the early days, the Hills would collect their limestone and take it by stone road to Plymouth works. The lower Taff Fechan feeder can be seen sweeping round to the right then being crossed by the tramroad as they both approach Pontycafnau. Courtesy Cyfarthfa Castle Museum

the upper section of the canal but, by reducing tonnage carried on the upper section, it potentially relieved the pressure on water supply.

It is not clear how much use, if any, Hill's Plymouth works made of the canal prior to the opening of the Merthyr Tramroad. The Plymouth company is not mentioned at all in the surviving tonnage book of 1797-8. Prior to the canal, when Anthony Bacon owned both Plymouth and Cyfarthfa works, Plymouth had sent almost all its output to Cyfarthfa for finishing. This seems to have continued after Bacon's death in 1786, when Richard Crawshay took over Cyfarthfa and Richard Hill took over Plymouth. It may not have been until the business received further capital, by bringing John Nathaniel Miers and Amos Struttle into the partnership and the Hills built rolling mills at Pentrebach in 1805/6, that they had products to sell regularly in markets foreign to Merthyr Tydfil.[52] On 5 June

1805, their request for their wharf at Cardiff to be extended was turned down by the canal committee. Until that time Plymouth did use the Merthyr Tramroad to carry raw materials. Imported iron ore, to supplement the Merthyr ironstone, was brought up the canal and tramroad to the works. Pit wood from the Plymouth estate, on the north-western outskirts of Cardiff, was also brought up the canal from the yards at Llandaff and Taffs Well.[53] Limestone was brought down Hill's northern extension of the tramroad from Lord Plymouth's quarries at Castle Morlais. In fact, for Plymouth works the tramroad offered three major advantages. Firstly, as we have seen, it indirectly relieved the canal's competitive pressure on Plymouth works' water supply. Secondly, it provided direct transport south to (and from) the canal at Navigation and thence to the sea at Cardiff, whereas Plymouth had been the worst located of the four Merthyr ironworks to be able to take advantage

A continuation of the previous photograph shows the upper water course in the foreground. The lower watercouse can just be glimpsed in front of the two Crawshay Bros railway wagons as it passes the brick works. On the hill in the left distance is Cyfarthfa castle and on the right is Cyfarthfa farm, with its clock tower. Courtesy Cyfarthfa Castle Museum

of the canal's upper section. Thirdly, it allowed Plymouth to at last escape the stranglehold of the growing Crawshay empire for its limestone supply. When Bacon owned both works, all limestone was quarried from Gurnos, just over a mile north of Cyfarthfa on the left bank of the Taff Fechan. This was Cyfarthfa land. When the two concerns were separated, following Bacon's death, Crawshay began to charge Hill. In 1793, Crawshay built the Gurnos tramroad to Cyfarthfa, not under the four mile clause but as a private tramroad not strictly connected to the canal. He proceeded to charge Hill 1/9d per ton for limestone delivered to Hill's road waggons at Cyfarthfa.[54] This was an exorbitant price and in 1802 Hill was only too glad to cancel the agreement to use Gurnos stone, after Lord Plymouth had been persuaded to open up more of the Morlais quarries for Hill's own use.[55]

Richard Hill senior died in 1806. For twenty long years Richard Crawshay had been a thorn in his side. Hill had been agent to Anthony Bacon and was married to the sister

of Bacon's long-time mistress and mother of Bacon's children. When Bacon died in 1786, there were three ironworks in his ownership – Cyfarthfa, Plymouth and Hirwaun. Bacon's heirs were minors and it fell upon Richard Hill to oversee the affairs of the three ironworks on behalf of the executors, until the Court of Chancery ruled how the Bacon empire would be divided. Hill was allowed to manage Plymouth and Richard Crawshay took over Cyfarthfa.

In a letter to Crawshay on 4 July 1786, Hill, concerned that Crawshay was putting about comments that Plymouth iron was not fit for the best melting purposes, had added the hopeful remark, '*Relying on your friendship respecting Plymouth furnace as soon as matters are settled in Chancery.*' Some chance! Also, in that same letter, possibly before a Merthyr to Cardiff canal had been dreamt of, Hill betrayed his works' vulnerability to drought: '*We are offering our prayers noon and night for rain.*' To Richard Crawshay, Richard Hill was not a rival worthy of respect. Rather he was an irritation

General View, Merthyr

Taken only a few years after the canal's closure at Merthyr, compare this photograph to the 1877 panorama by Harris on pages 48-49. Here the gates at Parliament Lock are closed and the water level lowered in the lock, so that the penstock of the side paddle gate on the lock wall can be clearly seen. This is the paddle demanded by the canal company's 1790 Act (hence the name of the lock) and through this sluice all water from the lock was meant to pass to the River Taff above Plymouth weir. The weir too is clearly shown, together with the entrance to the Plymouth feeder, protected by a building housing the mechanism for raising and lowering the sluice. In the left foreground, wagons stand on the railway from the Ynysfach casting houses, which crossed the canal at the lock's tail.

SR collection

and a hindrance to Crawshay's grand single minded ambitions. To Crawshay, Hill was '*a pitifull Fellow and may bluster as long as he pleases.*'[56]

Glyndyrus and Pontyrhun

If there had been any respite from water requirements by the upper section of the canal on the opening of the Merthyr Tramroad, it was short lived. On 23 July 1805, Philip Williams, the canal company's chief clerk and secretary to the committee, wrote to Richard Crawshay announcing that the navigation was open to Merthyr and three boats, loaded with iron at Cyfarthfa the previous night, were due at Cardiff the next morning. Three more boatloads would leave Cyfarthfa that night. He added a telling comment that he would defer repairing a lock further '*until we are Stoped for Want of Water.*'[57] Clearly water shortage on the canal was a predictably regular event. This July stoppage had been caused by Hill & Sons' clerk, Lancelot Steel, who was caught breaking open the padlock on the paddle of Lock 1 and letting out the water of the upper pond. In an uncharacteristic gesture of leniency, Crawshay declined to prosecute but used the incident to force a meeting with the Hills, when he announced his latest idea to build reservoirs for the canal's supply. The canal company appointed its solicitor, John Powell, to write to the landowners to canvass their support for a third Act of Parliament.[58]

By September, the site of one reservoir had been planned on Glyndyrus farm, land owned by Lord Dynevor and John Richards. Relations were not perfect with these landowners. They had contributed a great deal of land for the building of the canal and two disputes were outstanding. Dynevor and Richards had put in a claim that the canal had used 10,000 perches of stone from their land for which they charged 6d per perch; the canal company claimed the land had passed into their ownership before quarrying had begun. The second dispute was their claimed right as brinkers (owners of land adjacent to common land) to compensation for land taken by the canal company on Coedpenmain Common.[59] These joint landowners were not in a mood to give up further land to the Glamorganshire Canal. After an abortive attempt to meet on site at Glyndyrus, Philip Williams met Thomas Bold, their Brecon solicitor, at Cardiff:

'. . . . he seems to doubt our right of making reservoirs at Glynderris Farm, he ask'd me if we claimed ye Ground wanted as a matter of right or ask'd for it as a favour. I told him that the Act of Parliament impowered us to take any land within such a distance of the Canal that we claimed it as our right on paying for it. He'll throw any obstacle he can in the way.'[60]

As well as the Glyndyrus reservoir, a much grander scheme was planned to build a reservoir above Cefn, in the Great Forest of Brecknock. A special assembly was called for 19 April 1806, to discuss applying to Parliament for

powers to build it. On 29 March a letter was sent to the Hills informing them of the intention. It was estimated that the reservoir would supply 30 locks of water per day for eight weeks in the driest season.[61] No response having been received from the Hills, the meeting of 19 April was postponed. Crawshay spoke with Richard Hill senior on 6 May and the following day a letter was sent seeking a reply to the proposals and reminding Hill that the canal company was suffering from his works using too much water.[62] A reply was received on 20 May and, following their father's death, the two brothers, Richard and Anthony Hill, attended the 3 June canal committee meeting.[63] Their response was simple:

'They object totally to the making of the reservoirs as liable to such abuses that the rights they claimed cannot be protected. They make no complaints and only require that the whole of the Water sho'd be delivered to them above the Weir. But it is immaterial in what mode it is delivered provided the whole is delivered. In consequence of the above no agreement is entered into with them.'

That summer, too, was a bad one for the canal. On 12 July, Philip Williams wrote to Crawshay:

'I am fearful we cannot send ye Boats back to Merthyr being obliged to run so much Water from the ponds above to bring them down through the Locks & Ponds below which were all dry.'[64]

The canal company determined to progress with the reservoir schemes. Kaye & Co were confirmed as solicitors and Sir Samuel Romilly would take the Bill through Parliament. Advertisements were again inserted in *The London Gazette*. Benjamin Hall was instructed to visit Mr Fordyce in London, to obtain an order for Charles Hassall to survey the Crown land wanted for making the intended reservoir on the Great Forest of Brecon. Hall was also to deliver a letter from Richard Crawshay to John Rennie, the engineer, to request his attendance at Merthyr and prepare to give evidence before the House of Commons Committee.[65] Rennie had recently been retained by the canal company to resolve the water dispute at Melingriffith and they had been well satisfied with the agreement he had drawn up with Richard Blakemore's consultant engineer, William Jessop.[66]

Only six weeks later, on 24 and 25 October, John Rennie attended the GCC committee meeting where he presented recommendations which would not only at last provide the Glamorganshire Canal with ample water to its upper section for the years to come but would also be acceptable to the Plymouth company in maintaining their supply.

Rennie felt that the expense of making a reservoir in the Great Forest of Brecon, with the application to Parliament, would be of the order of £4-5,000. The idea should be abandoned entirely as being too costly and with no guarantee that they would get the necessary Act. Rennie believed that the rights of Plymouth should be honoured

For some reason John George Wood's lithograph of Pontyrhun was omitted from his published Rivers of Wales *in 1813. This is his original water colour. The smoke and grime of Merthyr has been left behind in the distance and what is presented is an arcadian setting viewed from the Cardiff to Merthyr turnpike. Above the river bridge of Pontyrhun is the canal company's pump house and the aqueduct which fed water from the pumps into the canal.* Courtesy Cardiff City Library

and that water from the canal should continue to be passed to Hills' works as at present or by new iron pipes from the side paddle of Lock 3. He did approve of the Glyndyrus reservoir scheme and to maximise their impact he advised that reservoirs there be made as extensive as possible. To supplement this supply to the pound below Lock 3, he proposed diverting water from the old Cyfarthfa Coal Canal.

Rennie's main recommendation was:

'an engine to be erected below Mr Hill's Water Course for supplying the canal with water into the Four Mile Pond with a Boulton and Watt 36 inch cylinder single stroke.'

If this water and that from

'the well sunk in the lock keeper's garden are found insufficient he also recommends a small Steam Engine to raise the Water from the said Well instead of the Machine now in use.'

This was referring to the well and pump at Parliament Lock, which had been providing emergency water to the pound. This had only just been installed but was not proving a success. It is unlikely that it was an implementation of the 1801 suggestion by Watkin George, to culvert water

from the Plymouth works tail race under the river to a well near Glyndyrus, as by 1806 Pentrebach rolling mills further down the valley were utilising the spent water from the Plymouth tail race. In fact the tail race did not enter the Taff until Pontyrhun and it was here that the Boulton & Watt engine would be erected. No other details of the type or method of operation of the pump at Parliament Lock seem to have survived. It was installed in 1805-6 at a cost of £300 and was, perhaps, one of Watkin George's few failures.[67]

The committee accepted Rennie's proposals with enthusiasm. Joseph Bailey would manage the Pontyrhun project, while Crawshay would negotiate with Lord Dynevor and John Richards for the Glyndyrus land, calling out the canal commissioners if he had to. John Rennie was paid £40 on account, and it seems this remained his total fee for his services.[68] On 3 November, Charles Hassall was written to at East Wood, Pembrokeshire, informing him that he would no longer be required to survey the land in the Great Forest.[69]

Plans were drawn up by Philip Williams for a single reservoir of 13 or 14 acres at Glyndyrus, being sent to John Powell (solicitor for the GCC), Thomas Bold (Lord Dynevor's solicitor) and John Wood (John Richards' solicitor).[70] Lord Dynevor and John Richards determined not to release more land for the canal and took counsel

A hundred years after Wood's painting and Pontyrhun shows quite a different aspect. The later pumphouse, with its tall chimney, is in the centre of this picture postcard view of Troedyrhiw. Above the line of the canal is the route of the joint GW & RR line from Merthyr to Quaker's Yard Junction; Troedyrhiw was served by a halt. Much closer to the photographer, on the east side of the valley, is the TVR station. The coal tips in the distant right are from Castle Pit, off picture.   SR collection

from Mr C. Abbott, while the canal company on their part took counsel from Sergeant John Williams. Abbott's opinion was that the powers of the second (1796) Act had expired because they required any additional work to be completed within two years; nevertheless he feared the commissioners would be called out. Bold's fanciful reading of the existing Acts as not empowering the proprietors to build within the parish of Merthyr Tydfil but only *from* that place was discounted. Williams' opinion was similar to Abbott's – the powers of the two Acts had lapsed (including raising the balance of capital of £6,400) and the commissioners now had no powers to seize the land at Glyndyrus; he advised that if terms could not be agreed with the landowners for the land to be paid for out of income, then a new Act would be necessary after all.[71]

Having only just abandoned the idea of another Act, the committee was therefore led into preparing fresh notices of application to Parliament for insertion in *The London Gazette* and *The Cambrian*, although it would have to wait to get such authorisation at a special or general assembly of the shareholders.[72] What really concerned them was their right to use the canal's revenue to finance capital projects. Several of the important freighters were challenging the annual accounts and were pushing for reductions in tonnage rates under Section XLIV of the first (1790) Act.

Notwithstanding the possibilities of a new Act, they would still call out the commissioners and tackle Lord Dynevor and John Richards head on for the Glyndyrus

land. Perhaps as a sop to these negotiations, the committee announced that two places had been surveyed for the site of the steam pump, the one on the premises of Lord Dynevor and John Richards having been rejected, in preference to the other on Lord Plymouth's land adjoining Pontyrhun. The canal company could not be accused of coveting all the land of Dynevor and Richards.[73]

On 3 June 1807 the annual general assembly authorised the erection of the Pontyrhun pump as recommended by Rennie. Lord Dynevor was expected in the country to view the site of the intended Glyndyrus reservoir.[74]

This was also the meeting when Watkin George left the committee. His Cyfarthfa partnership with Richard Crawshay was dissolved. Although retaining his interest in the Union ironworks, Rhymney,[75] George moved to the Pontypool Ironworks where he became a partner of Capel Hanbury Leigh.[76] It is not known exactly why Richard Crawshay lost such an able partner as Watkin George, one who had served him so well as chief engineer at both Cyfarthfa and on the Glamorganshire Canal. Unlike most of his contemporary ironmasters who were iron makers, Crawshay's background was in selling iron and establishing markets for his product. He had to rely heavily on others for developing the technical processes of iron production. Crawshay's acknowledgement of these contributions was grudging and it may be that Watkin George was one of the victims of this attitude. Perhaps George saw in Capel Hanbury Leigh a more amenable long-term partner.

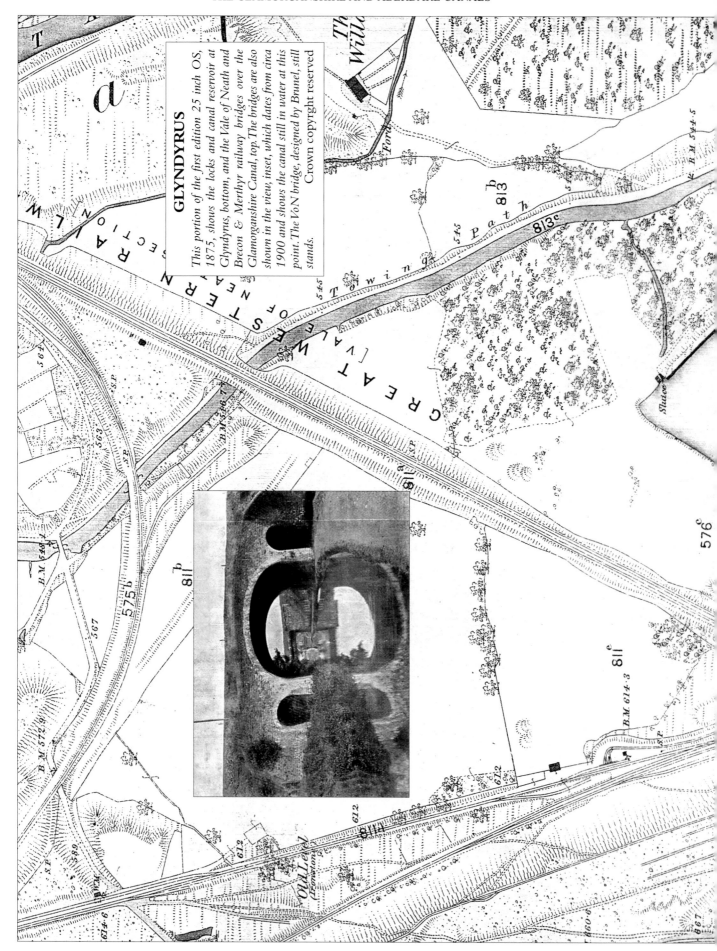

GLYNDYRUS

This portion of the first edition 25 inch OS, 1875, shows the locks and canal reservoir at Glyndyrus, bottom, and the Vale of Neath and Brecon & Merthyr railway bridges over the Glamorganshire Canal, top. The bridges are also shown in the view, inset, which dates from circa 1900 and shows the canal still in water at this point. The V&N bridge, designed by Brunel, still stands.

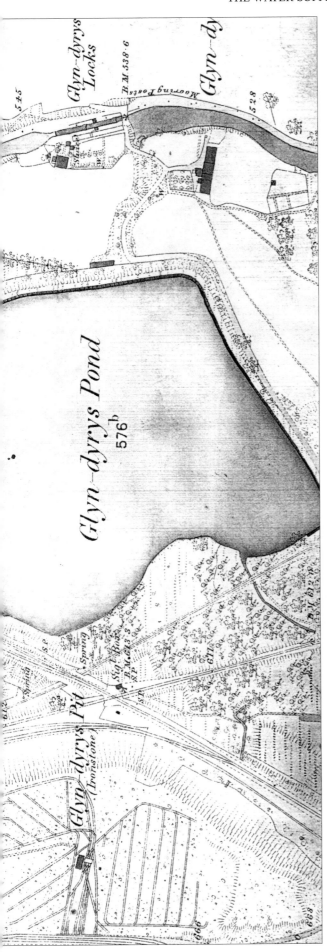

Meanwhile, although the canal company were actively engaged in securing better and alternative water supplies, they did not cease their vigilance at the source of the problem – Parliament Lock. The Hills had placed a flood gate on their feeder below the weir, which would reduce the supply of flood water to the canal above the weir. Threatening letters followed.[77] The pounds above Lock 3 were invariably dry, so that Cyfarthfa had commenced loading iron and unloading goods below this lock. The Merthyr clerk combined his job of providing boating permits with being lock keeper at Parliament Lock and, in June 1808, Crawshay successfully claimed a refund of 3d per ton on all his Cyfarthfa traffic, arranging that permits be granted from Parliament Lock and not from the Cyfarthfa yard in future.[78] In the summer drought of 1807, Philip Williams wrote to Crawshay from Navigation:

'The Rain in the Hills this morning has given us Water to fill the Canal from Merthyr to this place but I am fearful it will be of short duration. It will however enable us to take a trip of Iron down from Cyfarthfa.'[79]

A year later, Thomas Reece, who replaced Philip Williams as company clerk, wrote to Crawshay:

'The Water in the Canal from hence to Merthyr is so low that it will be impossible for the Boats to make one Trip more till rain, indeed some of the Ponds are so much under level that to make one Trip will be attended with a good deal of difficulty, therefore to make the most of the Water to prevent the least possible Waste I propose detaining the up Boats at this place till Saturday when I hope the 6 boats that left Cyfarthfa on Thursday will return so that we shall have a fleet of at least 12 boats to load Iron on Monday.'[80]

Making the best of the water supply to the upper section continued to be an art.

Letters to Lord Plymouth's steward Frances Webb, at Salisbury, for the land at Pontyrhun, did not receive a favourable response. Lord Plymouth had died and his estate was being managed by trustees while the new Earl was under age. The canal committee was still unsure whether it had the right to call out the commissioners. They pleaded to negotiate purchase or rental of the land:

'. . . from the late extension of Mr Hill's Works and increased consumption of Water (whether entitled by Law or not) the Canal will become absolutely dry and useless (it is now before he takes a greater quantity which he is preparing for) unless an immediate supply from the Taff (in the manner proposed) be obtained.'[81]

By August 1807, Dynevor and Richards, fearing that commissioners would undervalue their land, had agreed a rent of £100 per annum (i.e. £50 to each) for the 14 acres required for Glyndyrus reservoir. The agreement would run for the unexpired term of the Cyfarthfa lease, about 60 years.[82] When the agreement came to be drawn up, it was found that Lord Dynevor could not grant a lease of the land for 54 years but for only 21 years or three lives. Nevertheless, this was accepted on the understanding that, in future, Lord Dynevor would fulfil the original agreement.[83] A small amount of land was also taken from Lewis Lewis, for which a rental of £30 per annum was agreed.

This satisfactory outcome at Glyndyrus did not stop the canal company proceeding with plans for a third Act, to repeal the clause in the 1796 Act which limited completion of works to two years.[84] In February 1808, the canal commissioners were put on standby to value the Pontyrhun land.[85] What finally led to the abandonment of the Bill was Frances Webb's more positive letter of 5 Feb 1808 to Richard Crawshay, in response to Crawshay's latest offer. Webb proposed that the single acre of land needed at Pontyrhun be granted to the canal company under a 99 year lease at a rental of £50 per annum, although Lady Amherst would not object to a 1000 year lease. What was more, he reminded Crawshay of his request for a wharf on the canal at Merthyr, to be granted to Lord Plymouth at a favourable rent not exceeding £5 per annum. The minute books do not record whether the committee expressed any opinions, simply that the terms were agreed. The steam engine would be completed at Cyfarthfa and workmen would be employed forthwith to drive the level and shaft for the pump under the direction of Joseph Bailey – and the unfortunate William Williams, stone cutter, was to be given notice to quit his yard at Merthyr to make way for the Earl of Plymouth.[86]

Whilst work proceeded at Pontyrhun, the agreement with Lord Plymouth's trustees and guardians was changed to an outright purchase of the one acre for £1,000! Similarly, the wharf and yard at Merthyr Bridge was to be sold but only for £60. The difference of £940 between the two transactions was to be invested by the canal company in 3% Consuls on behalf of Lord Plymouth, still in his infancy.[87]

Such large items of expenditure caused the other freighters, led by Samuel Homfray and Richard Hill, to question the canal company's accounting conventions. Each year since the 1805-6 accounts were presented, they had been challenged by the freighters at the Michaelmass Quarter Sessions. Each time, the Justices had appointed independent auditors to inspect the accounts (George Lyndon for three years and William Harrison lastly). Yet despite severe doubts being raised at the authority of the canal proprietors' using income from tonnages to finance capital projects, the Justices declined to exercise their powers under the canal Act and reduce tonnage rates. Frustrated by these incomprehensible defeats, Samuel Homfray and his Penydarren company applied to transfer the proceedings from the Quarter Sessions, by certiorari, to the Court of King's Bench. This threat at last prompted the Justices at the Michaelmass session in 1809 to make the long-fought for order to the canal company to reduce tonnage rates. The rate for stone, iron, timber etc was to be 2¹/₂d per ton per mile and the rate for ironstone, iron ore, coal, limestone, lime and manure was to be 1d per ton per mile. By way of

appeal, however, the canal company themselves removed the proceedings to the higher court where they were indeed successful in having the judgement overruled![88] The delight of the committee is evident in Thomas Reece's reply to Samuel Church's letter of 8 Feb 1810, informing them of the result:

'. . . the contents of which has given me the greatest pleasure imaginable. The Victory over the Justices is so complete that I expect they will never attempt to control us any more – I am just returned from Cyfarthfa. Mr Crawshay is very much pleased at the Conquest he desires me to request you will use your best exertion to endeavour to saddle our opponents with the whole of the Costs.'

(The freighters had to wait until Michaelmass 1815 before the tonnage rates were to be next reduced with the assent of the canal committee.)

The investigation of the accounts by George Lyndon and William Harrison over this four year period has left us with a detailed breakdown of the costs of the Glyndyrus and Pontyrhun projects, whilst the original account books of the Glamorganshire Canal Company are assumed lost.

The cost of building Glyndyrus reservoir and feeder was £841 2s 1d, all expended in the accounting year September 1807 to August 1808. This included £60 for building the lock keeper's house, £22 6s 9d for timber for the feeder to the canal (18 feet of baulk, 60 feet of oak, 13¹/₂ feet of elm, and deal plank) and £10 15s for timber for grate and frame. The ironwork, comprising five 12 inch pipes, a drain and grate, was provided by Cyfarthfa at 15 shillings per ton, making £32 3s 3d. The canal company's favourite contractor, David Edwards, was responsible for the labour at a total charge of £658 16s 10d. Other costs were for white lead, lead washers, 248lbs of wrought iron screws, sawing timber, carpentry, fixing pipes and grates, fencing, surveying and for 19 wheelbarrows. The first year's land rent of £30 to Lewis Lewis and £50 to each of Lord Dynevor and John Richards are not included in these costs.

The 1808-9 accounts show an additional maintenance labour charge of £48 17s 7d charged by David Edwards.

The cost of erecting the Pontyrhun engine was £8,428 19s 6d, expended in the two accounting years September 1807 to August 1809. This was way in excess of Crawshay's original estimate of £5,000.[89] Cyfarthfa built the engine (by this time the Boulton & Watt licence patent had expired and 'Boulton & Watt type' engines could be made freely) which alone cost £6,882 15s 4d, of which £2,440 1s 5d was for the castings. £940 (being £1,000 less the £60 credit for the yard at Merthyr Bridge) was the cost of the land from the Plymouth estate. The labour costs were for sawing timber, carpentry, sinking shafts and pits, cutting the foundations and driving the drift to convey the water from the river to the engine. Edward Thomas superintended sinking the pit for the engine house, working under Joseph Bailey.[90] David Edwards and Rees Davies had the contract for cutting the foundations of the engine and James Nicholls drove the level from the river to the engine. T.E. Clarke recorded in 1848 that the engine had been erected by John

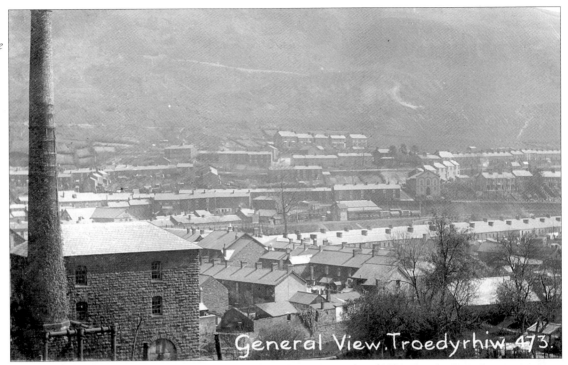

A closer view of the pumphouse and chimney taken from the canal bank. Note the fine masonry work.
SR collection

Griffiths, a Cyfarthfa engineer.[91]

Thomas Morgan, tenant of the farm on which the Pontyrhun engine was erected, was paid a total of £22 18s trespass compensation for damage and refencing after the canal company had attempted to make his landlord, the Plymouth estate, accept responsibility. The canal company chose to build a wall 5¹/₂ feet high and 2 feet thick to fence off the Pontyrhun land. John Robert was paid the surprisingly large sum of £10 for a cow lost in the canal there during the work.[92] At Glyndyrus, David Howell, tenant of Cwm Canaid Farm, claimed compensation for 1a 1r 12p of his land taken; when this was investigated by the committee, they established that Richard Crawshay himself was the tenant with the interest so no damages were paid.[93]

Lord Dynevor and John Richards, not to be left out of the Pontyrhun affair, were initially to claim rights to the land eventually taken for the engine and pump but were successfully subdued by John Oatridge's work on behalf of the Plymouth estate.[94]

In July 1809 the Pontyrhun engine was examined by the committee who gave a vote of thanks to Bailey 'for his judgement and care in constructing the same.' The following April it was decided to make a tramroad incline to carry the coal from the canal bank to the engine's boiler house. After a year's operation had proven the engine's success, Bailey was given a more formal vote of thanks and presented with a pipe of wine.[95]

It had taken four years since plans had been formulated but the Glamorganshire Canal Company now had an adequate water supply to its upper section, to enable it to cope with the rapidly increasing traffic to and from the metropolis that was Merthyr Tydfil.

Back at the Plymouth company, the Hills were continuing to expand their operation and were building a new weir on the river to supplement the supply to the Pentrebach rolling mills.[96] Reece wrote that the canal company's supply would be diminished. Reacting to the Hills and other freighters challenging the expenditure on Glyndyrus and Pontyrhun, the canal committee reported that they had been 'absolutely necessary from Messrs Hill & Co having extended their Watercourse to four times its former consumption.' Richard Hill's response, on 12 July 1809, was to prevent boat number 3, loaded at Cardiff, from entering Parliament Lock, claiming his works were not being delivered the full amount of water from the canal as per the Act of Parliament. After so many disputes the canal still had an illegal bypass feeder at the lock. The committee, in a mood of conciliation, resolved to implement what they had often before discussed[97] – to pipe the water from the paddle of Lock 3 to the Hills' feeder gate. Iron pipes 9 feet long and 15 inches in diameter were ordered and the Hills agreed to their being conducted through the wall of the watercourse.[98] With the reservoir at Glyndyrus having been operational for one summer, William Moses and Joseph Bailey were of the opinion that, if the canal feeder at Lock 3 were totally taken away, the reservoir would be sufficient to supply the canal for at least two months in a dry season.[99]

The Glyndyrus reservoir was not only the saviour of Cyfarthfa and Merthyr canal traffic, its water was relied upon by freighters the whole length of the canal. In 1821, when the committee were planning to raise the canal banks to permit greater tonnages to be carried, they considered raising the banks of the reservoir.[100] Evidence given by the Glyndyrus lock keeper, William Edmunds, in the Melingriffith dispute of 1827 proves how important was the reservoir's contribution.[101] Edmunds stated that it held between 700 and 800 locks of water. In the dry season of 1825, he had run down 732 locks from the reservoir and in the 1826 dry season, 1024 locks. Its use was simple – whenever Plymouth works required the water via the pipes from Lock 3, then an equivalent lock-full had to be drawn from the reservoir to allow the boat to pass Locks 4 and 5.

The Pontyrhun pump also made its valuable contribution. Costs of working the engine, including coal, were afforded a special line in the annual accounts. A new circular boiler was put in in 1824, when the decayed aqueduct was to be substituted for iron pipes by Cyfarthfa's engineer, William Williams.[102] However, it seems the wooden trough was retained, for T.E. Clarke described it in 1848:

'The engine throws up a ton of water at every stroke and makes eight to ten strokes a minute. There are three rods working perpendicularly, one through the cylinder, the diameter of which is 40 inches; the stroke is nearly eight feet. The water is conducted from the engine to the canal by a wooden trough about four feet wide and 240 feet in length.'[103]

The boiler was replaced again in 1841. In 1848, when running costs were becoming expensive, William Williams recommended a new boiler and a completely new engine from Maudsley & Field.[104] Whilst the old one continued to be maintained, the new engine was erected in a new engine house through the years 1850 and 1853, the work being superintended by Rees Davies. Williams and Davies were each paid £20 for their services.[105] The old engine was sold at auction in November 1854, being described as:

'a 60 HORSE POWER PUMPING ENGINE, Double-action, with Working-beam, Connecting-rod, Crank, Fly Wheel, and Shaft; Foundation Plates &c., complete; also the Boiler in good working order with Steam Pipes and other Fittings complete; about 90 feet of 2 feet 6 inch pipes in Pump Column.'[106]

Annual running expenses at Pontyrhun varied from about £100 to £400. For the six years from October 1849 to September 1855, costs of building the new engine are shown with these running costs in the canal company's accounts as:

1849–50	£2,480	7s 7d
1850–51	£2,804	17s 4d
1851–52	£3,184	18s 5d
1852–53	£2,665	19s 10d
1853–54	£1,416	10s 5d
1854–55	£ 470	9s 3d[107]

During building of the new engine, in 1852, the brothers Hill put the canal company into a panic when they announced that they were planning to divert their tail race to enter the Taff *below* the engine![108] The canal company were not sure of their rights but it appears that the Hills did not carry out their threat — indeed, water from the Pentrebach and Duffryn sites enters the Taff at the site of the engine to this day.

The 1850s also saw the canal company fight to protect its water rights at Merthyr against provisions of the 1848 Public Health Act. Sanitary conditions in the town were appalling, the lack of adequate supply of clean water, and poor sewerage and drainage all contributed to disease and regular cholera outbreaks. In 1849, 2,925 died of cholera in Merthyr parish. When the ratepayers elected their Board of Health in October 1850, it was inevitable that it be dominated by the four iron masters who contributed over half the district rates. When its first chairman, Josiah John Guest, died in 1852, his place was taken by Robert Crawshay. The ironmasters persuaded the board that the waterworks should be a private concern but the subsequent 1852 Act for supplying the people of Merthyr with water came to nothing, when only £4,000 was subscribed of the £50,000 required. A new Act was passed in 1858 and included a clause safeguarding the water rights of the Cyfarthfa and Plymouth ironworks, and the Glamorganshire Canal. The Board constructed the Pentwyn reservoir on the Taff Fechan above Dolygaer, with the ironworks and canal being allowed first call on its waters. An independent piped water supply to the inhabitants of Merthyr from the Callan Brook commenced in 1861, even then requiring the consent of the Crawshays and Anthony Hill because the Pentwyn reservoir was not yet complete.[109]

Pontyrhun pumping engine ceased to be used regularly in 1876,[110] by which time the struggling Plymouth works did not rely on water power and the dwindling traffic on the upper section of the canal was not demanding so much water. The detailed report on the state of the canal in July 1885 reported that, at Parliament Lock, *'pipe not now used can be filled with bricks til water is required by Plymouth Iron Works'* and *'paddle leading to river out of repair – new frame and paddle made ready to be put in.'* Glyndyrus reservoir was attended by David Jones and the carpenter was putting the paddle in repair. At Pontyrhun, the fact that an engineer, Theophilus Griffith, still lived there may be an indication that the engine was steamed occasionally. The report states, *'engine requires painting and windows should be boarded up from outside where practicable. Steam pipes require tarring outside. Engine in fair condition.'*[111]

Also in 1885, Crawshay Bros exchanged land at Cyfarthfa's former wharf at Cardiff (which was required by the canal company for a new timber pond) for the top-most 193 feet of the canal at canal head, Merthyr, which they planned to fill in for the use of Cyfarthfa works. This did not prejudice the canal's water supply at canal head and the agreement was formalised by an 1893 lease, whereby Crawshay Bros would maintain the watercourse through its works to the canal below Lock 2. They also returned water from Ynysfach ironworks to the canal below Lock 3.[112] Thus was the water supply continued until the Merthyr section was closed in 1898.

The Pontyrhun engine was not sold until 1915 (seventeen years after closure of that section of the canal), when the Merthyr Tydfil Council expressed concern at the safety of the engine house stack. The engine was bought by Mr John Paton of Pontypool. The engine house was demolished and the stone was used to build the church at nearby Merthyr Vale.[113]

NOTES TO CHAPTER 4

1 NLW MS 15334E Letterbook of Richard Hill 1786-1792.

2 CCL MS 2.716 Diary of John Bird, 6 March 1790.

3 Gwent RO D 2.162 Letterbook of Richard Crawshay, 6 March 1790.

4 For Smeaton see A.W. Skempton (ed) *John Smeaton, FRS.* London 1981. Smeaton died on 29 October 1792.

5 CCL Bute I 37 Thomas Dadford evidence 10 July 1794.

6 Gwent RO D 2.162 Letterbook of Richard Crawshay, 18 May 1790.

7 GCC minute book 6 June 1792.

8 GCC minute book 5 June and 13 July 1793.

9 GCC minute book 26 Oct and 14 Dec 1793.

10 Richard Hill's own plan recording this arrangement is copied with Sylvester Douglas's opinion in NLW Maybery 1889 p.76, 7 Nov 1793.

11 GCC minute book 7 Aug and 11 Sept 1818. Boats continued to use this feeder arm until closure.

12 CCL Bute I 14.

13 CCL MS4.596, 10 Jan 1794 Richard Hill to Messrs W. & J. Powell.

14 CCL Bute I 15 30 Jan 1794. A fine portrait of James Birch hangs in the Cyfarthfa Castle Art Gallery, Merthyr Tydfil.

15 Bute I 29, 9 Feb 1794 Richard Hill to Messrs W. & J. Powell.

16 CCL Bute I 30, 13 Feb 1794 Richard Hill to Messrs W. & J. Powell.

17 CCL Bute I 34, 17 March 1794 Richard Hill to Messrs W. & J. Powell with copy of John Inge's letter (no date) to Hill.

18 NLW Maybery 2482, 25 June 1794 Richard Hill to John Powell, quoted in Chris Evans *The Labyrinth of Flames*, Cardiff 1993, p.114.

19 NLW Maybery 94, 12 June 1794 James Davies' statement.

20 CCL Bute I 37, 11 July 1794 Affidavit of John Warwick, agent and supercargo to James Dadford.

21 GCC minute book 28 July 1794.

22 J. Lloyd *The Early History of the Old South Wales Iron Works, 1760-1840*, London 1906 p.77. See also Evans *The Labyrinth of Flames* p.112-5.

23 Brindley married Henshall's daughter.

24 Edward Paget-Tomlinson *The Complete Book of Canal and River Navigation*, 1978, p.342.

25 CCL Bute I 33.

26 CCL Bute I 21, 17 June 1795 Hugh Henshall to W. & J. Powell.

27 NLW Maybery 2500-2.

28 Copies in NLW Maybery 1221, 15 Aug 1795 and in CCL Bute I 7.

29 GCC minute book 25 August and 2 Sept 1795.

30 NLW Maybery 2503, 2 Oct 1795 Richard Hill to John Powell.

31 GCC minute book 7 Nov 1795 and CCL Bute I 36, 18 Nov 1795 John Allen, Clements Inn to Messrs Powell, Brecon enclosing copies of the sworn affidavits by William Williams and David Edwards.

32 NLW Maybery 92, 93 and 2507, 5 and 11 May 1796.

33 See plan prepared by Charles Hassall and William Pitt in April 1795. NLW MS11910E.

34 GCC minute book, 5 Sept 1797.

35 GCC minute book, 27 June 1798.

36 NLW Maybery 2525-8, 22 Jan - 14 Mar 1799.

37 NLW Maybery 2529-30, 20 May - 10 June 1799; GCC minute book 27 July 1799; NLW Maybery 2682, 16 Aug 1799.

38 NLW Maybery 97 and 98, brief and plan.

39 NLW MS 11910E. Written on a scrap of paper on which is also written '*at General Quarter Sessions Swansea Tues 6 Oct 35th year of George III's reign*'.

40 CCL MS 2.716.

41 GCC minute book, 9 Aug 1799; NLW Maybery 2682, 2532, and 2533 16 Aug, 17 Aug and 20 Aug 1799.

42 NLW Maybery 2523, 6 Nov 1798.

43 GCC minute book, 18 Oct 1799.

44 GCC minute book, 4 June 1800.

45 GCC minute book 3 Nov 1800.

46 GCC minute book, 4 June 1800.

47 GCC minute book 21 Jan 1801.

48 GCC minute book, 3 Mar 1801.

49 NLW Maybery 188-9, 22 April nd 2 July 1801.

50 NLW Maybery 102, 29 July 1801.

51 GCC minute book 24 June, 18 July, 19 Aug 1801, 24 Jun 1802 and 3 Sep 1802.

52 Accounts to Plymouth Forge in the surviving GCC letter book for the period 1805-15 show an increase in tonnage from £200 18s per quarter to a peak of £674 4s 10d in January 1814 quarter.

53 See Plymouth steward account books for the period. GRO D/D Pl 945 and 946.

54 NLW Maybery 1889, 2460, 2466.

55 See Plymouth steward account books for the volumes of limestone quarried by Hill. The comparative size of the two ironworks is clear when, for example, in 1822 14,794 tons $7^3/4$cwt were charged to Homfray's Penydarren works and 5,496 tons 10 cwt to Hill's Plymouth works, the royalty being 3d per ton. GRO D/D Pl 945 and 946.

56 Gwent RO D2.162 Letterbook of Richard Crawshay, 6 July 1791 Richard Crawshay to James Cockshutt.

57 GCC letter book 23 July 1805.

58 GCC minute book 5 June and 3 Aug 1805. GCC letter book 14 June and 12 July 1805.

59 GCC minute book 11 April 1805, 3 Aug, 11 Mar, 29 Mar, 29 Apr, 21 May and 3 June 1806.

60 GCC letterbook, 27 Sept 1805 Philip Williams to Richard Crawshay.

61 GCC minute book 29 Mar 1806. GCC letter book 15 Jan and 29 Mar 1806.

62 GCC letter book 7 May 1806.

63 GCC minute book 21 May and 3 June 1806.

64 GCC letter book 12 July 1806.

65 GCC minute book 3 Sept 1806.

66 See Volume 2 for a full discussion of the Melingriffith water supply.

67 GRO (formerly CCL) Kyrle Fletcher papers ms4.800 KF16 folio 4.

68 GCC minute book 24/25 October 1806.

69 GCC letter book 3 Nov 1806.

70 GCC letter book 10 and 31 Dec 1806 and NLW Maybery 2558.

71 GRO GCC Letterbook 28 Nov 1806 Philip Williams to Richard Crawshay and 3 Jan 1807, Philip Williams to John Powell; NLW Maybery 2559 9 Jan 1807, Benjamin Hall to W. & J. Powell; NLW Maybery 193 22 Jan 1807, case and opinion of Sergeant John Williams and Maybery 1222 and 1223; GRO CL/MS 4.800 (formerly CCL Kyrle Fletcher 15 and 16) case and opinion Wood & Son, Cardiff.

72 GCC letterbook 16 Feb 1807 and GCC minute book 17 Feb 1807.

73 GCC letterbook 10 June 1807, Philip Williams to Francis Webb.

74 GCC minute book 2 and 3 June 1807.

75 In 1816, John Llewellin, Union Ironworks agent, was still dealing with George's affairs. NLW Maybery 3824.

76 Lawrence Ince *The South Wales Iron Industry 1750-1885*, Merton 1993 p.113.

77 GCC letterbook 2 May 1807. GCC minute book 18 July 1807.

78 GCC minute book 3 July 1807 and 1 June 1808.

79 GCC letter book 20 July 1807.

80 GCC letter book 25 Aug 1808.

81 GCC letter book 10 June 1807, 3 July, 1 Aug 1807. GCC minute book 18 July 1807

82 GCC minute book 15 Aug 1807. GCC letter book 20 July, 15 and 20 Aug 1807.

83 GCC minute book 2 Sept 1808.

84 GCC minute book 27 Oct, 17 Dec 1807 and 19 Feb 1808.

85 GCC letter book 1 and 3 Feb 1808.

86 GCC minute book 19 Feb 1808.

87 GCC minute book 2 June 1808. GCC letter book 26 Apr 1808 and 12 June 1809. The company's seal was not affixed to the deed for the coal yard until 1829 which significantly was the year when Robert Thomas's export of Merthyr steam coal began in earnest (GCC minute book 22 April 1829).

88 GCC letter book 28 Nov 1 and 10 Dec 1806, 16 Feb, 9 April, 1 and 5 Dec 1807, 18 Oct 1809, 27 Jan and 10 Feb 1810. GCC minute book 17 Feb, 15 Aug 1807, 22 Apr, 2 Jun, 2 Sep and 25 Oct 1808, 25 Aug, 10 and 21 Oct 1809. GRO CL/ms4.800 KF16 and CCL Bute I 9.

89 GCC minute book 2 Jun 1808.

90 GCC minute book 22 April 1808.

91 T.E. Clarke *History of Merthyr Tydfil*, Merthyr Tydfil 1848.

92 GCC minute book 2 March and 12 July 1809. Also itemised in the accounts 1808-9.

93 GCC minute book 2 Sept 1808 and 7 June 1809.

94 GRO D/D Pl 945/10.

95 GCC minute book 12 July 1809, 24 April and 18 July 1810.

96 GCC minute book 1 June, 28 July 1808 and 6 April 1809.

97 At meetings 3 Nov 1800 and 24/25 Oct 1806.

98 GCC minute book 12 July and 25 Aug 1809. GCC letter book 11 Aug 1809.

99 GCC minute book 10 Oct 1809.

100 GCC minute book 10 May 1821. The original 2in. survey for the first edition OS map of 1813 shows the reservoir's reduced area while Harrison's 1830 map shows it to its full extent. Archaeological fieldwork during the destruction of the reservoir in 1995 indicated that the banks had been raised during its lifetime.

101 Dyfed archives Trostre 4734.47

102 GCC minute book 10 June 1824.

103 T.E. Clarke *History of Merthyr Tydfil*, Merthyr Tydfil 1848.

104 GCC minute book 2 June 1841, 7 June 1848, 27 Oct 1848 and 6 June 1849.

105 GCC minute book 17 Oct 1850, 1 June 1853 and 27 July 1853.

106 GCC minute book 7 June and 9 Nov 1854. Monmouthshire Merlin 17 Nov 1854.

107 GRO QAW 2/84-90.

108 GCC minute book 28 July 1852.

109 Raymond Grant *Water and Sanitation. The Struggle for Public Health in Merthyr Tydfil*, Cowbridge 1993 p.21-6.

110 GRO QWA 2/112-113.

111 GCC minute book. P.G. Harwood's report of 31 July 1885 presented to the committee 12 August 1885.

112 GCC minute book 21 Nov 1885 and CCC Blue box 2141 (since destroyed).

113 GCC Minute book 22 July 1915.

Chapter 5

MERTHYR COAL

The Merthyr ironworks were strategically placed where the coal seams and ironstone bands outcropped at the northern edge of the coalfield. For thirty years, from the founding of the ironworks to the building of the Glamorganshire Canal, there had been time for an infrastructure of waggonways and tramroads to develop to get the coal and ironstone to the furnace banks. Coal and mine (as the ironstone was called) was dug from levels or from patching and scouring. This latter method of securing mine was effected by suddenly releasing dammed up ponds of water, which caused the surface soil to be washed away leaving nodules of the heavy mine to be collected by hand. The ironmasters had systematically bought up leases of the mineral rights and agreed contracts with colliers and miners to work defined areas of their lettings. Drainage of the coal levels was conveniently by adits driven into the hillside below the workings, there being little need for pumping engines. For this reason, Merthyr Tydfil has no tradition of widespread use of early steam engines, or 'fire engines', of the Newcomen type.

Only Cyfarthfa and Plymouth had coal works close to the Glamorganshire Canal. Those belonging to the Dowlais and Penydarren concerns were across the river, clustered along and overlooking the valleys of the Dowlais and Morlais Brooks.

Cyfarthfa's coal and ironstone was mostly dug from levels on the hillside to the west of the canal and from as early as 1767 was delivered to the coking yards and furnace charging platform at Cyfarthfa by a tub-boat canal.[1] This Cyfarthfa Canal wound its way south along the 650 foot contour as far as Cwm Canaid, directly entering some of the coal levels in which the boats were loaded. Isaac Wilkinson, then in charge at Cyfarthfa, had opened a colliery at 'Comcaned' in 1768 and three local men had agreed to work it '*for the Consideration of four shillings per Dozen Coakes Delivered into the Boates in Raw Coal and likewise to be measured on the Bank of the Furnace*'.[2] Robert Clutterbuck's travel journal of 10 September 1799 describes the scene as he left Merthyr, for the Vale of Neath:

'*Understanding that it was impracticable for a Carriage to pass the Mountains, we left Merthyr Tydvil on horseback, keeping to the S.E. towards the Hills. About half a mile*

West of Cyfarthfa, the Canal over which we crossed made a very contracted circuit and offered us an ingenious contrivance in the conveyance of heavy Burthens. For the banks forbidding the use of barges commonly employed, there are seven or eight of a diminished length linked together by chains which acting as joints permit the floating Carriage to adapt to the stream.'[3]

F.J. Pedler, writing in 1930, describes the former route of the Cyfarthfa Canal in detail, and the coal and ironstone levels it served. At that time, Mrs Mary Simons of Brynteg Farm said she recalled helping her father, Howel Giles, hauling tub boats along the canal when she was a girl.[4] The canal went out of use as Cyfarthfa started sinking pits to the lower seams in the area from 1825 and laid more permanent tramroads to the furnaces. The full length of the canal, from Cwm Canaid to the point where it crossed the Aberdare road at Heolgerrig, is shown on the 1850 tithe map.

Richard Hill's Plymouth works obtained its coal from land on both sides of the river. Near to the Glamorganshire Canal, it had a colliery south of the Canaid Brook at Waun Wyllt, a tramroad being built to transport the coal across the canal and river to the works. In 1804, the Plymouth Estate paid for a survey to decide whether coal could be dug for sale at Waun Wyllt. Hill opposed the proposal, suggesting that all Waun Wyllt coal was needed by his works.[5] Hill's colliery was opened in 1805 at an annual rent of £50 but it was allowed to stand from 1811, after the Graig colliery was sunk near Pentrebach by the Hills. For £230 per annum they were granted liberty to take ten thousand tons of coal yearly from the Plymouth estate, any additional coal extracted being subject to a 9d per ton royalty.[6] By 1828, for example, the Hills were paying for an additional 11,932 tons.[7]

As can be seen, the Glamorganshire Canal could play little part in moving ironstone, coal or coke from pit to ironworks.

The vast quantities of coal dug in the area were consumed by the town's own iron furnaces (in the form of coke) but some was required by the many ancilliary industries and the hearths of the homes of the populace. The first sale coal to be carried on the Glamorganshire

THREE BRIDGES MERTHYR.

After 1898, as the abandoned section south of Merthyr quickly returned to nature, the towpath became a favourite country walk for those wishing to escape the smoke and noise of their workplace. At least four picture postcard publishers recognised the aesthetics of the massive stone bridge of the former Vale of Neath Railway, engineered by Isambard Kingdom Brunel. On 6 June 1849, the Canal Company's minute books record rejecting the dimensions of the Railway Company's first design and requiring an arch of 40 feet, to include the towpath unobstructed. The result is this beautiful elliptical arch flanked, east and west by the redundant semi-circular arches originally intended by Brunel to carry the towpaths. The broad gauge VNR climbed westerly out of Merthyr, across the canal and through the Aberdare Tunnel; it competed with the Aberdare Canal rather than the Glamorganshire, tapping the output of the ironworks and collieries at the head of the Cynon Valley and taking it down the Neath Valley to wharves on the river and also to Swansea Docks. The photograph is taken looking north. The next bridge is that of the Brecon & Merthyr Railway of 1866. They chose a lattice girder span and here the Canal Company refused them permission to lower its height. The B&M looped south and west of Merthyr, crossing Cefn Coed viaduct on its way north to Brecon and east to the LNWR lines out of South Wales. The third bridge, in the far distance, is the cast iron bridge carrying the parish road across the canal in front of Rhydycar Farm. The bridge frames are now removed and preserved across a section of the canal at Chapel Row Merthyr Tydfil. This section of the canal features on the OS map reproduced on pages 76-77.

SR collection

Canal at Merthyr was undoubtedly that from Thomas Key's colliery at Abercanaid. In October 1793, Key was granted a 21 year lease of a small wharf, 40 yards square, below Lock 2. From this yard he sold his coal to the village of Merthyr, it being particularly well-sited on the road which crossed the river by the stone Merthyr bridge (at Ynysgau), which, following its collapse in the 1795 floods, was replaced by Watkin George's iron bridge in 1800.[8] Some coal was sent from Abercanaid to Cardiff, where Key was also selling the output from his shallow collieries along the southern section of the canal.[9]

Thomas Key was Lord Plymouth's principal steward and agent in Glamorgan, and used his position to advantage in working sale collieries where the outcrops coincided with the line of the canal. When Thomas disappeared from the scene under a cloud in August 1799, his brothers John and William took over his business concerns.[10] In December 1804, the canal company were granting John Key permission to drive a level beneath the canal at Abercanaid.[11] Such wayleaves were to cost the Glamorganshire Canal dear in years to come, as colliery subsidence caused severe problems with the cut.

John Key died in 1809 and his modest coal empire was continued by his daughter and her husband, Brockett Grover, but this seems not to have included Abercanaid colliery. When the Merthyr coal yard lease expired, it was awarded to Daniel Williams, of Penlasgarn, Monmouthshire, for a further 21 years, where he was given permission to erect two houses.[12] Harrison's 1830 map still shows this as 'Daniel Williams Houses and Yard' and it remained the principal canal-side coal yard at Merthyr.[13]

The 1851 Public Health map shows a coal yard at the similarly-sited original Dowlais wharf, below Lock 1 and close to Jackson's bridge. By that time, both the Dowlais

A dramatic sky adds to this view of the staircase Locks 4 and 5 at Glyndyrus in about 1900, after the upper section had closed. The stonework of the locktail bridge has seen several major repairs in its 100 year lifetime. The most recent is that to the left, which may have blocked a onetime second boat arch that led to a curious cellar beside the lock chamber. The cellar, too small to take a full size boat, still exists. It may have housed a special boat for use by the canal company's committee in their official inspections along the canal. Beyond the stable and lockhouse on the left was the canal's Glyndyrus reservoir. These locks also appear on the OS map reproduced on pages 76-77.   Courtesy Merthyr Tydfil Library

Below Glyndyrus Locks and round a corner was Glyndyrus farm, seen here on the hillside in this circa 1910 view. Below that, the cottage marks the site of Cyfarthfa's pitwood wharf, from which a tramroad led northward around the reservoir to Ynysfach ironworks.   SR collection

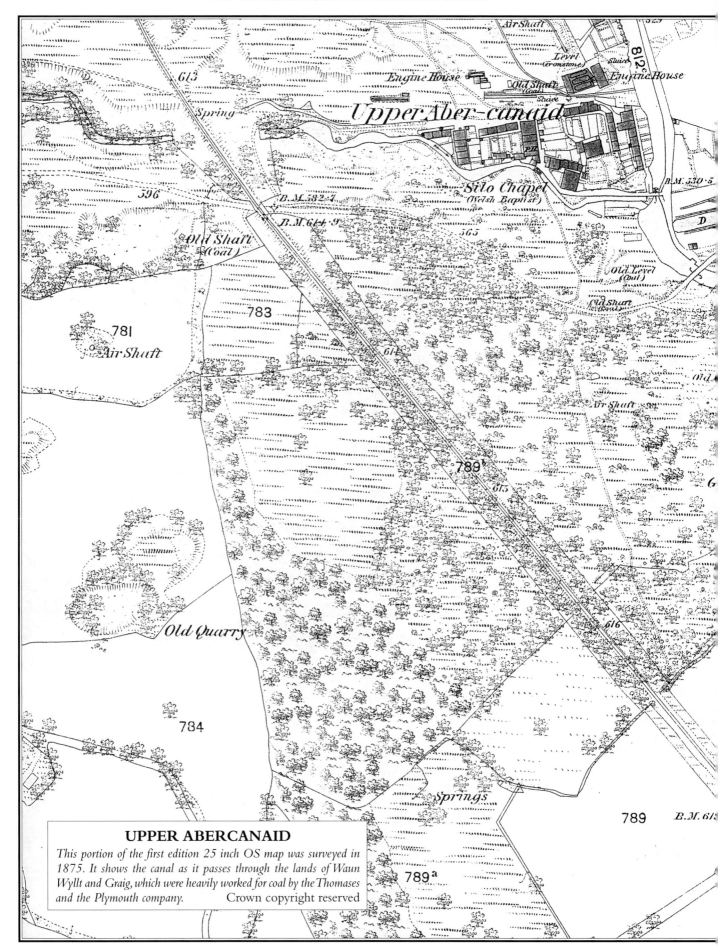

UPPER ABERCANAID

This portion of the first edition 25 inch OS map was surveyed in 1875. It shows the canal as it passes through the lands of Waun Wyllt and Graig, which were heavily worked for coal by the Thomases and the Plymouth company.   Crown copyright reserved

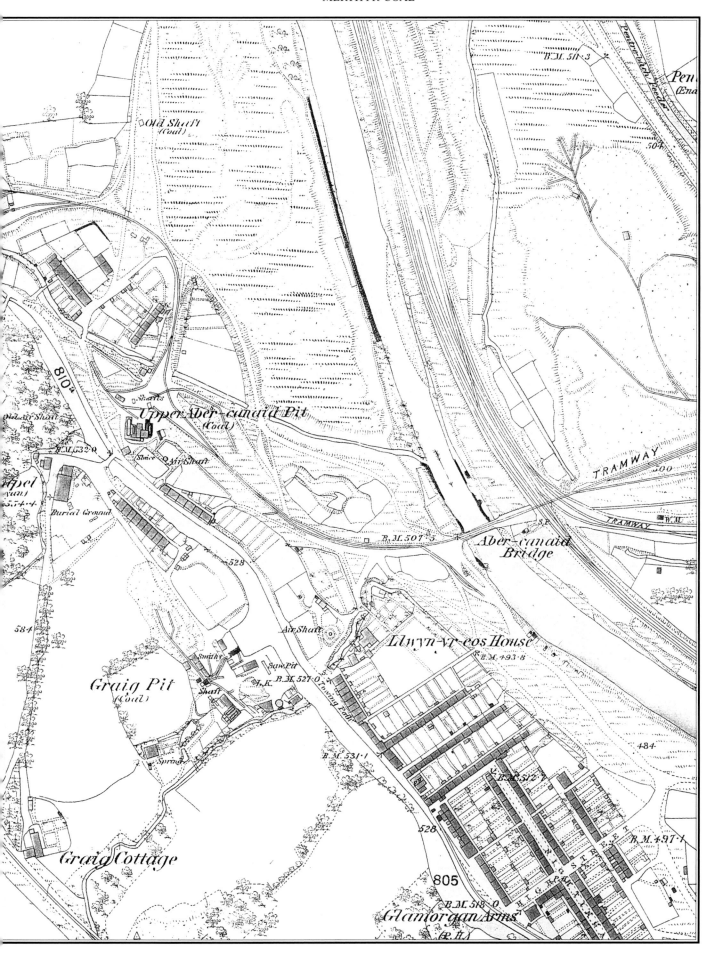

and Cyfarthfa companies were in the sale coal business, although the output was insignificant in comparison to that burnt in the furnaces. In fact, from as early as 1795 Dowlais had been selling coal to the inhabitants of Merthyr from a yard on its railroad at Pont Morlais. It also sent regular boatloads of Dowlais coal to Cardiff, for use at its own wharf and steam mill on the Sea Lock pond.[14] In 1809, an extension of the Merthyr Tramroad was laid south from Navigation to a canal basin, newly made specifically for the purposes of shipping Dowlais coal. When Josiah Guest, of the Dowlais works, established his glass works at Cardiff in 1824 it naturally used Dowlais coal, burning 2,039 tons in 1826.[15] By 1830, however, only 642 tons of Dowlais coal are recorded to have reached Cardiff by canal, as the needs of the growing Dowlais ironworks continued to demand almost all their coal.[16] Cyfarthfa did operate its own sale colliery to supply local needs at Merthyr but it had no connection with the Glamorganshire Canal.

Just below Glyndyrus farm, William Crawshay had a timber yard on the canal where pitwood was received for his coal works. A specially made tramroad led from the wharf, past the west bank of the canal company's Glyndyrus reservoir and then directly to the yard at Ynysfach ironworks.[17] At Glyndyrus, the lock keeper William Moses would, some years later, combine his canal employment with his talent as a local bard.

In 1824, Robert Thomas, a native of Llansamlet near Swansea who had been working at Cyfarthfa's collieries whilst living at Cwmcanaid, took on the old Waun Wyllt lease from Lord Plymouth to work coal and iron stone for sale. He was allowed to extract 4,000 tons annually under Waun Wyllt and Penylan farms, for which he would pay one shilling per ton royalty. The colliery was 320 yards from the canal and in 1825 he sought permission, under the four mile clause of the canal Act, to build a tramroad

Quay Row, Upper Abercanaid, facing the derelict and overgrown canal bed in 1972. These cottages housed colliers from the nearby pits. ILW photo 3 April 1972, neg 2286

to a wharf next to Glyndyrus farm, at what is now Upper Abercanaid. It took some time and expense from the Plymouth estate before the colliery started producing. His account with the Glamorganshire Canal was opened in July 1828 and his first royalties to Plymouth were for 882 tons large coal at 1 shilling per ton and 409 tons small coal at 4d per ton, raised from 23 June to 31 October. The coal was sold at Williams' yard in Merthyr.[18]

From February 1829 (when George Insole's extant coal account starts), Robert Thomas was sending the occasional boatload to George Insole's yard at the Sea Lock pound at Cardiff. By 26 April, Insole had received twelve 20 ton boatloads of Waun Wyllt coal and was able to sell his first full 125 ton shipment to Jeffrey Hooper, master of the *Alexander*, bound for Cork. The whole shipment was

Looking north at Upper Abercanaid about 1903. To the right is the entrance to the Plymouth company's basin and to the left is the old boathouse and Waun Wyllt dock. The small coal and ironstone mining community of Upper Abercanaid was large enough to sustain the Siloa Welsh Baptist chapel, built next to W.T. Lewis's grand house with its monkey puzzle tree. Alongside the pit pumping house can be seen the gable end of the aptly-named Quay Row.   SR collection

charged at £40 12s 6d (6/6d per ton) and Hooper was paid a gratuity of £3 2s 6d (6d a ton). Insole clearly made a loss on this first bulk sale because he was paying Robert Thomas £4 a boatload (4s a ton) and the boatage (or tonnage) fee to the GCC was £2 a boatload (2s a ton). On top of this were Insole's men's wages for unloading the boats onto his yard, then loading the sea-going vessel from his stage and finally trimming the coal in the ship. Who paid the boatman is unclear but it was probably Robert Thomas, who in these early months was using William Beynon.[19]

As well as shipping and selling coal from Cardiff, Insole ran a brick yard, boat yard and timber merchants business in partnership with Richard Biddle. On 1 July 1830 they completed a new canal boat for Robert Thomas, for which they charged £90.[20] Thomas may have had

A close up of the towpath bridge seen above, which spanned the entrance to the Plymouth basin. On the inside of the side members is cast 'A Hill Plymouth 1849'.
Courtesy Merthyr Tydfil Library

Upper Abercanaid colliery, circa 1905. The canal bank is on the right, just out of the picture.

Courtesy Merthyr Tydfil Library

In 1903, when this photograph was probably taken, Graig Welsh Wesleyan chapel was already showing signs of cracking from subsidence. The overgrown remains of the churchyard may still be seen but the buildings and cast-iron bridge are long gone. Upper Abercanaid colliery lay off on the right, across the bridge. SR collection

further boats built and repaired at the Old Boat Dock, which was just below his coal wharf on the west bank of the canal at Upper Abercanaid. In the last years of the canal, boatmen recalled a boat named *Lucy* being housed at this covered dock. Lucy was the name of Robert Thomas's wife and her name lives on even today in the folk lore of the South Wales steam coal industry, thanks to the influential writings of Merthyr historian Charles Wilkins and John Nixon's biographer, James Vincent.

Waun Wyllt was working the four foot seam, and the coal soon earned a reputation for its smokeless quality and steam-raising power, compared to the bituminous coals from the southern outcrop which were being sold for domestic use. Since moving to Cardiff in 1827, Insole's interests had shifted from the timber trade to coal. Rather than rely on selling loads of coal directly to ships' captains from his yard, he had travelled to Ireland and the South West of England to establish his own markets. Recognising the quality of 'Merthyr' coal, he now sought to enter the London market by supplying steam coal to the infant steam shipping business, particularly for the Thames tugs and packet boats. Some exploratory shipments to London soon created an eager demand and Robert Thomas's colliery became the focus for supplying the coal.[21] Wilkins, writing in 1888, quotes the *Cymmer Steam Coal Book* recording Insole making his first shipment of Waun Wyllt coal to London on 12 November 1830, when 414 tons were consigned to Samuel Welford per the *Mars* of Shields. This was already a significant tonnage, for the canal's capacity and loading had to be completed with three canal boats

The gravestone at the Graig cemetery (since removed) of Mary, wife of Morgan Morgan, lock keeper of Glyndyrus, 1857. W. Hamlin

acting as lighters outside the Sea Lock.

Not long afterwards, George Lockett, of the London coal merchants Edward Wood & Co, his agent James Marychurch and James Duke (later to become Lord Mayor of London), made a special trip to South Wales to seek out the source of this relatively smokeless Merthyr coal. The story told is that they stayed at the Angel Hotel, Cardiff, where the coal fire in their room instantly impressed them. They only needed to ask next morning (presumably at Insole's canal-side coal yard) and were directed to the Thomas's level at Waun Wyllt. There they negotiated with Lucy Thomas purchase of their total surplus output at 4

A view of the Plymouth company's village of Abercanaid, about 1912. The canal is still in water. Behind the chapel and across the River Taff can be seen the remains of Pentrebach ironworks and the spoil heaps of the Plymouth collieries.　　　Dave Thomas collection

Llwynyreos Inn, Abercanaid, photographed from the canal bank on 12 July 1947. The nearby Llwynyreos House was the residence of the Plymouth company's engineer.
ILW photo neg 476

shillings per ton at the pit, being able to sell it in London at 18 shillings. The first load went to George Lockett's Mitcham brewery. In August 1831, Insole complained to the Thomases that they were allowing '*Mr Noble, Mr Pryde and Mr George Lockett (Junior)*' to ship their coal after he had negotiated sole rights of shipment with them. That year we then find a contract between Insole and Edward Wood & Co for 3,000 tons of Waun Wyllt coal.

This method of personal bargaining at the pithead, with the merchants then arranging transport by canal and ship to the Thames, contrasted with the well-developed arrangements between the coalfields of the North East of England and London. Newcastle trade was highly organised, all the way into the hall of the Coal Exchange, and the masters of ships either acted for or were the servants of the coal owners.[22]

Although many of Insole's records have been destroyed since E.D. Lewis researched the business in 1938, some account books and daybooks survive in the Glamorgan Record Office. Entries for boat loads of coal received at the Cardiff yard in 1830 also record the name of the boatman. Loads from Merthyr were brought by Thomas Linnet, John Thomas, Edward Jenkins, Daniel Llewellyn, Hugh Steel, Evan Rees, William Beynon, James Noble, William Jarrett, Francis James, Phillip Fletcher, William Pride and John David. While Insole paid Thomas £4 per 20 ton load of large coal (i.e. 4s a ton), he generally sold it at 7s 6d and 8s per ton.

Insole's marketing was so successful in creating an immediate demand for Merthyr coal that, in 1830, Robert Thomas sent 10,476 tons to Cardiff.[23] In 1831 he applied to lease his own coal yard at Cardiff[24] (being initially refused) but he continued to supply Insole, who by now had dissolved his partnership with Biddle and was concentrating totally on coal. Thomas died in February 1833 aged 58 but his wife Lucy and their son William continued the business. In 1833, the Thomas's colliery sent 16,563 tons to Cardiff, increasing to 18,754 tons in 1834.[25] Loose sheets of Waun Wyllt accounts with George Insole survive for the eleven months Feb-Dec 1833 and they account for only 7,040 tons of the officially recorded total of 16,563 tons. In June, the accounts show 40 boats received at Cardiff and three of the boatmen (William Evans, Thomas Meredith and William Thomas) managed seven round trips in the month. Of the 41 boatloads received in October, William Evans managed eight round trips and Thomas Llewelyn seven.[26] Unless the coal was carried in baskets, for which there is no evidence, it must have taken several hours of several men's time to unload 20 tons from a canal boat onto the yard at Cardiff, remembering they had to take care to minimise breakage and were only using shovels and wheelbarrows. This would lead to the startling conclusion that the boatmen did not wait for their boats to be unloaded but took other ready boats, probably loaded with hay or timber or other provisions, back to Merthyr. An empty boat might be taken up the canal to one of the several loading wharves in the Taff Valley, where it would be exchanged for another boat ready-loaded with pitwood.

The boats were owned by the freighters but the men owned the horses. Even so it was more common for a boatman to keep to the same boat for several journeys. Depending how conveniently placed their homes were on the route of the canal, many boatmen probably slept on their boats during the working week, only returning home at weekends.

In 1838, the widow Thomas and her son took on a further mineral lease, that of the Graig farm adjacent to Waun Wyllt but with a different landowner – Margaret Morgan. The 99 year Graig rent was £1,000 per annum with royalties of 1s 3d on large coal and 6d on small coal. They opened a colliery on the bank of the canal near Key's old level. There, a large basin was built for the coal boats to draw alongside the tipping wharf within the colliery confines. Vincent tells a similar tale to Wilkins' of Lockett and Marychurch but Vincent's concerns the Durham mining engineer, John Nixon. Being so impressed by the smokeless properties of the coal on a Thames steamer, Nixon traced it to Wood & Co, and so back to South Wales and Lucy Thomas's Graig pit. Nixon's negotiations at the colliery were fruitless, however, since Thomas refused to increase output above 150 tons per day for which she had a ready market. Nixon would have to wait a few more years before he would be shipping coal down the Aberdare and Glamorganshire Canals.[27] Even so, output from the Graig colliery did grow through 1847, when Lucy died aged 66. The Graig Coal Company's account with the Glamorganshire Canal continued until January 1877.[28]

The Plymouth estate would not allow the Waun Wyllt lease to be renewed after 1837 but instead they let it to the Hills of Plymouth ironworks, who once again were hungry for coal from the west bank of the Taff but who also were keen to enter the sale business. They sank the Upper Abercanaid colliery beneath the banks of the canal near Key's old level and connected it to their tramroad, which crossed the river to the ironworks. The tramroad also connected the colliery to the ironworks' own basin on the canal, immediately opposite the old boat dock of Waun Wyllt. An iron towpath bridge across its entrance was cast at Plymouth with the legend 'A Hill Plymouth 1849' and survived well after the closure of the canal. The basin would have been used to import pitwood and other materials for the colliery, and possibly for the ironworks. Plymouth's iron output and iron ore imports were not carried on the canal north of Navigation, the Merthyr Tramroad being used instead.

In 1844, George Lockett contracted with Anthony Hill for 100,000 tons of Waun Wyllt steam coal at 4 shillings per ton. The quantity so alarmed the other directors at Wood & Co that they sent him back to Merthyr to ask Hill to reduce the order. Hill refused but this proved fortunate for the firm (and Lockett) because within six months the price of Merthyr coal had risen to 10s at pit. Such close contact with the pithead led George Lockett (junior) to join with others in sinking pits at Bwllfa (Aberdare), Blaen Rhondda, Mardy (Rhondda) and Harris Navigation (Treharris).[29]

From the 1870s Plymouth ironworks had its own private

GETHIN

Gethin pits at the southern edge of Abercanaid, again from the 1875 first edition 25 inch OS. The house at the apex of the two terraces of Park Square was Pond House, where the canal company's lengthman (John Rees in 1830) lived. Here was a large weir, necessary to release flood-water pouring into the canal from the slopes above, then out again, via a collecting pond, to the river below. When Gethin No. 1 was sunk in 1849, it was able to utilise this excess water and work as a balance pit. The canal pond was rebuilt by the Cyfarthfa company as a colliery reservoir and collected water above the canal (numbered 813 on this map and surviving to this day) but the canal weir was retained, as shown here. In 1885 the canal foreman, John Bodger, lived at Pond House.

Crown copyright reserved

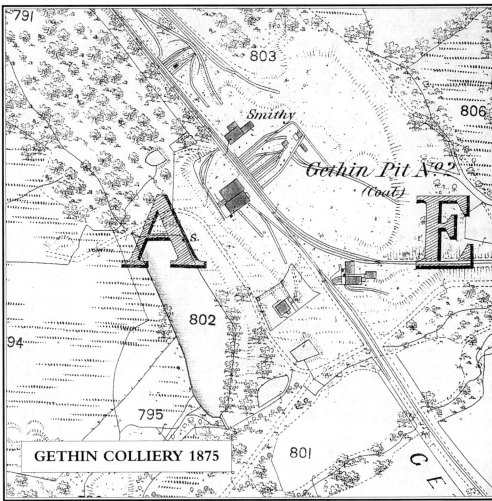

GETHIN COLLIERY 1875

Below: *William Crawshay sank Gethin No 2 pit high up the mountainside and connected it to Cyfarthfa by a railway. He also connected it with Gethin No 1 on the canalside by an incline and the canal did carry coal from this colliery.*

Brian Lewis collection

GETHIN PIT ABERCANAID.

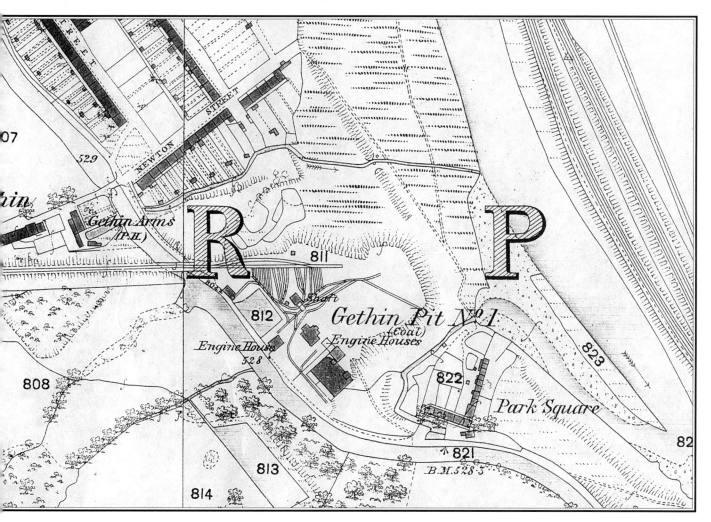

railway to connect to the Taff Vale Railway. Nevertheless, from the 1860s the Abercanaid canal basin was used for shipping the otherwise useless small coal from Plymouth's collieries to the patent fuel works at Maindy, a few miles north of Cardiff. Such traffic continued until the 1890s.

On the southern edge of Abercanaid lay the Gethin farm. In 1849 William Crawshay extended the area of Cyfarthfa's coal supply by sinking a pit at Gethin between the canal and the river. Gethin No 2 was later sunk from higher up the mountainside and an incline connected the two collieries, passing over the canal. Alongside Gethin farm was the Gethin Arms, with its own boat basin. Although this basin would have been used for bringing in beer, no doubt its convenience was also exploited by boatmen visiting the public house. The Gethin collieries had their own large basin alongside Gethin No 1 but William Gomer, interviewed by Ian Wright in 1949, said that coal from Gethin No 2 was actually tipped into boats

Pond House survives on the bank of the long-dry canal bed. This photograph, from the slip road off the A470, was taken when the tip at Gethin No 1 was being removed in July 1987. In the right foreground is the site of the pit and the incline from Gethin No 1 can be clearly made out. The canal bed snakes its way northward through Abercanaid to Merthyr. Since then the A470 has been continued northward to by-pass Merthyr and destroy the surface remains of Gethin No 2 and, further northward, the Glyndyrus reservoir.
SR photo 31 July 1987

Across the river, the Plymouth company sank a coal pit on the site of the disused Dyffryn ironworks. This photograph is believed to have been taken in 1909. The pit head frames of South Dyffryn colliery are in the right background, behind which runs the route of the Merthyr Tramroad. The stone blast furnace No 5 can be seen to the left of the nearest chimney. The Plymouth water feeder had earlier run at this lower level, in front of the furnaces, on its way further south to power Pentrebach ironworks. All surface remains at this site were swept away by a land reclamation scheme in the late 1970s.   SR collection

Castle colliery, Troedyrhiw, was the southernmost of Cyfarthfa's pits and the terminus of their private railway supplying coal to their ironworks. The canal is hidden below the tipping walls of the railway. Across the valley are more of the Plymouth company's many pits.   SR collection

Ash St & Castle Colliery. Troedyrhiw. 480.

Castle colliery from the canal bank a decade after closure of this section of the canal. The buildings on the towpath are Castle Houses. The stone building on the opposite bank may well have been stables connected to the quarry, which had a stone wharf there.

Bob Marrows collection

Bird's Eye View of Troedyrhiw. 472.

A fascinating distant view of Castle pit shows clearly the difference in levels between the canal and the higher railway, by that time continuing past Castle pit as the GW & Rhymney Joint railway on its way south to Quaker's Yard junction. The canalside Dynevor Arms public house is the leftmost building on Ash Road, with the canal bridge to its left. Behind this group of houses had been a massive pennant sandstone quarry and tramway incline to the canal, all of which, by the time this photograph was taken, seems to have been completely filled by waste from the colliery. Another large quarry can be seen behind the colliery and its steep incline to the canal can just be made out, including where it tunnelled beneath the railway. The remains of coal levels, which pre-date the Crawshay pit, are visible, with an eye of faith, between the two sets of housing on the slope of Ash Road. Finally, amongst Castle Houses lies a surviving limekiln from the canal's early days. It is conveniently just below the towpath from where it would have been charged with local coal and imported limestone.

Bob Marrows collection

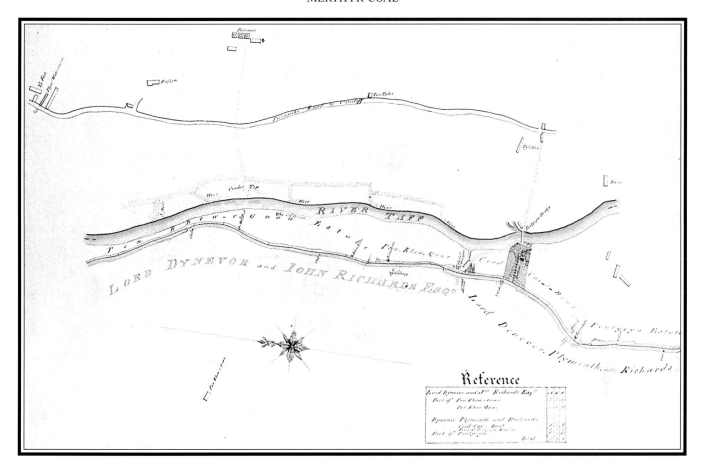

The Ashroad and Troedyrhiw section of the canal from William Harrison's 1830 survey. Note the canal pump at Pontyrhun, the limekilns beneath the canal towpath and the early coal level. Castell Gwewyer (Squirrel's Castle) is presumably the reason Castle Pit was later so-named – but what was Squirrels Castle? Harrison has also seen fit to show the long-defunct Troedyrhiw furnace on the bank of the Taff as well as the contemporary Dyffryn furnaces across the river.   Courtesy Glamorgan Record Office

directly through a hatch in the incline bridge. The canal coal trade from here ended in 1892.

The combined Gethin collieries proved very productive for Cyfarthfa, although the price was paid in human life. Underground explosions in 1862 and 1865 killed 47 and 34 men and boys respectively.

The Crawshays laid their own private railway in 1852, to run between the higher pit and the furnace coke ovens at Cyfarthfa. They extended it in the 1860s to their most southerly and deepest colliery, at Troedyrhiw – Castle pit. An earlier shallow Cyfarthfa colliery on the outskirts of Troedyrhiw was David Jenkin's pit near the Dynevor Arms, a canalside pub aptly named after the ubiquitous landlord, Lord Dynevor.[30] The canal company's own steam pump at Pontyrhun was supplied with Merthyr coal, delivered to a short tramroad at the canal bank.

Further south along the Four Mile Pond, there were several coal workings between Ynysygored and Aberfan. The iron bridge at Pant Glas led to a shaft across the stream from Hafod Tanglwys Uchaf. Just before the five mile mark, a coal level was operated on the site of the present Aberfan cemetery, opposite another canalside pub, the Red Cow, which would have slaked the dry thirst of colliers and boatmen alike. Between Perthygleision Upper and Lower bridges lay Perthygleision pit, shown on Harrison's 1830

map and included in the sale of the estate following William Williams' bankruptcy, and also advertised in *The Cambrian* of 17 Sept 1831. A request for a bridge here was turned down by the canal company committee in June 1828, the argument being that there were enough bridges in the vicinity. Coal from Perthygleision was boated to Merthyr for the brewery and even to Cardiff for smiths' use. When the Merthyr to Abercynon section of the canal was closed, Perthygleision's remaining two boats, numbers 19 and 386, were bought by James Jones of the Dynea boat yard. Boat number 373 also belonged to Perthygleision.[31]

In 1869 John Nixon, following his successes in the Cynon Valley, began sinking his Navigation colliery at Ynys Owen, later to become known as Merthyr Vale colliery. Coal production commenced in 1875. The shafts and surface buildings were situated on the valley floor across the river from Hafod Tanglwys, Perthygleision and Aberfan, and all output was sent via the Taff Vale Railway. The colliery affected the canal in another way. The workings were over 400 yards beneath the canal but they still caused severe subsidence between Nantymaen bridge and Perthygleision bridge. New retaining walls had to be built along the bank at Hafod Tanglwys Uchaf and the walling of the two bridges at Hafod Tanglwys and Pantglas was raised.[32] Ultimately, it was this subsidence which caused the abandonment of this

Left: Nant y Maen accommodation bridge, which carried a cart track over the canal, was already in a state of disrepair when photographed circa 1908. Right: Hafod Tanglwys iron bridge in 1924.   Both Leo Davies collection

This view over Merthyr Vale picks up the line of the canal in the far distance as it passes the northern outskirts of Aberfan. On the far right it is hidden amongst trees as it passes Ynysygored farm, at which point the line of the GW & Rhymney railway crosses over it. From here south, the railway is now on a lower level to the canal and is completely hidden by housing from Pantglas. The canal emerges from the trees at the point where the tipping tramway from Nixon's colliery has reached but not yet crossed it (middle distance, right). Just to the left, Pantglas bridge can just be made out behind the school buildings, followed by Hafod Tanglwys bridge which provided access to Hafod Tanglwys Uchaf farm. The photograph was taken in 1909 and it was another five years before the amount of waste from the colliery warranted extending the tramway across the canal and the beginning of tipping on the mountainside behind the farm. Long after the canal had closed, this was the site of the Aberfan disaster. The farm and most of the school (and the remains of the two canal bridges) were swept away on the morning of 21 October 1966 when the tips slid down the mountain.   Bob Marrows collection

A view of Nixon's Navigation colliery, Merthyr Vale, with Aberfan in the distance, taken around 1910. The line of the canal runs across the distant hillside in front of the cemetery and terrace of houses. John Nixon began sinking this colliery in 1869, after Thomas Powell had apparently declined to take the lease. Coal production started in 1875. The chimney on the right has the legend 'NN 1886' in its brickwork. This pit played a large part in the closure of the canal's upper section because of the subsidence it caused.

Bob Marrows collection

This general view of Aberfan circa 1910 shows the line of the canal as it passes the site of Perthygleision colliery, at the northern wall of Aberfan cemetery. The collapsed level entrance surrounded by its modestly sized waste tips is still visible today. A tramroad led directly from the level to a tipping wharf on the canal bank. The farm above and to the north of the colliery is Hafod Tanglwys Isaf. SR collection

section of the canal.

Merthyr Vale colliery was the cause of a tragedy which touched not just the nation but many people throughout the world. In the early years pit waste was tipped in the valley but in 1914 a tramway was built to bridge the canal, north of Pantglas bridge, and take the waste to the mountainside. From that time and for some fifty years until the fateful day, a succession of seven waste tips were created high above the level of the canal. At 9.15 on the morning of 21 October 1966, after torrential rain, the seventh tip slid down the mountainside, sweeping away Hafod Tanglwys Uchaf and its inhabitants, crossing the abandoned canal and railway embankment, and destroying Pantglas junior school and eighteen houses. In all, in the Aberfan Disaster, 144 people were killed of whom 116 were children.[33]

To the south of Nixon's Ynys Owen property was the Cefn Glas mineral property. A shallow colliery was sunk at the canal side in 1872 for Wood & Co of Dudley, the resident engineer being Thomas Heppell of Merthyr.[34] The shaft was only 45 yards deep and a drainage adit ran to the river, close to the foot of the railway viaduct. The colliery was very close to an earlier level. On 23 August 1836, the canal company refused the colliers, Messrs Sampson & Co, permission to use their own bridge here *'otherwise than the usual Stone Bridge* [Pontydderwen] *made by the Company and that any wharfing to be made by them must be made of stone under the direction of the Clerk of the Canal.'* Only 1,000 tons of coal were raised in the year 1861[35]. Advertisements appeared in the *Merthyr Express* through 1872-3 for *'excellent*

house, coking or smithy coal' for sale at the colliery (and canal) bank. Coal from the pit was taken by tramway bridge across to the towpath side of the canal and to a tipping wall on the Vale of Neath line, erected in the cutting as the railway approached Cefn Glas tunnel. Coke ovens were also built on the site. The railway tunnel passed beneath the canal on its route to Aberdare.

In 1884, Crawshay Brothers' Castle Pit railway became the Great Western & Rhymney Joint Railway, as it was extended south from Troedyrhiw to Cefn Glas, crossing the Taff Valley by a stone viaduct to its junction with the former Vale of Neath line above Quakers Yard. A siding from the joint railway entered the colliery, so that by 1890 there were three outlets for Cefn Glas coal – the Glamorganshire Canal, the GW&RR and the GWR.[36] In the 1890s, when the canal through the colliery was abandoned, Cefn Glas was left idle for long periods and changed hands several times. T.P. Jones & Co of Newport owned it in 1899, employing some 200 men, the output for 1898 being 11,739 tons large coal and 8,555 tons small coal. Weekly output fluctuated from 200 to 1,000 tons according to demand but by 1904 the colliery was closed for good and the plant disposed of.[37]

By 1904, of course, the upper section of the canal had closed so that all movement of Merthyr coal to market was by railway or road. Coal mining in Merthyr continued, the last pit near to the former canal being the Lucy Thomas No 4 which closed in 1955. Merthyr Vale colliery finally closed in 1989.

Aberfan Locks photographed circa 1890 by G.H. Bedford. Here is one of the few images of the canal at work north of Abercynon. A boat is rising in the lower lock and soon the massive gates (common to both upper and lower lock chambers in a staircase) will be opened to let the boat pass into the upper lock. The boat horse is completing its relaxed climb to the towpath above and there are plenty of onlookers to enjoy the occasion of the photograph. G.H. Bedford was an amateur photographer and member of the Cardiff Photographic Society. This may well have been a special trip for the society, although no other contemporary images of this stretch of the canal are known to survive. The functional simplicity of Dadford's architecture for the Glamorganshire Canal is encapsulated in this rural scene, where the lock keeper's cottage with its whitewashed walled garden is so much a part of the composition.   CCL collection

Inset left: *Aberfan lock keeper's cottage in the third quarter of the 20th century – many years after the canal's closure. The most obvious addition is the porch but ten-pane cast iron windows have replaced the twelve pane windows shown in the 1890 photograph. The house was demolished when the A470 dual carriageway was extended to Merthyr. Parts of the lock chambers survive and the canal bed can be walked from this point northward to Merthyr.*

Courtesy Merthyr Tydfil Library

A panoramic view south from above the canal at Pontydderwen to Cefn Glas in 1955. The parapets of the bridge can just be seen in front of the house, which protected the trunk and water race for emptying the canal. The slight widening of the canal's towpath on the left (near the second telegraph pole) marks the site of an early limekiln for burning limestone, brought by canal probably from the Aberdare Canal Company's Penderyn quarries. Just below and parallel to the curve of the towpath here is the line of the long-abandoned siding to Cefn Glas colliery from the GW & RR Joint line. The remains of the tipping wall can be seen at the end of the track, which can be traced from behind the roofless outbuilding. The site of Cefn Glas colliery is behind the tree on the right. The Joint line itself, known as the Quaker's Yard & Merthyr Joint Railway, was closed in 1951 and is visible on the left, with its severed double track crossing the viaduct to join the GWR at Quaker's Yard Junction. After leaving Quaker's Yard Junction, the GWR line, originally the Taff Vale Extension of the Newport Abergavenny & Hereford Railway, crosses the River Taff by its own viaduct and passes into a cutting to tunnel into the Aberdare Valley, on its way to join the former Vale of Neath Railway at Middle Duffryn. Just where the cutting starts was the colliery's tipping wall to a siding on that railway and the line of a tramway to it can also be traced from behind the roofless outbuilding. The line of the canal can be traced right round Cefn Glas, past the Powder Cottage and the

Prince Llewellyn, to a point in the distance beyond the water tank at Quaker's Yard (High Level) Station. Here, Pen Locks commenced to take the canal down to almost river level at Abercynon.

ILW photos 10 Aug 1955, negs 1439 and 1440

Pontydderwen still spans the long dry canal bed. Here it is photographed in April 1976.   Courtesy Merthyr Tydfil Library

Another panorama showing Pontydderwen (right) and Cefn Glas colliery site, taken from across the valley. A train bound for Pontypool Road is leaving Cefn Glas tunnel, while the timber strengthening of the RR & GW Joint Rly viaduct is clear evidence of mining subsidence. Cefn Glas farm nestles among the trees but dominated by the Penrhiwceiber waste tip.   ILW photos 10 Aug 1955, negs 1436 and 1437

This magnificent study is one of a series of views taken by the Cardiff photographer Joseph Collings of the widening of the Taff Vale Railway main line in the 1860s. Showing the reconstruction of Quaker's Yard viaduct, in the summer of 1862, it is also the first known photograph of the Merthyr Tramroad of 1800-2 in operation, on the right. A south-bound train of five drams, with its two horses and attendant drivers, stands in a passing loop, having just let a single horse-drawn dram go by heading north. Despite the fact the photograph was taken near the end of the tramroad's useful life, the track looks in superb condition and displays a well-metalled horse path between the tramplates. The Merthyr Tramroad used 3 foot cast iron tramplates throughout (they never converted to wrought iron), which were fixed to stone sleepers. This tramroad gained international fame as the scene of the world's first experiment with steam traction when, in 1804, a locomotive designed by Richard Trevithick hauled a loaded train of ten tons weight from Penydarren ironworks to Navigation. The 9 mile journey, which included the section pictured here, took just over 4 hours. On the old bridge stands a train of wagons in charge of a TVR 0-6-0 Standard Goods locomotive; the wagons most likely contain stone filling for the voids in the piers of the new viaduct. In the background, just above the tree line, the Glamorganshire Canal can be made out as it passes Powder Cottage (from which local quarries and collieries were supplied with blasting powder). Finally, note the man standing waving a flag on the crown of the third arch of the new bridge; he is the photographers assistant, indicating that the picture can now be taken. John Minnis collection

Another superb photograph of the widening of Brunel's Quaker's Yard viaduct, taken probably on the same day as the previous view. The TVR were able to keep the single line over the existing viaduct in operation whilst the widening proceeded alongside. Stone was quarried from the rock face beyond the viaduct, dressed, then winched aboard a 4-wheeled flat wagon, as seen on the right. This would then be pushed underneath one of the travelling cranes, which are ingeniously perched with their right-hand wheels on a rail running along the existing parapet. The crane's trolley would then lift one of the massive blocks, manoeuvre to the end of its run and gently lower it down to the masons. Just to the left of the viaduct can be seen the incline which was used to run materials down in the early part of the contract, when building in the river bed and as the piers started to progress. By the date of this view it was in the process of being dismantled. The tunnel beyond the viaduct is in the process of being opened out into a cutting as part of the widening. High up on the right above this scene of activity can be seen the revetment wall of the canal bank as it approaches Pen Locks, the top of a series of locks taking the waterway down to its own aqueduct across the river at Navigation.

SR collection

The Prince Llewellyn inn near Cefn Glas lock. The photograph is taken from the bed of the canal.
ILW photo 3 Apr 1972, neg 2289

NOTES TO CHAPTER 5

1 Charles Wood's diary of the building of Cyfarthfa ironworks has an entry for Saturday 30 August 1766: '*This day, Agreed with Abraham Evans & his partners to make the Cut . . . , in Length 1346 yards . . . at 6d per solid yard – Rock or Earth, as it may happen . . . they are obliged to finish it by the 11th day of february 1767.*' This may be for the first section of the canal or it may be for the feeder from the River Taff to provide water power to the works.

2 PRO E112/2094/75. Thanks to Chris Evans, Cardiff, for this reference.

3 CCL MS 3.277.

4 F.J. Pedler *History of the Hamlet of Gellideg*, Merthyr Tydfil 1930. Gellideg is that part of Merthyr west of the River Taff and north of the Graig brook.

5 GRO D/D PL945/5 p.40 and NLW Maybery papers 2006.

6 GRO D/D PL945/14 P.25.

7 GRO D/D PL946/7.

8 GCC minute book 26 Oct 1793.

9 Tonnage book 1797-9. GRO D/D Art O/21. See also Volume 2

10 John Evans, Blaenafon, believes Thomas Key's disappearance could be related to the bankruptcy of David Tanner.

11 GCC minute book 7 Dec 1804.

12 GCC minute book 3 Dec 1814, 31 Mar 1815 and lease GRO B/C GCo. 4/66

13 Also see Pedler *Gellideg*, p.43-4.

14 GRO Dowlais Letterbooks.

15 *The Cambrian*, 3 Feb 1827.

16 *The Cambrian*, 22 January 1831.

17 See Harrison's 1830 map and the 1850 Tithe map. The tramroad is clearly shown also on an unreferenced copy at Ynysfach Museum, Merthyr, of an 1860s map of Merthyr from the Glamorgan Record Office.

18 John Ballinger *Guide to Cardiff City and Port*, Cardiff 1908 p.15-16; NLW Lord Merthyr of Senghenydd papers 341 & 342; GRO Plymouth Estate books D/D PL946/4-7; Charles Wilkins *The South Wales Coal Trade & its Allied Industries, from the Earliest to the Present Time*, Cardiff 1888 p.71.

19 GRO D/D Xcv 1.

20 GRO D/D Xcv 1.

21 E.D. Lewis *Pioneers of the Cardiff Coal Trade*, in *Glamorgan Historian Vol. 11*, Barry nd p.43-52; Richard Watson *Rhondda Coal, Cardiff Gold*, Cardiff 1997 p.12-21; Eira Smith *Robert and Lucy Thomas*, in *Merthyr Historian Vol. 7*, Merthyr 1994 p.1-9; GCC minute book 21 Jan 1831; GRO Plymouth papers D/D PL946; GRO Insole Daybooks D/D Xcv 1.

22 Elspet Fraser-Stephen *Two Centuries in the London Coal Trade – The Story of Charringtons*, London 1952 p.51-2.

23 *The Cambrian*, 22 Jan 1831.

24 GCC minute book 21 Jan 1831.

25 *Cardiff & Merthyr Guardian*, 11 Jan 1834 and 10 Jan 1835.

26 GRO D/D Xcv2.

27 James Edward Vincent John Nixon *Pioneer of the Steam Coal Trade in South Wales – a Memoir*, London 1900 p.102-110.

28 This Graig should not be confused with the Graig across the river near Pentrebach, where Plymouth had one of its main collieries.

29 Fraser-Stephens *Charringtons*, p.52.

30 Clive Thomas in Perkins, Thomas and Evans *The Historic Taf Valleys, Vol 3*, Merthyr Tydfil 1986 p.107-112.

31 W. Gomer in conversation with ILW 7 Oct 1949.

32 WIMM 87.97I/14.

33 Melanie Doel and Martin Dunkerton *Is it Still Raining in Aberfan?*, Logaston 1991.

34 *Merthyr Express*, 9 Feb 1872. Thanks to Dave Thomas, Ponthir, for this and other newspaper references to Cefn Glas.

35 *Lawrence's Directory of the South Wales Coalfield*.

36 For a description of the joint railway see Eddie Evans *The Quakers Yard & Merthyr Joint Railway* and subsequent letters in *Archive*, The Quarterly Journal for British Industrial and Transport History, Issues 11 & 12, Lydney Sept & Dec 1996.

37 *Merthyr Express*, 5 Nov 1904.

A rare view by the photographer Richard L. Berry of Aberdare Canal Company architecture at the company's own wharf at Canal Head. Only a few years after the canal's closure, the canal had already become overgrown with weed. The cast iron post on which the massive wooden crane pivoted still survives but the buildings and the other two cranes beyond have, not surprisingly, disappeared.

Courtesy Aberdare Library

Chapter 6

THE ABERDARE CANAL
1812 - 1900

One traveller at the beginning of the 19th century described the valley of the River Cynon in Glamorganshire as '*a secluded retreat of nature*'. From time to time a few tourists and artists with their guides followed the rough horse track beside the Cynon. Benjamin Malkin commented '*In these wild districts the face of nature is enchanting but the state of accommodation is miserably poor.*' When Malkin reached the tiny hamlet of Aberdare in 1807, he found a cluster of ironworks where the valley opened out. '*I was glad to escape,*' he wrote, '*from the confusion of anvils, the blast of furnaces and the whirl of wheels.*'[1]

The Aberdare Canal, which opened for trade in these still rural surroundings in 1812, ran from near Aberdare, in a south-easterly direction down the valley, to join the Glamorganshire at Abercynon, a distance of only 6³/₄ miles. Although its mark on the canal map of Britain was small the waterway achieved great importance in its day.

The canal stimulated the expansion of the iron industry of the Aberdare region, particularly in the 1820s, by providing the ironmasters with access to their markets. By good fortune the canal also found itself ideally positioned in the valley to promote the development of steam coal mining during the 1830s and 40s. From 1846, the waterway faced competition from the Taff Vale Railway but so massive was the volume of coal production in the valley that the Aberdare Canal Company achieved its greatest prosperity during the 1850s and early 1860s.

Decline came in 1864, with the extension of the West Midland Railway into the Aberdare Valley from the east. Railways were demonstrating their superior coal handling facilities, particularly at the ports, and the diminishing iron industry of Aberdare, once providing the canal's staple trade, came to an abrupt end in 1875. The Marquess of Bute took control of the Aberdare Canal in 1885, along with the main canal, the Glamorganshire, and there was a brief renaissance in trading, this time by the Glamorganshire Canal Co itself. The GCC put on a regular service of boats from Cardiff to the by now well-established valley communities of Mountain Ash and Aberdare, the traffic now being almost exclusively up-valley consignments of market goods and general provisions. The revival was not to last for long. Intensive railway competition coupled with serious damage from mining subsidence brought an end to traffic on the Aberdare Canal and in 1900 the waterway was taken out of use in the interests of public safety.[2]

The Aberdare Canal Company: The Pre-Canal Years

The ACC was an unusual enterprise. From its incorporation as a canal company in 1793, it operated for 16 years without building a canal. Instead it conducted a trade from limestone quarries which it leased at Penderyn, raising stone and conveying it over its tramroad to the furnaces of the Hirwaun ironworks. The ACC also worked its own limekilns, supplying stone for road making and lime for building and agriculture.

The Act of 1793[3] authorised a canal to be built on the opposite side of the River Cynon from Aberdare and to follow the Cynon Valley southeast as far as Navigation (later to be named Abercynon), where a junction would be made with the Glamorganshire Canal. It also authorised a '*Railway or Stone Road*' to join the terminus of the Aberdare Canal with the Neath Canal at Abernant (near Glyn Neath – not the Abernant near Aberdare). The capital of the company was £22,500, with power to raise a further £11,000 if needed. There were 33 proprietors drawn from landowners, solicitors, bankers and industrialists, and among the subscribing ironmasters were the Homfrays of Penydarren, Richard Hill of Plymouth works, and John Partridge of Monmouth (later of Melingriffith), whose names are familiar from their involvement as shareholders in the neighbouring Glamorganshire Canal.[4] The Act, in common with others relating to South Wales canals, also authorised the building of feeder tramroads to coal works, iron mines, furnaces, quarries etc, lying within eight miles of the authorised route of the canal and rail road. This differed from the clause in the GCC Act, where the distance allowed was only four miles. The route was surveyed by John Dadford, for which he was paid £100 2s 6d. The ubiquitous canal engineering family – father Thomas Dadford and three sons Thomas, John and James – were promoters and initial shareholders too.[5]

In 1793, only one iron works existed in the Aberdare district; the Hirwaun works, established in 1757 by John Maybery and which, having passed through a number of hands, had been leased in 1780 to Anthony Bacon. On

Hirwaun ironworks lay in a constricted site on the Breconshire side of the stream, facing Glamorganshire. Although long-lived, it was never a great success even when in Crawshay hands. Ultimate closure came in 1905. By the time this photograph was taken, the casting sheds were gone and the four massive furnaces were already being robbed of stone. The rolling mills and puddling furnaces are situated on the platform beside the River Cynon. Behind, in the right distance, is the tramroad causeway, crossing the river. Courtesy Aberdare Library

Abernant ironworks closed in 1875 and the River Level colliery was sunk in its yard, in a similar way that South Dyffryn pit was sunk at the Dyffryn ironworks, in the Taff Valley. This photograph of about 1905 shows one of the furnaces, and the blast engine house and chimney. The ellipsoidal air reservoir controlled the blast to the furnace. Courtesy Aberdare Library

The cast iron wheel which powered the blast for the Llwydcoed furnaces.
Courtesy Aberdare Library

Bacon's death in 1786, a lease of the ironworks was granted to Samuel Glover of Abercarn,[6] who built (or inherited) a rail road there to bring in coal and ironstone from the south, at Bryngwyn. The Aberdare Canal Co considered that the traffic potential from the Hirwaun furnaces alone was too unpromising to cover the running costs of a canal and straightway it was decided to delay construction. Instead, the canal company, with Glover on its committee, resolved to build a rail road from the intended site of the canal head near Aberdare '*to join Mr Glover's Rail Road upon Hirwaun Common and from thence to the Lime Rock at Penderin.*'[7] The distinction between rail road and tramroad is important here and the minute books make it quite clear that it was an edge railway, not a plateway, they wanted – at the same cost per mile as John Dadford was then building to the Brecknock & Abergavenny Canal.[8] The contract for building the rail road was let to John Dadford's brother James (not Thomas Dadford junior as implied by Davies) and was completed in 1795, although the portion as far as canal head was not built.[9] The gauge is not explicitly stated but it must naturally have been the same as Glover's road. Waggons and a weighing machine were acquired through Samuel Glover, the company paying William Whitmore £52 10s for the weighing machine which was installed at the quarry, alongside a toll house for the weighing agent (Perequine Jones), built by John Watkins, mason for £27 9s 9d. A bye law was minuted on 3 July 1794 that '*no waggon but of proper width 3ft 2in be permitted to travel on the rail road.*' For opening the quarry Thomas John Llewelyn was paid five guineas, plus a three-year contract for raising the

Hirwaun High Street on a circa 1909 picture postcard, showing the tramroad passing through.   SR collection

High Street, Hirwain.

Llwydcoed (or Aberdare) ironworks closed in 1875. This undated photograph shows the three blast furnaces and the large diameter waterwheel (similar to Cyfarthfa's) which provided the blast to the furnace on the right.

Courtesy Aberdare Library

The classic photograph of a working tramroad in South Wales depicts a train of limestone on the Aberdare Canal Company's tramroad between Hirwaun and Penderyn. The train is passing a turn-out or passing place. The photograph shows clearly the way the flangeless tram wheels run on the outside of the tramplate flanges. The stone sleepers are evident on the passing loop and, considering the height to which the drams are loaded, it is not surprising that the odd lump of stone has fallen to the trackside. The haulier is riding the first dram. Courtesy Aberdare Library

A surviving structure of the canal company's tramroad of 1811 is the cast iron bridge across the River Cynon at Robertstown. It is one of the earliest iron railway bridges to survive. Cast into its central upright is 'Abernant 1811'.

W. Hamlin photo

limestone and delivering it to the side of the rail road at 3d per ton (each ton comprising 20 hundredweight of 120 pounds, whereas the company was to charge its customers tonnage rates based on 112 pounds to the hundredweight!). Llewellyn was loaned two planks and two wheelbarrows from the company.[10]

Philip Griffiths of Merthyr was appointed first Clerk to the Company of Proprietors of the ACC, at a salary of £20 per annum and he was paid an extra £10 to keep accounts of the amounts paid to James Dadford and his men. The committee could not have been unaware of the difficulties the Glamorganshire Canal was beginning to have in controlling payments to its engineer and contractor – Thomas Dadford, their man's father. Jeffreys and Walter Wilkins, the Brecon bankers who were already Treasurers of the Glamorganshire Canal Company, acted as Treasurers of the ACC and it was their difficult task to press the subscribing shareholders for their money each time there was a call on shares.

In 1799, Thomas Rees and Philip Watkins were paid 2s 6d per yard for extending the rail road 60 yards into the quarry. In July 1800, the Llwydcoed ironworks were under construction to the north-west of the 'canal head' and Thomas Dadford was retained to re-survey the line of the canal and a 'Dram or Rail Road' to the ironworks. By this time the edge rail road was generally losing favour to the plateway and this factor preoccupied the Aberdare Canal Company, rather than cutting the canal:

'the present Rail Road being imperfect and inadequate to the purpose for which it was intended. Resolved that the Rails be forthwith taken up and disposed of in such a manner

as the Committee shall think proper and that it be referred to the Committee whether it not be expedient to make a Tram Road from Hirwaun to the Limestone quarry according to Mr Outram's plan.'[11]

However, Llwydcoed was not the only new ironworks in the area. At Abernant, a partnership of Jeremiah Homfray and the engineer James Birch, from Penydarren, was being formed, with finance provided by the Tappenden family (brothers James and Francis, and their uncle James Tappenden) of Faversham, Kent.[12] Homfray, with Tappenden money, seized the initiative from the Aberdare Canal Company and planned a tramroad from Abernant and Llwydcoed, westward over the mountain, negotiating with the Neath Canal Company (so as to utilise that company's 8-mile clause) the building of the eastern portion, including a long incline down to their canal. At this time, George Overton was building the Merthyr Tramroad from Dowlais and Penydarren to the Glamorganshire Canal at Navigation, and all parties acceded to his superior type of track. Overton even moved into the Aberdare area and became a partner in the Hirwaun ironworks. The Tappenden tramroad opened in 1805 and the ACC's tramroad also was converted by them *'at an expense not exceeding Fifteen hundred pounds per mile'* and of *'Iron rails cast in flasks at Ten pounds per Ton the quantity for each rail not exceeding 69 tons per mile or to contain less than 60.'* Five guineas per ton were allowed as scrap for the old edge rails.[13]

By 1805, three iron producers were now active in the Aberdare neighbourhood, encouraged by an improvement in the iron trade: the Hirwaun works, managed from 1805-13 by Francis William Bowzer, Lionel Oliver & George

Overton; the Aberdare Iron Co at Llwydcoed (Scale & Co.); and the Abernant Iron Co, managed by Jeremiah Homfray, James Birch and Francis Tappenden, who had not begun production until 1804.[14] By the Tappenden tramroad route, all these Aberdare producers were able to send iron for shipment at the river port of Neath. The Aberdare Canal Company was still carrying little iron but its sale of limestone had increased substantially since its rail road had been converted to a tramroad and extended to deliver the flux for the furnaces at these ironworks. At the quarry, in 1801, the canal company's land-owner there (Watkin Powell) was appointed Clerk and Weighing Agent at a guinea per week but nevertheless had to provide £100 security, devoting his time fully to the company. He lived a charmed life for, when Philip Griffiths died in May 1803, he was made Clerk to the committee and then survived an incident when the canal company caught him selling lime and limestone for himself from the very quarry they rented from him.[15]

Meanwhile, in the Aberdare Valley there were stirrings for improvement in communications. A turnpike road down the valley to Navigation, whose Act had been passed the same day as the canal's Act in 1793 but whose start was then delayed until 1803, was at last taken in hand and completed by 1810.[16]

Evidence points strongly towards Richard Crawshay of Cyfarthfa being instrumental in the final push to persuade the Aberdare Canal Company to construct their canal. The three ironworks had been in full production since 1806. Although some of their iron was sent overland to Merthyr for finishing, most was consigned as pig iron via the Tappenden tramroad to the Neath Canal. Annual freight charges paid by the three works to the Neath Canal Navigation had by the end of 1808 reached over £2,100.[17] The Tappendens, whose partnership with Homfray and Birch was dissolved, had invested heavily in constructing the tramroad but the further costs of operating and maintaining the route, and in particular the long Penrhiw incline to the Neath valley at Pont Walby, were not being rewarded even by the growing tonnage receipts from the other two iron companies. In addition, the Tappendens seem to have been heavily in debt to Richard Crawshay for rolling their iron at Merthyr.[18] Crawshay must have realised that the tramroad to Glyn Neath was a drain on the Tappendens' resources but that something extra was needed to persuade them to redirect the export of their iron, from Neath to the Crawshay-controlled Glamorganshire Canal and Cardiff. In what must have been the last grand plan of his life, Richard Crawshay purchased Tappendens' tramroad for the unrealistically high price of £26,000 and re-let it to them at a peppercorn rent from 1 January 1810.[19] In addition, Crawshay gave up his nail works on the Glamorganshire Canal at Ynysangharad to the Tappendens, for them to build their own rolling mills for the Abernant Iron Company there. Thus were the Tappendens relieved of their financial millstone and were enabled to focus on Cardiff to export their produce. Francis Tappenden bought shares in the Aberdare Canal Company in 1809 and was voted on to their committee, where he supported his rivals in trade, John and George Scale of the Aberdare Ironworks, who were already pressing for canal-cutting to commence. Joseph Bailey indirectly represented the Crawshay interest. On 19 September 1809, a Special Assembly of the Aberdare Canal Company resolved to start constructing the canal. The committee also agreed to make a direct tramroad from Scales' works at Llwydcoed to the canal head.[20] Within six months, Richard Crawshay had died and he bequeathed the former Tappenden tramroad to his son-in-law, Benjamin Hall (rather than to his son William who received only a limited inheritance after having fallen out with his father).

Construction and Route

The Aberdare Canal Company now felt confident that it could attract all iron produced by the three ironworks away from the Neath Canal. The committee decided that a new survey was required and, after Thomas Cartwright the Neath Canal engineer had declined the offer, Edward Martin of Morriston was appointed to the task for a £20 fee. Thomas Sheasby junior was engaged as engineer. The survey was complete by 9 Jan 1810, when Evan Hopkin of Llangyfelach and his son David, who had already worked on the Neath Canal, won the contract. On 21 Dec 1810 the local members of the committee met to fix where to build the bridges:

'Evan and David Hopkin having proposed to build six Bridges more than they were engaged to do in consideration of being allowed to make the Two Lower ponds four feet deep instead of five feet and to make the Farmers Bridges eight feet wide in the Clear instead of twelve feet.'[21]

In response to what was a land valuation dispute, the minute book records that valuation was entrusted to Edward Edmunds of Nantgarw, as commissioner on behalf of the canal company, and Samuel Rees of Werfa, for the main landowner John Bruce Bruce, who had inherited his shareholding and from 1809 became a principal committee member.[22]

From the Glamorganshire Canal Company's minute book we learn that help came from the larger company when the GCC agreed to the request of Messrs Scale and Tappenden *'to carry stone, lime etc. free of tonnage for making the Aberdare Canal.'[23]* The Glamorganshire Canal Company was of course only too happy to encourage the Aberdare Canal promoters. Not only would the GCC benefit from tolls on Aberdare traffic passing on to its canal to Cardiff, but it would also get all the Aberdare Company's water at the Abercynon flight. That the GCC should receive all ACC water was not a foregone conclusion, because Richard Blakemore of the Melingriffith tinplate works and Pentyrch ironworks had petitioned the ACC for any excess water at the stop lock between the two canals to be directed back into the rivers Cynon and Taff, rather than flow into the Glamorganshire Canal; his works were already suffering from the GCC removing water from the River Taff. At

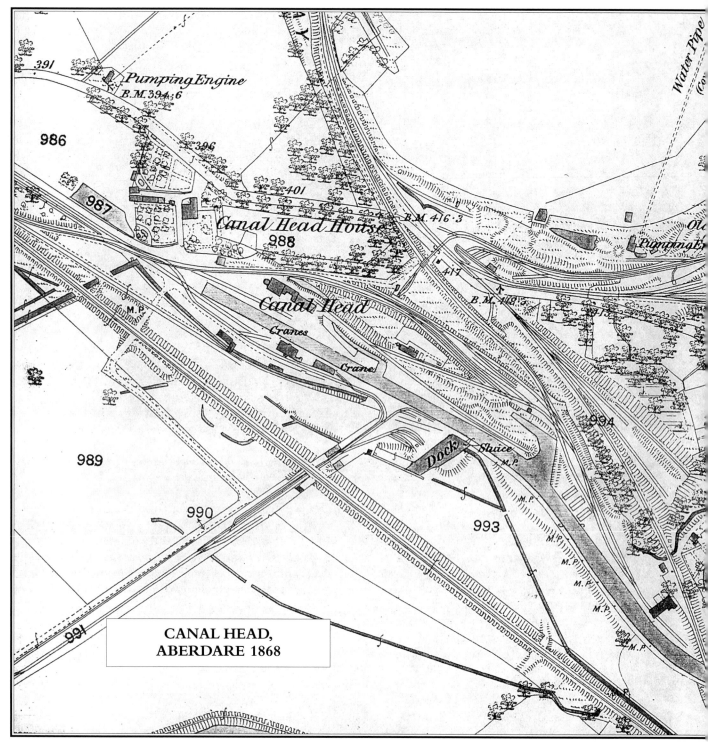

CANAL HEAD, ABERDARE 1868

Canal Head on the Aberdare Canal as surveyed for the first edition 25 inch OS in 1868. The canal is surrounded by the railway lines of several companies. The southern-most line, running from the north-west to the south-east, is the main line of the mixed gauge Vale of Neath (by then operated by the GWR, it being only a few years before the abandonment of Brunel's broad gauge in South Wales). Branches from the VNR can be seen serving both sides of the canal. The Aberdare Canal Company's tramroad (from Hirwaun and Llwydcoed) also enters from the north-west and crosses the VNR to serve just the southern side of the canal and the canal company's warehouse. The tramroad continues along the wharf to join the long straight Blaengwawr tramroad which enters from the south-west and whose loading dock is clearly marked. The canal feeder enters from the west, flowing beneath the main line of the VNR. From the north, the Abernant Railway (from the Abernant ironworks) serves the canal wharves and transshipment sidings, with the VNR on the north bank. Another line of the Abernant Railway bypasses the wharves and crosses the canal at Ynyscynon to continue south-east (off map) in parallel to the VNR, to serve High Duffryn colliery. It then continues past the other canal-side collieries before turning south, crossing the VNR and the River Cynon, and joining the TVR's Aberdare Railway. Ynyscynon House was the residence of David Williams, proprietor of High Duffryn colliery. This whole section of canal from the road just south of Ynyscynon House to Canal Head has been preserved as a nature reserve.

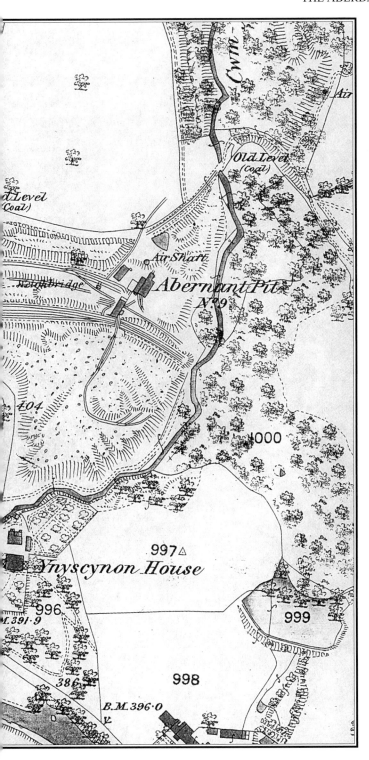

Canal Head house, Aberdare Canal.
ILW photo 18 April 1973, neg 2332

Aberdare to the junction with the Glamorganshire Canal, the level of the Aberdare Canal fell by only 13 feet. Two locks were needed, one at Cwmbach with an ultimate fall of 9 feet 3 inches and the other bordering the Bruce estate at Dyffryn, which lowered the canal by only 3 feet 10 inches.[25] The additional regulating or stop lock was at the approach to the junction, where the canal entered the Glamorganshire Canal at the tail of the GCC's Lock 17. The route of the canal was generally easy and followed hill slopes above the northern bank of the River Cynon. A small aqueduct carried the waterway over Nant Pennar and as originally built the canal was crossed by eighteen bridges, which are clearly shown on the unpublished 1814 OS 2 inch to 1 mile map.[26] Water supply to the canal was from a feeder off the River Cynon at Canal Head and the canal company in its latter years maintained reservoirs of 47 acres at Hirwaun Ponds.[27] In August 1811, Sheasby resigned to take up a post as clerk and engineer to the Severn & Wye Railway & Canal Company[28] and his place as engineer was taken on a part-time basis (two days per week at two guineas per day) by George Overton.[29]

At Canal Head, wharves were allocated at the basin, just 80 feet long and 60 feet wide, to each of the main freighters – Hirwaun, Aberdare, Abernant and John Bruce Bruce. Overton made sure that his Hirwaun company's yard was enclosed by a wall. The canal head at Aberdare was the most important transshipment point on the canal until the steam coal era and the arrival of railways in the valley. At the wharves were laid out tramroad sidings, a warehouse, and a crane to deal with outgoing and incoming traffic. Operations were superintended from Canal Head House, a residence and office for the company clerk, built at a cost of £150 on rising ground overlooking the site. In preparation for the expected traffic from the Aberdare Canal, the GCC had in November allocated 190 feet of wharfage, in the Sea Lock pound in Cardiff, to each of the three iron freighters. In July 1812, Overton reported to the committee that some six weeks of mason's and other

first the ACC was sympathetic to Blakemore and the committee directed that proper articles of agreement be drawn up but, after John Bruce Bruce and John Scale had listened to the GCC's side of their dispute with Blakemore, they took a more disinterested line. Although Blakemore's complaints continued to be heard at the Annual General Assemblies, they were rejected each time and nothing more is recorded in the ACC papers after July 1814. Instead, Blakemore chose to continue his fight solely with the Glamorganshire Canal Company.[24]

In the course of the 6³/₄ miles from the canal head at

When photographed circa 1890 by Richard L. Berry, Canal Head house was a picture of rustic charm which belied its industrial surroundings.
Courtesy Aberdare Library

work remained to be completed but by that time it is believed that the Aberdare Canal was already open for traffic.[30]

By October 1813 the ACC decided to settle with Overton and did not feel it necessary to continue with a permanent engineer, rejecting Overton's offer to undertake the task at £50 per annum.[31]

Boats, Trade and a period of Idleness.

The boats used on the Aberdare Canal were identical in design to those on the Glamorganshire. They were wood built, 60 feet long, 8 feet 9 inches wide[32] and were generally loaded to 20 tons. Because the dimensions of the ACC locks were slightly wider and longer than those of the GCC, the limiting factor on Aberdare boats was the tighter measurements of the Glamorganshire locks. Boats belonged to the various freighters or to independent boatmen, who each paid tolls to the canal company on the basis of so much per commodity per ton per mile. The canal company merely provided the way and acted as toll taker. Byelaws directed that each boat should be in charge of a capable boatman and an able haulier who must at no time be absent from the horse. The progress of a horse-drawn boat was around two miles per hour, so that a journey

between Aberdare and the junction at Abercynon, allowing for time to work through the two locks, would take between three and four hours. With overnight stops, boatmen working through to Cardiff from Aberdare would generally be expected to complete two return journeys in a week. A good deal depended on the state of the water supply, the congested traffic conditions on the Glamorganshire Canal and the time it took to work through the 35 locks on the 23-mile passage between Aberdare and Cardiff.

Trade on the canal in 1812 began hopefully with the carriage of iron. Iron was shipped down the valley at a tonnage rate of $2^1/_2$d per ton-mile – half the maximum rate the Act allowed and the same rate as charged for iron on the Glamorganshire Canal. Lime and limestone were also carried and possibly some coal. David Jones, a provisions merchant in Aberdare village, had bought one canal share in 1810 and he was probably also a customer or freighter, who would have been a regular user of the canal head wharf for receiving goods sent up from Cardiff.[33]

Comparison of the movement of traffic away from the Neath Canal to the Aberdare Canal and of return traffic to and from Tappendens' rolling mills at Ynysangharad, is not possible given remaining records.[34] It is also immaterial because, although the Aberdare Canal Co ran its canal business successfully and profitably in later years, its experience in trade between 1813 and 1818 was catastrophic. As soon as the canal opened, the iron industry, on which canal traffic depended, went into deep depression and two of the three ironworks, Hirwaun and Abernant, bankrupted their proprietors, leaving the canal company with no traffic and with unpaid bills for tonnage. The Scales at Llwydcoed fared not much better and their works ceased production. The Aberdare Canal, with no income, suffered with its creditors and from 1814 fell into virtual disuse, only a couple of years since its opening. Similarly, the former Tappenden tramroad to the Neath Canal also became derelict.

Iron Revives

Better days eventually dawned for the iron trade when the economy recovered and in 1819 the powerful Crawshay interests re-emerged in the Cynon Valley, buying the lease of Hirwaun and setting about reconstructing and expanding the works.[35] William Crawshay II now set his eyes on the Aberdare Canal Co to secure Hirwaun's transport outlet, just as his grandfather had done for Cyfarthfa with the Glamorganshire Canal. He soon had a controlling interest and by 1826 had purchased 96 of the shares in the Aberdare Canal Company.[36] In 1820, his initiative in undertaking to keep the canal tolls for all goods at 50% below the Parliamentary rates for three years, earned him the agreement of the revived Aberdare Iron Co (which had purchased the bankrupt Abernant ironworks and had consolidated them into the one company) to ship by the Aberdare Canal, in preference to the Neath Canal.[37] Scale & Co (now managed by Rowland Fothergill) were unable to re-open the former Tappenden rolling mills at Ynysangharad because Benjamin Hall, the Tappendens assignee and inheritor of Crawshay's land at that place, had meanwhile leased the site to Samuel Brown for chain making. However, in later years the Aberdare Iron Company did establish similar rolling mills at Treforest, with the canal linking their two centres of production.

The canal way and works were now in good condition as the company enjoyed a cycle of boom in the iron industry. At the 1 July 1819 Annual General Assembly it was resolved to increase the canal's water supply by tapping the River Aman, a tributary on the opposite side of the Cynon to the canal. Presumably, this would have necessitated an aqueduct for the feeder to cross the Cynon; no evidence has been found that these works were undertaken.

In March 1823, in order to keep in line with the Glamorganshire Canal which was raising its banks to enable boats to carry 25 tons, the ACC resolved to pay for such work by auctioning eleven shares still standing in the company's name and then to pay any additional amount required out of revenue. For this reason no dividend was paid in 1826. In only a few

years the fortunes of the canal had changed for the better.

The amount of trade independent of the iron companies was not sufficient to support a private boat-building yard on the $6\frac{3}{4}$ mile long canal. In 1825, when the canal company itself needed a 10 ton boat, it took tenders from three boat yards on the Glamorganshire Canal – Tredwin, Rugg and Lewis Williams. Williams' tender secured the work and he charged the ACC £50, including delivery of the boat to the bottom of the canal.[38] Williams, whose yard was at Llystalybont near Cardiff, also ran a carrying service between Cardiff, Merthyr and Aberdare, and leased the warehouse at Aberdare at £18 per annum. The canal company's tonnage book for July 1827 shows him using several boatmen, including Daniel Meredith, Jonas Williams and John Osland. Also at this time, Lewis Thomas was carrying regularly to Aberdare, using boatmen William Lewis, Edward Richards and Daniel Thomas, their shipments including flour, malt and oats, earthenware, timber, hemp, bricks, pantiles and tilestones.[39] Thomas seems to have been a local builder for it was he, with his gang of temporary labour, who carried out many of the repairs to the canal banks, to Thomas Reece's plan. In 1828, also, a house was to be built for the lock keeper '*near Mr Bruce's limekiln*', the tramroad was continued to the wharf on the lower side of the warehouse, and an office was built with small bedroom above. The mason was to be David Williams and the total cost of the office was not to exceed £20.[40]

The following figures are available for traffic in this period:[41]

1828 .... 59,525 tons
1838 .... 60,898 tons

These modest figures show almost no movement over the decade and refer mostly to iron. It is worth noting that not all the iron was exported via Cardiff. By 1838, the

This photograph is believed to show the footbridge at Well Place, Ynyscynon. Apart from the later Abernant Railway bridge, this was the first bridging point on the canal. The decking would probably have been changed at least once in its long existence.

Courtesy Aberdare Library

Crawshays had established the tinplate works at Treforest, which they were supplying with iron from Hirwaun, both centres being under the management of Francis Crawshay.

Canal Management

The Aberdare Canal Company had a similar but simpler management structure to the Glamorganshire Canal's. The Company of Proprietors (the shareholders) appointed a committee of its own members at the Annual General Assembly. The day to day management of the business was entrusted to salaried employees – the Clerk and, to a lesser extent, the Treasurer. Watkin Powell was the clerk in 1812, when the house was built for him at the basin (canal head). Powell continued as Clerk throughout the moribund period (but his salary and that of the lock keeper at that time were referred to the committee) and survived the period when William Crawshay, with his trusted cashier at Cyfarthfa, George Forrest, took control of the committee. At the July 1824 assembly John Lewis was appointed to take over from the Wilkins' as Treasurer and Collector. On 11 Jan 1825, Powell was suspended '*in consequence of his incapacity to conduct the company affairs*' but the committee '*allowed him to remain as Assistant*' at one guinea per week wages until 31 March, to give him time to find another situation and while he handed over to his nineteen year old successor James Peirce, whose salary was to be £75. Although this may have been to the company's advantage, it is unusually lenient for those days and suggests that the company was either particularly grateful to Powell for his past loyal service or that Powell continued to have some hold over the company in respect of his land-holding at their quarry.

James Peirce may have been the son of Thomas Peirce, cashier at Cyfarthfa and treasurer of the GCC from 1801 to January 1823, when George Forrest took over (from 1803 to 1807 a John Peirce had been GCC Clerk at Merthyr). During James Peirce's brief period of office on the ACC, he was several times referred by the committee to seek engineering advice from the GCC's Clerk, Thomas Reece. Thus it can be seen how closely William Crawshay controlled the management of both canals. On 19 June 1827, Samuel Ball succeeded Peirce at the same salary but with a coal allowance of £9 per annum. His contract stipulated that no horse or sporting dogs were to be kept and that he must work exclusively for the company. He also had to give £500 security for his integrity. These conditions might suggest that the committee already knew of Ball's weaknesses. Peirce had left for the more lucrative position of Clerk to the Brecon & Abergavenny Canal Co, at £200 per annum plus house. When Crawshay caught Ball drunk in August 1828 it was deemed sufficiently serious to minute the fact. Ball was later discharged and Thomas Wayne was the next appointment, on 5 November 1829. He was the son of Matthew Wayne, Richard Crawshay's trusted furnace master and book-keeper. On Crawshay's death, Wayne had, with Joseph Bailey, bought Nantyglo ironworks and then moved to Aberdare to found the Gadlys

ironworks in 1827, which he joined to the Aberdare Canal by tramroad.[42] Wayne was to bring some valued authority to the post of Clerk to the Canal's Committee and he was rewarded in 1830 with a salary of £100. In August 1836 the position of Treasurer, after being with John Lewis since 1824, was re-entrusted to the Wilkins family.

At this time the committee comprised William Crawshay Junior, his sons William, Francis and Henry, John Bruce Bruce, Rowland Fothergill and Morgan Morgan. The improved canal was now in good heart and the man behind its efficiency and good performance was Thomas Wayne. By prudent management he had been able to keep expenditure on the canal and its tramroads below the £350 per annum stipulated by his committee.[43] For this reason, from 1833 he was regularly rewarded with an annual 20 guinea bonus. But Wayne was not to stay with the canal company. As we shall see, the name Wayne was to have pioneering significance in the next phase of industrial development in the Cynon Valley – the birth of the Aberdare steam coal trade.

James Petherick took over from Wayne as Clerk, receiving a 20 guineas bonus in August but by the following year he too had been replaced. There then followed another settled period throughout the 1840s under Edward Lewis, who was assisted by his son Evan.

Aberdare Steam Coal

In 1837, Thomas Wayne left the canal company and joined his father, brother and others in sinking the first export steam coal pit in the Aberdare Valley, at Abernant-y-Groes (later to become known as Cwmbach Pit of the Aberdare Coal Company). A short tramroad incline took the coal down past the Colliers Arms, to their wharf on the north (left) bank of the canal. At that point a bridge already existed which allowed them access across the canal to their own dry dock.[44] In January 1837 Bruce had successfully applied for the canal company to erect a drawbridge to take a tramroad across the canal, from the small colliery on his Dyffryn estate near the later site of Middle Duffryn, the cost being estimated at £32 11s 3d. The Waynes had been encouraged to branch out from iron making by the success of Robert and Lucy Thomas and their son William, who had pioneered the production and marketing of Welsh steam coal from the same seams lying under the Taff Valley near Merthyr. Thomas Wayne's good fortune was not lost on the already well-established Monmouthshire coal entrepreneur Thomas Powell, who was already shipping coal down the Glamorganshire Canal from his Gelligaer colliery. He wisely followed the Waynes into the Aberdare steam coal trade. In 1840 he started sinking a pit at Tyr Founder (or Old Dyffryn) and two years later he struck the famous Four Foot seam.[45] Powell was granted permission to cut the canal bank to make his boat dock in July 1841. His coal wharf was on the canal's right bank, just up-stream from the coal wharf and boat basin of Lletty Shenkin Upper and Lower collieries of 1841. These collieries were sunk by William Thomas, while his widowed

The underground explosion at Middle Duffryn colliery in May 1852 claimed 65 lives. The event was recorded by The Illustrated London News *and is the finest we have of the Aberdare Canal in operation. It shows a drawbridge and the high-level bridge used to take waste to the riverside dump, which was the precursor of the bridge to take coal to the later railway connections. In the centre background is the ventilation furnace – the cause of the explosion.*   ILW collection

mother, Lucy, continued to manage the Graig pit in the Merthyr Valley. Permission was given him for the Lletty Shenkin basin in July 1843. In 1844, David Williams of Ynyscynon sank the Ynyscynon (or High Duffryn) colliery, again sited practically on the canal's towpath.

In these few years a string of collieries had been sunk in the valley, almost all of them virtually on the banks of the Aberdare Canal. It had taken fifty years for the preamble of the Aberdare Canal Act to at last have a ring of truth. Back in 1792 the promoters had exaggerated, if not lied, to the unsuspecting investor that '. . . *the making and maintaining of a Canal . . . will open Communications with several extensive Iron Works and Collieries.*' At a Special General Assembly in January 1840 it was resolved to raise £7,380 as further capital '*to accommodate the increasing Coal trade on the Canal*', which brought the total issued capital to the £33,500 authorised by the Act. Crawshay's committee decided to accept an offer to purchase, for £5,000 from Sir Benjamin Hall, the former Tappenden tramroad and so have complete ownership of the line from the limestone quarries at Penderyn to all the ironworks in Aberdare.[46] The canal also delivered limestone for agricultural and

domestic use to several limekilns built along its length. Lias limestone, for making mortar, was brought up the canal from the Bristol Channel and the committee saw fit to minute its instructions to Edward Lewis that Lias limestone should not exceed 3s per ton and '*3s for sawing Oak and 2s per hundred for sawing Deal shd be the highest price.*'[47] Carrying coal on the canal, together with the increasing population of the district, encouraged pilfering from boats and in July 1846 the committee resolved to appoint two policemen at wages not to exceed 15s a week.

Between 1840 and 1853, sixteen steam coal pits were sunk in the Cynon Valley[48] and feeder tramroads were built to connect some of the more distant collieries with wharves on the canal. Two of the more important of these tramroads ran from David Davis's colliery at Blaengwawr[49] (1844-5) and by incline from John Nixon's Werfa colliery (1844). John Nixon had moved to the district from the north-east of England, where he had worked for the Marquess of Bute's agent and then for a period in France. Through his own initiative, Nixon opened up the market for Welsh steam coal in France and started by shipping coal as an agent for Thomas Powell. Soon he was able to organise enough

One of the collieries sunk by the Aberdare Iron Company close to Canal Head was Abernant No 9, seen here before its closure in 1910. It was actually winding when this photograph was taken – note the flat ropes. The cylindrical chimney was for ventilation; a fire was kept burning in a furnace at a side entrance to the shaft and so drew stale air out of the pit (thus forcing clean air down into the workings). SR collection.

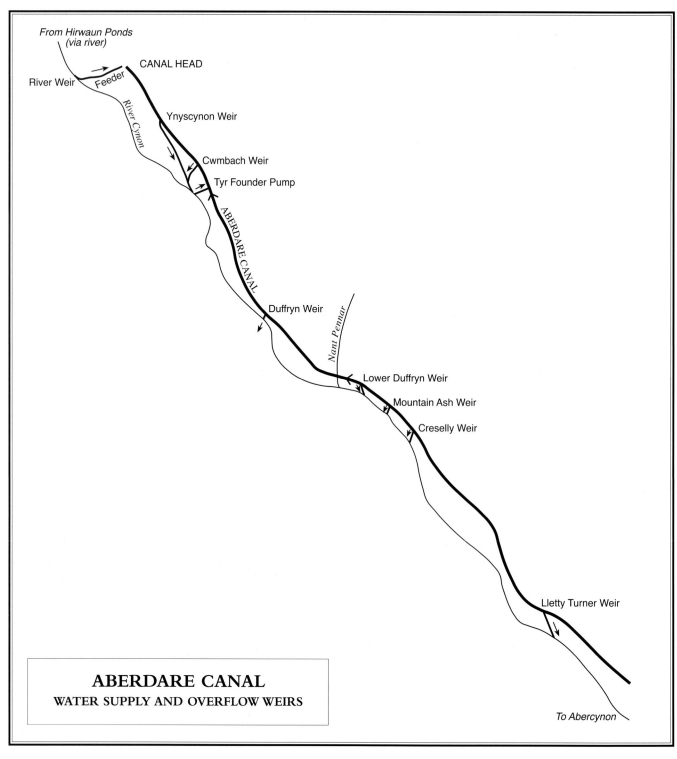

ABERDARE CANAL
WATER SUPPLY AND OVERFLOW WEIRS

capital to become a colliery owner in his own right. The Marquess of Bute had taken a lease of the Werfa property, to prevent the Aberdare Iron Company from working it in preference to the coal it was already working on Bute land at Abernant No 9 colliery. Arrangements were made with John Nixon to sink the Werfa and to then export his coal through the new Bute dock at Cardiff (the coal reaching Cardiff via the canal).[50]

At the same time that the Blaengwawr tramroad was first sanctioned, the committee gave permission to John Bruce Pryce (Bruce had changed his name in order to receive an inheritance!) to build a railway or tramroad from his property in Cwmaman. Seven years later, in July 1851, Crawshay Bailey was given permission for joining the canal at Ynyscynon from his estate at Cwmaman, at his own expense, but there is no evidence that this was for shipping coal or was even built for, as we shall see, by that time there were other means of transport out of the valley.[51] A footpath runs on a causeway across the water meadows from Thomas Powell's 1854 colliery at Abergwawr, to the canal's first bridge at Ynyscynon and there is a suggestion of a wharf below the bridge on the first edition 25 inch OS map of the 1870s, although this wharf may have been connected to the nearby High Duffryn colliery. The 1854 deposited plan for the Aberdare Valley Railway clearly identifies this as an occupation road, leased by David Williams to serve his farm at Ynyscynon from a wharf upstream from the footbridge there. Although it is tempting to speculate, we have no evidence that this footpath was ever a tramroad.

The mid 1840s proved to be a busy time for the Aberdare Canal and it was becoming clearer that the traffic provided by export steam coal would soon outstrip the tonnages for iron. As early as 1842, Thomas Powell, anxious to expedite loading coal into boats with ease of handling and reduced breakage, asked the canal company if it would agree to his carrying coal in the boats in boxes and also allow him to carry back the empty boxes free of tonnage charges. The canal company did agree to this request and in 1843 the expanding trade was further encouraged by a 25% reduction in tolls on coal, iron, iron ore, ironstone, limestone, pitwood and quarry stones.[52] In July 1846 the General Assembly re-affirmed the arrangement with Powell for free carriage of empty coal boxes. No equivalent agreements have been found between the Glamorganshire Canal Company and Powell, and there is no suggestion that he was using coal boxes on the Llanfabon tramroad from his Gelligaer colliery. Nevertheless, there is some evidence that the boxes were getting as far as the Sea Lock pound at Cardiff from both Thomas Powell's and John Nixon's collieries.[53]

Throughout this period of expansion, Edward Lewis continued to be a satisfactory Clerk and was regularly awarded a 20 guinea annual bonus. The 1842 Annual General Assembly added the proviso that Lewis must keep expenditure on the canal and tramroads below £80 per four week period. The following year his son was awarded 10 guineas for his assistance and Lewis was instructed to keep the wages of his workmen in line with those for the Glamorganshire Canal, where George Forrest had been Clerk since 1830, when he had changed jobs from Treasurer upon Reece's retirement. Forrest seems to have had a great influence in the financial management of both canals for a twenty-five year period from the early 1820s until his death in 1848.

Water Supply

Demand on water supply was now a serious issue. In July 1841 a sub-committee, consisting of Henry Crawshay and Rowland Fothergill, was formed to look into the provision of more water for the canal. The engineer Edward Powell was asked to report on the possibility and expense of pumping water from the Cynon and Aman into the canal, while they also investigated 'what can be done with Messrs Tappendens' old Pond on Hirwaun Common.' Two years later, the reservoir at Hirwaun was supplying water to the canal indirectly via the feeder from the River Cynon; Edward Powell was paid 10 guineas for his contribution and William Llewellyn was paid £5 for surveying and mapping the reservoir. The lock keeper, William Thomas, was expected to 'attend as before, not only to the Locks, but to the Bank Fences and Canal generally', whilst Rees Williams

was to be employed at 10s per week 'to do what Wm Thomas is now doing in watching the water at the Aberffrwd Canal.' The Clerk was instructed not to exceed 7 shillings in future for the hire of a man, two horses and a cart and not to exceed 4d a quart for labourers' beer 'when absolute occasion requires beer to be given.'[54]

By September 1844 the sub-committee was seeking an estimate

'for erecting an Engine to raise Water from the River Cynon for the Canal at a point below the site of Mr Powell's intended Engine on Mr Bruce's land.'

In April 1845, the canal company's solicitor was instructed to prepare a formal lease to the company from Thomas Powell, of the ground at Tyr Founder which they required for the engine and pump. The rent was to be £20 per annum and the committee resolved to approach the Glamorganshire Canal Company (who would also receive the benefit of the water) to contribute towards the total costs. In July 1846, the shareholders were informed that the GCC had agreed to paying £2,761 14s 2d, being two thirds of the total cost, in return for the GCC actually being granted ownership of the engine and pump.[55]

From July 1848, William Thomas's Lletty Shenkin colliery was allowed to use the waste water passing the Upper Lock, the colliery paying 8s 6d per calendar month.

Railways Move In

The boom in Aberdare steam coal, coupled with the traffic from the ironworks, attracted railways to the Aberdare valley and in May l846 the canal company's first railway competitor, the Aberdare Railway, entered the scene from Abercynon (Navigation House).[56] Here it branched away from the Taff Vale Railway's main line between Cardiff and Merthyr, and climbed steeply through the valley to a terminus in Aberdare. The Aberdare Railway was leased to the TVR in 1847 and before long a number of canalside collieries were linked up to the railway by branch lines, sidings and canal bridges. The bridges were not built without the canal company putting up a fight, to prevent its custom passing to the usurper. As early as July 1846, the Marquess of Bute's land agent applied for the canal to be bridged on Cwm Bach farm and the company took counsel's opinion respecting its right to withhold consent. The bridge was not built. After the landowners failed it was left to the colliery companies to fight their case in court. It was not until 1851 that John Nixon's Wyrfa Coal Company finally won the right at the Queen's Bench 'to erect a bridge across the Aberdare Canal, in order to convey the produce of their coal works to the railway for conveyance to the port of Cardiff.'[57] Once the precedent had been set the other collieries to the north of the canal, and even the Aberdare ironworks, were linked by bridges to the railway, the canal company stipulating that the tow path should not be narrowed and that the headroom be at least nine feet.[58]

In 1851, a second railway competitor arrived in Aberdare,

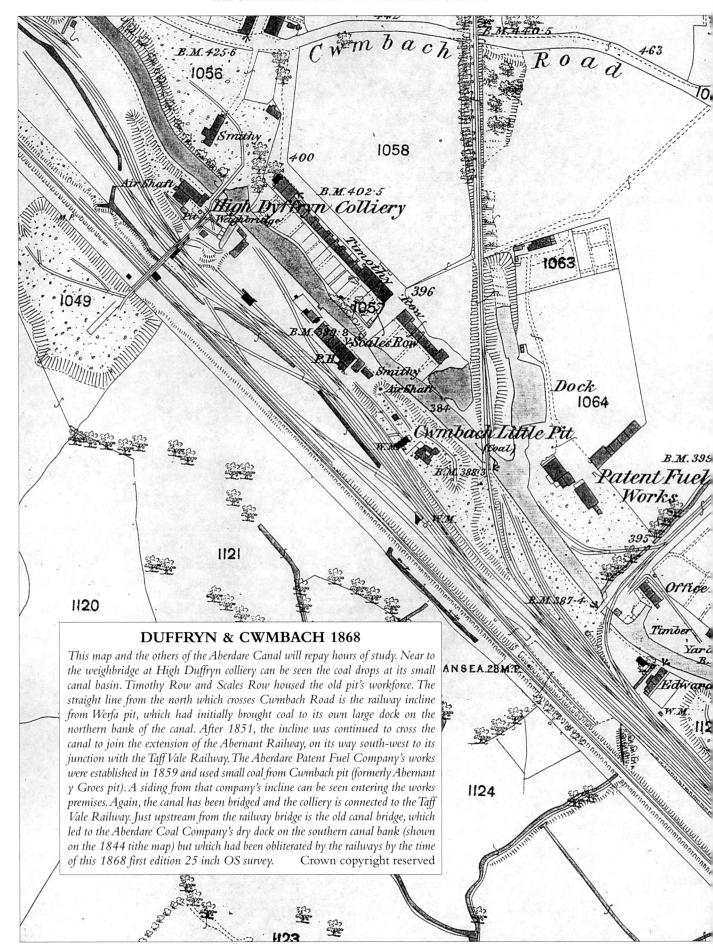

DUFFRYN & CWMBACH 1868

This map and the others of the Aberdare Canal will repay hours of study. Near to the weighbridge at High Duffryn colliery can be seen the coal drops at its small canal basin. Timothy Row and Scales Row housed the old pit's workforce. The straight line from the north which crosses Cwmbach Road is the railway incline from Werfa pit, which had initially brought coal to its own large dock on the northern bank of the canal. After 1851, the incline was continued to cross the canal to join the extension of the Abernant Railway, on its way south-west to its junction with the Taff Vale Railway. The Aberdare Patent Fuel Company's works were established in 1859 and used small coal from Cwmbach pit (formerly Abernant y Groes pit). A siding from that company's incline can be seen entering the works premises. Again, the canal has been bridged and the colliery is connected to the Taff Vale Railway. Just upstream from the railway bridge is the old canal bridge, which led to the Aberdare Coal Company's dry dock on the southern canal bank (shown on the 1844 tithe map) but which had been obliterated by the railways by the time of this 1868 first edition 25 inch OS survey. Crown copyright reserved

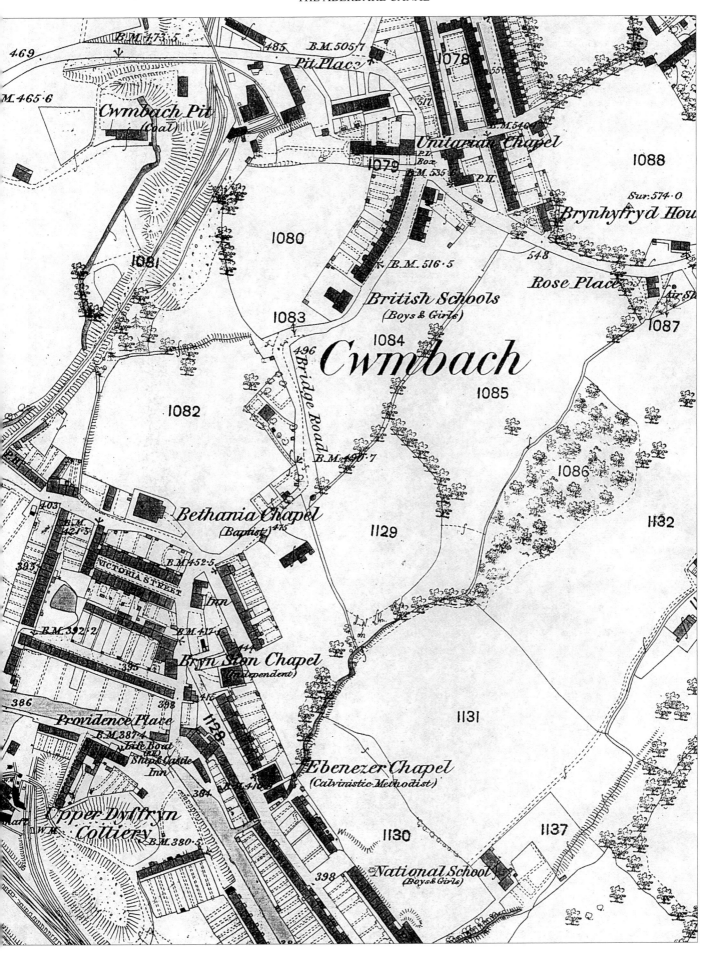

this time from the Neath direction, in the shape of the broad gauge Vale of Neath Railway, whose engineer was Isambard Kingdom Brunel. The VNR's ambition was to develop a coal traffic from the Dare and Cynon Valley pits and to carry the coal to Swansea for export but by 1852 its line still terminated in the station yard at Aberdare. For the time being the VNR could load only the coal brought up the canal to the Canal Head and tediously transferred to tram wagons for the final half mile to the VNR yard at Aberdare.[59] This process was partly simplified in 1853 when the VNR opened its broad gauge extension directly into the Canal Head yards.[60] Here, it could facilitate the transfer of Francis Crawshay's Hirwaun iron from tramroad to rail and Thomas Powell's coal boxes from boat to rail wagon. The VNR, receiving complaints *'respecting the limited accommodation for loading Mr Powell's and other Coal at the Canal Head'* gave orders for working night and day *'until the permanent accommodation is provided for the exchange of traffic between the Canal and the Railway'*.[61] Lletty Shenkin coal was passing this way for shipment at Swansea, being loaded into boats in containers for transfer to the Vale of Neath's flat wagons, which could convey them four at a time. The Canal Head siding would seem to have had less use after 1856 when the Vale of Neath line, in the name of the Aberdare Valley Railway, extended its broad gauge rails from Canal Head directly to Middle Dyffryn colliery. Thomas Powell had sunk this colliery in 1850 right alongside the canal, but on its northern bank. The coal was trammed across the canal bridge to the railway.

A Share in the Coal Boom

Competition from the Taff Vale and Vale of Neath railways was certainly intensive, yet the Aberdare Canal managed to keep its hold on sufficient coal loadings from the older collieries along its path to compensate for the dwindling traffic in iron. All this was made possible by the phenomenal export figures for the steam coal of the Aberdare Valley coalfield, which had reached one million tons by 1854 and had expanded to two million tons by 1862.[62] Tonnages on the canal rose accordingly, from 159,653 in 1848 to 216,704 in 1858.[63] It was a good time for shareholders. Their dividends rose to a maximum of £10 per £120 share for the financial years to March 1857-59.[64] Delays to traffic must have been considerable. In 1853 John Nixon had written to the Glamorganshire Canal Co complaining of delays to his boats due to congestion at the canal junction and had received the reply:

'The Committee consider that passing every other boat to the Aberdare Canal is a fair arrangement and also that they will jointly with the Aberdare Canal Co, erect a shed for the horses while delayed there.'[65]

Although the volume of coal carried on the canal was considerably smaller than that carried by the railways, the 1850s and 1860s proved to be the most prosperous years for the canal. Records of loading steam coal by canal from David Davis' Blaengwawr colliery for this period make interesting reading.[66] In March 1855, 111 boatloads of large coal, amounting to 2,314 tons 18 cwt, went by canal. The colliery was connected to the railway in March 1856 and this stimulated production.[67] As the months passed, the railway was able to take up the colliery's increased output while the quantity shipped by canal did fall. In a sample month, August 1859, 7,947 tons 17 cwt went by rail and only 885 tons 15 cwt by canal. In March 1858, 113 two-way trips were made by a total of 26 different canal boats, six of them managing eight trips and one managing nine trips in the one month. The majority went to Cardiff but there was some traffic to Brown Lenox and other loads carried by bye traders. From April 1857, the company began to rely to a large extent on Insole & Sons' boats. This coincides with the date when James Insole and David Williams sold the Deep Duffryn colliery at Mountain Ash to John Nixon and William Cory, which would have freed up Insole's boats to carry for others. Insole had invested in the concern while Williams was sinking the pit, which took from 1850 to 1855. While Insole had inherited from his father George his own bituminous colliery at Cymmer in the Rhondda, he acted as agent for other colliery companies and continued to carry steam coal on the Aberdare and Glamorganshire Canals, to be sold and exported from Cardiff.[68]

The surviving Glamorganshire Canal Company tonnage book for down traffic in August 1863 gives another glimpse into coal and residual iron traffic on the Aberdare Canal, as it joined the Glamorganshire at Lock 17.[69] Those who shipped that month were:

Aberdare Iron Co	Iron
Lletty Shenkin Coal Co	Coal
Aberdare Coal Co	Coal
David Davis	Coal
George Insole & Son	Coal
Thomas Powell & Son	Coal
Nixon Taylor & Co	Coal
Morgan Edwards & Co	Coal
Crown Preserved Coal Co	Coal
Chivers Todd & Chivers	Coal
Evan Williams	Coal
William Morgan	Coal
George Steele	Coal
Brown Lenox & Co	Coal
Gadlys Iron Co	Iron
William John	Coal

Some of these shippers seem to have been companies collecting their own coal, whilst others were bye traders.

Market boats, Builders, Pitprops and Limestone

The dash for coal was already transforming the Cynon Valley. No longer the *'secluded retreat of nature'* that Malkin had discovered, the valley was now home to an expanding immigrant population in rapidly growing urban

Lettyshenkin Colliery.

Upper Lletty Shenkin colliery of 1841, which had a direct link to the canal by a rope-worked incline, the top of which can just be glimpsed as it heads into the corrugated sheet-clad sheds in the centre. This postcard view dates from just before the First World War.

Bob Marrows collection

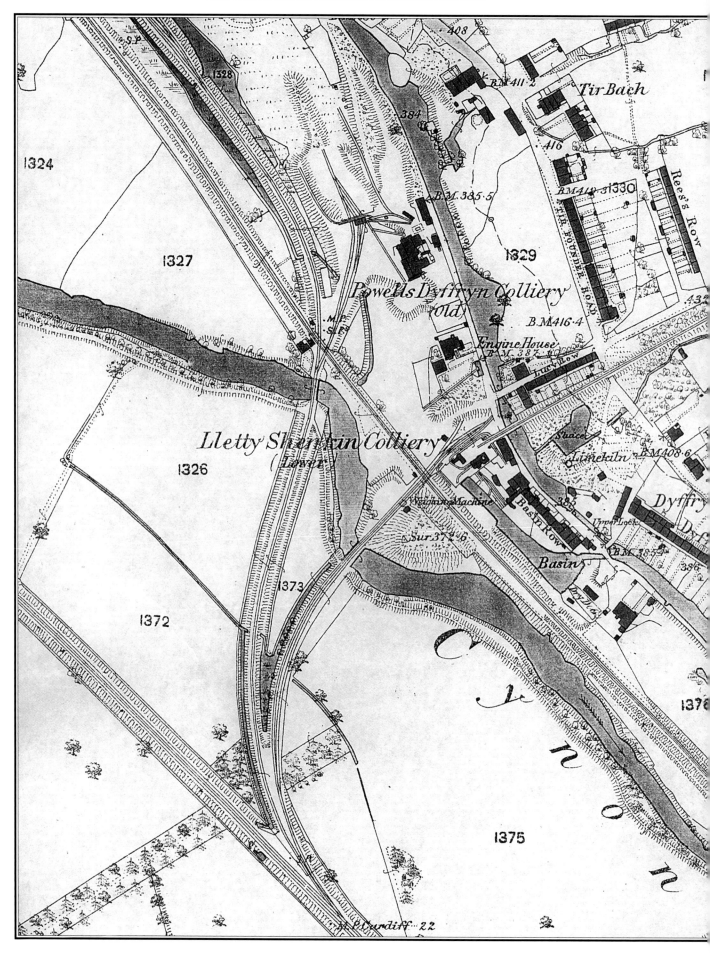

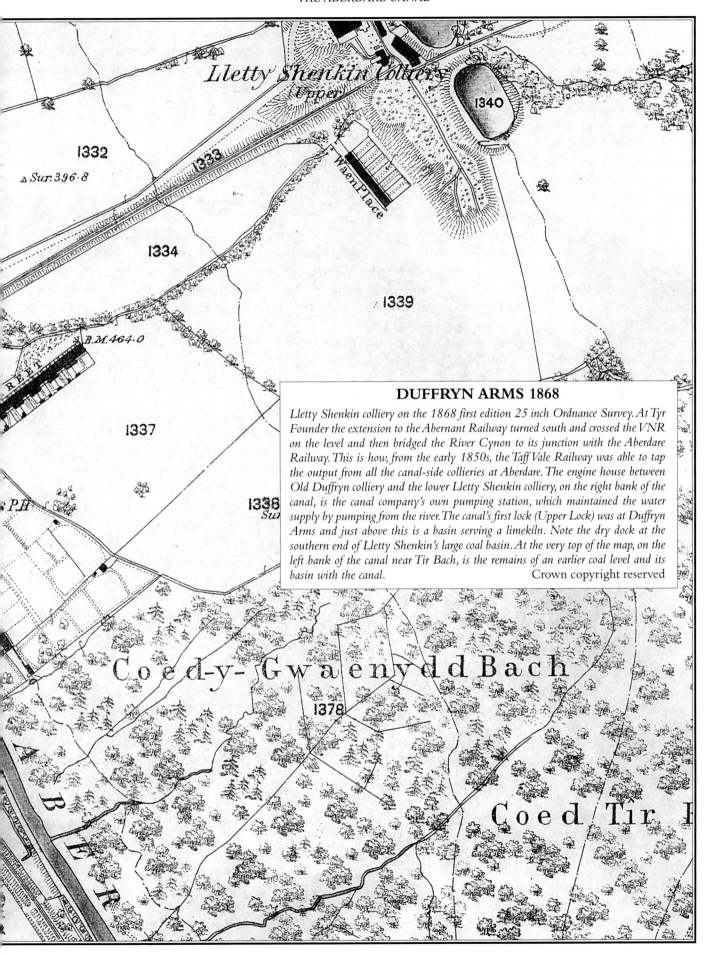

DUFFRYN ARMS 1868

Lletty Shenkin colliery on the 1868 first edition 25 inch Ordnance Survey. At Tyr Founder the extension to the Abernant Railway turned south and crossed the VNR on the level and then bridged the River Cynon to its junction with the Aberdare Railway. This is how, from the early 1850s, the Taff Vale Railway was able to tap the output from all the canal-side collieries at Aberdare. The engine house between Old Duffryn colliery and the lower Lletty Shenkin colliery, on the right bank of the canal, is the canal company's own pumping station, which maintained the water supply by pumping from the river. The canal's first lock (Upper Lock) was at Duffryn Arms and just above this is a basin serving a limekiln. Note the dry dock at the southern end of Lletty Shenkin's large coal basin. At the very top of the map, on the left bank of the canal near Tir Bach, is the remains of an earlier coal level and its basin with the canal. Crown copyright reserved

Middle Duffryn colliery. The coal wagons are on the GWR lines and beyond the fence runs the Aberdare Canal. Coal ceased to be raised here before 1885 but it retained importance for ventilation and pumping, and as the site of the Powell Duffryn coal washery, which was built in 1903 after this photograph was taken. The main road from Mountain Ash to Aberdare now runs past this site on the bed of the canal and railway but the retaining walls of the bridge can still be seen. W. Hamlin collection

settlements. The population of Aberdare, only 4,000 in 1831, had mushroomed to over 32,000 by 1861,[70] and a significant function of the railways and the canal was to bring in provisions for the shops of the new mining communities. In 1850, for instance, we find the canal carrier Evan Griffiths trading regularly between Cardiff wharf and Aberdare, and the barges of the Hirwaun Boating Co providing '*conveyance by water*' to Aberdare three times a week. These freighters loaded in the Cardiff Sea Lock pound from the coastal craft of such Bristol traders as James Pride and William Pritchard, while Williams & Co were still in business operating '*Fly Boats, daily*' to Merthyr, so probably carrying perishable goods.[71] As well as their concern with shop goods, it is possible that Bristol Channel traders like the Bridgwater Shipping Company would have brought in consignments of bricks and tiles to the Glamorganshire Canal from the River Parrett, for onward conveyance to the valley communities. Timber and slates were imported through Cardiff, much of the traffic to Aberdare and Merthyr being handled by independent owner boatmen or '*hobblers*'. These boatmen were usually able to secure a back load of small coal for the various patent fuel works established to the north of Cardiff.[72] The canal also played

its part in the urbanisation of the valley by providing transport for building stone from the Pennant sandstone quarries lying along its path.

The Aberdare Canal made itself useful to canal bank colliery proprietors in some less obvious ways. Pitwood was at that time an important up-valley freight imported through Cardiff, the timber forming support for the roofs of underground galleries and at Mountain Ash we find '*Nixon's Navigation Colliery, Pitwood Wharf*' listed as a location on the canal company's table of distances.[73] Mining activities stimulated a continuing demand for building lime and it is noticed, again at Mountain Ash, that there is a reference to a '*Nixon's Upper Limekiln*'. Nearby is '*Nixon's Lower Limekiln*', which corresponded closely to the position of Watson's timber yard, satisfying the needs of the domestic timber trade. The deposited plan for the NA&HR 1858 Act (see below) shows three Thomas Powell docks connected to the canal downstream of Duffryn Lock, the lowest one serving his timber and stone yard complete with limekilns.[74]

In this highly volatile period, with competition from the railways on all sides, it suited the Crawshays to view both the Aberdare and Glamorganshire Canals more and more as one unit. The salary of the long-serving Clerk,

Middle Duffryn colliery, viewed from the towpath of the derelict and overgrown canal around 1910. John Mear collection

Edward Lewis, was increased in 1848 to £150 plus £50 gratuities, until in 1853 Lewis's son Evan took over completely as Clerk and was allowed an assistant '*to superintend out of doors labourers*', which may have been what he himself had been doing while working with his father. But Evan Lewis did not last the year. John Forrest's first audit in February showed that he had been '*signing Vouchers for Stone and Materials received for the Company's service previously to their being paid for.*' Lewis's resignation was accepted and he was allowed to stay until 30 June. At the adjourned Annual General Assembly in August 1854, Thomas Shepherd (already Clerk to the Committee of the Glamorganshire Canal Company) was appointed Clerk, while a Mr Vaughan was appointed under Shepherd and allowed to live at the Clerk's house with the usual coal allowance. Probably it was the volume of paperwork resulting from the increased traffic which belatedly caused the committee to divide the labours of its Clerk between two men, in a similar way that the Glamorganshire Canal had for many years employed clerks at both Merthyr and Cardiff, in addition to the main position of Clerk to the Committee. So it was that Thomas Shepherd was able to manage both canals from his residence at Navigation House. The ACC paid him £50 per annum while paying Vaughan, the man on the ground, £70 per annum. At the same time Shepherd was receiving £400 per annum from the GCC. From then until at least 1867, John Forrest, the late George

Forrest's son, received from the ACC a yearly gratuity of £20, which the Annual General Assembly minutes state was '*on account of the satisfaction he has given to the Company and the high rate of provision during the last year*', although the exact nature of this service is not made clear. Forrest had at first taken over his late father's position as Clerk to the GCC but had resigned due to ill health – he seems to have found working for the ACC less arduous. Wilkins & Co remained as treasurers. Shepherd's salary was increased to £80, backdated one year, in July 1857 and to £100 in July 1863.

In the 1850s the Aberdare Canal, like the Glamorganshire Canal, found itself having to safeguard its water supply against provisions of the 1848 Public Health Act. A waterworks company was formed, which proposed to build a reservoir for the town of Aberdare at Nantmelin, in the Dare valley. In order to replenish what would otherwise be a diminished supply of water from the Cynon to the canal, the 1858 Waterworks Act stipulated the building of a second canal reservoir at Hirwaun. This compensation reservoir was built over part of the route of the derelict Tappenden tramroad which, on William Crawshay's death, Sir Benjamin Hall had transferred to the ACC in 1840. The remnants of the tramroad were of no use to the canal company and, after several offers having come to nothing in past years, this occasion prompted its final sale to Francis Crawshay, who wished to use it to bring coal from Rhigos to his Hirwaun ironworks.[75]

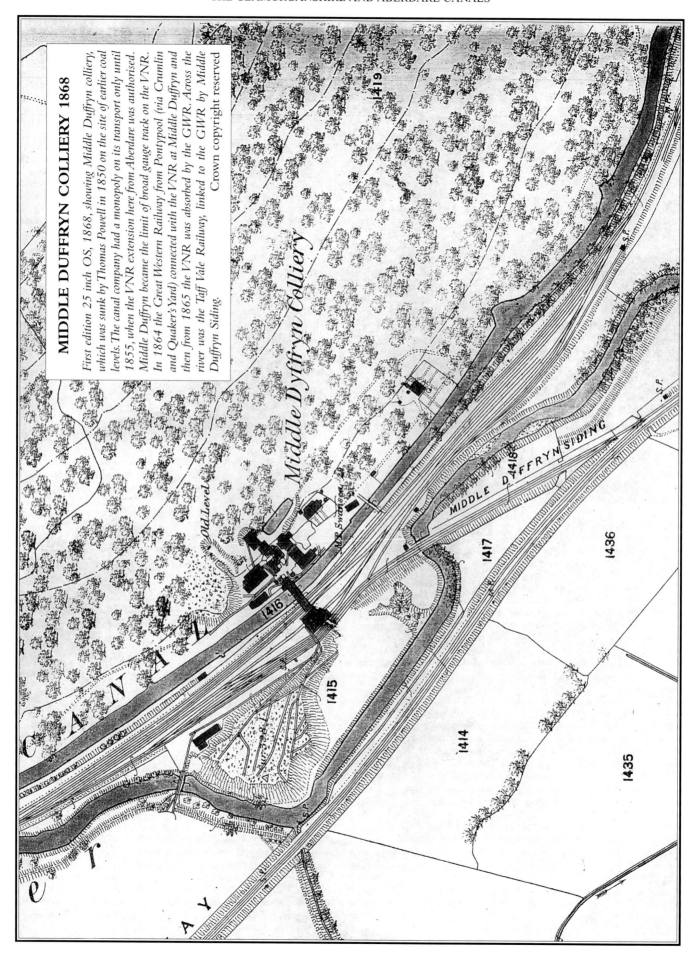

MIDDLE DUFFRYN COLLIERY 1868

First edition 25 inch OS, 1868, showing Middle Duffryn colliery, which was sunk by Thomas Powell in 1850 on the site of earlier coal levels. The canal company had a monopoly on its transport only until 1855, when the VNR extension here from Aberdare was authorised. Middle Duffryn became the limit of broad gauge track on the VNR. In 1864 the Great Western Railway from Pontypool (via Crumlin and Quaker's Yard) connected with the VNR at Middle Duffryn and then from 1865 the VNR was absorbed by the GWR. Across the river was the Taff Vale Railway, linked to the GWR by Middle Duffryn Siding.

This strangely posed group photograph, in obviously freezing conditions, shows an unidentified footbridge on the Aberdare Canal in the 1880s. It may be Cae Draw Nant bridge near Lord Aberdare's residence, Dyffryn House. The Aberdare professional photographer Richard Berry captioned this fine photograph 'Frost and Fog' in his own family album. Other photographs in the album show skaters on the frozen flooded meadows between canal and river.
Courtesy Glamorgan Record Office

In taking a broad view of the canal at this time, it will be seen that signs of decline, so long delayed by the steam coal boom, were already evident by the mid 1860s.

Years of Decline

The year 1864 was a defining one in the career of the Aberdare Canal Co, for it witnessed another railway invasion – an assault from the east by the Great Western Railway. The GWR, which had absorbed the West Midland Railway's line from Pontypool Road to Middle Duffryn (Mountain Ash), now began to syphon off its share of the coal traffic from the intensively worked collieries of the Mountain Ash district, in particular the Middle Duffryn, the Deep Duffryn, and John Nixon's Navigation colliery, all of which had been sending some coal by the Aberdare Canal. The GWR line ran closely parallel with the canal in the valley, in some places squeezing it tightly for space. Indeed, the original promoting company, the Newport, Abergavenny & Hereford Railway (NA&HR) had obtained parliamentary powers in 1858 to divert the course of the Aberdare Canal, to provide room for the railway at the site of Deep Duffryn colliery.[76] By 1872, 13 coal trains a day were being moved eastwards out of the valley and in 1885 the number of coal trains on the line was close to 40 daily.[77]
In 1858 the canal company's receipts stood at a healthy £4,352. By 1868, with tonnage down to 93,542, receipts had fallen to £2,837.[78] Then, in 1870-71, an old customer, Samuel Thomas of Ysguborwen, withdrew the last of his coal traffic from the canal in favour of the railway. Thomas, and his erstwhile partner Thomas Joseph, had opened coal levels

at Ysguborwen in 1840-1 and ran their coal down to the ACC tramroad by an incline. By 1852, the collieries were connected to the VNR and, in 1854, Thomas and Joseph extended their railway across the River Cynon to the Aberdare Railway, crossing the canal company's tramroad on the level. For this privilege the ACC were able to charge five shillings wayleave each year. Their response to his leaving the canal completely was to attempt to change the wayleave to a penny per ton. Naturally this ended in court and, as for previous cases where the Glamorganshire Canal had an obvious interest, the larger canal company was requested to pay half the legal fees.[79] The strike and stoppage at the Aberdare ironworks in 1875 then produced a desperate situation for the canal company. Shepherd wrote to Fothergill asking his company to formally give up its tramroad connection to the canal since '*trade on the Canal is so bad that the Company may be compelled to shut it up or sell it and such case the Company would like to have all their property in hand*.'[80] From the end of the mid sixties the canal was in serious trouble from a new and growing problem – mining subsidence – and the company's efforts to get compensation from the larger coal owners were unsuccessful.[81] Burnyeat & Co (since 1872 the owners of Lletty Shenkin colliery) paid a paltry £23 7s 5d in September 1878 but the main culprits were Powell Duffryn & Co, the company that had been formed on the death of Thomas Powell.

The Marquess of Bute

In 1885 the Marquess of Bute gained control of the Aberdare and the Glamorganshire Canals by acquiring the shares of both waterways from the Crawshay family.

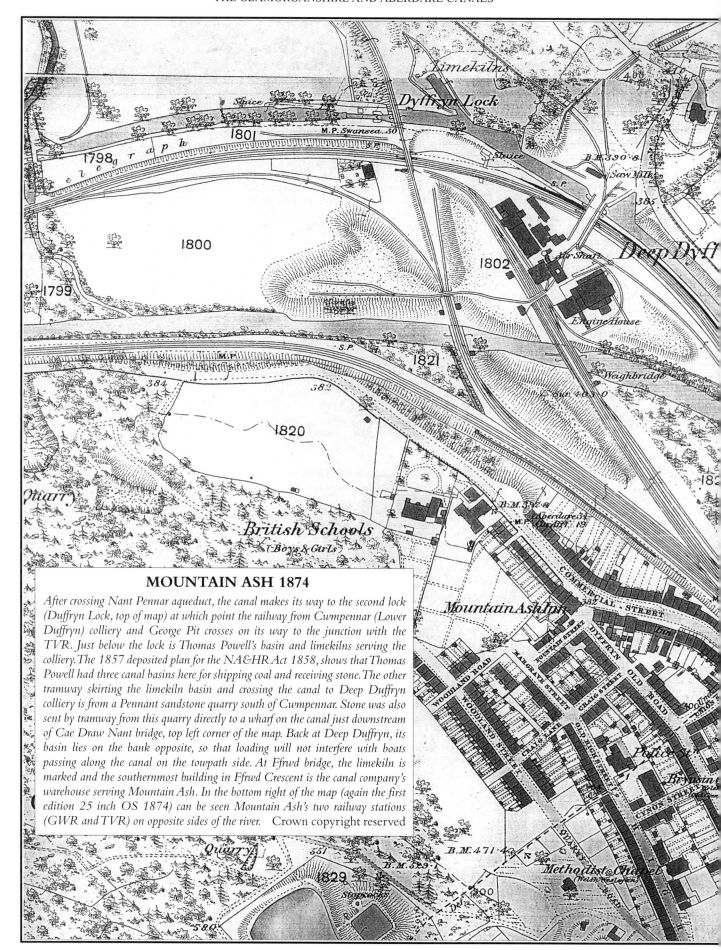

MOUNTAIN ASH 1874

After crossing Nant Pennar aqueduct, the canal makes its way to the second lock (Duffryn Lock, top of map) at which point the railway from Cwmpennar (Lower Duffryn) colliery and George Pit crosses on its way to the junction with the TVR. Just below the lock is Thomas Powell's basin and limekilns serving the colliery. The 1857 deposited plan for the NA&HR Act 1858, shows that Thomas Powell had three canal basins here for shipping coal and receiving stone. The other tramway skirting the limekiln basin and crossing the canal to Deep Duffryn colliery is from a Pennant sandstone quarry south of Cwmpennar. Stone was also sent by tramway from this quarry directly to a wharf on the canal just downstream of Cae Draw Nant bridge, top left corner of the map. Back at Deep Duffryn, its basin lies on the bank opposite, so that loading will not interfere with boats passing along the canal on the towpath side. At Ffrwd bridge, the limekiln is marked and the southernmost building in Ffrwd Crescent is the canal company's warehouse serving Mountain Ash. In the bottom right of the map (again the first edition 25 inch OS 1874) can be seen Mountain Ash's two railway stations (GWR and TVR) on opposite sides of the river.   Crown copyright reserved

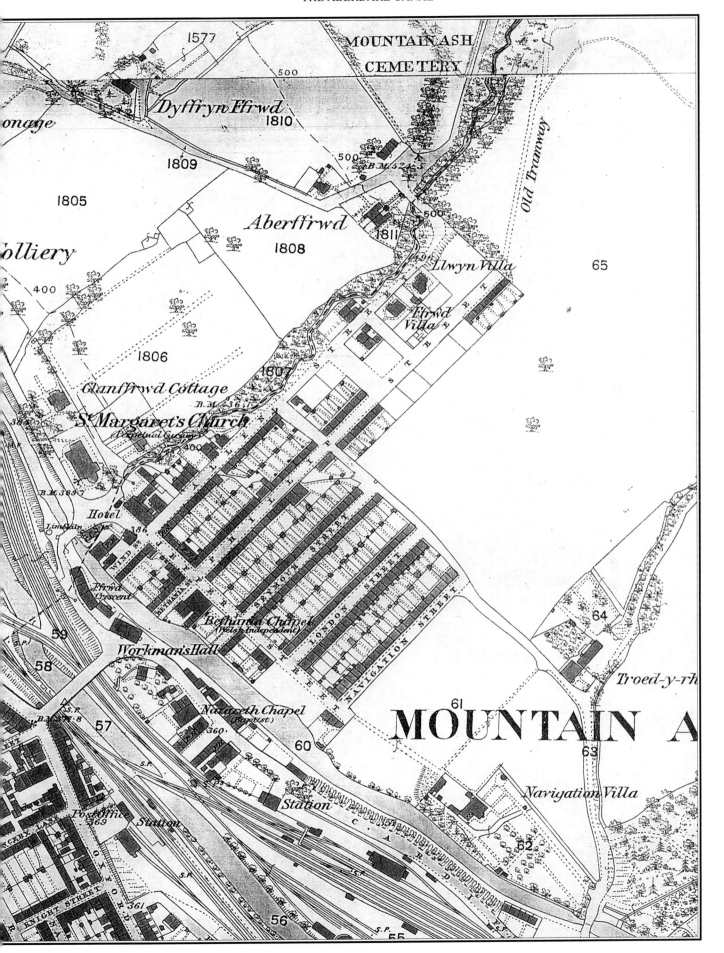

Deep Duffryn colliery taken from St Margaret's church before closure of the canal, probably circa 1890. The GWR found a narrow way between canal and colliery, the canal being protected by a high masonry revetment wall. To the right, before the bridge, was the colliery's canal basin. Beyond the bridge to the right are the saw mills.

John Mear collection

The main road from the river bridge to St Margaret's church passed over the canal on Ffrwd bridge, seen here to the left of Ffrwd Crescent in the early 1900s. The limekiln and stone yard were on the left.   SR collection

Bute himself became chairman and the two canal companies were run by the same managing committee of Bute employees. Thomas Shepherd, an old Cyfarthfa man, was forced to resign and Charles Evans, a Cardiff solicitor, became Clerk. The Brecon bankers of Wilkins & Co, as Treasurers, were the only survivors.

Bute's motive was possibly to secure the water supply to feed his Bute docks, although later he presented an unsuccessful Bill in Parliament to convert both the canals into railways. Lord Bute merged the operation of the Aberdare and Glamorganshire canals into one and in 1887 the GCC began regular carrying of merchandise between Cardiff, Pontypridd and Merthyr, and on the Aberdare Canal between Cardiff, Mountain Ash and Aberdare.[82] Boats were reconditioned, new ones were built, warehouses were established and improvements made to the canal. Although the Aberdare and the Glamorganshire canals were now worked as one, they were still separate companies in the legal sense and this gave rise to an interesting position for the Glamorganshire Canal Co. On its own canal it acted as toll taker but on the Aberdare Canal it became a toll payer.[83]

The Bute management's effort to revive the Aberdare Canal proved ultimately to be unsuccessful. As we have seen, the competition from the railways in the Aberdare Valley was now overwhelming and the canal company had to bow to the more direct and efficient port handling facilities offered by the railways. In 1888, the tonnage on the canal was 102,805, a figure that seemed buoyant enough, but because the company's rates for all classes of goods had been cut several times below the parliamentary rates to encourage the traffic, the receipts for 1888 were only £750, – not enough to cover the running expenses of the canal.[84]

Ironically, however, for a canal that had prospered on coal, it was ruinous damage from mining subsidence that would bring an end to canal traffic, which by 1897 had dwindled to only 7,855 tons.[85] With sinking towpaths and subsiding bridges, the working of the boats was becoming intolerable for boatmen and horses. A report of 1891[86] highlighted the situation:

'. . . *the company's Storehouse at Canal Head is sub-siding rapidly towards the south west.*

. . . [at Yniscynon Bridge] *the horseway is under water for about 40 yards on the upper side of the bridge. Bank requires to be raised and walled for 60 yards.*

. . . [at Cwmbach Pit] *towing path continually subsiding from the bridge at Scales Arms for a considerable distance down and has to be constantly raised and repaired.*

. . . [next to the Aberdare Coal Co incline bridge] *the horseways under these bridges are two feet or more under water owing to subsidence. The bank will have to be raised and a wall put in to face it.*

. . . [second bridge below Mountain Ash] *this bridge is too low for traffic and should be pulled down and a girder bridge substituted for it.*

. . . [opposite the lime kilns] *the bank has subsided and must be raised for a distance of 50 yards.*

. . . [Nixon's boat dock, Newtown] *canal subsided for 30 yards on upper side of the bridge and must be raised and repaired.*

For a considerable distance below Mountain Ash where the turnpike road runs parallel to and close under the canal bank, there is constant leakage and the embankment is in a bad state. The towing path has recently been raised 18 inches on account of the subsidence.

The only photograph we have of a boat on the Aberdare Canal, taken just downstream of Ffrwd bridge, Mountain Ash. It may well be a Whitsun treat for the congregation of St Margaret's church or Bethania chapel. The terraces in the background are Wind Street and Bethania Street (the lower ends of Allen Street and Phillip Street respectively). The canal was officially closed in 1900 and it is unlikely that boat outings were allowed after that time. The photograph was taken by G. Davies.

Courtesy The Boat Museum, Ellesmere Port, photo ref R0525

This aerial view of Mountain Ash was taken in about 1930, after much of the closed canal had been converted to road and Ffrwd bridge had been demolished. Nevertheless, the line of the canal can be made out clearly as it sweeps in from the top left, past St Margaret's church to the site of Ffrwd bridge. Both Mountain Ash railway stations are also shown in this picture, the GWR to the NE between canal and river, and the TVR on the SW bank of the river.
Bob Marrows collection

… [opposite Pontcynon] the embankment is leaking slightly.'

Between 1891 and 1897, the annual engineering bill for stopping leaks and raising towpaths on the canal rose from £28 to £46 a mile,[87] as boat crews and horses continued to wade through flooded towpaths and under the sinking arches of such bridges as 'Breeches and Leggins bridge' at Mountain Ash. In 1900, the canal had become unworkable and the decision was taken to close it in the November of that year for reasons of public safety. An interesting entry, dated 11 November 1915, in the company's minute book records an offer by telephone made by the Powell Duffryn Company to buy Canal House.

The limestone traffic meant that the canal company's tramroad between Penderyn, Hirwaun and Aberdare remained in use after the abandonment of the canal. In January 1904, the Penderyn-Hirwaun portion was converted to a standard gauge railway to link the quarries with the GWR at Hirwaun, any onward traffic to Aberdare then having to be transferred to the continuing tramroad.[88] This transshipment could not have been satisfactory and the tramplates on the section from Hirwaun to Aberdare are said to have been taken up in 1916. This information came from an Ian Wright interview on 30 Dec 1949 with Ivor Llewelyn, Traffic Manager of the Glamorganshire Canal Company from 1912 to 1944. He had succeeded his father Lewis Llewelyn, whose own father had worked on the Penderyn tramroad. It seems likely that the family are the descendants of Thomas John Llewelyn, who opened up Penderyn quarry in 1793.

While the quarry railway prospered, the disused canal quietly mouldered in decay, until it was bought by the Urban District Councils of Aberdare and Mountain Ash in 1923. The Aberdare Canal Act of 1924 confirmed the sale, which was soon followed by the conversion of the canal into a relief road up the valley designated the A4059 and B4275. For this reason, the visitor to the Cynon Valley will find very few traces of the canal, except an excavated portion in water from the site of Ynyscynon bridge to Canal Head, where Canal Head house survives as a habitation. But, with an eye of faith, the pedestrian can look along the road today and see it as a ribbon of water.

The Penderyn railway was sold to the quarry owners in 1944. The old Aberdare Canal Company finally went into voluntary liquidation in 1955.

Some Aberdare Canal Boatmen – a postscript by ILW

Since the closure of the Aberdare Canal happened a century ago, communication with living boatmen, even the oldest of the retired men, has long been impossible. It was my good fortune in 1943, whilst at school in Cardiff, to make contact with the last of the canal workers and boatmen at Gabalfa and Llandaff on the Glamorganshire

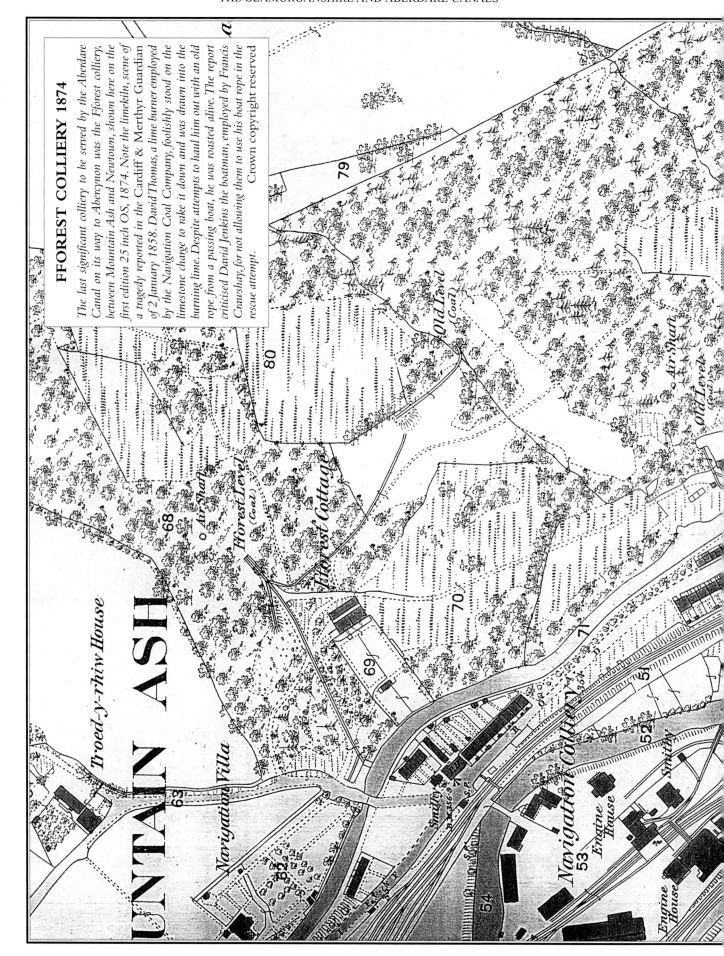

FFOREST COLLIERY 1874

The last significant colliery to be served by the Aberdare Canal on its way to Abercynon was the Fforest colliery, between Mountain Ash and Newtown, shown here on the first edition 25 inch OS, 1874. Note the limekiln, scene of a tragedy reported in the Cardiff & Merthyr Guardian of 2 January 1858. David Thomas, a lime burner employed by the Navigation Coal Company, foolishly stood on the limestone charge to rake it down and was drawn into the burning lime. Despite attempts to haul him out with an old rope from a passing boat, he was roasted alive. The report criticised David Jenkins the boatman, employed by Francis Crawshay, for not allowing them to use his boat rope in the rescue attempt.

Crown copyright reserved

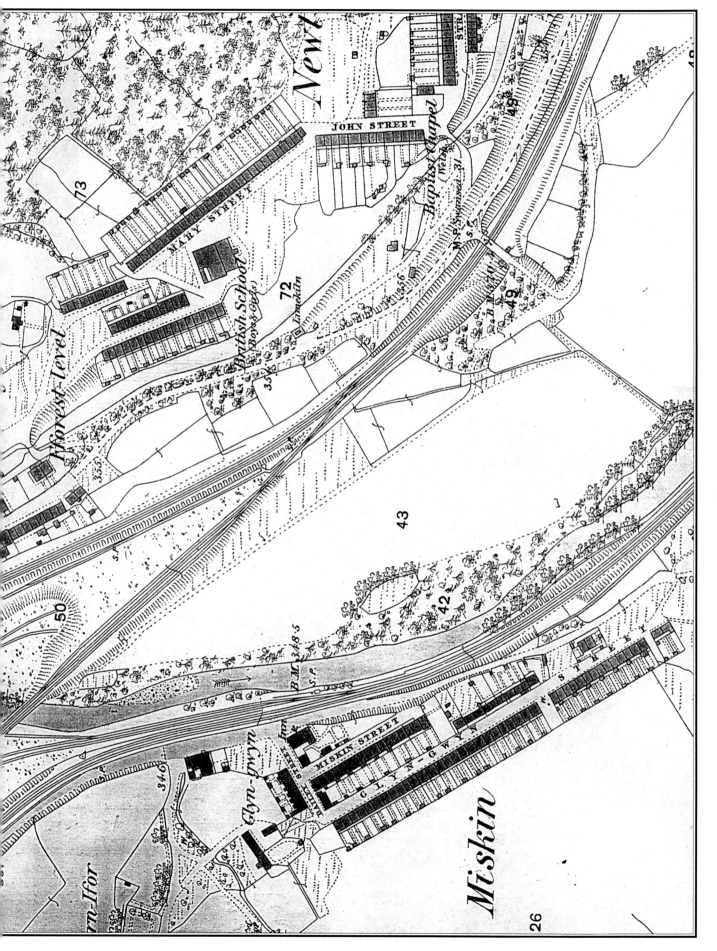

Three views of Troedyrhiw Forest or Creselly Arms bridge, with the photograph, **left**, taken in September 1898, showing the the canal still in water. The picture, **top right**, shows the upstream side of the bridge. There were so many engineers and contractors involved in the building of the Aberdare Canal that it is difficult to decide who was responsible for the bridge designs. Was it Sheasby, Overton or Hopkin? There seem to have been two general types. The road bridges are quite substantial stone arches – of a heavier design than those on the Glamorganshire – whilst the foot bridges consisted of vertical stone abutments and a flat deck. At Creselly Arms bridge, a truffin led from the canal to the river and would have been used to drain the section of canal when maintenance was required. In the view, **above right**, the parapets are shrouded by an overhanging tree (much grown since the earlier picture) but the towpath and rubbing stones on the approach to the bridge are clearly visible. The two photographs right are circa 1925.   Left: SR collection. Right: Both collection of the late G. Davies, courtesy A. & R. Williams

Interaction between road, rail and people at Creselly Crossing, Mountain Ash on the former GWR Vale of Neath line in 1962. Pannier tank 3753 is propelling coal wagons in the direction of Aberdare and the gates are closed to protect the road through Nixon's Navigation colliery which lies behind the photographer. "Crossing No Gates" is not a contradiction. The road sign refers to the unprotected National Coal Board line running in front of the gates. This private railway, built by John Nixon and later operated by Powell Duffryn, ran from Pontcynon to Deep Duffryn colliery, a distance of 3 miles. The photograph is taken from the river bridge. The site of Creselly bridge on the Aberdare Canal was close to the pub and terrace of houses seen behind the locomotive.
Alan Jarvis photo 1427, 31 May 1962

Canal. Talking with the boatmen was resumed after the war and was later extended to the canal community at Rhydyfelin, near Pontypridd. Most of the retired boatmen I talked to had homes on the bank of the Glamorganshire Canal and had been regular traders to Aberdare. Ivor Llewelyn, the Glamorganshire company's last manager, with whom I had an interview in 1949, his father Lewis, also manager before him, and Lewis's father, too, all appeared to have owned canal boats and were bound up in one way or another with the running of the Penderyn-Hirwaun tramroad.

In 1948, Henry 'Harry' Watts recalled his time on the boats. Harry was born in 1879 and was already working as a steerer for a Mynachdy boatman at the age of 10. He recalled:

> "I've taken Irish hay to Merthyr and barrels of oil to Aberdare. I boated for the company [GCC] for a time and we got a bonus for taking an 'express' load from Cardiff to Aberdare or Merthyr. The rate was 5s for the boatman and 2s 6d for the boy."

As a hobbler Harry had worked boat No. 50 *Wide Awake,* and another boat, No. 82. Harry's father had also owned and worked his own craft, trading between Aberdare, Merthyr and Cardiff with boats named *Perseverance, Providence* and *Fiery Dragon.* Amongst Harry's memories of the Aberdare Canal was *"water running uphill."* This happened as a boat coming down from Aberdare was nearing the junction with the Glamorganshire and coinciding with a boat crew emptying Lock 17 on their way down from Merthyr. The discharged water, bouncing off the top gate of Lock y Waun, had nowhere to go except to push its way up the Aberdare Canal.

It is 50 years since my conversation with Thomas Jones, a retired boatman of Llandaff North, whose memories have resulted in a remarkably long journey into the past. In 1874, at the age of 11, Tom started as a boat boy on boats working up from Cardiff to Merthyr and Aberdare. He recalled:

> "I was hauled in for school soon after, but I was back on the boats when I was 13, helping on Powell Duffryn boats with coal from Middle Dyffryn pit."

Thomas Jones became an independent owner boatman when he was 16, working imported pitwood up from Cardiff for the

Top: *The Colliers Arms (or Cat) bridge when the roadworks were just beginning which were to obliterate the Aberdare Canal. The headframe of Navigation colliery can be seen in the distance.* **Centre:** *Strand bridge, Newtown, spanning the dried up and filled in canal bed.* **Bottom:** *The road aspect of Strand bridge on the same day. All three views are circa 1925.*

All collection of the late G. Davies, courtesy A. & R. Williams

Cwmcynon colliery, pictured around 1905 and situated a quarter of a mile up the valley from Penrhiwceiber High Level station, lay between the River Cynon, seen here, and the canal, which was up on the bank on the right. The colliery opened around 1890 and was served by both Nixon's private railway and the GWR (ex-VNR). It was another of John Nixon's pits but, due to its proximity to the GWR (ex-Vale of Neath) line which ran alongside on its way up the valley to Aberdare and beyond, its output was despatched to the docks at Cardiff by rail. The level of the canal is just discernable in the background, in line with the roof of the building on the right.

Neil Parkhouse collection

Taken not that long after the canal's closure, this photograph shows both railway stations at Penrhiwceiber. The closer High Level station is the GWR's (Cwmcynon colliery was off to the right), whilst the one in the valley, across the river, is that of the TVR. At this spot on the canal (shown clinging to its hillside ledge lower right) there was a stone wharf and tramway leading from a quarry.   SR collection

A remarkable image from when the Aberdare Canal was still in operation and indicating how rural was much of the route it followed. The view is from its last bridge (Quarry bridge) as the Aberdare Canal approached its junction with the Glamorganshire Canal. The River Cynon below, in its turn, is winding its way to its confluence with the Taff, whose valley can be seen in the distance. The image is so remarkable because it shows how little development had taken place at the future Abercynon before the sinking of the Dowlais Cardiff colliery in the 1890s. By contrast, the settlement at the basin at Navigation can just be made out.   Courtesy Aberdare Library

The junction of the Aberdare Canal with the Glamorganshire Canal in 1948. The Aberdare Canal sweeps in from the left and the ruined locks are numbers 17 and 16 of the Glamorganshire Canal. The house was built on an island, for the bypass weir from above the locks passed it on the left into the Aberdare Canal. ILW photo neg 489

Nixon's Navigation colliery at Mountain Ash.

> *"I would bring coal down to Cardiff which I had loaded at the Blaengwawr Basin at Aberdare. Most of it went to the patent fuel works at Maindy and Blackweir but the coal boats stopped when the fuel works got linked up to the railway. One of my boats was the* Lady Margaret. *I bought another, a Nixon's boat, from the railway contractors Meakin & Dean after they had finished building the GW & Rhymney Joint line. I went to Aberfan to buy it. The management wanted £30 for it but I bargained with them they agreed to let the boat go for £13. That would have been about 1885 or 1886."*

Tom Jones remembered the Aberdare-Hirwaun tramroad working during his trips to load coal at Davis Blaengwawr on the 'Upper pond.' He went on:

> *"the present Llewelyn's [Ivor's] grandfather worked stuff over the Hirwaun Railway [the Aberdare-Hirwaun tramroad]. I remember the horse working and I have taken timber from Watson's Timber yard to the tramroad."*

Ben Gould of Treforest was another boatman who was engaged in the up-valley timber trade to the Aberdare

Canal. Bill Gomer of Rhydyfelin recalled him taking cog wood to Mountain Ash for the timber merchant Edward Ashton and coming up from Cardiff with pitwood for Nixon's Navigation colliery. Ben Gould's boat at that time was No. 392 Comet, a boat Ben later sold to an owner on the Monmouthshire Canal at Risca. Bill Gomer had spent his early life working as an independent or 'hobbler' and for some years he was the holder of a contract to work the GCC goods boats between Cardiff, Merthyr and Aberdare. He was well aware of the hardships of the last years of boating to Aberdare, when the effects of subsidence could prove dramatic:

> *"The going was bad* [to Aberdare] *as soon as you left the junction. It was hard going and very shallow. Just above the lock at Dyffryn the canal was very deep. To get under the bridge arches the company had to cut down the boat stove pipes level with the cabin roofs when boats were empty and the water was high in the ponds."*

Bill remembered seeing the old Aberdare Canal Company's 10 ton maintenance boat when boating to Aberdare. The initials ACC were carved into the top planks near the bow. The foreman in charge of the Aberdare Canal during its last years was Noah Fletcher.

NOTES TO CHAPTER 6

1 Benjamin Malkin *The Scenery, Antiquities and Biography of South Wales*, London 1807.

2 There are two important published works dealing with the Aberdare Canal to which the reader is referred: Charles Hadfield *The Canals of South Wales and the Border*, Cardiff 1960 p 66-70 and 118-126; and Alun C. Davies *A Welsh Waterway in the Industrial Revolution. The Aberdare Canal 1793-1900*, in *The Journal of Transport History New Series IV Vol 3*, Leicester 1978 p 147-169. The latter is a particularly scholarly analysis, drawing from the minute books and share transfer books of the ACC, which the present authors see no need to attempt to duplicate here.

3 Aberdare Canal Act 1793. 33 Geo III cap xcv.

4 See Davies *Aberdare Canal* for a more detailed analysis of the canal's promoters and shareholders.

5 WIMM 80.71/2 *Plan of a Canal and Railroad for forming a Junction between the Glamorganshire and Neath Canals in the County of Glamorgan by John Dadford 1792*; ACC minute book first Tues May 1793.

6 John Lloyd *The Early History of the Old South Wales Iron Works, 1760-1840*, London 1906.

7 ACC minute book 20 June 1793. GRO D/D B Ca 1-4. The GRO holds the original two volumes of the Aberdare Canal minute books plus the two-volume certified copy which was made when the Marques of Bute acquired the canal with the Glamorganshire Canal in the 1880s.

8 See Gordon Rattenbury *Tramroads of the Brecknock and Abergavenny Canal*, Oakham 1980.

9 ACC minute book 20 June 1793; John F. Mear *Aberdare. The Railways and Tramroads*, Aberdare 1999 p 18. This fine book unravels the history and archaeology of the tramroads associated with the Aberdare Canal. Again, the reader is referred to this book for more detail than the present authors intend to repeat here.

10 ACC minute book 8 May 1795.

11 ACC minute book 10 July 1801. Benjamin Outram was one of the earliest proponents of the plateway (in the latter half of the 18th century) to the extent that many thought, erroneously, that the term 'tramroad' was derived from his name. For Outram see R.B. Schofield *Benjamin Outram - 1764-1805*, Cardiff 2000.

12 For the Tappendens' disastrous financial ventures in South Wales see Peter Tann *The Tappendens and the Abernant Iron Company, 1801-15*, in *Morgannwg Vol XL*, Cardiff 1996 p 40-63; *The Tappenden Tramroad to the Neath Canal, 1800-14*, in *Journal of the Railway and Canal Historical Society Vol 32 Pt 2 No 164*, July 1996, p 88-102.

13 ACC minute book 31 Aug 1801, 29 July 1803, 1 Mar, July 1806, 13 June 1807; John F. Mear *Aberdare Railways* which uses the NCC minute books and Maybery papers.

14 For the history of ironworks at Hirwaun and Aberdare see Lloyd *Old South Wales Iron Works*; Lawrence Ince *The South Wales Iron Industry 1750-1885*, Merton 1993; Raymond Grant *Cynon Valley in the Age of Iron*, Aberdare 1991.

15 ACC minute book 29 July 1803.

16 Hadfield *Canals of South Wales*, p119-120, citing D.E. Fraser *The Development of the Road System in Glamorgan up to 1844*, University of Wales thesis 1944 and Enid Walker *The Development of Communications in Glamorgan . . . between 1760 and 1840*, University of Wales thesis 1940.

17 See table of Neath Canal Company income from the three ironworks in Davies *Aberdare Canal*, Appendix A.

18 Mear *Aberdare Railways*, p58.

19 GRO D/D B Ca 66 and 67.

20 ACC minute book 18 Aug and 19 Sept 1809.

21 ACC minute book 19 Sept, 25 Nov 1809, 9 Jan, 17 Jan, 15 Feb 1 July and 21 Dec 1810.

22 ACC minute book 20 July 1813.

23 GCC minute book 18 Jan 1810.

24 ACC minute book 19 Sept 1809, 9 Jan, 17 Mar 1810, 1 July 1811 and 1 July 1814. The canal fell into disuse in 1814 and, when revived, it became managed by the same family Blakemore was fighting on the GCC – the Crawshays. For this dispute, see Volume 2.

25 Board of Trade Returns 31 Dec 1888 *Aberdare Canal*.

26 NLW.

27 Board of Trade Returns 31 Dec 1888 *Aberdare Canal*.

28 Hadfield *Canals of South Wales*, p122 and 213; Harry W. Paar *The Severn and Wye Railway*, Dawlish 1963 p27 .

29 ACC minute book 20 Aug 1811.

30 ACC minute book 22 May and 24 July 1812, GCC minute book 23 Nov 1811.

31 ACC minute book 29 Oct 1813.

32 The Board of Trade Returns of 31 Dec 1888 for the Aberdare Canal record the maximum size of boats as 66ft 0ins long and 9ft 0ins wide. A copy in ILW's possession has 66ft deleted in red ink and 60ft 0ins substituted. The Glamorganshire Canal locks would not accommodate a boat longer than about 62ft.

33 Davies *Aberdare Canal*, p155.

34 See Davies *Aberdare Canal*, for his worthy attempt.

35 Ince *South Wales Iron Industry*, p34.

36 Davies *Aberdare Canal*, p156-7.

37 ACC minute book 26 Mar 1819 and 27 Oct 1820.

38 ACC minute book 29 Mar, 21 June and 28 June 1825.

39 Information kindly supplied by Keith Jones. Unfortunately the authors have not been able to locate this Aberdare Canal Tonnage Book which was formerly in the possession of the late Mr Howells of Newport.

40 ACC minute book 3 April, 28 Aug and 1 Sept 1828.

41 Hadfield *Canals of South Wales*, p123.

42 Charles Wilkins *The South Wales Coal Trade and its Allied Industries, from the Earliest to the Present Time*, Cardiff 1888 p80-4; Lloyd *Old South Wales Iron Works*, p127. Additional information on Peirce from Ray Haydon via John Norris.

43 ACC minute book 9 Aug 1832.

44 NLW unpublished 1814 OS Map and Aberdare Tithe Map 1844.

45 Wilkins *Coal*, p90-4; J.H. Morris & L.J. Williams *The South Wales Coal Industry 1841-1875*, p106.

46 ACC minute book 18 July 1839, Jan 29 1840, 18 Sept 1841; GRO D/D B Ca 66 and 67. See also Mear *Aberdare Tramroads*, p60-3.

47 ACC minute book 25 July 1843.

48 D.S. Barrie *The Taff Vale Railway*, 2nd edition, South Godstone 1950, p14.

49 ACC minute book 25 July 1844, 17 April and 8 May 1845.

50 James Edward Vincent John Nixon *Pioneer of the Steam Coal Trade in South Wales – a Memoir*, London 1900, p120-65.

51 Tom Evans included this conjectured tramroad in his map for Alun Davies' article *Aberdare Canal*.

52 ACC minute book 28 July 1842, 25 July 1843. Contrary to the assertion in Davies *Aberdare Canal*, p159, the minute books do explicitly grant Powell's request.

53 Samuel W. Allen *Reminiscences*, Cardiff 1918 p172.

54 ACC minute book 25 July 1843

55 ACC minute book 25 July 1843, 11 Sept 1844, 17 April 1845, 30 July 1846.

56 Eric R. Mountford & R.W. Kidner *The Aberdare Railway*, Headington, nd (c1995).

57 *Cardiff & Merthyr Guardian* 8 Feb 1851. Mountford & Kidner *The Aberdare Railway*, p26-8.

58 ACC minute book 1 Dec 1852.

59 Vale of Neath Rly Directors' minute book 11 Nov 1851.

60 ACC minute book 21 July 1853. E.T. McDermot *History of the Great Western Railway*, 1931, Vol 2 p11.

61 VNR Directors' minute book 9 Jan 1854.

62 Morris & Williams *South Wales Coal Industry*, p108.

63 Hadfield *Canals of South Wales*, p125.

64 Hadfield *Canals of South Wales*, p125.

65 GCC minute book 7 June 1853.

66 GRO D/D NCB 16/32 Blaengwawr Steam Coal by Canal, Nov 1851-Sept 1859.

67 Mear *Aberdare Railways*, p118.

68 Richard Watson *Rhondda Coal, Cardiff Gold. The Insoles of Llandaff, Coal Owners and Shippers*, Cardiff 1997, p73-4.

69 GRO D/D X296.

70 Census returns cited in T.J. Evans & J. Yockney *Aberdare: An Excursion in Industrial Geography*, in *Fieldworker Magazine*, University College Swansea 1969 p26.

71 Slater's *South Wales Directory 1850*, Carriers, Traders and Agents under Cardiff.

72 Information from Thomas Jones, retired boatman engaged in Bridgwater brick trade and the Cardiff timber trade, Cardiff to Merthyr and Aberdare, between 1879 and 1898. There was also a patent fuel works on the Aberdare Canal.

73 R. de Salis *Bradshaw's Canals and Navigable Rivers of England and Wales*, 1918, p114.

74 GRO Q/DP 167.

75 Mear *Aberdare Railways*, p63-4, 61-2. ACC minute book Jan 29 1840, 26 Aug 1858.

76 The Newport, Abergavenny & Hereford Railway Act 1858. 21 and 22 Vic Cap cxxvi.

77 Gwyn Briwnant Jones & Denis Dunstone *The Vale of Neath Line. Neath to Pontypool Road*, Llandysul 1996, p91 and 99.

78 Hadfield *Canals of South Wales*, p125.

79 ACC minute book 31 Aug 1870, 23 Aug 1871, 14 Aug 1872, 19 Aug 1874.

80 ACC minute book 15 Sept 1875

81 First mention in the minute book is 17 August 1864.

82 *Western Mail* 7 April 1893.

83 Board of Trade hearing of objections to Rates, Tolls etc 1894 (Llewellyn 15332) p2.

84 *Canals and Navigations in the UK*, 1888, p810-1, cited in Davies *Aberdare Canal*, p162.

85 Royal Commission on Canals 1906 Q10808.

86 W.T. Lewis and Mr Harwood's report of 4 August presented to the Annual General Assembly, GCC minute book 26 Aug 1891.

87 Royal Commission on Canals 1906 Q10809.

88 Mear *Aberdare Railways*, p148-150.

The seal of the Aberdare Canal Company, entitled Aberdare Canal Navigation and Rail Roads.
Taken from the canal company's minute books.   Courtesy Glamorgan Record Office

Chapter 7

THE WATER SUPPLY TO THE CANAL AT NAVIGATION

The canal crossed the Vale of Taff at what is now Abercynon. Just beyond the canal aqueduct, on the left bank of the river, the Glamorganshire's primary water feeder south of Cyfarthfa entered the cut. Nearby were the company's administration offices and workshops. The locality was christened Navigation.

The feeder took its water from the right bank of the river, opposite the flannel mill where the Nant Mafon enters the Taff at Fiddler's Elbow. It then ran downstream through Goetre Coed and crossed the river by its own aqueduct.[1]

Unfortunately the feeder and wooden aqueduct were prone to be damaged when the river flooded, and it was soon found necessary to survey a replacement feeder. The proprietors ordered Patrick Copeland, appointed to the newly-created position of Clerk and Cashier to the company, to seek proposals for its making.[2] Seven more acres of Jenkin Jenkins' land were purchased for this new feeder[3] and in September 1796 the contract was placed with David Edwards, at his estimate of £679 0s 6d, for which he was also to maintain it in good repair for two years. Watkin George, effectively the canal company's engineer at this time, gave security for Edwards' completing the contract, a fact which may indicate that the latter was a Cyfarthfa man.[4] More likely is that Edwards was in fact the well-respected bridge builder and son of William Edwards. William Edwards had built the world famous arch at Pontypridd (or Newbridge) and, together, father and son had worked on the watercourses to the original forges at Cyfarthfa in 1766.

The new feeder's intake was higher up the Taff at Quaker's Yard, at the confluence of the Bargoed Taff and the main river. Immediately below this point the river drops sharply, and so allowed the feeder to maintain high ground on the right bank and to enter the canal between the two pairs of locks (20-21 and 22-23) in the Abercynon flight. This gave welcome water where it had been difficult for the Dadfords to provide much in the way of sideponds between locks. However, either the engineering was more difficult than Edwards had expected or he had simply over-extended himself in this and his other contracts, for by July 1799 it was still unfinished and he is reported to have defalcated (broken his contract with a suggestion that he had embezzled the monies already paid to him). This lends

weight to the argument that this was the same David Edwards who, at that time, had been awarded the much more prestigious contract of bridging the Usk at Newport; experienced water engineers were at a premium in South Wales in the late 18th century.

Thomas Roberts was hired as *'foreman merely as timekeeper and head labourer'* and the completion of the feeder was entrusted to Copeland and Watkin George, with the canal company paying the labourers through Copeland.[5]

Meanwhile, the original feeder had to be made to perform. George sought to protect it from the Taff floods by building a wall along its length at an estimated cost of £50 10s 6d.[6] The feeder was placed in the charge of the Caedudwg lock keeper, Thomas Edmund, who also looked after the short feeder from the Caedudwg Brook which ran through Cwm Ellen Deg.[7]

Thus by 1800 the canal company had the luxury of two water supplies at Navigation.

It was in 1800 that the new feeder became an unwitting party in the canal company's attempts to prevent the Merthyr Tramroad being built.[8] The tramroad route to the interchange basin at Navigation caused it to cross the feeder, just before the tramroad made its second crossing of the river. The tramroad had no Act of Parliament as the Earl of Plymouth's trustees had granted the company use of his land for the greater part of its route and the partners were confident of persuading other landowners to co-operate similarly.[9] The canal company saw this feeder crossing as their best opportunity in opposing the tramroad and they focussed their efforts on pressing Jenkin Jenkins to sell them the required portion of his land; he declined, indicating that he was willing only to sell them the useless slip of land lying between the feeder and the river. Meanwhile they warned the tramroad company that any attempt to bridge the feeder would be met with force.[10] However, the tramroad company carried on regardless so that, at the canal company meeting on 3 March 1801, Copeland was ordered to *'without delay demolish all works that may be erected across our new Feeder and continue to remove everything that may encroach upon the same and its Banks.'* At the same meeting, it was realised that no legal conveyance existed for the lands Jenkins had sold to the canal company in 1797. Copeland was ordered to complete the conveyance and, if there was

The route of the canal from Pontcaederwen to Cefn Glas and Goetre Coed from Harrison's 1830 survey. At lock 9 (Cefn Glas) the canal started its descent to the river crossing at Navigation.
Courtesy Glamorgan Record Office

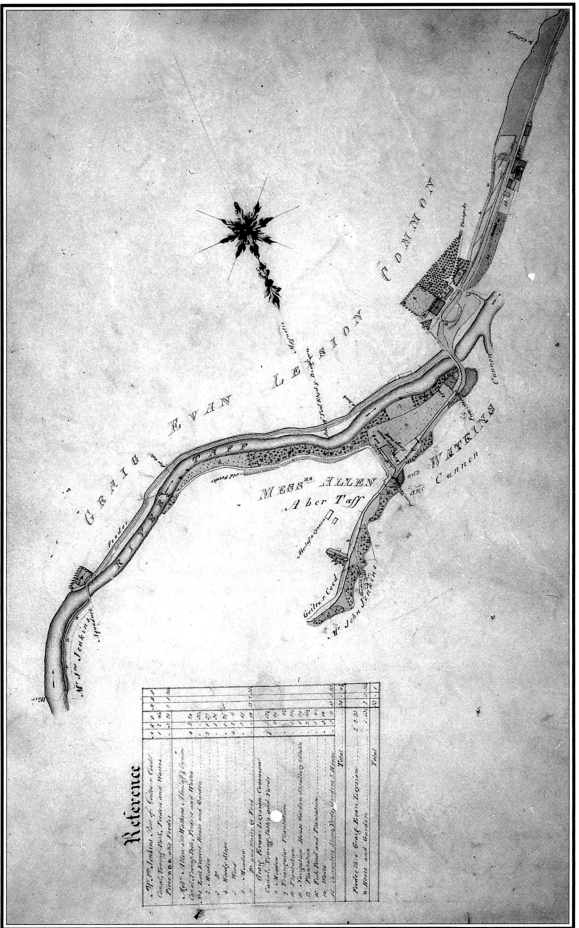

Harrison's 1830 survey shows the Abercynon flight, the aqueduct and the coal transshipment wharves at Navigation and also the water supply to the latter place. The abandoned upper feeder is still shown in part.
Courtesy Glamorgan Record Office

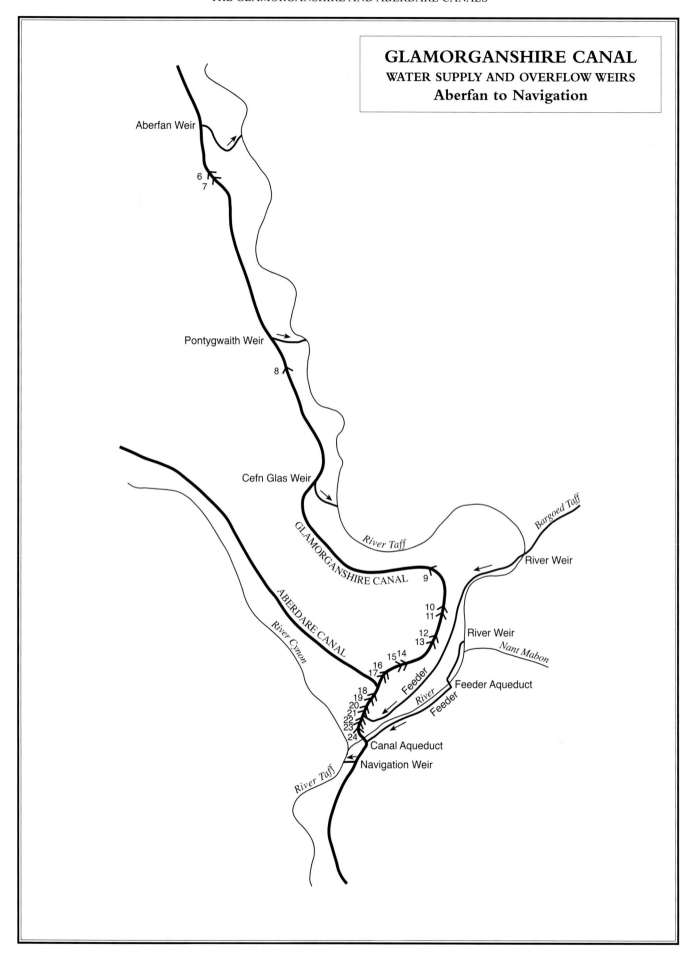

GLAMORGANSHIRE CANAL
WATER SUPPLY AND OVERFLOW WEIRS
Aberfan to Navigation

A view on the Abercynon Eleven Locks, looking up the flight to Aberdare Canal Junction, taken by W. Rowlands in October 1913. In the foreground is Lock 20, the top lock of the two-rise Lock Odyn-galch (Limekiln Lock). Next ahead is Lock y Waun, another two-rise or double lock, with the turnover bridge for the Aberdare Canal crossing the lock tail. Above, the line of the Aberdare Canal can be seen running left and in front of the Junction Cottage (top centre of picture). Dock cottages and the dock workshop (the low white building) can be seen on the right. Locks 16-17 and 14-15 are the two-rise pairs seen climbing the hillside at the top of the picture. After a half-mile pause, five more locks complete the 207 feet rise of the Abercynon Sixteen.   ILW collection

Another photograph by W. Rowlands, looking down the Abercynon Eleven lock flight from Locks 20 and 21 (Lock Odyn-galch) in October 1913. In the foreground is the lock-tail bridge carrying Alexandra Place (the old Aberdare road to the Taff Valley) and the towpath over Lock 21. The arm of the canal running left, was the outlet of the upper or Quaker's Yard feeder and formed a basin serving a limehouse, storehouse and a limekiln. As the collection of stone blocks indicates, this wharf was used by the GCC stonemasons. This stone wharf was effectively the terminus of the canal by this time. Lock Stackhouse is the next two-rise lock and at the bottom of the flight is Lock Isaf (No. 24), where a GCC goods boat is seen unloading its cargo into a warehouse.

When the Marquess of Bute took over the canal, the story of Abercynon as a canal settlement was not quite over. This was due to the enthusiasm of one man, Lewis Llewelyn, who believed in canals and had served the GCC all his life. Made traffic manager in 1885, Llewelyn realised that the canal had a place in delivering foodstuffs to the new and booming mining populations. The GCC itself started carrying in 1887 and by 1895 a number of depots had been set up along the line, including one at the new settlement of Cilfynydd and another at Abercynon. The latter's transit sheds at Lock Isaf (near Imperial Square) were served by an 'express' horse boat from Cardiff that did not call at Pontypridd. Jack Herbert was the first GCC boatman to work the Abercynon boat and Bill Herbert, Jack Williams and Bill Thatcher were other regulars. The boats brought in flour, bran, oils, Indian corn and sacks of barley meal for fattening Abercynon's backyard pigs. These goods remained in store until called for. Perishables such as bacon, butter and cheese were carriage paid and would be sent out by the GCC's horse and cart. In the good times two boats provided a regular daily service to Lock Isaf.

At the left of the picture the Taff Vale Railway will be observed descending its own incline to Abercynon on its way from Merthyr to Cardiff. In the distant left the Basin can be discerned across the river at Navigation. The canal company's warehouses and Navigation House are all visible and, in the far centre distance are the headframes of the Dowlais Cardiff colliery.

ILW collection

GLAMORGANSHIRE CANAL.

Summary of DAILY TRAFFIC passing through *Abercynon* Lock, Month of *May* 190 9

Lockage

	UP BOATS.			DOWN BOATS.			Total.	
	Laden.	Empty.	Total.	Laden.	Empty.	Total.		
1	1	.	1	.	1	1	2	1
3	1	.	1	.	1	1	2	1
5	1	.	1	.	1	1	2	1
8	1	.	1	.	1	1	2	1
12	1	.	1	.	1	1	2	1
13	1	.	1	.	1	1	2	1
14	1	.	1	.	1	1	2	1
29	1	.	1	.	1	1	2	1
	8		8		8	8	16	8

Movements through locks were recorded by lock keepers at certain key points along the canal and in order to conserve precious water supplies the GCC would order 'working turns', i.e. a keeper would not allow a descending boat down through his lock until an up boat had passed. In this way a lock of water (estimated at about 30,000 gallons) would be saved. The operation of Abercynon Lock (Lock Isaf) was unusual. Since 1900 it had been the virtual head of navigation and the unloading point for the Abercynon warehouse. As shown in this Summary of Daily Traffic through it, only eight boats unloaded in the lock during May 1909. ILW collection

meeting received the inevitable body blow when it was informed that Jenkins had indeed sold land to the tramroad company and that it even included the land on which the feeder was already made, and for which the canal company still had no legal conveyance.[14] Charles Brown, recently appointed to replace John Wood as Law Clerk, had a job to do. An action of trespass was brought against the tramroad company, not only for crossing the feeder but for digging the boat basin at Navigation to communicate with the canal. A meeting of the commissioners was convened to legalise the canal company's appropriation of Jenkins' land.

The tramroad was built and commenced operation. The feeder continued to function also. The tramroad basin was connected to the canal and Philip Williams, replacing the retiring Patrick Copeland, was awarded an addition of £5 to his £100 annual salary, to account for all the canal transshipment traffic using the tramroad.[15] When the suit went to the King's Bench in 1803, the canal company showed it meant business by again attempting to remove the bridge across the feeder.[16] Finally, in September 1804, articles of agreement were signed between the two companies and the dispute was settled. Jenkin Jenkins' conveyance of land for the feeder had been ratified in July 1803; the tramroad company would pay an annual rent of twenty shillings to the canal company for the privileges of bridging the feeder and connecting its basin to the canal.[17]

Interestingly, when the turnpike from Aberdare was being built in 1809, the trustees applied for permission to bridge

any difficulty, the canal commissioners would be called out to value the same land for compulsory purchase under the terms of their Acts.[11] The resultant draft conveyance, dated 4 May 1801, includes a plan showing both the new and old feeders.[12]

Richard Hill junior and William Taitt attended part of the canal company's meeting on March 25 as representatives of the tramroad company. Taitt's terse reply to Copeland's threats was that they had ordered their engineer George Overton not to 'desist from going on'. When asked for the names of the tramroad company's proprietors they refused to divulge them, leaving the canal company in a position that they were unable to serve writs, not knowing who to serve them to.[13] Then, in, August the canal company

After the Taff Bargoed joins the River Taff at Quaker's Yard, the river drops appreciably as this circa 1911 photograph shows. The houses of Quaker's Yard are in the distance, whilst the iron pipe marks the confluence of the rivers on the right and the take-off on the left for the later (upper) feeder to the canal at Navigation. SR collection

The Victoria bridge carrying the Merthyr Tramroad across the River Taff. In the foreground are the stone piers of the earlier wooden tramroad bridge which the stone arch replaced, probably in 1815. The stone pier has now gone but the foundations of the cutwaters can be seen from the bridge when the river is low.

Photo P.G. Rattenbury

the new feeder and take the road via the old bridge across the Taff. The canal company offered an alternative suggestion, that the turnpike cross the Taff further south, on an extension to the downstream side of the canal aqueduct itself.[18] This was accepted and today, since closure of the canal, the whole of the original aqueduct and turnpike is utilised by the road.

The lower feeder continued to give trouble when the Taff was in flood but was maintained as the preferred feeder to the upper one. Further work was needed on the protecting wall and in March 1809 Thomas Reece, the clerk, reported that the weir had been destroyed and '*he has cleaned out the new Feeder and which now supplies the Canal with Water.*' The weir would have to be repaired in May when the river allowed.[19] Three years later there was a similar occurrence when the trough carrying the feeder over the Taff was very decayed; a new one was ordered to be '*put up as soon as the Canal can be supplied with Water from the new Feeder which Mr Reece is desired to get cleaned with all convenient speed*'.[20]

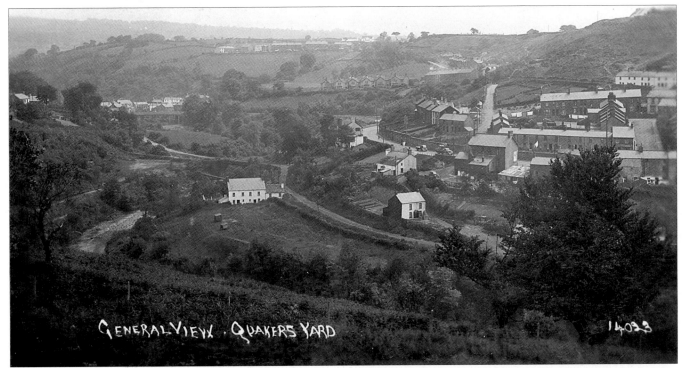

GENERAL VIEW, QUAKERS YARD

14023

This general view looking north at Quaker's Yard, probably taken in the mid 1920s, bears some study. The track passing between the two whitewashed houses in centre-picture is the former Merthyr Tramroad. Behind the leftmost house the tramroad makes a dog leg and crosses the river by the Victoria bridge, then continues round the corner and crosses back on a second bridge north of Quaker's Yard. The dog leg is there because Victoria bridge replaced the earlier wooden bridge on the tramroad, the line of which is shown by the iron water pipe crossing the river. Quaker's Yard is in the distance, nestling at the river's side. The line of the upper feeder can be seen above the bank of the river, on the left, after it has been crossed by the tramroad. This was the spot where the canal company had hoped to stop the Merthyr Tramroad but had failed, because Jenkin Jenkins sold his land to the tramroad company.

SR collection

The Water-Falls, Abercynon.

The earlier (and longer surviving) canal feeder to Navigation was taken off the River Taff's right bank (left of picture) at this weir at Fiddler's Elbow. The overgrown remains of the weir house can just be seen in this circa 1910 postcard view. Immediately below the weir the Nant Mabon enters the Taff, where there was a woollen mill and mill pond. The house on the right fronts onto the route of the Merthyr Tramroad.

SR collection

1688

The Aqueduct, Abercynon

To take it to the Basin at Navigation, the lower feeder crossed the river by a wooden aqueduct which was rebuilt several times in its lifetime. Here, a 1906 picture postcard shows the timber trough, shortly to be replaced with cast iron pipes.   SR collection

Close up of the feeder aqueduct pipes of 1908. They carried a timber walkway and railings but river floods have taken their toll.
Courtesy Merthyr Tydfil Library

It seems from this evidence that the new feeder was prone to blockage, probably from earth, stones, leaves and branches being swept into it from the steep bank to which it clung on its way to Lock Stackhouse. In 1812, the Aberdare Canal finally made its junction with the Glamorganshire Canal above Lock 18 of the Abercynon flight. This indirectly provided another feeder to the Glamorganshire Canal, with a steady flow of water from the Cynon Valley catchment area. Richard Blakemore of Melingriffith was wise to this fact. From 1809, he was demanding a stop lock and overflow weir to the river from the Aberdare Canal, thereby limiting the flow of water into the Glamorganshire which he felt would prejudice his works' water supply from the Taff, much further down the valley.[21] No evidence has been found of this overflow weir, however, or what would have been a long watercourse to the River Cynon. In 1814, Blakemore sought compensation

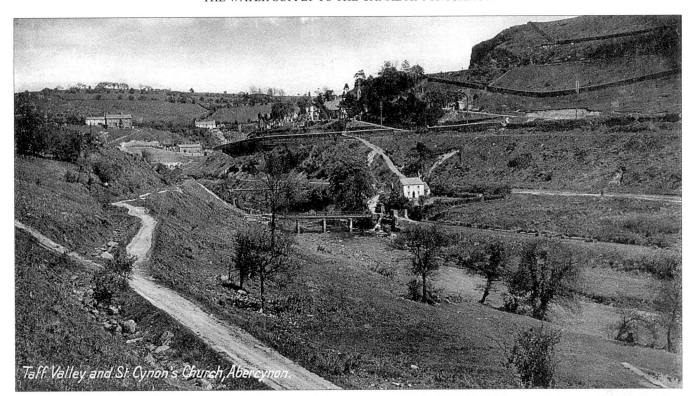

Looking north towards Fiddler's Elbow, in the distance, this late 1940s postcard shows it all. The photograph is taken from the footpath forming the outer slope of the upper feeder's dry bed, as it winds its way round the hillside to the canal at Lock 21, in the Abercynon flight. At the river, the lower feeder crosses and makes its own way downstream to the Basin at Navigation. The whitewashed house on the river's left bank, between the feeder and the line of the Merthyr Tramroad, is the canal company's Ty Feeder, built in 1828. A footpath takes a steep line from Ty Feeder to the road and St Cynon's church. At the point where this path meets the road, the line of the Llanfabon tramroad, which has skirted the churchyard on its way from Nelson, starts to drop into the Taff Valley, also making its way to the Basin. Finally, above the road and through the quarry runs the Taff Vale Railway's branch from the Taff main line to Nelson and Llancaiach.   SR collection

Looking down the valley from St Cynon's church in the 1920s, showing the lower feeder in water in the foreground and the converging lines of river, lower feeder, Merthyr Tramroad and Llanfabon tramroad. On the opposite side of the valley, the upper feeder keeps its height as the river drops to the Basin. On the bend, the line of the ancient parish road from Aberdare to the Merthyr - Cardiff road makes its steep way to the river ford, seen between the two leftmost piers of the bridge, before reappearing on the left bank and crossing the canal feeder. This old route (which crosses the canal at Lock 21) was superseded when the GCC allowed the turnpike to share the aqueduct crossing at the Basin.   SR collection

The Basin, Abercynon.

The River Taff is prone to flooding so Thomas Dadford cleverly chose to cross it where it flowed through a relatively deep ravine. This is graphically shown in another late 1940s postcard view. The canal aqueduct (by then taken over totally for road and pedestrian traffic) can be seen crossing from Abercynon to the small canal-side settlement at the Basin. The lines of the feeder and Merthyr Tramroad show clearly.

SR collection

Below left: The downstream side of the canal aqueduct before road widening. ILW collection, copy neg 2269

from the Aberdare Canal Company but when their committee rejected his claim he reverted to his court battles against the Glamorganshire alone.[22]

Whether or not Blakemore had his weir, the additional water flowing into the Glamorganshire from the Aberdare Canal would have sufficed to replace the intermittent supply from the inefficient new feeder, particularly since the steep lock bypass weirs on the Abercynon flight may not have had the capacity to carry both supplies without significant wastage. By 1817, the new feeder was sufficiently redundant for John Guest to make an unsuccessful application to lease the weir and part of the feeder at Quaker's Yard.[23] The full report of the state of the canal in June 1818 does not mention the new feeder but with regard to the old feeder states 'The Weir and Aqueduct on the River Taff are in very good repair and also the banks and hedges'.[24] Harrison's survey of 1830 tellingly marks part of the abandoned route of the new feeder near Lock Storehouse as 'Old Feeder'. A small basin remained where the feeder had entered the canal. Here was the canal company's limekiln, limehouse and stonemasons yard, an outpost of their workshops down

the hill at Navigation. In 1843, the Jenkinses of Goetre Coed, who had recently lost yet more of their land, this time to the Taff Vale Railway, attempted to buy back the route of the former feeder but the canal company's committee, perhaps with some malice, declined their offer.[25] Thomas Evans, in his history of Abercynon, wrongly suggests that it was the building of the Taff Vale Railway which caused the feeder to be 'transferred to the other side of the valley.'[26]

The importance of the remaining, original watercourse is shown by the canal company's continuing to employ full time superintendents. In 1825, the retiring feeder tender, Thomas Evans, was awarded a pension of six shillings per week.[27] In 1828, a cottage was ordered to be built for the feeder tender at the mouth of the feeder near Navigation House;[28] Harrison's survey shows this to have been built at the feeder aqueduct on the left bank of the river. The house, naturally named Ty Feeder, is now a ruin but the aqueduct, in its 1851 rebuilt form, remains. Persistent destruction of its wooden troughs by flood and rot must have prompted the decision to replace them in October 1908 with two riveted cast iron pipes on stone piers.[29] In this form the feeder survived to supply the canal with water even after closure of the canal north of Pontypridd in 1915. The main supply to the new canal head was water from this feeder channelled along the old canal bed. A wooden launder was built to take water through the breach at Cilfynydd. In 1921 it was estimated that the flow of water along the Navigation feeder was 7 million gallons per day.[30] But the canal was breached again on Cilfynydd Common in 1922 and not repaired. From that time the canal head at Pontypridd had to rely solely on the Caedudwg Brook. To prevent trespass at the dangerous area of the breach, the towpath above Holly Cottage was blocked by fencing and railings.[31]

The feeder to Navigation did continue to flow after the

1922 breach, the water being diverted from the canal to supply the Dowlais Cardiff colliery at Abercynon. This continued until 1960, after which the National Coal Board pumped water directly from the River Taff to meet their requirements.[32] The pipes making up the feeder aqueduct originally had a wooden walkway with iron railings placed atop. Remnants of the walkway and railings can still be seen and there is an overflow weir into the river at the mouth of the pipes. The river weir and feeder intake sluice also remain.

Of the second feeder, its course from the Merthyr Tramroad crossing can still be walked to the site of the Abercynon flight, where a footbridge takes its route over the railway cutting. The weir at Quaker's Yard has disappeared and the short stretch to the Merthyr Tramroad crossing has been filled in. This fact may have contributed to the view expressed by some observers[33] that this feeder came not from Quaker's Yard but from the Nant Mabon at Fiddler's Elbow. The feeder was thought to have travelled upstream and crossed the river below the tramroad bridge, making a hairpin bend to continue its course to Lock Storehouse. The main archaeological evidence to support this novel argument was the high water intake (now obliterated) on the Nant Mabon and the existence of remains of an old bridge downstream of the tramroad bridge. In truth, the water leat was that serving the flannel mill which is actually recorded as having had a 'very high wheel'.[34] The bridge remains are not of an aqueduct but of an earlier tramroad bridge. In February 1815, the upper tramroad bridge collapsed under a train of Penydarren trams and the wooden bridge was rebuilt in stone; the lower bridge was inspected at the same time and also found to be dangerous and required rebuilding.[35] The collapsed upper bridge was rebuilt immediately wholly in stone and the stone abutments still betray where the fatal timbers had been fastened. However, the lower bridge had not collapsed and the tramroad company chose to build its replacement alongside, whilst continuing to use its fragile wooden predecessor. There is no evidence that the abutments of the still-existing stone bridge originally supported a wooden bridge. Moreover, the line the remnants of the old bridge take across the river is a natural continuation of that of the tramroad, whereas a noticeable bend now exists to take the route onto the replacement stone bridge.

NOTES TO CHAPTER 7

1 GCC minute book 26 October 1793, itemises the costs of land purchased from Jenkin Jenkins for this purpose.

2 GCC minute book 1 June and 30 July 1796.

3 GCC minute book 25 March 1797.

4 GCC minute book 11 Feb 1797.

5 GCC minute book 27 July 1799.

6 GCC minute book 15 July 1797.

7 GCC minute book 18 October 1799.

8 GCC minute book 1 March 1800.

9 This agreement was formalised 20 June 1801. GRO D/D Pl 733.

10 GCC minute book 1 March and 25/26 November 1800.

11 GCC minute book 3 March 1801.

12 GRO B/C GCa 4/53.

13 GCC minute book 25 Mar 1801.

14 GCC minute book 19 August 1801.

15 GCC minute book 6 June 1802.

16 GCC minute book 13 April and 21 July 1803.

17 GRO GCa 4/58.

18 GCC minute book 25 August 1809 and 18 April 1812.

19 GCC minute book 23 Dec 1808, 2 March 1809 and 12 July 1809.

20 GCC minute book 3 April 1812.

21 GRO D/D Art O/24; ACC minute book 19 Sept 1809,1 July 1811; GCC minute book 18 Jan 1810.

22 ACC minute book 1 July 1814. For the Blakemore's disputes with the Glamorganshire Canal see Volume 2.

23 GCC minute book 1 Nov and 6 Dec 1817.

24 GCC minute book 3 June 1818.

25 GCC minute book 7 June 1843.

26 Thomas Evans *The Story of Abercynon*, 3rd edition, Risca 1976, p.41.

27 GCC minute book 3 Feb 1825.

28 GCC minute book 28 July 1828.

29 Diary of Ivor Llewelyn, last manager of the GCC, related to ILW 30 Dec 1949. The rebuilding is not recorded in the company's minute book.

30 Cardiff City Archive (since destroyed) Blue Box 2530, *Report on suggested purchase of second portion of the Glamorganshire Canal between Abercynon and Pontypridd*, Cardiff Corporation Waterworks, Nov 1921.

31 ILW in conversation with Gilbert Randall, canal foreman at Cilfynydd, in 1949.

32 *Aberdare Leader*, 4 June 1960.

33 Notably Gordon Rattenbury, Michael J.T. Lewis and Howard Meyrick.

34 NLW Bute Collection Box 141 Parcel 6, Report Relating to the Water Power of the River Taff, 1842.

35 Josiah John Guest to William Taitt, 16 Feb & 18 Feb 1815, quoted in Madeleine Elsas *Iron in the Making, Dowlais Iron Company Letters 1782-1860*, Cardiff 1960.

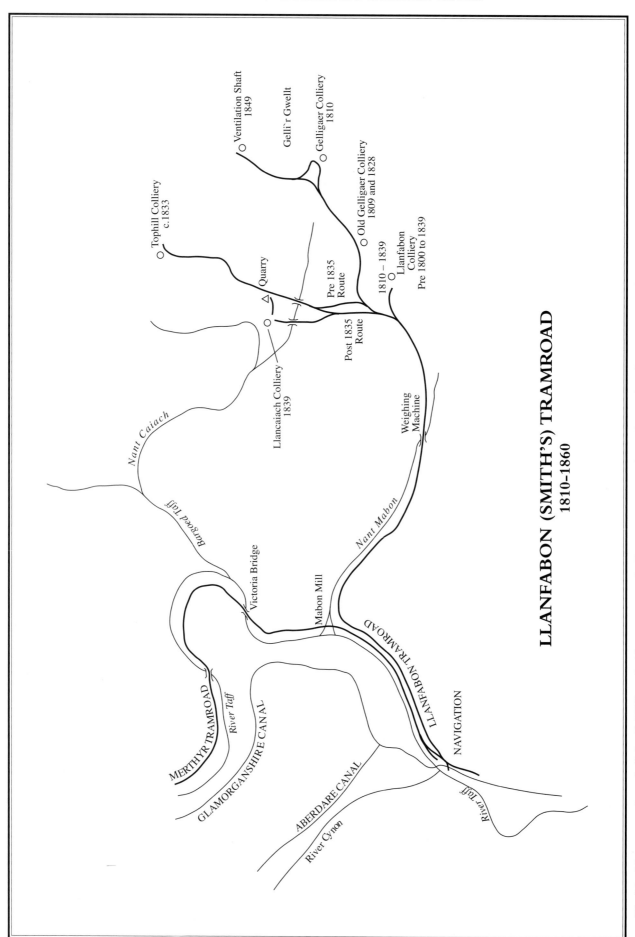

LLANFABON (SMITH'S) TRAMROAD
1810–1860

The Llanfabon tramroad was built by Sir William Smith to serve several collieries near present-day Nelson and Gelligaer. It remained a private concern throughout its life, which was from 1810 to perhaps as late as the 1850s.

Chapter 8

COAL FROM GELLIGAER

The A472, which follows Cwm Mafon from the site of St. Cynon's church, at Fiddler's Elbow, to the village of Nelson, has been a road only since 1865. Prior to that year, public road traffic to the Taff Valley, from the area around Nelson and Llancaiach, took the ancient route from Caerphilly north to Quaker's Yard. The modern A472 lies on the abandoned route of the Llanfabon tramroad of 1810, which carried coal to the canal until the 1850s.

The tramroad was built by a Worcestershire gentleman, Sir William Smith of Eardiston (an estate in the very north of the county near the Shropshire border). Smith celebrated his baronetcy of 1809 by taking on the Llanfabon colliery, to work as a sale-coal business. Along with many outsiders with capital to spare, he sought a better rate of return through supporting the war economy by industrial investment, rather than leaving it on the land. The colliery lay on the watershed between tributaries of the River Taff and the River Rhymney. With the Glamorganshire Canal only a few miles away, Smith chose Cardiff as his port – despite coal exports from Newport being free of tax at that time. The quiet valley of the Mafon offered a direct route to the canal for his private tramroad. The Plymouth Estate charged Smith £10 per annum, from 29 September 1810, for a 31 year lease of its portion of the land needed to build the Llanfabon tramroad. It ran from his colliery to the Dowlais company's newly completed coal basin at Navigation.

Coal for local consumption had been dug from outcrops in the Llancaiach area for years before the coming of the Glamorganshire Canal. The Colliers' Arms may mark one early coal level – on the road along the Caiach Valley past Ton Teilwr and Forest Farms, to which the Llanfabon colliery eventually extended. Account books from 1800 to 1812 for the Plymouth Estate, show the old Llanfabon colliery on their land as '*not worked*'. There is no mention in subsequent years' accounts. Smith's colliery worked the same coal but from neighbouring property. To ship the coal, he was granted a coal wharf at the Sea Lock in Cardiff and at the committee meeting of 3 April 1812, he was permitted free tonnage of 80 tons of material for covering the new yard.

In *The Cambrian* of 18 July 1812, '*Llanvabon Colliery*' was advertised to be sold by private contract. It was described as:

'*..now in regular work, and capable of being considerably extended.*

The above Mines are in part held under a lease of which eleven years are unexpired and the other part for the lives of William Thomas and Mary Jones, under the annual rents together of £40 15s and lie under about forty acres of land.

There is a Railway from the Works to the Glamorganshire Canal, for which annual compensations are paid to different persons amounting in the whole to about £20 per annum.

The coal is of excellent quality, supposed to be superior to any in the neighbourhood, and of great thickness.

An extensive trade is now carried on from the port of Cardiff, and any quantity of coal may be got to extend the same.

There are nine canal boats, various tram-waggons, and a spacious yard with a counting-house, at the Sea lock, Cardiff, attached to the above Works, and many other conveniences for carrying on the same.

The purchaser will have to take the Machinery, Utensils, Implements etc of the present proprietor, employed in the said Works, at a fair valuation, and the purchaser may be accommodated with any part of the purchase-money on good security.

In case the above Works are not Sold by the 25th day of August 1812 the same will be LET by PRIVATE CONTRACT.'

Why Sir William Smith should attempt to sell the concern when he had only just completed laying down the tramroad and setting up the yard at Cardiff is unclear. There are no clues as to what markets Smith sought to supply with his coal. He may have planned to ship coal up the Severn to markets near his Worcestershire estate but they were much closer to the Black Country collieries. Alternatively, he may simply have relied upon the usual method of selling coal to ship captains from his Cardiff yard. In 1812, Smith may have foreseen the repercussions of the collapse of the Aberdare iron industry and the Tappenden bankruptcy. Even if not directly affected, confidence must have been shaken and his advisers may have counselled him to withdraw from South Wales. In fact Smith was not a casual observer but was much closer to the root of the Tappenden bankruptcy, for the owner of the neighbouring colliery to Llanfabon was none other than Sir Jeremiah Homfray. It seems more than a coincidence, and a lot like *déjà vu,* that (the also newly-knighted) Homfray should lease Gelli ar Gwellt colliery

The private transfer dock at Navigation, owned jointly by the Dowlais, Penydarren and Plymouth companies, whose Merthyr Tramroad was completed to this point by 1802. Universally known as the Basin, the canal and tramroad terminal handled bar iron and rails which were put onto boats for onward carriage to Cardiff. In the opposite direction iron ore, imported through the Cardiff Sea Lock, was boated to Navigation and transshipped to the tramroad for haulage up the valley to the ironworks. On 21 February 1804, the Basin was the destination for Richard Trevithick's epic journey down the tramroad with his steam locomotive, hauling successfully 10 tons of bar iron in waggons and 70 passengers – the first steam locomotive to run on rails. This reconstruction is based on the artist's visits to the infilled site in the 1940s, when almost all of the original cottages, smithy, warehouses and stables were still in existence including the base of the crane. The design of the crane is not known but the example depicted is from one by Thomas Telford. The viewpoint is from the canal towpath bridge which crossed the dock's entrance. The nature and design of the bridge is not known. Navigation – the name of the settlement around the Basin – owed its existence to the business of canal and tramroad transfer, and possessed a mill, three pubs, a post office and a general store, in addition to the smithy and tramroad buildings. The dock went out of use when traffic down the Merthyr Tramroad ended in 1875, the last freighter almost certainly being the Plymouth Forge Co. As for modern Abercynon, this settlement did not begin to take shape until the 1890s, with preparations for the sinking of the Dowlais Cardiff colliery.

from 29 August 1810, at the same time as an English newcomer invested the capital in developing the transport infrastructure to allow Homfray to ship his coal. Homfray had done it to the Tappendens at Hirwaun and was also taking advantage of Dr Richard Griffiths' tramroad in Cwm Rhondda. It is therefore easy to surmise that it was Jeremiah Homfray who had been instrumental in persauding Smith to invest in South Wales coal. Homfray went down with the Tappendens and when his effects were auctioned they included three iron and two wooden boats on the Glamorganshire Canal and his coal yard at the Sea Lock.[1] The 32 tram wagons for operating on a '*three foot road*' would have been from Griffiths' tramroad rather than the Llanfabon tramroad, which is assumed to have been to the same gauge as Overton's Merthyr Tramroad (4ft 2ins).

With Homfray's bankruptcy and the closure of Gelli ar Gwellt colliery, Smith was set to lose income from traffic on his tramroad but he must have been unsuccessful in finding a buyer at that difficult time for he continued to operate the colliery and the tramroad.

Entries in the Plymouth Estate account books show Smith buying pit wood[2] and an entry in the canal company's minutes for 16 June 1819 reads, '*Mr Reece* [to] *inform Mr Robt Thomas that when a plan is submitted to the committee on the part of Sir Wm Smith Bart an answer will be given to his application.*' This may well be the application to allow the Llanfabon tramroad its own coal yard and tipping wharf on the west bank of the canal at Navigation and to free it from sharing the Dowlais facilities. The tramroad was allowed access to the new yard, crossing the Merthyr

Above: The canal community at the Basin was always something apart from the coal town of Abercynon. Here it is photographed from Incline Top. The building on the right was that of the Dowlais company, backing onto the canal and whose pine end overlooked the dock (here filled in). The next large building was Penydarren's, followed by Plymouth's. The terrace in shadow included a public house and brewhouse.

ILW collection, copy neg 2343

The former Penydarren and Plymouth ironworks properties at the basin. The viewpoint is similar to that of the sketch, page opposite. ILW collection, copy neg 2342

Site of the canal/tramroad transshipment basin in 1946, looking west, with the three iron companies' properties and the base of the crane. Photo Stanley Mercer

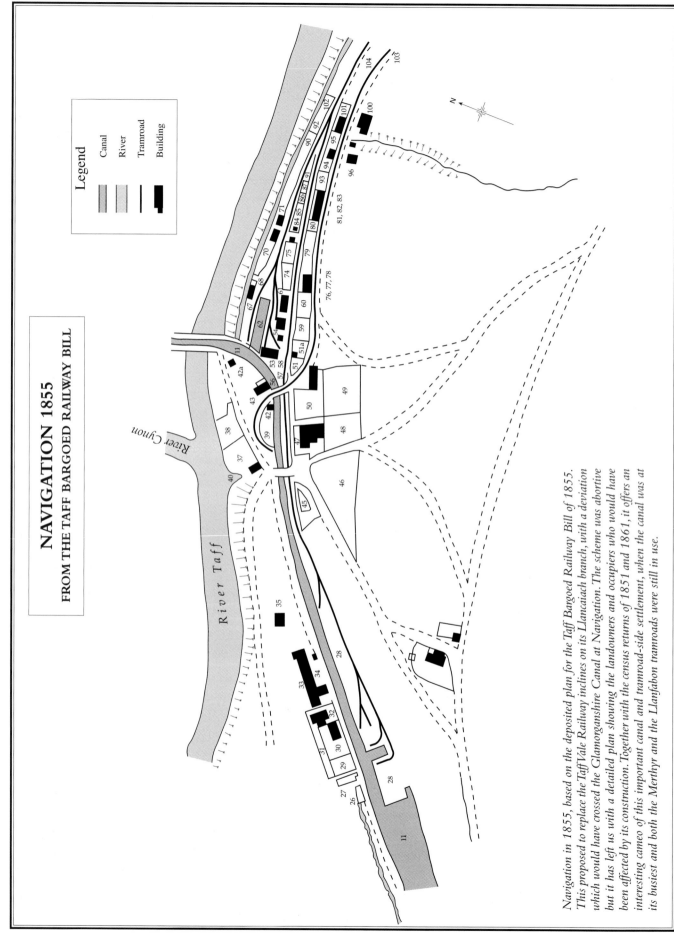

NAVIGATION 1855
FROM THE TAFF BARGOED RAILWAY BILL

Navigation in 1855, based on the deposited plan for the Taff Bargoed Railway Bill of 1855. This proposed to replace the TaffVale Railway inclines on its Llancaiach branch, with a deviation which would have crossed the Glamorganshire Canal at Navigation. The scheme was abortive but it has left us with a detailed plan showing the landowners and occupiers who would have been affected by its construction. Together with the census returns of 1851 and 1861, it offers an interesting cameo of this important canal and tramroad-side settlement, when the canal was at its busiest and both the Merthyr and the Llanfabon tramroads were still in use.

In the centre of this re-drawn plan, the canal crosses the river and makes its way south-west, beneath the Llanfabon tramroad bridge and in front of Navigation House before passing the canal company's maintenance yard opposite the Merthyr Tramroad's lower basin. The towpath is on the up-stream side of the aqueduct, while the turnpike from Aberdare is on the down-stream side. Both towpath and turnpike cross the bridge at Navigation in opposite directions, the turnpike making its way up the hill to join the Merthyr-Cardiff turnpike at Travellers Rest. By that time, of the three co-owners of the MTRC, the Plymouth Company was by far the main user – Dowlais had its own railway connection to the TVR and Penydarren was in the process of closing. Note that the dry dock next to the canal overflow weir is shown as Plymouth property and not the canal company's.

The Llanfabon tramroad is shown as still being in the ownership of John Berry, Sir Christopher Smith's executor, while Duncan & Co (Lancaiach colliery) continued as its users to their tipping wharf opposite the basin. Although Thomas Powell's coal wharf is shown, by that time all Gelligaer coal was using his Tophill colliery to the TVR. Robert Beaumont was losing his Tophill colliery and the canal. On the original plan Cartwrights, who had also ceased to use Smith's tramroad and the canal. On the original plan the centre of deviation crosses the canal at the tramroad bridge and it is unclear whether a junction might have existed between the two tramroads. The Lanfabon tramroad crossed the MTR on a draw bridge but it is not known what form the canal crossing took – stone, wood or iron.

Copies of the deposited plan are at Glamorgan Record Office (Q/DP 150) and at the House of Lords Records Office. The railway was never made. The numbers refer to the schedule which accompanied the deposited plans and are summarised in the accompanying table.

	DESCRIPTION	OWNER	LESSEE AND OCCUPIER
11	Glamorganshire Canal	GCC	GCC
26	Overflow weir and watercourse	GCC	
27	Dry dock, shed and yard	Plymouth Iron Co	
28	Lower basin, wharf and tramways	MTRC	Plymouth Iron Co
29	Garden	GCC	Joseph Green
30	Dwelling house, out-buildings, yard and gardens	GCC	Joseph Green
31	Yard	GCC	Joseph Green
32	House, outbuildings, yard and gardens	GCC	David Leyshon
33	Sheds and garden	GCC	
34	Carpenters shop, smiths shop, sheds and yard	GCC	David Leyshon
35	Saw pit	GCC	
37	Cottage, outbuildings, yard and garden	Bute trustees & John Berry (executor of Sir Christopher Sydney Smith)	
38	Garden and shed	Bute trustees	Thomas Powell (lessee), Isaac Price (occupier)
39	Coal wharf, tramway, shipping place and coal tip	Bute trustees, GCC & Smith's executor	Duncan & Co
40	Warehouse and cut	Bute trustees and GCC	
42	Coal wharf, tramways, weighing machine house and shipping place	Bute trustees, GCC & Smith's executor	Duncan & Co
42a	Coal wharf and shed	Bute trustees & GCC	Thomas Powell
43	House, stable, outbuildings, coal wharf and shed	Bute trustees & GCC	Thomas Powell (lessee), Isaac Price (occupier)
45	Plantation, pasture and pond	GCC	Thomas Shepherd
46	Plantation	GCC	Thomas Shepherd
47	Dwelling house, office, outbuildings and garden (Navigation House)	GCC	Thomas Shepherd
48	Plantation, bath house and walks	GCC	Thomas Shepherd
49	Pasture	GCC	Thomas Shepherd
50	Stabling, outbuildings, garden, plantation bank and yards		Thomas Shepherd
51	Plantation	GCC	George Knill
51a	Garden	Dowlais Iron Co	Thomas Shepherd, George Knill
53	House, stable, pigstye and wharehouse	Dowlais Iron Co	Thomas Thomas
54	House, shop, outbuildings and yard	Penydarren Iron Co	Thomas Powell and Duncan & Co
56	Bridge	GCC & Smith's executor	
57	Draw bridge and tramroad	Sir Christopher Smith's executor	Plymouth Iron Co
58	Tramroad and bridge	MTRC	Thomas Thomas
59	Garden	Penydarren Iron Co	Robert Scott
60	Garden and sheds	Plymouth Iron Co	Robert Scott
61	House, office, outbuildings and yard	Plymouth Iron Co	Plymouth Iron Co
62	Basin, wharf and tramways	MTRC	
67	Carpenters and smiths shop & yard	Plymouth Iron Co	Edward Davies, Edward Watkin Scale
68	House and yard	Plymouth, Dowlais	Edward Jenkins
69	Stable and yard	Plymouth, Penydarren	Edward Jenkins
70	Public house, outbuilding, yard and garden	Bute trustees & Mrs Hopkins	Edward Jenkins
71	Brewhouse, stable and yard	Bute trustees & Mrs Hopkins	Robert Scott
74	Garden	MTRC	William Lewis
75	Garden and piggery	MTRC	Morgan Ellis
76	House, outbuilding and yard	Bute trustees & Richard Davis	William Lewis
77	House, outbuilding and yard	Bute trustees & Richard Davis	William Edmunds
78	House, outbuilding and yard	Bute trustees & Richard Davis	William Edmunds, William Lewis
79	Garden	Bute trustees & Richard Davis	Thomas Oriel
80	Garden	Plymouth Iron Co	Moses Miles and Evan Jones
81	House and yard	Plymouth Iron Co	Thomas Oriel
82	House and yard	Plymouth Iron Co	Moses Miles and Evan Jones
83	House and yard	Plymouth Iron Co	
84	Ruin and rough pasture	MTRC	Thomas Thomas
85	Stable and garden	MTRC	Thomas Oriel
86	Garden	MTRC	Moses Miles
87	Garden	MTRC	Evan Jones
88	Garden	MTRC	Vacant
89	Smiths shop	MTRC	
90	Rough pasture bank	GCC and MTRC	William Richards, Thomas Smith
91	Rough pasture bank	MTRC	Evan Jones
92	Garden	GCC and MTRC	William Richards
93	Garden	Plymouth Iron Co	William Richards
94	Garden	Bute trustees & William Richards	
95	House, stable, outbuilding, yard & gardens	Bute trustees & William Richards	William Richards
96	Smiths shop and yard	Bute trustees & William Richards	William Richards
97	Pig stye	Bute trustees & William Richards	William Richards
100	House, shop and yard	Bute trustees & William Richards	William Richards
101	House, outbuildings, yard & garden	Bute trustees & Daniel Jenkins	Daniel Jenkins
102	Garden	MTRC	Daniel Jenkins
103	Tramroad and banks	Smith's executor	Duncan and Co
104	Tramroad and banks	MTRC	Plymouth Iron Co

In 1809, the canal company allowed the Merthyr Tramroad to be extended south alongside the canal to a coal wharf below Navigation, where coal from the Llanfabon tramroad was also shipped initially. The bridge shown here, spanning the tramroad extension and the canal, was built to link the administration offices in Navigation House with the canal company's workshops. The towpath also changed sides here. It led beneath the bridge on the Navigation House side, the horse then having to be led across the tramroad track and over the bridge. The hawthorn trees mark the line of the path linking the towpath to the higher level of the tramroad. Navigation House, purpose-built by Thomas Dadford and administrative headquarters of the canal company from 1792 to the early 1880s, has been a public house for many years and is still an imposing building.

ILW photo 27 Aug 1948, neg 500

The line of the 1809 extension of the Merthyr and Llanfabon tramroads passing under Navigation bridge. The canal span is on the left, in this 1946 photograph, and St Thomas's Roman Catholic church is beyond, standing on the site of, what was from 1819, the Llanfabon tramroad's tipping wharf. Photo Stanley Mercer

Tramroad by a drawbridge and the canal by what also may have been a drawbridge.

The 1813 unpublished first OS survey of 2 inches to 1 mile shows Llanfabon colliery (Smith's) on the Caerphilly road, just south of the junction with the road to Ystrad Mynach. Strangely, no tramroad connection is shown but the tramroad rounds the low watershed to the north and terminates on the side of the Caiach Valley, at a second colliery near Wern-caiach (Homfray's).

Sir William Smith died in 1820 or 1821[3] and his 22 year old son Christopher Sidney Smith became the second baronet, inheriting his father's South Wales undertakings. Sir Christopher extended the Llanfabon colliery in September 1822, by taking out a 14 year lease under the whole of Ton Teilwr Farm from Matthew Matthews, at a yearly rent of £100. Annual royalty payments were to be 4$\frac{1}{2}$d per ton for the first 7,000 tons and 8d per ton thereafter. The lease is witnessed by Smith's Cardiff agent, Robert Thomas.[4] During the 1820s, the neighbouring Plymouth Estate took trial borings at Llanfabon, under the direction of Robert Thomas of Waun Wyllt, and in March 1829 Smith took a 21 year lease of 25 acres of Forest Fawr. This time the royalty was 1s per ton for the first 1,000 tons and 8d per ton thereafter. Because the colliery extended over the two properties, Smith's coal bailiff had to arrange for separate accounts to be kept for the two landlords. The tonnages removed from beneath Forest Fawr land for each month of the years 1830-1 are recorded in the Plymouth papers, witnessed by Robert Thomas.[5] Smith continued to purchase pit wood from the Plymouth Estate.[6]

Samuel Lewis's *Topographical Dictionary of Wales*, 1833 edition, states under Llanfabon, '*A colliery belonging to Sir C. Smith, Bart., from which a tram-road communicates with the Glamorganshire canal, affords employment to about twenty men.*' In the same Dictionary, the entry under Gelligaer records '[a tram-road] *from the collieries on the west side of the parish extends a distance of nearly three miles, to the Glamorganshire canal, between Cardiff and Merthyr-Tydvil.*' The first of these Gelligaer collieries had been sunk near Jeremiah Homfay's former level at Gelli-ar-gwellt. *The Cambrian* of 21 November 1829 reported the occasion:

'*Gellygare. Nov 17 1829. There has been for some days past a very pleasurable excitement among the peaceful inhabitants of this neighbourhood, occasioned by the persevering efforts of Mr Thomas Powell being crowned with the most complete success. This public-spirited gentleman, to whom Newport is mainly indebted for its present prosperity and its extensive commerce in coals, has sunk two shafts of a hundred and twelve yards each to discover a vein of coal, the existence of which has heretofore been a problem. His most sanguine expectations have been realised; for at this depth he has discovered a vein of coal of nearly six feet thick, equal, if not superior, in quality to the best Newport coals. Mr Powell intends shipping this coal at Cardiff; for which purposes he has made a tramroad to connect his colliery with the Glamorganshire Canal. He will be able in a very short time to send down to that port from two to three hundred tons a day, where their superior quality will no doubt, ensure them a ready sale.*'

This 1880s photograph will make comparison with the one on the following two pages. It was taken before the sinking of Dowlais Cardiff colliery which created the village of Abercynon. The footbridge across the river is the most obvious feature common to both photographs. It led from Navigation to Aberdare Junction, whose original station buildings are shown. Martin's Terrace has not yet been built alongside the towpath. Let into the towpath wall can be seen a horse pool (alternatively called a horse slip). These served two purposes – firstly to allow horses to drink at the canal but secondly to allow any which fell into the canal to get out. The canal company's yard is off-picture to the left, where the logs may indicate the site of the carpenters' saw pit.

Courtesy Aberdare Library

Abercynon from Travellers Rest taken at the turn of the century. At the middle right is the Basin and the wooded line of the ravine through which the River Taff flows. The Glamorganshire Canal can be seen passing under the TVR main line, crossing the river, then swinging south past Navigation House and continuing by the newly-built colliery terraced housing, to the canal company's workshops at Navigation Yard. Behind, in turn, are the sidings of the Dowlais Cardiff colliery, the River Taff, Abercynon railway station canals locomotive depot, and Abercynon proper. The TVR line to Aberdare branches off the main line just north of the station. In the right distance is the beginning of the Abercynon Sixteen flight of

locks leading past Aberdare Canal junction, where a group of white-washed canalside cottages can be made out easily. The line of the Aberdare Canal can be seen leading into the Cynon Valley. In the foreground, the TVR branch to Nelson climbs past Travellers' Rest. The tramroad extension from Navigation House to the coal wharf on the extreme bottom left was still in situ when this photograph was taken. The trees hiding Navigation bridge mark the site of a fish pond between road and canal. As can be seen, Abercynon was an important focus of routes from the south to the Cynon Valley, the Taff Valley and, via the Mabon Valley, to Llanfabon and Gelligaer.

SR collection

Dowlais Cardiff colliery in 1905. The low quality of the printed image on this picture postcard means it cannot take too much enlarging. A boat is moored at the colliery company's wharf where a train of loaded trams stands alongside a covered shed. It is difficult to tell whether the boat is loading coal or is unloading stone. The possible answer is that Aberthaw limestone is being delivered for burning in the colliery's limekilns for use as cement. The boat would have turned in the old coal dock before tying up at this wharf. SR collection

On 21 November the paper further reported:

'*Mr Powell has erected two steam engines of considerable power, one for pumping the water, the other for winding the coals. He has also built several very convenient cottages near the colliery for the workmen, and we may expect that what has heretofore been a houseless wild, will soon be a populous hamlet.*'

It was an easy task for Powell to lay a tramroad extension from Sir Christopher Smith's Llanfabon tramroad at Werncaiach, on a causeway across the flat valley, to serve this New Gelligaer colliery. At Navigation, he arranged with the canal company for his own coal yard and their minute book records on 4 June 1828:

'*Ordered that the land adjoining the yard occupied by Sir C. Smith opposite the Navigation House and extending to the Aqueduct Bridge be let to Mr Powell or the proprietors of the Gellyher Gwelt colliery subject to such power as the Act for the Aberdare Road provides to that Trust at the annual rent of 2 guineas and during such time as they ship thence not less than 50 tons of coal per week.*'

On 23 December 1829 Thomas Powell applied to the canal company for his own coal wharf at the Cardiff Sea Lock and on 13 November of the following year he was advertising in *The Cambrian*:

'*Powell's Main Coal, Cardiff. T. Powell begs to inform Ship Owners, masters of Vessels and Purchasers of Coal in general,*

that having completed his colliery at Gelligare he is enabled to keep, at his Wharf at Cardiff, a Constant Supply of very superior Bituminous Coal, equal in size and quality to his best Newport Coals being worked from the same vein.

From facility of conveyance and other advantages, T.P. is enabled to offer his Coal at Cardiff sixpence per ton under the price of Newport Coals and to give 21 cwt weight to the ton with the usual gratuity, and a bonus or present in addition, to every Master of Vessel for the first cargo, whether taken on freight or his own account.'

The success of the great Thomas Powell brought others to the area. One of these was Robert Beaumont, a mineral surveyor from Newcastle upon Tyne, who had come to South Wales in 1827 as mineral agent to the Marquess of Bute. In 1833, he lost his full-time job with the Marquess and turned coal owner, opening a colliery at Tophill and laying a tramroad connection which ran past Llancaiach Isaf to Smith's tramroad.[7] Finally (as far as the Llanfabon tramroad is concerned), came Llancaiach colliery, sunk just south of Llancaiach Fawr by Duncan & Co between 1836 and 1839. Thus the Llanfabon tramroad carried the produce of five collieries to the Glamorganshire Canal, *viz*. the old Llanfabon colliery, the old Gelligaer colliery, the new Gelligaer colliery, Tophill colliery and Llancaiach colliery.

When the Taff Vale Railway was promoted in 1835, Thomas Powell was a prominent member of the provisional committee. It was no surprise, therefore, that he pressed for a railway branch to Gelligaer. At their meeting of 23 October 1835, it was resolved '*that a branch to the collieries of*

Another view of the colliery at Abercynon, showing the overhead ropeway to take waste to its tips on Graig Evan Leishon. On the canal towpath, two colliers walk away from the cameraman, whilst a loaded boat approaches along the waterway. SR collection

The Colliery. Abercynon.

Mr Powell and Sir Christopher Smith and Mr Beaumont and the Bargoed Vales be made in such a way as shall be determined after a further view of the locus by Mr Brunel.'[8] The Act so obtained authorised the TVR branch to be taken through Nelson to the older Llancaiach colliery at PontySquire, near to the valley of the Bargoed Taff. However, in 1839, when land for the branch was being acquired and contracts were being let, the directors decided it should terminate short at Duncan & Co's new Llancaiach colliery, which had been sunk during the TVR Bill's promotion and was then being connected to Smith's tramroad. The TVR agreed with Smith for a realignment of the tramroad, so that only two tramroad bridges need be provided to cross the TVR as it cut its way through Nelson towards Llancaiach. The line from Tophill was diverted westward to join the new line from Duncan's colliery, which then joined the main tramroad south of Nelson. Thomas Powell also arranged for a tipping wharf to be built, where the tramroad from his Gelligaer colliery ran close to and above the TVR branch in Nelson. Thus was he prepared to divert all his coal from Smith's tramroad (and therefore from the Glamorganshire Canal) to the Taff Vale Railway.

At this time the Royal Commission on Children's Employment published their first report which gives one measure of the size of each of the Gelligaer collieries:

	Gelligaer	Tophill	Llancaiach
Adults	127	50	40
Under 18 yrs old	13	11	10
Under 13 yrs old	10	6	6

Wages fluctuated and depended on the price coal sold for at Cardiff. In the period 1836-1841, colliers were paid from 1s 4d to 2s per ton and could expect to cut 15 or 16 tons weekly (or 3 tons daily) by working 10 hours per day. The seam was nearly six feet thick, including one foot of soft shale nearly in the centre. In March 1841, the cost of Gelligaer coal at Cardiff was calculated at 6s 6d per ton:

Price paid to collier per ton 1s 5d
Drawing coal to the level mouth 1s 4d
(allowance for tram plates, pit wood repairs and oil etc)★
From the level to the canal Basin 9d
including wayleave *(Llanfabon tramroad tonnage charge)*
From the canal Basin to Cardiff 1s 11d
Rent 1s 1d
TOTAL 6s 6d

★ *For Llancaiach and Gelligaer Collieries, where pits were used, the cost of bringing coal to the surface was an additional 3d or 4d per ton.*

The expense at Cardiff of removing coal from the canal boats and loading the ships, with allowances to captains and other expenses, amounted to about 10d per ton. While the Gelligaer collieries were paying colliers 1s 5d per ton, Walter Coffin in the lower Rhondda was paying the same and George Insole was paying 1s 10d but his colliery was on stop awaiting a rise in the market.[9]

Sir Christopher Smith died in 1839, aged 41.[10] His eldest son was only 15 and the executors understandably chose to liquidate his South Wales assets. The Llanfabon colliery had already closed. From peak years of 1826 and 1827,

General View Abercynon.

The foreground of this general view of Abercynon of about 1910 shows the canal company's former maintenance yard and workshops, by then the property of the colliery. The site had been chosen by Dadford as the highest point in the Taff Valley with room enough for the yards. The earliest group of buildings was the central complex, dominated by the standard GCC pattern house set back from but facing the canal. The large house to the left, with the two bays, and the two-storey chimney-less range, were a much later addition but pre-dated the colliery. At the far end of the wall a crane survives on the towpath. Here, during canal days, work went on in a rural setting echoing to the sounds of blacksmiths, sawyers and lock gate makers, and the shouts of men with horses. The June 1885 survey indicated that the whole canal was operated in a run-down state, with buildings and works very dilapidated. The canal administration had already moved from Abercynon to Cardiff and Navigation House was reported 'let to Mr Wm Jones'. This brought an end to the long reign of Thomas Shepherd, who had been appointed Clerk at Navigation House in 1851. Navigation Yard was in a depressing state with the covered saw pit and the fitters', smiths' and carpenters' shops 'all out of repair'. Among the men serving the company at Abercynon in 1885 were George Lewis – the mason, Williams – a book keeper and Thos. Edwards – the carpenter. Known as 'Tom One Flasher' by the boatmen, Tom was responsible for disconnecting one of the top gate paddles (or 'flashers') on the locks in an effort to keep down maintenance costs.
SR collection

GENERAL VIEW ABERCYNON

This apparently tranquil scene would have been photographed to a background of incessant noise from coal trains on the Taff Vale Railway and from pit-head activity at the Dowlais-Cardiff Colliery. In this photograph a canal boat is using the old loading dock of the Dowlais Company to turn. Here in days past were the sidings of the southern extremity of the Merthyr Tramroad and Llanfabon tramroad, where sale coal from the Dowlais and Gelligaer pits was transshipped to canal for Cardiff. In the 1880s the Dowlais Company built a steelworks at a new seaboard site at East Moors Cardiff, destined to replace the works at Dowlais itself. To supply this new works with coking coal they sank the Dowlais-Cardiff Colliery at Abercynon – then the deepest pit in the coalfield. The pit was conveniently sited between the railway and the canal and led to significant expansion of the village of Abercynon, including the building of the massively impressive

Miners' Institute in 1905, just to be discerned in the centre distance. A large stock of Baltic timber pit props is stacked between the road and the railway sidings at the station beyond. The crew are turning the boat before unloading their cargo at the colliery wharf, just left off picture, where there was a connecting tramway. Immediately opposite the dock and below the walled yard, is the Canal Company's old dry dock. Steps can be seen descending into it and there is a protective railing on the towpath where once a bridge would have been at its entrance. Next to the steps is the paddle for draining the dock into the river. In 1893, with the impending abandonment of the upper section of the Glamorganshire and the whole of the Aberdare, the company's workshops were closed at Navigation Yard and were moved down the valley to the vacant premises of the Cambrian Patent Fuel Works at Gabalfa.

SR collection

179

when the canal respectively carried 8,500 and 10,660 tons of his coal to Cardiff, exports slumped to just 607 and 60 tons in 1833 and 1834.

As far as the tramroad is concerned, it is still recorded as being in the hands of Smith's executors in 1855 and continuing to be used by Duncan & Co. No records have been found for its operation. A weighing machine was situated on the tramroad, just west of the junction to the old Llanfabon colliery and where all traffic would have passed. Houses on the site were named appropriately Tai Machine. The route was a gentle gradient down the valley as far as Fiddler's Elbow, where the tramroad crossed the Cardiff to Merthyr turnpike and turned southward to drop by a steep incline to the canal Basin.

Beaumont's letter (written when Powell was operating the tramroad) suggests that the tonnage rate was 3d per mile but no accounts have survived. Howard Meyrick wrote that '*in its heyday, it was a scene of much activity when as many as 63 'journeys' weekly, averaging 48 tons each and pulled by teams of six horses, passed over the weighing machine.*' His source is not stated and may simply be calculated, for there must certainly have been a high level of traffic to support the figures in annual returns of the Glamorganshire Canal – 18,246 tons in 1830, 69,840 tons in 1833 and 71,710 tons in 1834. The 1834 figure is made up predominantly of Thomas Powell's coal and compares with coal shipments by canal to Cardiff from the other main coal owners in that year – 56,432 tons by Walter Coffin, 18,754 tons by Lucy Thomas and 11,772 tons by George Insole. It was not long before the highly successful Powell moved further westward in the coalfield and was sinking pits in the Cynon Valley, to add to his coal shipments down the Glamorganshire Canal.

Although it has previously been supposed that the Llanfabon tramroad was horse-drawn throughout its history, a report in the *Cardiff & Merthyr Guardian* of 8 August 1840 describes a boy being run down and killed by an engine on the tramroad. Edward Williams, a 12 year old, was returning three horses from his work. Hearing the engine coming down after him, he turned the horses into a parting of the tramroad. As the engine approached, one of the horses turned back towards the main line and in trying to stop him the boy got caught in the engine. This report is too early for it to refer to the, as yet unopened, TVR branch, which was also worked by horses.

Most coal traffic diverted from the tramroad to the TVR branch in the 1840s, although this was slow to happen because of Thomas Powell's dispute with his own TVR who would not allow him to run his own trains and use his own locomotives.[11] Tramroad branches remained to connect collieries with the railways but the main tramroad to the canal fell into disuse. In 1862, a movement, supported by Thomas Shepherd who was also Clerk of the GCC, began to persuade the Plymouth Estate that the '*Old Tramway leading from Cardiff Road towards Nelson Village . . . be made into a Turnpike Road to avoid the dreadful Hill at Quakers Yard.*' Final agreement to build the road was reached on 2 February 1864, after the route had been secured from the possibility of subsidence from coal mining beneath it.[12] The incline portion of the tramroad from Fiddlers Elbow can still be walked as it makes its way above the line of the Merthyr Tramroad to the site of the basin.

An enlargement of the boat from the picture on the previous page. It appears to be a standard provisions boat with cabin and is carrying casks, possibly of grease for the Dowlais-Cardiff colliery. The load is not particularly heavy, as the boat floats relatively high in the water. The boatman is on the towpath leading the horse, whilst his butty, having helped in the winding operation, is standing on the dockside about to rejoin the boat.

SR collection

NOTES TO CHAPTER 8

1 *The Cambrian*, 6 Nov 1813.
2 For example GRO D/D Pl 945/22.
3 Burke states 1821 but a copy of his will in Worcester Record Office (705:847) is dated 7 Feb 1820 with a codicil dated 23 May 1820.
4 GRO D/D Tho 1108.
5 GRO D/D Pl 580, Pl 945/26,28,30, and Pl 620A/1-3.
6 GRO D/D Pl 946/7.
7 John Davies *Cardiff and the Marquesses of Bute*, Cardiff 1981, p236 and 222.
8 PRO RAIL 684.1.
9 Letter from Robert Beaumont to Lord Bute 5 March 1841, CCL Bute VII 44 (7) and from the Children's Employment Commission Report, 1842.
10 Copy of his will in Worcestershire Record Office 705:847, dated 7 April 1839, with a codicil dated 9 July 1839, probate granted 3 Sept 1840.
11 See Colin Chapman *The Nelson and Ynysybwl Branches of the Taff Vale Railway*, Oxford 1997 for a full account.
12 GRO D/D Pl 819, 820, 821.

Chapter 9

TO PONTYPRIDD

When William Edwards completed his new stone arch at Pont y ty Pridd in 1756, it was purely to replace a succession of earlier wooden structures and a ford on the Taff river, where the ancient route to Eglwys Ilan, from Llanwonno and the farmsteads of the lower Rhondda, crossed. For some time after the Glamorganshire Canal was built to pass close by, the locality remained a rural setting and the celebrated 'Newbridge' was simply a mecca for British artists seeking an Arcadian atmosphere for their paintings.[1]

From Navigation the canal was now on the east bank of the River Taff, heading south towards Newbridge, keeping to the western edge of Graig Evan Leyshon common and, for most of the 19th century, travelling through unspoilt countryside. This rural interlude was finally to change in the mid 1880s, with the sinking of Albion colliery on Ynyscaedugwg farm, just below the lock of that name. The mining community of Cilfynydd was quickly established here, complete with rows of terraced houses above the canal where it clung precariously to the side of the valley. The settlement was served by a warehouse provided by the Marquess of Bute who, following his purchase of the Glamorganshire and Aberdare Canals, sought to run market boats to some of the canalside communities. Boats continued to arrive at Cilfynydd until the breach there in 1915 led to the canal's closure above Pontypridd.

Pontypridd

Between Cilfynydd and Coed Penmaen, the canal passed Pont Shon Norton and the Pontypridd Chemical Works. This was a wood distillery owned by Chivers, Todd & Chivers, who also had a vinegar factory (the Cambrian Vinegar Co) on Merthyr Road and at the wharf in Cardiff. In Kelly's 1871 Directory they advertised as '*manufacturers of acetate of Lead, soda and lime, vegetable naphthas, solvent and miscible, mineral naphtha grease, vegetable oils, pitch etc*'. Some of their shipments, including receipts of coal and wood via the Aberdare Canal, are shown on the August 1863 GCC down tonnage book. Glan Ely bridge, on the canal close by the works, later became known by boatmen, quite naturally, as 'Distillery Bridge'.

The canal next skirted the common lands of Coed Penmaen, to round which boats were slowed down by a series of seven locks (numbers 26 to 32), past Trallwn to below Ynysangharad. This, coupled with the canal's proximity to the river bridge, was therefore a natural spot at which a community would be born. In fact, three communities with quite separate characteristics formed along this short stretch of canal. These were Coedpenmaen, Trallwn and Ynysangharad.

Lock 28 was the site of a pair of limekilns built on the edge of Coedpenmaen Common as early as 1796, by Edward Edmunds.[2] Here, imported limestone was burned for use on the farm and also, increasingly, for the building industry. The GCC minute books record an incident at the Limekiln Lock when Thomas Jones, in charge of boat number 7, was pressed for damage caused by his boat.[3] In later years Ashton's timber yard was situated here, initially on the towpath side, before moving to a site across the canal.[4] At this place too, Coedpenmaen foundry was established to provide ironware for the building trade and the other industries, including coal mining. Harrison's 1830 map shows an arm of the canal serving these premises, although nothing is mentioned in the minute books. The nearby public house bore the name Newbridge Arms. A lock keeper's house was not built at Coedpenmaen until 1834.[5] By the 1840s, the Davies family had a boat yard here and the family were still in business through the 1880s. Boat 501, one of the last to work on the canal, is said to have been built here.[6]

In 1893, when the town of Pontypridd was approaching its population peak, the local baker Hopkin Morgan had the old foundry arm dug out and lined, so the canal could serve his steam-powered bakery. Some of the last canal deliveries to Pontypridd were of Spillers flour from Cardiff docks. The building contract for the Hopkin Morgan canal arm and its towpath bridge are in the Glamorgan Record Office.[7] Bertie (Robert) Parry is the boatman remembered as having taken the first load into the basin. He lived at a house near Pwllywhyad bridge (Treforest) and would sleep in the boat at Melingriffith or Tongwynlais. 'Billy Ringtail' was his butty[8].

In 1817, the growing amount of traffic through the Newbridge locks caused the canal committee to appoint a second lock keeper and to have a cottage built to house

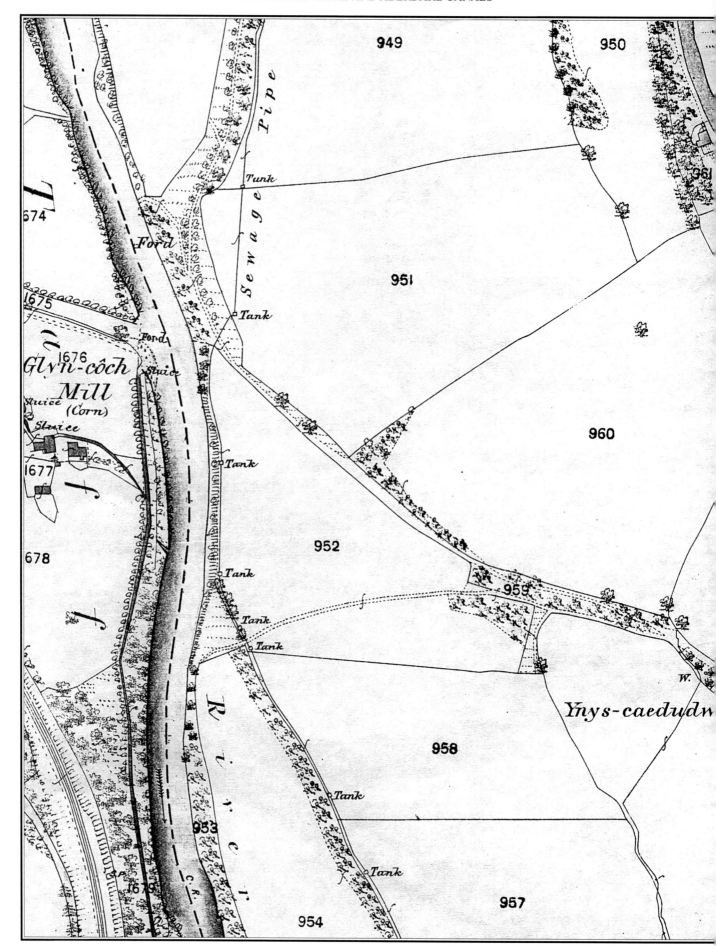

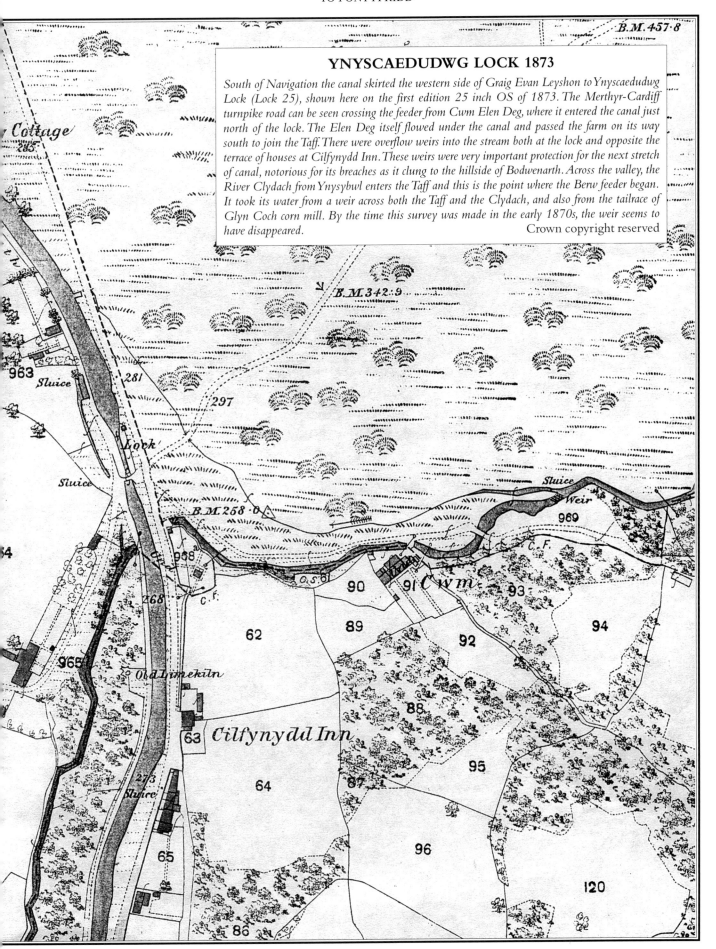

YNYSCAEDUDWG LOCK 1873

South of Navigation the canal skirted the western side of Graig Evan Leyshon to Ynyscaedudwg Lock (Lock 25), shown here on the first edition 25 inch OS of 1873. The Merthyr-Cardiff turnpike road can be seen crossing the feeder from Cwm Elen Deg, where it entered the canal just north of the lock. The Elen Deg itself flowed under the canal and passed the farm on its way south to join the Taff. There were overflow weirs into the stream both at the lock and opposite the terrace of houses at Cilfynydd Inn. These weirs were very important protection for the next stretch of canal, notorious for its breaches as it clung to the hillside of Bodwenarth. Across the valley, the River Clydach from Ynysybwl enters the Taff and this is the point where the Berw feeder began. It took its water from a weir across both the Taff and the Clydach, and also from the tailrace of Glyn Coch corn mill. By the time this survey was made in the early 1870s, the weir seems to have disappeared. Crown copyright reserved

The valley floor stretch of canal from Navigation south to Pontypridd was broken in 1885-7 by the sinking of the Albion colliery, adjacent to Ynyscaeduduwg Lock (number 25). The open lower lock gates can just be seen to the right of the bridge in this postcard of 1906, one of a series of the locality published by Curtis. The photograph depicts a bye trader's boat being loaded with small coal, probably destined for one of the patent fuel works lower down the canal. The man in the bow, near to the horse and cart, is using his shovel to trim the load round the towing mast. The boat's horse is presumably resting in a field or at stables nearby. The coal wharf would have been sited on the opposite side of the canal from the colliery in order not to restrict the towpath. Adjacent to the coal heaps can also be seen the terminus of the electric passenger tramway from Pontypridd. The colliery was sunk at Ynyscaeduduwg farm, and the stone hut on the canal bank beyond and to the left of the leftmost telegraph pole is the site of one of the many agricultural limekilns which served the farms along the path of the canal. The stone wall, to be seen above the horse-cart, marks where the Caeduduwg Brook passes beneath the canal. The main trestle footbridge over canal and railway from village to colliery can be seen in the southern distance. At the Albion, in 1894, occurred one of South Wales' worst underground explosions, killing 287 colliers. The colliery was also the source of much concern to the canal company as they suffered regularly from subsidence, from as early as 1890. In July 1915, a serious breach, swept away the railway also. The breach was never repaired and the canal became effectively closed north of Pontypridd.

SR collection

Cilfynydd photographer Curtis's study of colliers on the early shift, making their way from the village across the canal to Albion pit. Brian Lewis collection

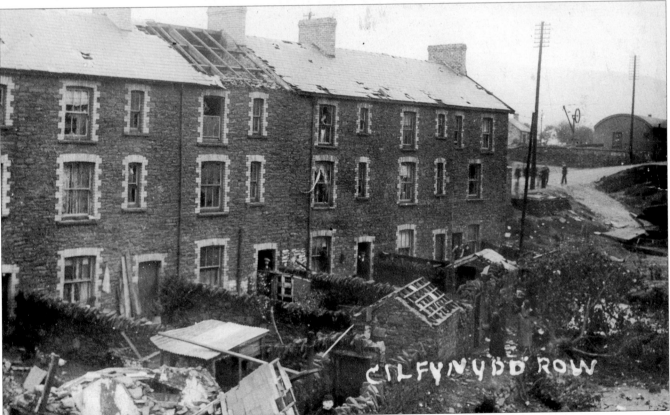

On 27 October 1913, about eleven miles of the Taff Valley experienced a serious tornado, whose devastation was well-photographed by the local postcard publishers. Here at Cilfynydd, the photographer has incidentally captured part of the canal at Ynyscaedudwg Lock for our benefit. The crane and warehouse (similar to those at Abercynon and Pontypridd) are remaining evidence of the late 1880s push by the Marquess of Bute to increase market traffic on the canal. Dave Morgan collection

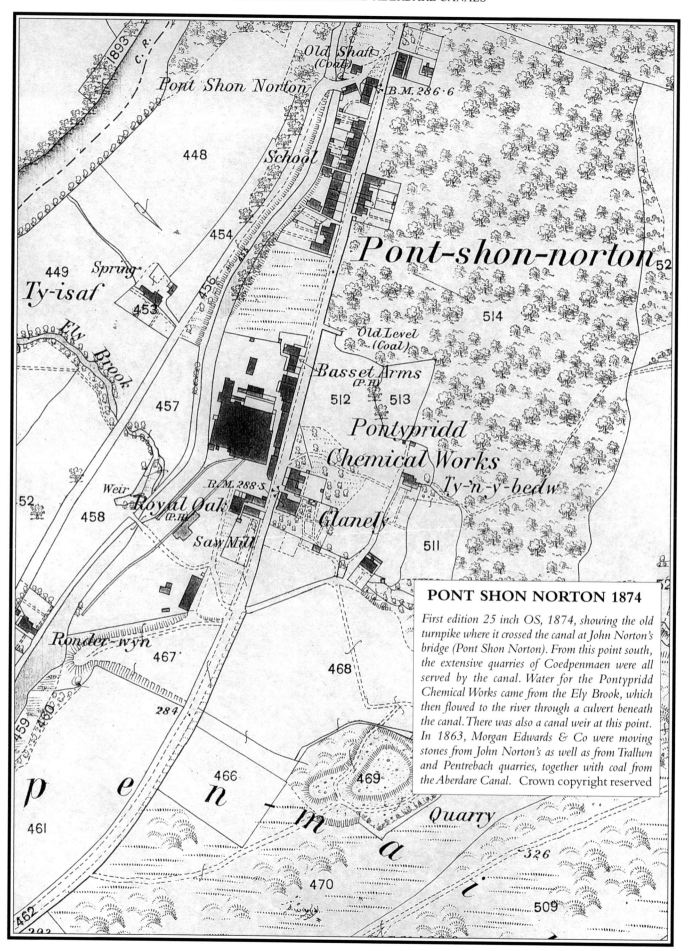

PONT SHON NORTON 1874

First edition 25 inch OS, 1874, showing the old turnpike where it crossed the canal at John Norton's bridge (Pont Shon Norton). From this point south, the extensive quarries of Coedpenmaen were all served by the canal. Water for the Pontypridd Chemical Works came from the Ely Brook, which then flowed to the river through a culvert beneath the canal. There was also a canal weir at this point. In 1863, Morgan Edwards & Co were moving stones from John Norton's as well as from Trallwn and Pentrebach quarries, together with coal from the Aberdare Canal. Crown copyright reserved

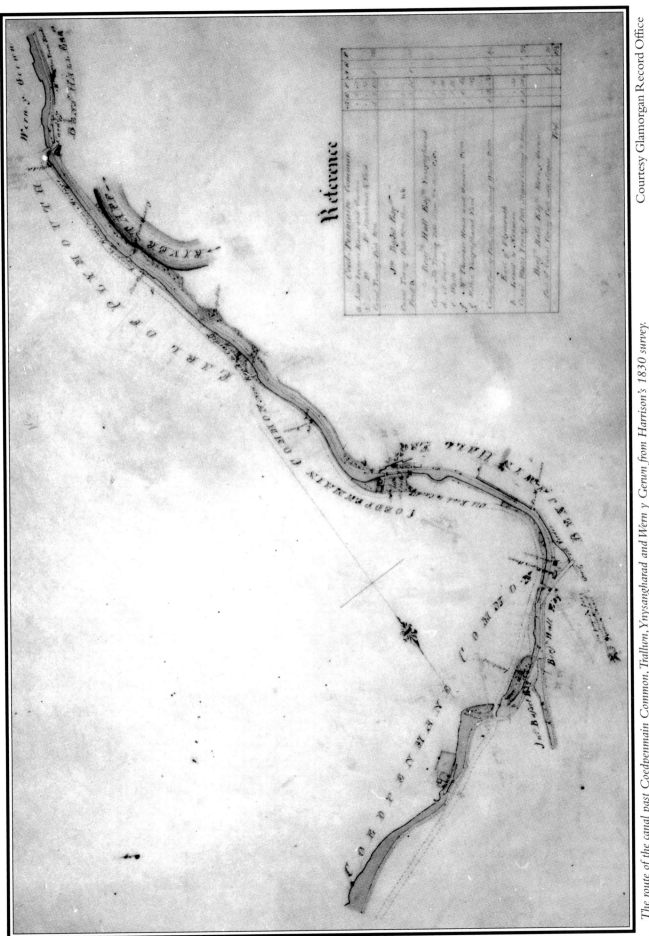

The route of the canal past Coedpenmain Common, Trallwn, Ynysangharad and Wern y Genun from Harrison's 1830 survey.

Courtesy Glamorgan Record Office

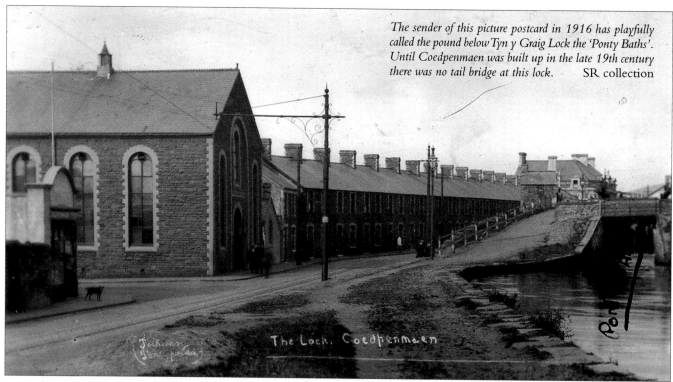

The sender of this picture postcard in 1916 has playfully called the pound below Tyn y Graig Lock the 'Ponty Baths'. Until Coedpenmaen was built up in the late 19th century there was no tail bridge at this lock.   SR collection

The Lock. Coedpenmaen

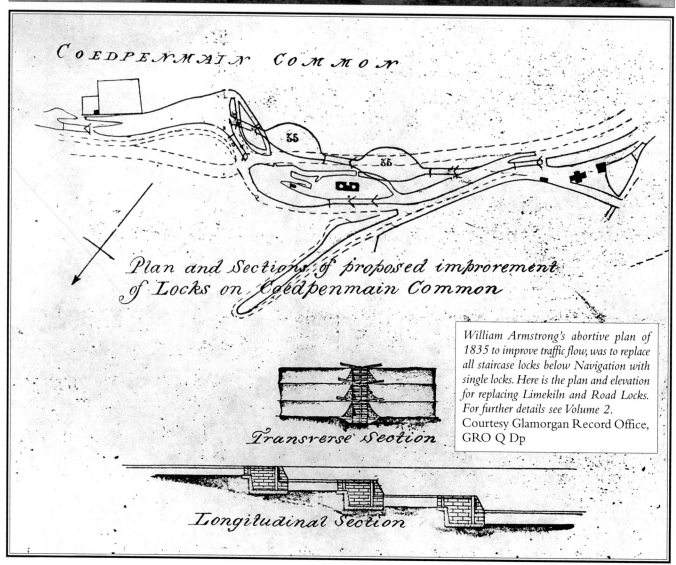

COEDPENMAIN COMMON

Plan and Sections of proposed improvement of Locks on Coedpenmain Common

William Armstrong's abortive plan of 1835 to improve traffic flow, was to replace all staircase locks below Navigation with single locks. Here is the plan and elevation for replacing Limekiln and Road Locks. For further details see Volume 2.
Courtesy Glamorgan Record Office, GRO Q Dp

Transverse Section

Longitudinal Section

Where the canal passed through what became urban areas, it was inevitable that the over-bridges would require alteration to accommodate the changing road traffic needs. In 1899, Pontypridd Urban District Council was given permission by the canal company to widen the four main canal bridges in its area – Pont Shon Norton, Coedpenmaen, Trallwn and Gwern y Geryn. This is Coedpenmaen Road bridge, which took the original Cardiff-Merthyr turnpike across the canal. The lock was known as Road Lock. The photograph is one of the series taken by Cardiff Corporation for their 1943 survey, when they purchased the canal from the Butes.
Courtesy Cardiff City Library

Taken at the same time and from the same spot on the towpath as the view on above, this photograph is looking 'downstream' and shows the entrance to the top of the double staircase Limekiln Locks (Locks 28 and 29). On the left was the small basin where boats delivered limestone and coal for the kilns. These were built against the bank of the locks, allowing them to be charged from the top and the burnt lime to be raked out from the bottom. Between the upper lock chamber and what might be the remains of the kilns, a canal company cast iron lamp post can just be made out.
Courtesy Cardiff City Library

Hopkin Morgan bakery, East Street, Pontypridd circa 1960. The single storey buildings in the foreground stand on the filled-in canal basin.
J. Gross photo

189

A dramatic representation of the depth inside a staircase of locks – numbers 28 and 29.
Courtesy Cardiff City Library

him at Trallwn.[9] There is a dearth of information in the canal company minute books relating to activity at Trallwn, any development in the movement of shop goods taking second place to the main function of the canal. Nevertheless, through the early decades of the 19th century, Newbridge gradually took over from Llantrisant as the market town for Rhondda. The main impetus for this shift was not just the Glamorganshire Canal but the building of Dr Richard Griffiths' tramroad, which ran from coal pits at Dinas and Porth along the right bank of the Rhondda, past Newbridge, to his coal canal at Treforest, which then linked with the Glamorganshire Canal.[10] From its opening in 1809 until well after the opening of the Rhondda branch of the Taff Vale Railway, the Doctor's tramroad offered a convenient method of passenger transport, its trains of empty coal drams accommodating womenfolk returning

into the hills with their shopping from markets at Treforest and later from Newbridge.[11] By the 1830s, Trallwn had its own canalside community supporting the handling of incoming merchandise. In June 1833 it is recorded that the canal company's warehouse there was to be let and the following year permission was given to Nathaniel Jones to put in steps to his granary on the canal company's land.[12] This granary gave the name to Cornstores Hill. whose road rises steeply from this point on the canal to the turnpike and the common beyond. In later years it was occupied by William Lewis.

The growth of the Rhondda steam coal industry from the 1830s really began to put Newbridge on the map. Edwards' high river arch proved an inconvenience to modern traffic and in 1853 a public subscription was organised in the town for another new river bridge.[13] The GCC committee minuted that they would 'cheerfully' increase warehouse accommodation for goods at Trallwn when a site for the bridge was agreed. To their delight the new bridge was built, unsympathetically, right alongside the old one, so the established route from the canal wharves at Trallwn needed no alteration. In 1856 Newbridge's postmaster decided that the town should revert to its old name to differentiate itself from all other Newbridges and so, abbreviated slightly, it gained the name by which it is still known today – Pontypridd.[14]

For many years, market boats from Cardiff delivered to Trallwn to a regular timetable. In the 1870s and 80s, Thomas Thomas, J.J. Thomas and Davis & Son are listed as canal carriers here. When the Marquess of Bute took over the canal in the mid 1880s, the canal company itself commenced carrying to Pontypridd and Abercynon. Six horses were stabled at Trallwn for GCC deliveries to town and district. Bill Gomer started with the canal company in January 1901 and was put in charge of the chain horse delivering to Hafod and Graig. The chain horse was put in front of the horse in shafts, to assist on the steep hills in these districts. At this time, Martha Thomas was GCC agent at the Trallwn canal office. Several pubs and beer houses clustered around the canal company's own buildings at Trallwn, including the Llanover Arms, the Crown Inn and the grand Queens Hotel (all three on the road to the river bridge).

In 1800, round the corner from Trallwn, at Ynysangharad, Richard Crawshay built a small iron forge, which he subsequently sold in 1810 to the Tappendens of Abernant ironworks (on the newly-opened Aberdare Canal) for them to convert to rolling mills. Following the Tappenden bankruptcy, the

The surviving corn stores at Trallwn on 17 April 1971, still identifiable in design as a grain warehouse. The photograph is taken from the slope of the horse path; the chamber of Lock 30 is on the right.
ILW photo, neg 2261

Trallwn bridge, at the foot of Corn Stores Hill and the tail of Lock 30, connected the centre of Pontypridd with the old Cardiff road through Coedpenmaen. The road ran adjacent to the canal at this point, behind William Lewis's 1850's corn stores which are seen beyond the lock. Trallwn bridge had already been rebuilt at least once in its lifetime, from what was originally probably close to the usual pattern of over-bridge at a lock tail, to the elegant low elliptical arch which appears in the background of the 1893 publicity shot of Trallwn wharf overleaf. This present photograph shows how the 1899 widening was undertaken by replacing the stone parapets with latticed wrought iron and by building additional stone abutments to take the bridge extension on the downstream side. The electric tramway to the Albion colliery, Cilfynydd, was laid across the new bridge and opened in 1905. The picture is by local photographers Thos. Forrest & Sons.   Courtesy Pontypridd Heritage Centre

The same photographer took this view of the widened Trallwn bridge circa 1902, looking from the Corn Stores towards Pontypridd. Between the bridge and the lock keeper's house on the left was Canal Place, which led from the public wharf servicing Pontypridd. The importance of this area as a gateway to Pontypridd is perhaps indicated by the existence of the three inns – the commodious Queen's Hotel, the more modest Crown Hotel and, hidden by the lock keeper's house, the Llanover Arms. The canal is now lost under the new road but the Llanover Arms remains in business.

Courtesy Pontypridd Heritage Centre

Although this is quite clearly a publicity photograph, it well presents industry and prosperity at Treflum wharf in 1893. The canal was now in the hands of the Marquess of Bute, who had been thwarted in his attempt to close it and convert it to a railway. Forced to make a go of it, he offered support to Lewis Llewelyn's proposals for a regular service of market boats to serve Pontypridd, Cilfynydd and Abercynon, from Cardiff. The steam boat Bute was purchased for this purpose and she puts on as modern a face as was possible on a narrow canal of the day. The photograph was again taken by Thos. Forrest & Sons.

A drawing made in 1943 by J.K. Roberts of the old GCC warehouse and crane at Trallwn wharf.

Trallwn bridge and a portion of the Queen's Hotel can be seen at the end of Ynysangharad Street in this photograph, the main subject of which is the canal company's fine warehouse of Pennant stone, roofed with Welsh slate. ILW photo, neg 2262

Below: *Trallwn wharf in 1943. On the left is the canal company's warehouse and crane (in the shadow of the building). Closer to the camera, on the extreme left, are some of the cottages of Canal Square. The photograph shows clear evidence of dumping taking place into the canal, from alongside the company's other warehouse in Ynysangharad Street.*
Courtesy Cardiff City Library

The rear of Canal Place, Trallwn in 1945, showing the collection of canal-side buildings which formerly housed a thriving community who helped supply Pontypridd with produce imported via the Glamorganshire Canal.
Courtesy Pontypridd Library

site became the Brown Lenox chain and anchor works from 1816. Brown Lenox were based on the bank of the Thames at Millwall, manufacturing chain cable with iron supplied by the Crawshays from their nearby George Yard in London. By founding a new works on the canal at Ynysangharad, they became much closer to their Cyfarthfa point of supply, while also being close to the seaboard for exporting their finished products via the canal through Cardiff. It was the chain works which provided further impetus for the growth of a settlement at Newbridge and particularly round the chain works itself. Brown Lenox were the premier manufacturers of chain cable. One of their most famous orders was for Brunel's steamship *Great Eastern*. Others included the Cunard liners *Mauretania* and *Aquitania* and the battleships *Lion*, *Dreadnaught*, *Rodney* and *Hood*.[15] Among the many pubs associated with the chain works were the Bunch of Grapes, Cable & Anchor and Union Bridge Inn. The latter was named after the chain suspension bridge over the River Tweed, which was one of many chain bridges also built by Brown Lenox.

Another main employer at Newbridge was the quarrying industry, as the route of the canal conveniently passed close to what became commercially obvious spots to start cutting the Pennant sandstone from Coed Penmaen common. The stone was used for constructing the canal locks and banks, and later for building houses for the Chain Works' workforce but was also sold further afield through the availability of canal transport. John Morgan was possibly one quarry owner when he was granted a 99 year lease in 1814, for a piece of land 90 feet long between the canal

and the turnpike road near Ynysangharad, for building a house and perhaps a stone wharf.[16] Alternatively, he may have been the John Morgan, lock keeper since 1801, who at last was being allowed a house at Ynysangharad and who the following year was moved to Cardiff and appointed Pool Master. He died in 1838 after a long career at Cardiff and the canal company paid his widow £50 to show their gratitude for his service.[17]

After 1915, when the canal was permanently closed above the Cilfynydd breach, the effective terminus was at Coedpenmaen. Sporadic traffic continued to the warehouses at Trallwn and to Hopkin Morgan's bakery, until the outbreak of the Second World War. Tom Frazer, with his son Cyril as butty, was the last boatman to call at Trallwn. The boat was number 451 and the date was Saturday 23 May 1942. They returned empty to their house at Treble Locks the same day. On Monday he took No. 451 empty to Cardiff and was told when he got there that the canal had breached at Nantgarw.[18]

An Insight into the Timber Trade

John Daniel's account book for the period 1817-1857 is a surviving detailed record of a timber and coal merchant's business in the Pontypridd district. The cost accounts of pitwood purchases indicate how much he relied upon the canal for transport.[19]

Pitwood was bought by the short cord from farms over a wide area – from Bodwenarth to Llandaff – and each lot was invariably paid 'delivered to canal side'. On 26 March 1819 there is even an entry where he has purchased 26

This is a fine view of the extent of the Brown Lenox chain and anchor works. The many chimneys are evidence of the chain-makers' forges. Until 1902, the works relied totally on canal transport. This photograph shows, in the top left, the connection to the Pontypridd, Caerphilly & Newport Railway. Even then, the canal remained the most important means of getting chains to the proving house on the Sea Lock pond at Cardiff. The light on the water shows clearly the lower basin and the towpath bridge over its entrance. Water continued beyond the basin, beneath the floor of the covered test shop, where the boats were loaded. Above the canal locks a north-bound boat can be seen waiting near the whitewashed buildings. The route to the works entrance for its employees and visitors was from the main road, between the Bunch of Grapes public house and Underhill cottages, across the canal lock tail bridge and through a modest entrance near the proving shed. ILW collection

cord 2 qtrs from the GCC itself – at a cost of 12/6d per short cord.[20]

Most entries do not specify who was the ultimate customer but a 6 October 1820 account records Daniel arranging 501 cords of pitwood from Wm. Vaughan's Penriewchybir (*sic*) farm, to be delivered direct to Cyfarthfa works at a net cost of 17/6d per cord (totalling £438 7s 6d, of which Vaughan was paid £260 11s 6d for the standing wood). The net cost includes Daniel's costs of paying his man Morgan Llewellyn 2d per cord for cutting the wood and 48 days @ 2/6d per day for cording the wood at Penriewchyber. He then paid Llewellyn £27 10s for carrying the wood to the canal and 10/- for ale (this was thirsty work). Finally, the boatage to Cyfarthfa was a hefty 4/- per cord.

Daniel also dealt in bark. A 22 June 1819 entry records his costs for stripping 12 tons of bark on Craig Alva and Brintail farms (near Glyntaf). Morgan Llewellyn's men were paid £18 9s 2d for stripping, 18s for cording, 4 guineas for hauling it to the canal, £4 15s 7d for carrying to Cardiff, 18s for loading and weighing the bark in Cardiff, and 6s for ale at Cardiff. In addition, Thomas Thomas was paid 5s to allow them to cross his field with the bark to reach the canal. This particular account does not specify the destination of the bark but a later entry of 2 October 1837 is for a consignment from three farms to J. & E. Jenkins,

Bristol tanners. To ship it from Cardiff, Daniel used both Prichard's and Pride's Bristol trading vessels. It was no doubt the ready availability of bark in the Pontypridd district which attracted the Pontypridd chemical works to a canal-side site at Pont Shon Norton.

Daniel's account book also records the timber cutting and clearance by Morgan Llewellyn's team of William Crawshay's Forest Isha farm in 1831, to make way for the building of Treforest tinplate works.

As well as pitwood and bark, there are a few entries for the purchase of cordwood in 1821-2 for charcoal burning, for Richard Blakemore of Melingriffith tinplate works. Also, Daniel dealt in hardwood, buying 108 oaks from William Williams' colliery site at Perthygleision in 1828. From 1822 to 1825 there are a number of transactions with William Rugg and in 1835 a sale of timber to Jenkins shipyard on the Sea Lock pound.

A quite separate part of the account book, although perhaps not directly related to the canal, is a fascinating record of domestic and small business coal sales in Pontypridd in the 1850s. Daniel's primary supplier was John Calvert's pit.

Arbitrarily surviving records such as this account book leave us important glimpses of what incidental traffic the canal carried, alongside the mainstream commodities of iron, stone and coal.

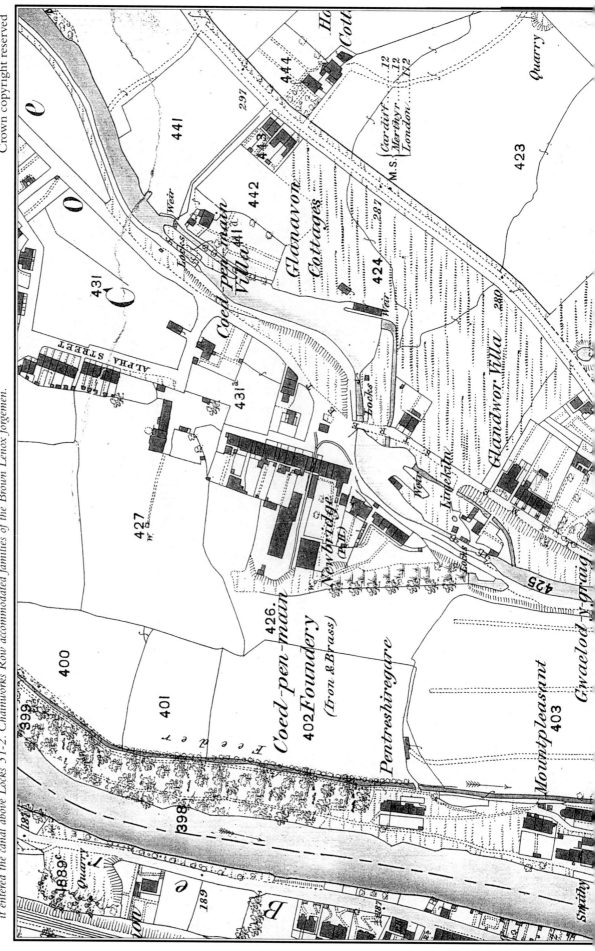

The 1874 first edition 25 inch OS of the three canal-based communities at Pontypridd. Workers housing had sprung up around Limekiln Locks and Coedpenmaen foundry. Alongside the entrance to the bypass weir at Lock 28 can be seen a small basin where the limestone boats would have unloaded. This has been thought the site of the carpenters shop, boat yard and dry dock occupied by the Davies family through the 1840s and 1880s, although Harwood's 1885 report suggests it was alongside Lock 27, which places it as the covered dock and accompanying building by the lock by-pass weir. The north-south line of trees from below Lock 29 to Coedpenmaen foundry marks an abandoned basin (shown on Harrison's 1830 plan and Armstrong's 1835 plan) but which was later dug out again in 1894 to form the canal basin to serve Hopkin Morgan's bakery. The next set of locks is at Trallwn, which was a thriving canalside community serving the needs of Pontypridd proper across the river. The upstream bridge is William Edwards' span of 1756, now supplemented by the 1857 New Bridge. The Berw feeder can be seen following the left bank of the river, having crossed it by the Berw Aqueduct. It passes beneath Llanover Street and continues closely parallel to the canal until it reaches the upper basin of the chain works, where it entered the canal above Locks 31-2. Chainworks Row accommodated families of the Brown Lenox forgemen.

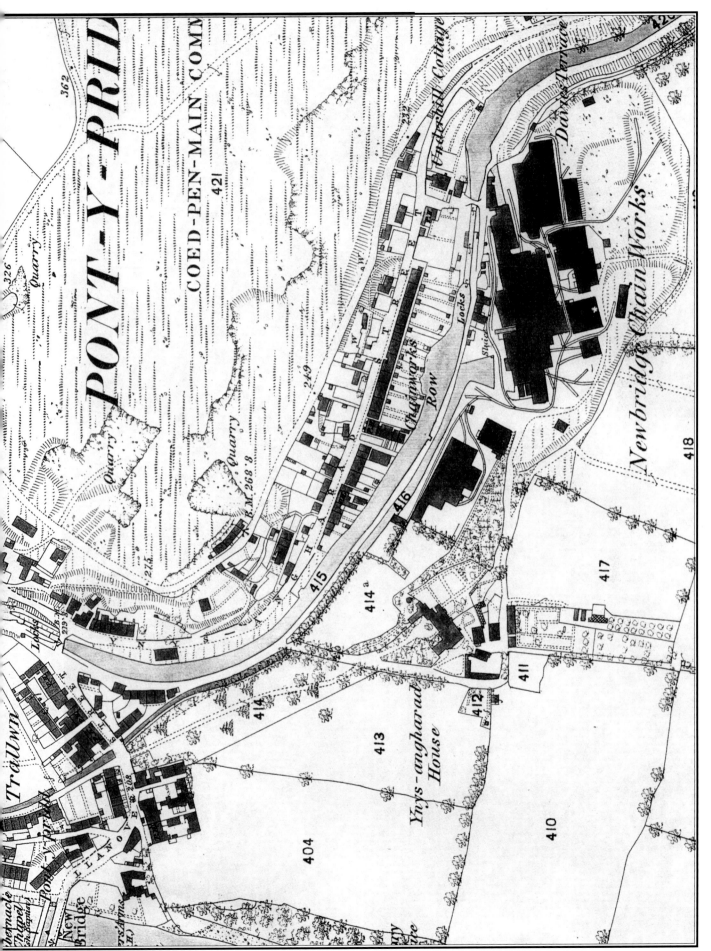

A damp day circa 1916 at Ynysangharad Locks has not prevented housewives from hanging out their washing in the back gardens of Chainworks Row. The top gate of the lock staircase is open. Note the whitewashed lock keeper's cabin and the wall with closed door to keep the public from trespassing at the lock-side. The path on this side of the canal allowed access to the back gardens from Ynysangharad Street where, in the distance, the tall GCC warehouse can be made out. The humped bridge on the towpath marks the entrance to the upper basin, which received boatloads of iron and steel from the ironworks of Merthyr and Aberdare. The large bite in the canal bank opposite allowed boats to enter and leave the basin with ease. Stocks of iron bar can be seen in the yard alongside it, near the corrugated iron canopy. The Berw feeder finished at this basin and

View of Ponty from the

partially emptied into the canal underneath the towpath bridge. A horse slip can be seen where the boy on the towpath is standing. Most of the feeder water, however, bypassed the locks and powered the works' turbines, before emptying into the canal below via the lower basin. There was also a weir here from which overflow water made its way below the canal bank, past Grove House, to the river at Pentrebach. The lock keeper's cottage is below the locks, facing the canal and alongside Underhill Cottage, partially hidden by trees. Just in picture, on the opposite bank from the lock keeper's cottage, there are two boats awaiting loading in the lower basin of the chainworks. In earlier years, from beyond the church spire in the left distance, came the Doctor's tramroad, bringing coal to the Canal from the Rhondda valleys. *SR collection*

No. 698 GLAMORGANSHIRE CANAL. UP.
PERMIT BROWN, LENOX & Co., Boat No.
Master, to pass this   day of   189

SPECIES.	T.	C.	Loaded.	Landed.
			SEA LOCK.	YNYSYNGHARAD.

GLAMORGANSHIRE CANAL.
2340 (CARRYING DEPARTMENT.)
Goods Warehouse, Cardiff.
Permit Boat No. 88 W. Thatcher June 15 1927

	TONS	CWT.	FROM	TO
Sundries	12	"	Wharf	Trwidd

Per pro Glamorganshire Canal Co.

78
GLAMORGANSHIRE CANAL.
(CARRYING DEPARTMENT.)
Goods Warehouse, Cardiff.
Dec 10 1917
Permit Boat No. 382 W. Bladen June

	TONS	CWT.	FROM	TO
Sundries	1 3/3	"	Wharf	Trwidd Trefoust

Per pro Glamorganshire Canal Co.

Top left: *An unused Brown Lenox permit of the 1890s, for carrying up the canal from the Sea Lock to the Newbridge works.*

Top right: *Bill Thatcher, of Rhydyfelin, took flour and groceries from Cardiff wharf to Trallwn on 15 June 1927, as recorded on this GCC waybill for boat No 88.*

Middle right: *William Bladen Junior, of Llandaff, is the boatman leaving Cardiff for Pontypridd with bagged flour and groceries on this GCC waybill of December 1917. The company referred to such commodities as Sundries.*

Bottom right: *There must have been an economy drive at the GCC's Pontypridd wharf in 1904, because Mrs Martha Thomas, the canal's agent at Trallwn, is recycling six-year old bill heads from the defunct Merthyr office, closed in 1898. This GC note permits a chainworks consignment to pass from Ynysanghard to the Sea Lock pound in (unusually) a canal company's boat, 1 June 1904. All ILW collection*

A delightful Brown Lenox publicity shot of mooring swivels made for the port of Calcutta in 1905. The chain-makers' shops are to the right. Faintly visible is a cabin boat lying in the basin beyond the testing shop, left. SR collection

Glamorganshire Canal Navig.
CANAL STORES,
MERTHYR TYDFIL.
No. 492 June 1st 1804
To the Warehouseman!
Please deliver to bearer allow
Boat 502 to pass
with Ton 16 - 0 - 15
Shackles &c for Lenox
to Cardiff from
Lenox & Co chain works
Ponty Prdd

for the Glamorganshire Canal Co.,
(Signed) M Thomas

NO GOODS TO BE GIVEN
WITHOUT AN ORDER.

THE CANAL LOCKS, PONTYPRIDD. 35222

A quintessential canal scene at Ynysangharad Locks on a picture postcard from the 1930s – staircase lock architecture, locktail bridge, boat, boatmen and horse. The boatman is Bill Bladen with his horse Dick. The man in the boat is thought to be Vernon Burdett and Bert Bladen is at the tiller. In recent years the photograph was published in the South Wales Echo and a staggering number of people claimed to be the boy at the lock gate.
SR collection

This is the earliest photograph so far discovered of the Glamorganshire Canal at Ynysangharad. It shows a boat leaving the lower basin, sometime before 1900. The horse is straining at the rope to bring the boat round to begin its journey south, probably down to Cardiff. The standard Glamorganshire Canal boat was ten feet shorter than the 70 foot narrowboats of the English canals. Nevertheless, this length demanded some

manoeuvrability when turning in the cut or entering basins. In the left distance, beyond the chainworks is St. Catherine's church, standing at the gateway to the Rhondda. St Catherine's architect was John Norton, after whom Pont Shon Norton was named. Its stone is likely to have come from Bodwenarth quarry.

Doug Williams collection

Bert and Willian Bladen with a loaded boat, No. 502, bound for Pontypridd in the 1920s, passing through Gabalfa towards the Cambrian Yard. The load is likely to be flour for the Hopkin Morgan bakery at Pontypridd. Note the tarpaulin at the bow, ready to cover and protect the load in bad weather. The design of the Glamorganshire Canal boat is dealt with in Volume 2. The picture was taken by S.C. Fox, an amateur photographer who worked as a journalist with the Western Mail.   Courtest Cardiff City Library

NOTES TO CHAPTER 9

1 H.P. Richards *William Edwards, Architect, Builder, Minister*, Cowbridge 1983.

2 GCC minute book 15 Jan 1796.

3 GCC minute book 29 Aug 1811.

4 Bill Gomer in conversation with ILW in 1949.

5 GCC minute book 7 Feb 1834. However, Jeremy Lowe and David Anderson, surveying the building prior to its demolition in 1971, state that the method and materials of construction suggest a date earlier than 1811; see J.B. Lowe and D.N. Anderson *Iron Industry Housing Papers 2*, Cardiff 1972.

6 ILW in conversation with Bill Gomer 2 Dec 1949.

7 GRO B/C GCa 4/116.

8 Bill Gomer in conversation with ILW in 1949 and John Close in conversation with ILW, 19 Feb 1948.

9 GCC minute book 6 Oct 1817.

10 The Doctor's tramroad and canal will be covered in Volume 2.

11 E.D. Lewis *The Rhondda Valleys*, London 1959 p114 and John Charles *Pontypridd Historical Handbook*, Pontypridd 1920 p23-4.

12 GCC minute book 5 June 1833 and 30 Dec 1834.

13 Don Powell *Victorian Pontypridd*, Cardiff 1996 p50.

14 Huw Williams *Pontypridd: Essays on the History of an Industrial Community*, Cardiff 1981 p3.

15 S.K. Jones *A Link with the Past: The History of the Newbridge Works of Brown Lenox & Co, Pontypridd*, in Glamorgan Historian Vol 11, Cowbridge 1984 and Morien *A History of Pontypridd and Rhondda Valleys*, Pontypridd 1903.

16 GCC minute book 27 Nov 1813 and 1 Mar 1814.

17 GCC minute book 25 June 1801 and 9 March 1838.

18 Tom Frazer in conversation with ILW 24 April 1948.

19 GRO D/D Xdm

20 A cord is a unit of measure equivalent to 128 cubic feet of round or split wood. A standard cord measures 4 feet by 4 feet by 8 feet. A short cord is 4 feet by 8 feet by any length of wood under 4 feet.

Chapter 10

THE WATER SUPPLY TO THE CANAL AT NEWBRIDGE

The history of the Graig yr Esk feeder, from the confluence of the Nant Clydach and the River Taff to the canal north of Ynysangharad, is bound up with the succession of ironworks that operated on the site at Newbridge, which ultimately became occupied by the Brown Lenox Chain and Anchor Works.

In 1800, when Richard Crawshay built his forge at Ynysangharad, he arranged with the Glamorganshire Canal Company that water from the canal could drive his mills, providing it returned to the canal below the double Locks 31 and 32.[1] Details of the operation of this forge, nail works or rolling mill are scant. Crawshay had had ideas for 'iron manufactures' closer to Cardiff right from the early years of planning the canal. His letter of 14 August 1788 to James Cockshutt states '*I believe he* [John Kemeys Tynte] *has the very spott on which I wish to build a Mill below new Bridge*'.[2] John Bird's diary entry of 7 October 1790 includes '*Mr Crawshay and Mr Homfray are looking out for a place near the Town* [Cardiff] *to errect a manufactory for nails and Hardware*'.[3] Although Crawshay is said to have acquired land, including the Forest Estate, further down the valley in 1794,[4] it seems his intentions to build the forge did not reach fruition until the transport arrangements were firmly established and he was confident he had the people to manage an extension of his empire away from the Cyfarthfa site. The Newbridge works was built on land purchased by Crawshay in 1799 from Lord Dynevor and John Richards. The works is referred to obliquely in G. W. Manby's 1801 tour: '*turning down a lane beyond MR CRAWSHAW'S new Forge, the beautiful structure of Pont-y-Pridd bursts on the sight.*'[5]

This is quoted in Brooke's *Chronology of the Tinplate Works of Great Britain* (p117). He cites this quotation mistakenly as referring to Treforest Tinplate Works but this was not built until the mid 1830s. Wilkins' *Iron, Steel, Tinplate* (p228) states incorrectly that the Treforest works were acquired by the Crawshays in 1794 and he goes on to confuse Treforest with the Newbridge site. This confusion is repeated in Charles' *Handbook* (p14) and in Brooke's second edition of his *Chronology*, whereas his first (of 1932, p95) does not include the references and is closer to the truth. A further unsourced reference in Charles and in Brooke's second edition maintains '*he* [Crawshay] *built large tin mills which were in 1806 the largest in the kingdom*' (Charles) and

'*A writer in 1806 stated that Mr Crawshay's tinplate works at Treforest had greater production than Melingriffith*' (Brooke). Brooke's source is an interpretation of Charles, who had confused Malkin's observations in his 1803 tour, published in 1807, which referred to Melingriffith, not Treforest. Charles further confuses his sources, for he first quotes (p16) Lewis's *Topographical Dictionary* of 1833 incorrectly as being of 1813; later (p25) he again quotes Lewis '*the establishment of tin mills* [at Treforest], *which are now completed and in full production, and they are said to be the largest tin mills in the world.*' This quotation is from Lewis's third edition of 1843, whereas Charles leaves the reader to believe it to be 1813. The truth is the only tinplate works in the Taff Valley before 1834 was the Melingriffith Works and that Crawshay's only ironworks south of Merthyr was the forge at Newbridge. The only mill on the Forest estate in 1794 was a corn mill and its demise during the building of the tinplate works is recorded in William Crawshay's correspondence.[6]

Little further has been found to substantiate the operation of this Newbridge works. The nature of its water supply would have restricted the scale of the concern, as Crawshay would have had to be careful not to run the pounds dry above the double Ynysangharad Locks when operating his mills. Surface water channelled to enter the canal from Coedpenmaen Common might have helped but the fact that little documentary evidence survives suggests that the operation was not important to the Crawshay empire. It is difficult to believe there was enough water to drive substantial rolling mills. The likelihood is that the forge was a nailery with small rolling and slitting mills.[7] Wilkins and Morien, both writing in 1903, imply that there was '*a small blast furnace*' on the site but this is doubtful and they are probably confusing a blast furnace with a remelting furnace.[8]

Crawshay had purchased the land on which the forge stood. In 1808, the canal company questioned whether his land included the yard behind the lock keeper's house.[9] Richard Crawshay died in June 1810 and bequeathed the lands at Newbridge to his son-in-law Benjamin Hall. Just before his death, Crawshay sold the Newbridge Works to the Tappendens, whose blast furnaces operated at the Abernant ironworks at Aberdare. The Aberdare Canal was

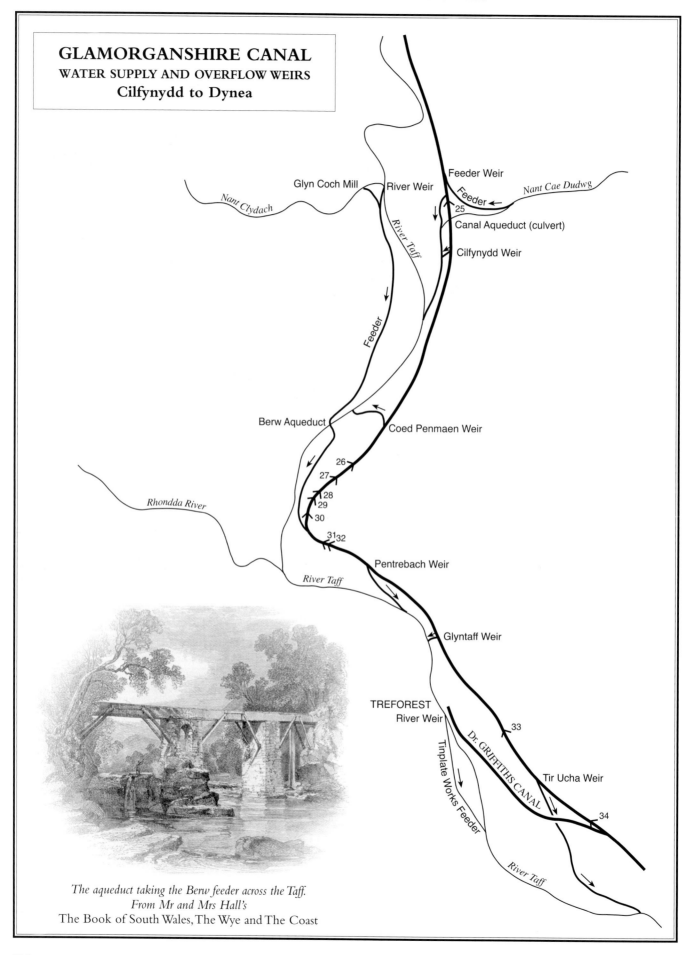

GLAMORGANSHIRE CANAL
WATER SUPPLY AND OVERFLOW WEIRS
Cilfynydd to Dynea

Nant Clydach

Glyn Coch Mill

River Weir

Feeder Weir

Feeder

Nant Cae Dudwg

River Taff

25

Canal Aqueduct (culvert)

Cilfynydd Weir

Feeder

Berw Aqueduct

Coed Penmaen Weir

26

27

28

29

30

Rhondda River

31 32

River Taff

Pentrebach Weir

Glyntaff Weir

TREFOREST
River Weir

Dr. GRIFFITHS CANAL

33

Tinplate Works Feeder

Tir Ucha Weir

34

River Taff

The aqueduct taking the Berw feeder across the Taff.
From Mr and Mrs Hall's
The Book of South Wales, The Wye and The Coast

The Caedudwg feeder in 1907, flowing through Cwm Elen Deg. The spoil tips from the Albion colliery can already be seen on the hillside to the right. SR collection

The dam on the Caedudwg Brook created an acceptable open-air bathing pool for residents of Cilfynydd. The feeder left the stream on the left. SR collection

finally being built after almost twenty years of procrastination and the owners of the three ironworks at the head of the Cynon Valley were planning to re-direct the majority of their raw output from the Neath Canal, and its connecting tramroad, to the Aberdare and Glamorganshire Canals.[10] More land was leased to the Tappendens from the Glamorganshire Canal Company, to allow warehouses and workmen's houses to be built on the east bank of the canal and a wharf to be laid down at the double locks.[11] A tramroad was laid from above Gwern y Gerwn bridge to bring Rhondda coal to the works from Griffiths' Tramroad, the canal company allowing this on payment of tonnage, as if the coal had been hauled along the canal.[12]

The 1800 rights to use the canal water were perpetuated in the agreement with the canal company but Tappendens were planning a much grander operation than the former Crawshay forge and they needed an independent water supply.

Meanwhile, Doctor Richard Griffiths had completed his short coal canal from Treforest to Dynea and, from 1810, was seeking permission from the Glamorganshire Canal Company to make a junction between the two canals. The GCC wanted assurances that there were no leakages and, in particular, they required guarantees of a good independent supply of water – even though there were no locks on the Doctor's Canal.[13]

Griffiths, Francis Tappenden and Benjamin Hall together, came to an opportunist agreement regarding the sale of the Newbridge works. Griffiths would be allowed by the Glamorganshire Canal Company (on whose committee Hall sat and whose chairman, Rev'd Benjamin Hall, was Hall's father) to make his canal connection if he provided land on which the Tappendens could bring in a new supply of water to the Newbridge works (the tail races emptying into the canal), so encouraging Tappendens to lease the site from Hall. The successful result of the agreement is summed up by the canal company minute of 3 February 1813, signed by Richard Griffiths and witnessed by the canal company's Clerk, Thomas Reece:

'Messrs Tappendens having constructed a Weir on the Taff on the Lands of Mr Griffiths and brought Water to their Works which is afterwards brought into the Canal and affords a good supply. Ordered that Dr Griffiths have leave to join the Canal giving to the Company the right to the Water brought by Messrs Tappendens and indemnifying them when necessary against any claim of Messrs Blakemore and Co. respecting the granting Dr Griffiths a supply of Water for his Canal.'

It was as well that they included a clause protecting them against Blakemore's claims of water for his Melingriffith works, further downstream.

Thus, in 1813, the two canals were joined. The head of the Doctor's Canal was connected to the River Taff by a sluice and short feeder above the weir, where water was also taken off the opposite bank of the river to the Forest corn mill (and later the Treforest tinplate works). Surplus water from the GCC's Deniah pond was allowed to pass to the Doctor's Canal by a new overflow weir.

Unfortunately this agreement did not last long for, by late 1814, the Tappendens were bankrupt; it may well be that the costly expansion of the Newbridge works as rolling mills and the provision of the new water supply contributed to the affair. In 1814, immediately prior to the bankruptcy, Edward Williams' diary remarks:

'The largest ironworks here [Aberdare Valley] of Messrs Scale [and] of Tappenden & Co are inferior only to those of Merthyr Tydvil.

The Ironworks belonging to the above Tappenden & Co. at Newbridge, twelve miles below Merthyr Tidvil are on a larger scale. These consist of rolling mills for making bar and plate iron, but very few years ago there were only about four or five scattered cottages. Here now there are not less than two hundred houses, many of them very respectable buildings, and a large and very commodious Market Place is now nearly finished here. The market was first opened in August 1814, and promises from its favourable situation to become one of the first Markets in the Principality.'[14]

The implication is that the Tappendens' Newbridge ironworks (and perhaps the Crawshay forge before it) was the impetus for the growth of that area of Pontypridd. The sale notice following the bankruptcy gives some idea of the scale and capacity of the undertaking:

'The extensive FORGES at NEWBRIDGE, attached to these [the Abernant] Works, and having Communication by the Glamorgan and Aberdare Canals, capable of Rolling One Hundred Tons of Finished Bar Iron per Week, with a HOUSE for a Manager, and sundry WORKMEN'S HOUSES, &c. Together with an eligible FREEHOLD FARM adjoining consisting of about 60 Acres; distant from Merthyr and Cardiff 12 Miles. The LEASE of a WHARF at Cardiff . . . .

On the same day will be sold VARIOUS IMPLEMENTS. Smiths, Carpenters', and other Workmen's Tools, &c. Twelve Horses, a Quantity of Hay, Three Acres of Potatoes, a Quantity of Mine, Trams, and an Iron Boat, suited to the Glamorgan and Aberdare Canals. Sundry Stores, &c. &c . . . .

Also will be Sold at Newbridge Forges and Farm, (of which public Notice will be given on or about the End of October next) the FARMING STOCK and IMPLEMENTS, a Quantity of Oats stacked, Barley do. Hay do. and After-Grass, &c. Cast Iron Rolls, Standards, and sundry Machinery, with a Quantity of Wrought Iron, Coal Trams, &c. Seven Freehold Workmen's Houses, situate at Gwern-gerwn, near the Newbridge Forges.'

It is interesting to note that the sale notice included one boat only (an iron one), perhaps indicating that the Tappendens, rather than run their own fleet, had relied on carriers who owned their own boats. The Glamorganshire Canal Company restrained boats loaded with Abernant iron to pay the tonnage debts due to them.[15]

Samuel Brown, in partnership with Samuel Lenox, took over the site for their Chain and Anchor works[16]. Whether they bought the works at the auction or later treated with the assignees is not known. By November 1817, Brown had been building on the site and was leasing further land from the canal company *'between the Wall lately erected by him and the feeding Weir and water course at the Ynysangharad lock'*.[17]

It seems that the canal water supply from the 1800 agreement was sufficient to drive the machinery for the chain works, as Samuel Brown & Co did not continue the watercourse agreement with Dr Griffiths.

The canal company also survived without this extra water until, in 1819, it was forced to find a supply to accommodate Richard Blakemore's Pentyrch ironworks (see Melingriffith and Pentyrch section in Volume 2). The scheme included the recommendation *'that an additional supply of Water should be procured by resuming the Feeder made by Messrs Tappenden near Newbridge.'* Benjamin Hall junior had died in 1817 but his executors consented *'that the Canal Co shall have such part of the Ynysangharad estate as may be necessary for the intended feeder at the same rate per acre per annum as paid to other proprietors whose lands are used for the same purpose'*.[18] Griffiths made similar allowances for his land when the feeder was being planned in 1820. A new aqueduct, taking the feeder over the River Taff, was built of Memel pine at an estimated cost of £200.[19] So in 1820 the restored feeder came under the ownership of the Glamorganshire Canal Company.

From the aqueduct, the feeder passed through John Bassett's Coedpenmaen Estate before entering Hall's land. In the autumn of 1823 a breach occurred here and the Canal Company were forced to pay £10 damages to Bassett.[20] Harrison's 1830 Canal survey includes the feeder and shows by this time the late Dr Griffiths' land had been disposed of to William Crawshay, whilst Thomas Walters, of nearby Ty Berwdy (through which the feeder passed), and Evan Griffiths (Richard Griffiths' brother) were the

Within four years from sinking the Albion, over 500 houses were built there to create the village of Cilfynydd. This view of young lads at the Albion pit also shows water entering the lower canal pound from the lock bypass weir.   Brian Lewis collection

main feeder at Navigation. In 1833, a new overflow weir was made on the Ynysangharad pond, to ensure water from the feeder passed through to the lower pond and did not go to waste.[22] In 1834, the weir across the Taff at the head of the feeder was renewed.[23]

In 1826, Rev'd George Thomas, Dr Richard Griffiths' nephew, who had inherited his uncle's estate, was permitted to extend his tramroad from Ynis Geryn (Gwaun Geryn) bridge to supply Brown Lenox's works with coal. The route taken was along the canal towpath, on the same line which the Tappendens had used in earlier years to supply their rolling mills.[24] The coal was not only for the forges but was probably used by the growing number of steam engines on the site. Nevertheless, Brown Lenox continued to use the canal water supply and, in 1842, the canal company were concerned when the chain works removed their water wheel, presumably for replacement.[25] Jones states that steam hammers were installed in 1845 but that waterpower was used at Brown Lenox well into the 20th century.[26] In 1847, a Mr Austin was refused permission to rent the feeder water for his own use. In 1851, the company unsuccessfully sought to alter the course of the feeder near their works, whilst in 1881 the canal company made representation to Brown Lenox on the amount of water they were extracting from the canal.[27] By the time Morien was writing in 1903, waterwheels had been replaced by turbines.[28]

Although the feeder appears from photographs of the aqueduct to have been in good order well into the 1880s, the survey report of the whole canal, commissioned in 1885, when the Marquess of Bute took over the canal company, shows that at that time it was out of repair:

'THE BERW FEEDER I have inspected this throughout and for a moderate outlay it can be put into working order and very materially assist the supply of Canal water, by directing the Clydach river into the Millstream and blocking up the sluice without passing over the Mill Wheel if permission can be obtained from the Merthyr Tydfil Sanitary Board to do this.'[29]

There is no indication that this work was done but the first edition 25 inch OS map of 1875 suggests that the river weir was already gone and the only source of water supply was indeed via the mill. Photographs and picture postcards from the early 1900s show the aqueduct rapidly

other landlords. In 1825 Thomas Walters claimed damages caused to his land by the flooding River Taff entering the feeder and spilling onto it.[21] The feeder took water where the Nant Clydach from Ynysybwl joined the River Taff. At this point also was a corn mill, whose pond was fed by the Clydach and whose tailrace emptied into the feeder. The route then followed the right bank of the Taff, round Graig yr Esk and crossed the river by way of the Berw Aqueduct, to enter the canal above Brown Lenox's Newbridge works. It is assumed that this is the identical route the earlier Tappenden feeder took and that the 1820 aqueduct was a rebuilding of the wooden troughs on stone piers on the site of the original structure.

For several years the Graig yr Esk feeder served as an important water supply for the canal, supplementing the

The 1915 breach at Cilfynydd which caused closure of the canal above this point. The canal had already been badly breached at the same spot in 1896 (see Volume 2) and the company chose not to invest any more in its repair. The photograph, taken on 16 Jan 1932, shows the wooden flume, built to span the 1915 breach to continue to provide water from the Elen Deg feeder to the southern stretch of canal. Below the canal, through the breach in the towpath and bank, can be glimpsed the former railway branch to the Albion colliery, seen in the right distance. The Dowlais-Cardiff colliery is in the far northern distance.

Courtesy Welsh Industrial & Maritime Museum

Bank slippage at Cilfynydd was continuing even to 1932. An abandoned boat lies in the ice.

Courtesy Welsh Industrial & Maritime Museum, BB 242/36

deteriorating and clearly not in use.

Today there are substantial remains of the feeder and its stone revetment walls from its source as far as the aqueduct but the route on the left bank of the River Taff to the canal has been lost to housing development. The weir on the Taff is no more but the corn mill survives, converted to a residence; the sluice where water entered its pond from the Clydach can be seen in the stone wall on the river bank below the railway bridge. Remains of the stone piers of the aqueduct can be seen upstream of the 1885 railway bridge which took the Taff Vale Railway branch to the Albion Colliery at Cilfynydd.

A photographic view of the Berw aqueduct in the 1860s. The aqueduct and the picturesque rocky river bed was something of a site for visitors to the Taff Valley. Penry Williams painted it in the 1820s, whilst Henry Gastineau published a lithograph in 1830 and sketches of it appeared in traveller's books. Francis Bedford and Thomas Forrest published cartes de visite depicting photographs of it in the 1860s. Bedford even published it on a stereograph in the early 1860s. In the early part of the 20th century, when the aqueduct was completely derelict, it still attracted the attention of picture postcard publishers. SR collection

NOTES TO CHAPTER 10

1 GCC minute book 1 March 1800.

2 Chris Evans and G. Hayes *The Letterbook of Richard Crawshay 1788-1797*, Cardiff 1990 p23-4.

3 Hilary Thomas *The Diaries of John Bird of Cardiff, Clerk to the First Marquess of Bute, 1790-1803*, Cardiff 1987 p63.

4 Charles Wilkins *The History of the Iron, Steel, Tinplate and Other Trades of Wales*, Merthyr Tydfil 1903 p228 and J. Charles *Pontypridd Historical Handbook*, Pontypridd 1920 p14.

5 G. Manby *An Historical and Picturesque Guide from Clifton, through the Counties of Monmouth, Glamorgan and Brecknock*, Bristol 1802 p174.

6 E.H. Brooke *Chronology of the Tinplate Works of Great Britain*, first edition Swansea 1932 and second edition Swansea 1944; Wilkins *Iron, Steel, Tinplate*, op cit; Charles *Handbook* op cit p14; Benjamin Malkin *The Scenery, Antiquities and Biography of South Wales*, London 1807; Samuel Lewis *A Topographical Dictionary of Wales*, first edition London 1833 third edition London 1843. NLW Crawshay letterbooks.

7 Morien *History of Pontypridd and Rhondda Valleys*, 1903 p160.

8 Wilkins *Iron, Steel, Tinplate*, p.235.

9 GCC minute book, 25 Oct 1808.

10 See chapter on Aberdare canal.

11 GRO, D/DB Ca 23.

12 GCC minute book, 3 Feb 1813.

13 GCC minute book, 7 June 1809, 22 Sept 1810, 18 April 1812, 3 Feb 1813; GCC letterbook 2 Aug 1809.

14 NLW Llanover Estate Archives, MS 13089 E, Diaries of Edward Williams, alias Iolo Morgannwg. Thanks to Peter Tann and Brian Davies for this reference.

15 GCC minute book, 12 Jan 1815 and 31 Mar 1815.

16 Stephen K. Jones *A Link With the Past: The History of the Newbridge Works of Brown Lenox & Co., Pontypridd*, Glamorgan Historian vol 12 Barry 1982 p27-46.

17 GCC minute book, 1 Nov 1817.

18 GCC minute book 16 June 1819.

19 GCC minute book 21 Sept 1820, 23 Nov 1820, 15 Feb 1821 and 12 July 1821.

20 GCC minute book 2 Oct 1823.

21 GCC minute book 7 April 1825.

22 GCC minute book 25 Oct 1833.

23 GCC minute book 7 Feb 1834.

24 GCC minute book 7 June 1826.

25 GCC minute book 1 June 1842.

26 Stephen K. Jones *A Link With the Past*, p36.

27 GCC minute book 2 June 1847, 31 July 1851 and 11 May 1881.

28 Morien *Pontypridd and Rhondda*, p159.

29 GCC minute book 10 Aug 1885.

Chapter 11

LIMESTONE, PENNANT SANDSTONE AND THE QUARRIES

The Glamorganshire Canal is rightly remembered as an 'iron and coal canal'. However, this rather tabloid description over-simplifies the varied carrying activity on the waterway and the business conducted along its floating harbour in Cardiff. During the course of over 150 years, the up traffic included iron ore, timber, pitwood, bricks, domestic foodstuffs, beer, porter, hay, corn and animal feeds. To the down consignments of iron and coal were later to be added the considerable trade in patent fuel, whilst throughout the life of the canal there were significant movements of stone, or 'stones' as the commodity is often expressed in the canal company's documents, loading bills and boat passes.

Two principal types of stone were to be found naturally outcropping along the line of the canal:

(1) The carboniferous limestone of the southern coalfield edge, which stands out dramatically north of Cardiff at Castell Coch, where the River Taff passes through the Garth Gap.

(2) The Pennant sandstone of the coal measures, which is still prominent in quarries and outcrops along the Taff Valley between Merthyr and Taffs Well.[1] The Pennant stone was not just an important source of traffic to the canal; its ready availability, and easily workable and durable nature made it the obvious first choice of the canal engineer-contractors Thomas Dadford & Son, and almost the whole of the Glamorganshire Canal was built of it.

Cardiff Lime

A third source of stone traffic was provided by Aberthaw lias limestone, which was brought in to Cardiff by sea from beaches and cliffs near the harbour at the mouth of the River Ddawan (or Thaw), some five miles west of Barry.[2] For many generations, Aberthaw limestone had been a well-known import at Welsh and Westcountry harbour limekilns for, when burnt with imported anthracite coal from West Glamorgan, it produced a high quality hydraulic lime which would harden under water. It was consequently much sought after by the builders of river bridges, harbour works and canals. For example, we hear of the stone pier at St Agnes in Cornwall, finished by Thomas Tonkin in 1710 at

a cost of £6000, with foundations of

'great rocks buoy'd up with casks and brought there and the superstructure laid in hot lime, made of what they call lyas stone, brought from Aberthaw in Wales, which by experience I have found to be the best for these sort of works, it growing hard as the rock itself.'[3]

Nearer to home, lime-burning in kilns must have been a familiar sight at the little river port of Cardiff, on the Taff, where, in 1774, the Melingriffith Company of Whitchurch was obtaining building lime which had been produced at a kiln near the Town Quay by Thomas Williams, a lime-burner. The same company, in 1775, rented a limekiln from the Corporation of Cardiff for 6d a week, the limestone being brought in by coasting vessel from beaches at Lavernock, in Glamorgan. From the same Melingriffith tinplate works accounts, E.L. Chappell records that, in 1774-75, the proprietors of this water powered establishment were reconstructing Radyr weir on the River Taff, building and acquiring boats, and promoting navigation on their water feeder and along the Taff as far as a landing place at Cilynys Farm. It seems beyond reasonable doubt that the hydraulic lime made from Lavernock limestone was providing an hydraulic mortar for securing masonry at the weir and for building the adjoining navigation lock. It is an interesting thought that this small-scale canal and river navigation was at work perhaps 20 years before the opening of the Glamorganshire Canal.[4]

Earlier still, Charles Wood's diary (1766-7)[5] of the construction of Cyfarthfa furnaces and watercourses abounds with references to this 'Cardiff Lime' (burnt lias limestone from Aberthaw). On 9 May 1766, 'Cardiff Lime costs in Cardiff 6d a horse load which is about 2 Winchester bushels and for carriage [to Merthyr] 2d a load.' Wood goes on to discuss mixing quantities and the building qualities of the lime. On 13 May 1766, 'This day came a load of Cardiff Lime . . . . by William Richard, carrier, from Wm James, Limeburner. NB This load described here is a load paid for at the kiln and measures 32 bushels each basket containing 8 quarters of Sand.' Again, Wood goes on to discuss mixing recipes and finishes with, 'This William Edwards informs me from a long experiment he has had in the use of this Lime.' William Edwards, of course,

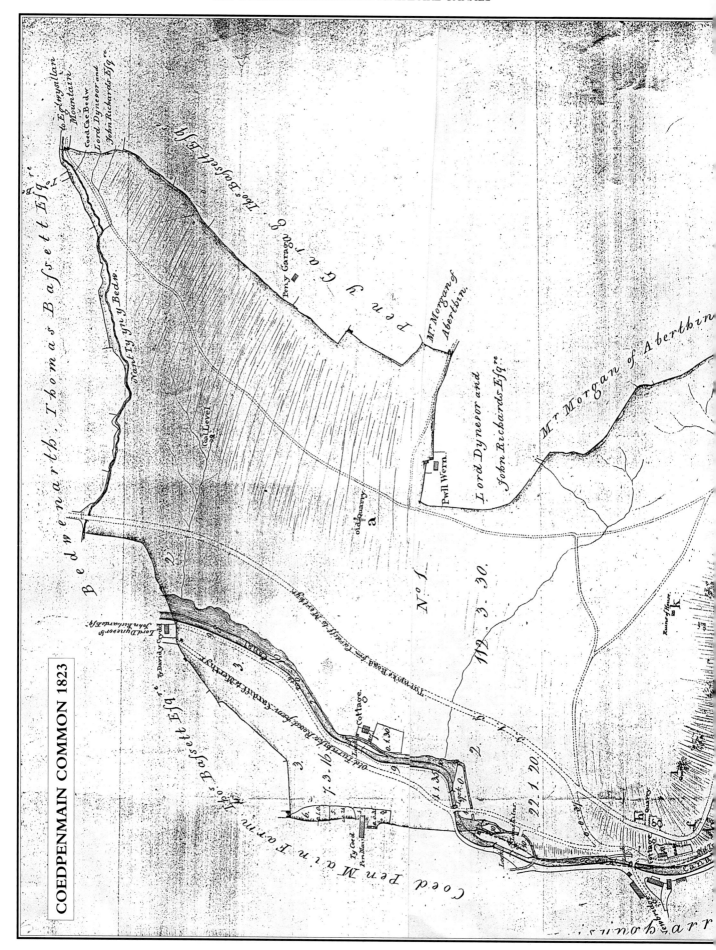

COEDPENMAIN COMMON 1823

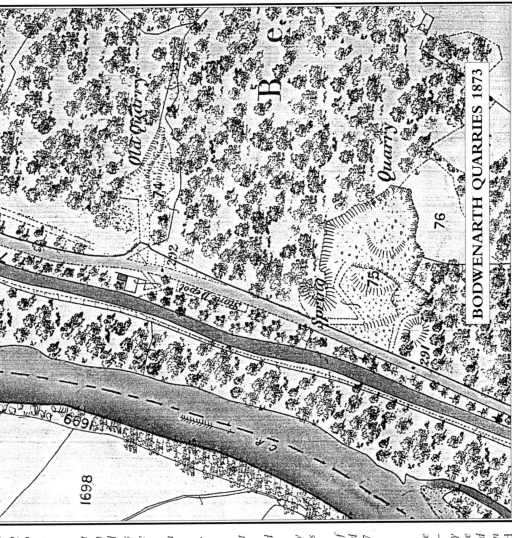

BODWENARTH QUARRIES 1873

Above: This map of Coedpennaen common was prepared in 1823 for the Marquess of Bute, as part of the continuing dispute amongst the land-owners of bordering property over how the common should be carved up between them. Of concern to them was the brinkers, or those who were already living or working on the common. Thus the map reference lists the various quarries on the common as follows:

(a) Quarry worked by the Canal Company for the purpose of Building Locks.
(b) Quarry also worked by the Canal Company to a very great extent. It is said that the Ground occupied by the Canal Company on Coed Pen Main and Graig Evan Leyshon Commons was formerly surveyed and found to contain about 30 acres and that Five Pounds per Acre was the Sum fixed to be paid by the Canal Co. The deeds had been drawn up but then it had been found that Bute had no right to lease the stone on the commons.
(c) Quarry first opened by the Canal Company and afterwards worked by William James who sold the Stones.
(d) Quarry worked by the Newbridge works Company to build Workmens Cottages . . .
(e) Quarry where Stones were worked to build the Newbridge Works;
(f) Quarry worked by William Jones who sold the Stones.
(g & h) Quarries now working by Thomas Edward and Miles Miles who pay Rent of £5 a year to Mr Bold.
(i) Quarry where Thomas Rees (employed by Mr Stewart) worked and was stopped by Mr Thomas.
(13) David Hopkins Garden was formerly a Quarry where stones were got by Nathaniel Jones, William Williams and Adam Rowland and used for building Houses on the opposite side of the Canal on Mr Hall's property.
The map covers the canal from Tyn y Graig Lock (Lock 26) through to the site of Ynysangharad Locks (Locks 31-32) at Newbridge works. Also of interest are the old and new turnpike routes.
Courtesy Cardiff City Library, Bute I 37

Right: Before the massive ribbon development of Cilfynydd had started with the opening of the Albion colliery, two quarries were served by the canal at Bodwenarth – the site of the Cilfynydd breaches. William Morgan was moving stones from here by canal in August 1863 and David Davies had Bodwenarth Quarry in 1875. Note the stone depot beside the turnpike and the track leading to the yard, buildings and wharf on the canal. Security on the canal was maintained by the towpath being on the far side, away from the road.
Crown copyright reserved

Castell Coch quarry, at Tongwynlais, was the southernmost quarry on the Glamorganshire Canal. This had a long history, stretching back to before the opening of the canal, when William Price operated it. The photograph dates from the mid 1890s, poorly reproduced on a picture postcard almost a decade later. Note the limekiln and the incline from the quarry to the canal wharf (shown on the Table of Distances as John Thomas's quarry). The river bridge is the Pentyrch ironworks' Ynys bridge, leading to the canal's Pentyrch bridge and beyond to the Castell Coch iron mines. The large Ynys House was formerly occupied by the proprietor of the Pentyrch and Melingriffith works, T.W. Booker (see Volume 2). The castle itself was restored by the Marquess of Bute in the 70s (compare to the Ibbetson painting on page 19). SR collection

was the well-respected bridge-architect and mason who had built the famous river arch at Pontypridd in 1756. Thus the tradition of using Cardiff Lime and knowledge of its properties was well established in the Taff Valley, long before Dadford arrived to build the Glamorganshire Canal.

We know from Thomas Dadford's reports that, from the beginning of canal construction in August 1790, he was using hydraulic lime mortar which he does refer to as 'Cardiff Lime'.[6] In October 1793, Richard Crawshay arranged that a double limekiln be built 'at the end of the company's warehouse and a house at one end'.[7] This is likely to refer to the limekiln halfway down the 16-lock flight at

Abercynon, needed by Dadford to supply mortar to complete this massive lock construction project and also to provide for its future maintenance. The canal company's stone masons yard was then permanently established here. David Edwards, William Edwards' son, would have used the kiln when he was building the new (upper) feeder in 1796. The feeder enters the canal at the limekiln, and Harrison's 1830 plan shows the kiln and limehouse separated from the storehouse by the feeder arm. The limehouse is significant, for when limestone is burnt in the kiln it produces quicklime, a caustic and potentially dangerous material which must be kept dry in storesheds.

The canal and Taff Vale Railway facing north from Pentyrch bridge about 1905. Road, canal and railway are passing through the Garth Gap. Castell Coch quarry is out of picture on the right but its canal loading tip wall and tramway are clearly visible. W. Hamlin collection

216

From the same viewpoint as the previous picture, this poor quality but rare photograph shows a boat waiting at Edmund Thomas's quarry tipping wall, whilst a passenger train heads north on the TVR main line. The quarry seems to have closed by 1907, when the Cardiff Railway cut off its canal access. The photograph was copied from Glamorgan *by A. Thomas, published in 1907.*

The limeburner may also have lived there, although it was a dangerous place because carbon dioxide could leak through the walls from the burning kiln, and asphyxiate the sleeping man and his family. The 1873 OS map shows the limekiln re-sited across the canal and alongside the double Locks 20-21, which appropriately had become known as Lock Odyn-galch.

Quicklime becomes extremely volatile when water is added to it and for this reason it was not generally carried by boat but when this became unavoidable the lime was transported in barrels or waterproof bags in a covered boat. For example, on 11 April 1795, Henry Charles, Cardiff agent to the Dowlais ironworks, wrote to Robert Thompson that 20 sacks with 92 bushels of oats had been sent on the boat which was formerly number 9, with Hugh Mellor as master (boatman). He remarked that it was the only boat sealed properly for taking up loose lime but that John Key, the canal carrier for whom Mellor worked, refused to take lime which was not in bags. Thompson was to send bags and then the lime could be sent up in the Dowlais company's own boats.[8] The supplier of lime was named as B. Williams, who may have been a relative of Thomas Williams, the Cardiff town limeburner in the 1770s. At the Sea Lock pound, the limekiln was operated for some thirty years by James Parry. Parry owned his own coastal vessel to bring in the stone from Aberthaw.

Although the solidity of limekilns suggests a permanent presence, sometimes they were built as temporary structures for a specific building programme. Thus, in April 1838, when the canal company was rebuilding the Sea Lock, the Clerk, George Forrest, was instructed '*to fix on the most eligible Site near the Sea Lock for building a Limekiln.*'[9] The kiln did not last long after its purpose had been fulfilled.

Agricultural Lime

The building of limekilns was conceived as an integral part of the economy of many canal and tramroad companies, and proprietors frequently built kilns or financed their erection by others in order to stimulate trade.[10] In January 1796, Edward Edmunds of Penrhos (near Nantgarw) was granted a lease of canal land to build limekilns on the south west of Coedpenmaen, between the canal and the common. In March, the opportunist Thomas Key was quick to apply to erect several more kilns along the canal and particularly more at Coedpenmaen but since the contract with Edmunds had already been made, Crawshay's committee declined to lease more land there. Instead, they asked Key to stipulate where else he wanted to build them. Nothing further is minuted.[11] The 1798 deposited plan for the Cardiff to Merthyr Tramroad shows that Thomas Key was then occupying William Bassett's land, bordering the canal north of Coedpenmaen Common.[12] A map of 1823 records that Edmunds occupied his Coedpenmaen kilns '*for about 10 years without paying any rent. Mr Edmonds then sold to William Crawshay Esq and they are now in the possession of John Williams*'.[13] In 1871, Evan Williams is recorded as the limeburner at Coedpenmaen.[14]

The position and frequency of kiln sites along a canal was determined largely by the location of the points of sale, the location of the quarries, the ease of access to coal, the unstable nature of quicklime, and the handling costs and tonnage charges on the canal.[15] Kilns for agricultural lime were usually built closest to the point of sale, so that it was the stone and not the quicklime which travelled by water. Of the 14 kilns that have been identified on Harrison's plan of the canal in 1830, almost all must have been small-scale operations working seasonally to provide lime for farmers. Lime was an essential element in increasing crop yields and correcting the acidity of poor hill land. The limekilns were stone structures with cone-shaped internal chambers, which were charged from the top with broken limestone and coal, the reduced quicklime being removed after burning by means of a draw hole under an arch at the base of the kiln. Farmers usually 'quenched' the

The Glamorganshire Canal from Walnut Tree bridge, Taff's Well, looking towards Cardiff on 6 May 1899. The photograph appears in an album entitled 'Cardiff Railway Company Vol 1' (of five), which between them record in great detail the construction of the railway company's new dock at Cardiff between 1899 and 1907. Being on Bute land, Castell Coch quarry was worked extensively to supply Cardiff's dock projects. In this instance, the photographer was sent here to record the removal of carboniferous limestone boulders by the dock contractors Topham Jones & Railton. The quarry, now disused, is still a prominent feature of the Garth Gap, where its face provides adventure to the present generation of rock climbers. The construction of Walnut Tree viaduct, carrying the Barry Railway's Rhymney branch across the Taff Valley, happened to coincide with the quarrying and it is the massive brick pier and high girder of the partly built bridge, completed in 1901, that dominates this quiet canal scene.   Courtesy Public Record Office, PRO RAIL 97/22

caustic quicklime with water to form slaked (hydrated) lime and in this state it was safe to be carted off to the fields for dressing the land.

The coal for lime burning along the Glamorganshire Canal's upper pounds could well have come from coal levels, like the small canal-bank colliery on Edmund Williams' land at Perthygleision, where in 1830 there was a rural limekiln. Single limekilns predominated along the Taff Valley canal bank and were a reflection of the narrow and somewhat limited agricultural opportunities of the coalfield. Perhaps there could be no greater contrast than with the wharves of the Brecon & Abergavenny Canal, 20 miles away, where there are the remains of substantial banks of multiple limekilns at Gilwern, Llangattock and Talybont. These are witness to the big business in canal-borne lime to the more favoured farms of the Vale of Usk, and to the coal and lime also distributed onward to farmers along the line of the Hay Railway and the Govilon-Hereford tramroads.[16]

At Ynysygored farm, 4½ miles from Cyfarthfa, the limestone may have come to the kiln from quarries north of Merthyr or from Penderyn (via the Aberdare Canal) on the northern outcrop. The kiln on the canal at Graig Evan Leyshon common was built and operated by Thomas Thomas, at an annual rent from April 1820 of five shillings.[17] The GCC Table of Distances continued to refer to it as Thomas Thomas's limekiln, and in 1855 it is recorded as being leased to William Morgan and worked by Lewis Thomas.[18] It no doubt used coal from the level on the opposite bank, although no bridge is known to have connected them. At Ynyscaedudwg, at the north end of Cilfynydd, a kiln was producing lime for the widely scattered hill farms of Llanfabon parish and business was brisk enough here for the GCC to provide a house for a resident lime burner. Edmunds' two limekilns at Coedpenmaen were to serve the emergent industrial and communications centre of Newbridge, at the meeting of the Rhondda with the Taff. The twin Newbridge limekilns stood next to a two-rise pair of locks and it was not long before the canal boatmen, as at Abercynon, had given Locks 28 and 29 the name 'Lock yr Odyn', the Kiln Lock.

The role of limestone as a fluxing agent in iron and steel making is well known. It might have been expected that the Glamorganshire Canal, so intimately bound up with the iron industry, would have played a part in bringing furnace limestone from the quarries to the ironworks, as happened on the Caldon and the Peak Forest canals in England. In fact the canal is unlikely to have taken part in this traffic. The canal head at Cyfarthfa works terminated too far south to serve the Gurnos quarries and the works received all its limestone by way of the Gurnos tramroad, which crossed the Taff on the Pont y Cafnau (an early iron tramroad bridge and aqueduct which was expertly restored *in situ* in 1994-95). Limekilns and a tramroad siding were built on the Gurnos tramroad, where the route ran close to the Brecon to Merthyr turnpike and this point was probably where stone destined for Plymouth ironworks was transshipped to road waggon. At the southern outcrop of the limestone, the Pentyrch ironworks of Richard

Blakemore similarly had no need of the canal to bring in fluxing stone, the local mines and quarries in the shadow of the Garth mountain ensuring sufficient supplies of iron ore, coal and limestone – which was, of course, the very reason why the ironworks had been established there.

Limestone Quarries

We now look at what is known of the canal-served limestone quarries of the southern outcrop, which are still so much a part of the drama of the Castell Coch landscape. Thomas Dadford even saw fit to indicate the quarries on his original survey of the canal route in 1790. William Price of Ivy House, Tongwynlais, gave up land here when the canal was built but his quarrying continued so close that, in the first three decades, the canal suffered breaches as a direct result of Price's activities. The canal company claimed compensation from Price in 1812, then in 1820, when it threatened an injunction for further undermining the canal. Price retaliated by claiming he himself had not been paid the agreed £7 7s 6d trespass when an overflow weir had been built across his property. The weir was built on the site of the 16th century Taff iron furnace at Ivy House, where the Ton Brook, which had powered the furnace bellows, enters the River Taff. The drop to the river was steep here and the problems with Price at one stage caused the canal committee to consider diverting the canal, when John Hodgkinson was asked to survey the new line.[19]

The family names of Morgan, Thomas and later Edwards have long been synonymous with quarrying in Taffs Well and Tongwynlais. In 1824, John Morgan leased a lime quarry in Castell Coch forest for seven years, from the Marquess of Bute and he received an allowance of £3 out of the first year's rental for putting the limekiln into good repair.[20] In all probability this is the kiln whose curling smoke among the beech woods was noticed by romantic writers and artists of the 18th and 19th centuries, touring this valley in search of picturesque scenes and awe inspiring effects of nature; among them was the painter J.C.Ibbetson (1759-1817).[21]

Five named limestone quarries appear in the Glamorganshire Canal Company's *Table of Distances from Cyfarthfa*, between Caeglas Lock, Taffs Well and the 18½ milepost at Tongwynlais. Listed are the quarry owners John Morgan, Evan Morgan, Thomas Thomas and John Thomas, and it would seem reasonable to suppose that appearance in the Table (which could date from 1851) is an implication that these owners were consigning stone from their quarries by canal.

Jacob Harris and William Morgan were certainly working as lime merchants and burners in Taffs Well in 1875, with Morgan's son Isaac still carrying on the trade of lime merchant there in 1895.[22] In 1885, John Thomas of the Castell Coch quarry was sending around three boats of limestone a day to the North Road wharves in Cardiff, two of the boatmen concerned being J. Harris (could he be Jacob Harris the lime merchant?) and J. Stephens.[23] By

Castell Coch quarry on the east side of the Garth Gap at Tongwynlais, being worked for limestone for the Cardiff Railway's new dock project, again photographed on 6 May 1899. The canal and the Cardiff-Merthyr Road are in the foreground. On the higher bank, in front of the quarry, the steam cranes are for moving the stone and loading it onto wagons on the temporary railway, laid to take the stone and burnt lime out by rail for direct consignment to the Cardiff dock site. Note in the quarry (right) a double limekiln and a row of wagons probably owned by the dock contractors. In 1906, this quarry site was used again by the builders of the Tongwynlais-Treforest section of the Cardiff Railway.
Courtesy Public Record Office PRO RAIL 97/22

DAN-Y-CRAIG HOUSE, TAFF'S WELL, GLAM.   No. 663

The temporary timber bridge, crossing the Glamorganshire Canal at Walnut Tree bridge (Taff's Well), giving direct rail access from the Rhymney Railway to Castell Coch quarry, for loading stone and burnt lime for the Cardiff Railway Company's new dock project at Cardiff from 1899. The dock was opened in 1907 by the King and Queen, and named the Queen Alexandra dock. In the distance, the Portobello quarries can be seen behind the terrace of houses called Forest Row. On the left is part of the Garth ironworks (see Volume 2).

SR collection

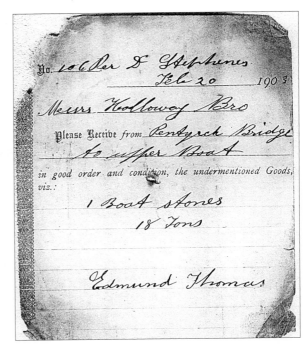

Permit dated 20 February 1903. Stone from Edmund Thomas, Castell Coch quarries, consigned from Pentyrch bridge to Upper Boat for Messrs. Holloway Brothers. ILW collection

Left: *Two Castell Coch quarry permits of 1885 for 20 ton loads of limestone delivered to Cathays (North Road, Cardiff). The quarry owner was John Thomas, Cwm Nofydd, and the boatmen were J. Harris and Jack Herbert.* ILW collection

this time, the stone from the Castell Coch and Portobello quarries was being shipped chiefly for road stone but prominent limekilns in Castell Coch quarry were still a feature here until 1971, when they were swept away for the building of the Cardiff–Merthyr trunk road.

The building of the Cardiff Railway from Heath to Treforest in 1906 considerably altered the approaches to the Garth Gap quarries and the 1971 A470 trunk road has made modern identification of their sites even more difficult. Portobello quarry may have sent its last canal loaded stone to the contractors building the Cardiff Railway. Owned by Thomas Edwards, the quarry was later connected by a siding to the CR but the rail traffic did not develop and the last wagons of stone left Portobello in 1927. John Thomas of Tongwynlais appears as a quarry owner in Kelly's Directory of 1914 but it is unlikely that any stone traffic was being handled by the boatmen after about 1911.[24]

Pennant Sandstone

'The wall on your left and the farm buildings are made of local Pennant sandstone which breaks easily into flat blocks and is the best building stone within the Coalfield'[25]

The writer of the guidebook was standing on Pontypridd Common and his Pennant sandstone was well known as 'Newbridge Stone' among the 19th century building contractors of Cardiff. Newbridge was a

particularly active place for quarrying, with a string of stone workings lying close to the Glamorganshire Canal from Cilfynydd to Coedpenmaen, Pentrebach and Treforest.

Thomas Dadford knew the virtues of the Pennant stone and opened quarries to build his locks and bridges as the canal navigators cut their way down the Taff Valley between 1790 and 1794. Naturally, Dadford and the canal company would open the quarries only after acquiring the land from the existing landowners, under the powers of their Act. In this way they would not be liable to pay the landowner for the tonnage removed. One of Dadford's carriers, who moved materials into position for the masons, was the ubiquitous Thomas Key. During the period of the extension of the canal from Cardiff to the Sea Lock in 1797 - 98, the sum of £88 was paid '*To Thomas Key for boating stones*'[26]. At this time the Pennant stone was playing its part in facilitating the industrialisation of the valley and Richard Crawshay's nail forge at nearby Ynysangharad was an example of the common use of stone for building. The local quarries on Coedpenmaen Common provided the stone and the further supplies required to build the row of workers cottages in what later became Ynysangharad Street, in Pontypridd. In 1809, Pennant stone was being used to construct the stone arches of the Machine bridge at Treforest, carrying Dr. Griffiths' coal tramroad over the Taff. The quarries at Newbridge were so near to these sites that haulage of stone was probably done by road. By 1830, there is evidence at Pentrebach of a well established canal

223

The only photograph of a loaded stone boat known to the authors. A bye trader eases his boat out of Lock Lewis, Rhydyfelin, on his way to North Road, Cardiff, with another load of building stone from the Pontypridd quarries, circa 1910. Note also the excess water by-passing the lock and re-entering the canal from the right. This was something of a design fault and caused boatmen a lot of trouble at several locations on the canal, since the force of water would drive the boat into the bank as it left the lock.

David Wilkins photo

business at the quarry, with a 'wharf' marked on Harrison's map, which had an environmentally-unfriendly 'quarry tip', where stone rubbish was discharged across the canal straight into the river. Pennant sandstone splits easily and is also ideal for paving stones; several of the quarries specialised in their production.

Meanwhile, in Merthyr, by 1800 one of the world's leading producers of iron and from then until 1850 the largest town in Wales, it is not surprising to find that the Glamorganshire Canal was stimulating the trade in building stone. In 1830, Williams & Co were renting three stone yards on the canal's east bank, above Lock 2 in Merthyr, just below the Penydarren yards. By 1851, the GCC *Table of Distances* shows two named quarries at Pont Rhun and another at Cnwc, and it could be expected that boatloads of stone from these sites would be shipped to the stoneyards of Merthyr. Canal-served stoneyards still existed in Merthyr in 1875 but by this date they seem to have moved nearer to the timber yards above Parliament Lock and had become general builders' yards.

Some quarry owners may have had their own boats but the majority probably relied upon independent owner-boatmen working for them under contract. A quarry owner like John Gibbon of Pentrebach, Glyntaff, would find a 'regular' who would boat his stone to the North Road wharf in Cardiff. Gibbon, in 1904, had two boatmen working regularly for him and at busy times in the quarry he could call on the services of two or three more.[27]

In mid-Victorian times, we have some evidence of named carriers of the Pennant stone, such as Morgan Edwards & Co, who in 1863 were doing some carrying from quarries at Lock 9, John Norton's bridge, Trallwn, Pentrebach and from the Aberdare Canal. Also in 1863, we find John Llewellyn boating stone from Squirrel's Castle (Castell Gwewyer, Pontyrhun), William Morgan carrying from Cilfynydd, and David Thomas operating from Navigation.[28]

If the boatmen of the Glamorganshire Canal were good horse traders, they were also skilled at buying and selling stone to their advantage. "*How much do you want for a hundred ton?*" was a common enough call to the quarry owner, in times when business on the canal was still very personal. Having bought and loaded his stone, a boatman would leave Pentrebach and, on arrival at North Road wharf in Cardiff, he would pay 6s 8d tonnage on the 20 tons cargo, and an additional 1s 8d wharfage (1 old penny per ton) on 20 tons landed and put out for sale on the wharf. The figures quoted refer to the rates in operation on the canal about 1890. The marketing procedures at the North Road wharf are not fully understood through lack of evidence

Another poor quality but rare view. showing the North Road stone wharf, probably in the 1880s, seen from above the lock and gate lodge to Cardiff Castle. On the bank are stacks of Newbridge stone, brought down by boat from the Pontypridd quarries and identifiable as kerb, channel and paving for Cardiff streets. The stone, which was sold to builders on this public wharf, was dressed on site by the masons. Pennant sandstone from Pontypridd changed the face of developing Victorian Cardiff and the canal's key part in this transformation is still only poorly recognised. ILW collection

but certain information is of great interest. Twenty masons are said to have been at work there dressing Newbridge stone in the 1890s.[29] A boatman engaged in the trade quoted the following figures:

14s 0d for 20 tons of rough walling
15s 0d for 20 tons of cuttings and shoddies
£1. 00 for kerb, channel or paving (heavier, measured by the yard) *'it would run 21 ton'*
(Note: Owing to inadequate note-taking some 50 years ago it is now uncertain as to what stage of marketing the stone these figures refer.)

The phenomenal growth of Cardiff was accelerated by the opening of the West Bute dock in 1839, the East dock (1858), the Roath dock (1887) and the Queen Alexandra dock (1907). Coal shipments rose from 200,000 tons in 1840 to 3 million tons in 1870 and in this period Cardiff's population rose from 11,000 to 57,000. The expansion of

In 1949, Cardiff Corporation re-used stone from the walls of the disused Glamorganshire Canal at North Road wharves and constructed stone seating for the city's Maindy Stadium (itself, now replaced). Frederick Francis was one of the masons working on the wharf. ILW Photo 30 Nov 1949, neg 911

Since 1793, the Aberdare Canal Company had been in the business of working limestone quarries, operating limekilns, and distributing lime and limestone over its system of tramroads. Only after long delay was the canal built and opened in 1812. The process of distributing limestone from Penderyn was extended along the company's canal and kilns were erected for the burning of lime for building and agriculture. One such kiln site was set up on the canal bank at Ffrwd bridge, Mountain Ash, where blocks of limestone, brought by boat, are seen stacked near the kiln in this photograph dating from around 1880. In the distance, looking towards Aberdare, is the Deep Dyffryn colliery.   ILW collection

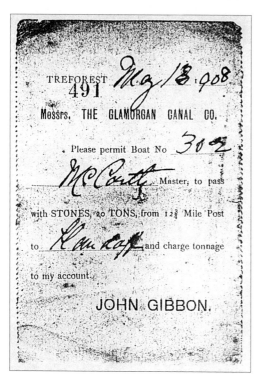

A John Gibbon quarry permit for boatman McCarthy to bring 20 tons of stone from the Pentrebach quarry to Llandaff wharf, 13 May 1908. ILW collection

its docks promoted further dramatic urban growth in Victorian Cardiff and 52,000 people were added to the city's population in the 20 years before 1881, with another 79,000 in the next 20 years. Growth of this kind produced an average of 30 new streets, and 1,274 new houses and shops each year in the period 1884-1888.[30] The Glamorganshire Canal's contribution and the part played by its hard-working boatmen to the growth and character of Victorian and Edwardian Cardiff is not widely appreciated. Look for the evidence in the Pennant sandstone in Roath, Cathays, Heath, Roath Park, Canton, Pontcanna, Gabalfa, Llandaff and Whitchurch.

From around 1860, Pennant sandstone began to be the dominant building stone used in Cardiff's inner expansion. The railway could have brought some of this material close to the building sites but it is also very clear that the Glamorganshire Canal, with its Pontypridd quarries, was in an advantageous position for delivering Cardiff's building stone. Most of the Pennant quarries were convenient to canal wharves. The quarries were only 12 miles from central Cardiff, which allowed the average boatman and his butty some 5 - 6 hours to reach the point of sale. The Pontypridd

Albion colliery, Cilfynydd. A cart collects a load of stone just delivered by canal to the towpath. Also, on the extreme left, a pile of limestone can be seen on the towpath next to the Caedudwg limekiln, which appears to be in use.
Brian Lewis collection

quarries remained relatively free from railway competition. There were convenient wharfage arrangements in Cardiff between Blackweir, Cathays and North Road Lock, with new bays being provided for stone to be delivered directly into builders' carts. Finally, there was the heavy demand for building stone to stimulate the trade. Figures for tonnages of stone carried on the canal are lacking until the late 19th century, a period of decline, but the following table can be given for stone and gravel loaded and discharged on the canal by bye traders[31]:

1894 .... 65,041 tons
1898 .... 46,086 tons
1906 .... 35,427 tons

In spite of its rather sombre appearance, the Pennant stone remained an important and fashionable building stone in Cardiff for over 60 years, with the wall surfaces and mullions of buildings often enlivened by dressings of yellow brick or Bath stone. Finally, it is a sad reflection on modern day planning that many of Cardiff's street pavements of Pennant flags are being needlessly replaced with less durable concrete slabs.

By good fortune a complete set of boat permits exists for the traffic from John Gibbon's quarry at Pentrebach, Pontypridd to North Road, Cardiff (February-December 1904). In the 11 month period of the permits, which are consecutively numbered, John Gibbon sent down 4,400 tons of stone in 220 boats to Cardiff. Presuming a traffic of 10 boats for January 1904, the tonnage sent from the quarry in the complete year 1904 would be 4,600 tons. The permits show that the majority of the loadings were handled by two Llandaff-based boatmen, William Bladen and his son or nephew, also William, working with two boats and a boat boy in charge of each horse. The name of another boatman, Henry Herbert, occurs twelve times in the year, when he was in charge of the GCC's goods boats Nos. 100 and 503. True to a boatman's instincts, Herbert was keen to pick up a back load for Cardiff and in 1904 he brought down 240 tons of stone to North Road in the company's boats, rather than return to Cardiff empty.

The Gibbon quarry was the last of the canal served quarries to give a livelihood to the bye traders and the stone traffic on the canal seems to have ended about 1914. It seems that the Pennant stone had lost its attraction to builders and canal-carrying from the Newbridge quarries ended, not so much through competition from railways but because of the growing fashion for building in brick.

NOTES TO CHAPTER 11

1 For further reading see John Ballinger (Ed.) *Cardiff: an Illustrated. Handbook*, Cardiff 1896 p188-190 and John W. Perkins *The Building Stones of Cardiff*, Cardiff 1984.

2 Susan Campbell-Jones *Welsh Sail*, Llandysul 1976 p23 and Colin Chapman *The Cowbridge Railway*, Poole 1984 p52.

3 M. Nix & M.R. Myers *Hartland Quay*, Hartland Quay Museum, 1982 p7 quoting R. Pearse *Ports & Harbours of Cornwall*, 1964 p124.

4 Edgar L. Chappell *Historic Melingriffith*, Cardiff 1940 p33-4.

5 Charles Wood *An Account of the Material Transactions at Cyfarthfa in the Parish of Merthyr Tidvil - Commencing April 11th 1766*, microfilm copy at GRO.

6 GCC Thomas Dadford's Report Accounts for Extra work: item 24 Aqueduct at head of Lock 2. GRO QAW 2/118

7 GCC minute book 26 Oct 1793.

8 GRO Dowlais Letters folio 301, 11 April 1795.

9 GCC minute book 10 April 1838.

10 For comprehensive information on the properties, production, uses and transport of lime see Stephen Hughes *The Brecon Forest Tramroads*, Aberystwyth 1990 p355 and R. Williams *Limekilns and Limeburning*, Princes Risborough 1989.

11 GCC minute book 15 Jan and 12 March 1796.

12 GRO Q/Dp 8b.

13 CCL Bute 1 37.

14 Kelly's South Wales Directory, 1871.

15 Hughes *Brecon Forest Tramroads*, p193.

16 See Gordon Rattenbury *Tramroads of the Brecknock and Abergavenny Canal*, Oakham 1980 and Gordon Rattenbury & Ray Cook *The Hay and Kington Railways*, Mold 1996.

17 GCC minute book 6 April 1820.

18 GRO Q/Dp 150.

19 GCC minute book 15 July 1797, 6 Nov 1812, 22 April 1813, 2 March, 6 April and 20 July 1820.

20 NLW Bute MS 6323 cited in Roger Brown *More about Ton*, Tongwynlais 1983 p46.

21 Ibbetson's oil '*Return from Market*' (NLW) and his watercolour '*Damsels on a Horse*' (NMGW) depict this pre-canal limekiln at Castell Coch c1790 (see page 19).

22 Worrall's Directory 1875 and Kelly's Directory 1895.

23 GCC down boat passes, John Thomas's Quarry 1885, ILW collection.

24 J. Tyler *Iron in the Soul*, Taffs Well 1988; Eric Mountford *The Cardiff Railway*, Oxford 1987 p79.

25 Glam Nat Trust:3 *Walks in the Coalfield*, pp4-5.

26 Dadford's accounts for Mar 1797-Mar 1798.

27 GCC boat passes from John Gibbon quarry, Pentrebach 1904. ILW collection.

28 GCC Down tonnage book Aug 1863, GRO D/D X296.

29 ILW interview with Frederick Francis, mason, North Road wharf, Cardiff, 1949, working reclaimed Pennant stone for Maindy Stadium. His father was one of the 20 masons on the wharf "*working for the Bute*".

30 M.J. Clark *Cardiff*, in G. Humphreys (ed) *Excursions from Swansea*, University College Swansea Geography Dept 1978. See also M.J. Daunton *Coal Metropolis Cardiff 1870-1914*, Leicester 1977, which covers the development of Cardiff housing in detail, whilst ignoring the source and supply of building materials.

31 1894 Board of Trade: Hearing of Objections to Tolls etc; 1898 Board of Trade: Canal Returns; 1906 Royal Commission on Canals.

Chapter 12

ARCHITECTURE – THE BRIDGES

It is generally agreed that the most familiar and attractive feature of British canal architecture in the countryside is the gently curving canal bridge. When a canal was cut through open landscape or through urban settlement, it became the responsibility of the canal engineer to provide bridges over the navigation where parish roads or landowners fields were to be cut in two. This requirement, outlined in both canal and railway Acts of Parliament, was to be repeated throughout the Railway Age, and in our own day the Department of Transport and its agencies have to consider the provision of accommodation bridges across the routes of all motorways.

Thomas Dadford built the majority of the Glamorganshire Canal's bridges in stone. They were arched bridges, adequate enough for the horse drawn road traffic of their day and they were constructed in the local Pennant sandstone of the Taff Valley. In 1793, the cost of building a stone bridge was quoted as £40.[1] Some of the canal company's early bridges were built of wood, as at Aberfan and Rhydycar,[2] but possibly because of problems from wear and tear and the Welsh climate they did not last long. In 1843, the GCC ordered that their wooden bridges be replaced with iron ones.[3] Iron bridges were generally flat decked, as at Melingriffith, and presented a rectangular space for the boats to pass under. The usual construction was a simple one of three elements – a cast iron deck over the water, which located into two cast iron openwork parapets. Bridges of this kind would be supported on masonry piers built high enough to give headroom for boats. There is also some evidence of movable bridges on the Glamorganshire Canal but they were rare. A swing bridge of some kind existed at Melingriffith in 1806[4], whilst at Merthyr a drawbridge carried the Cyfarthfa works railway over the canal's upper pound until the 1890s.[5] A late Victorian swingbridge at James Street, Cardiff, served the needs of road traffic and shipping.

In June 1818, the GCC committeemen's 3-day annual survey throughout the navigation reported that there were 83 bridges along the whole line of the waterway, between Cardiff and Merthyr.[6] These 83 bridges would have been canal company structures, for which the GCC was responsible for maintenance. Additionally, there were quite a number of privately owned bridges on the canal. For the most part these were towpath bridges, designed to carry the company's horse path over the entrance to private works basins. Examples of this type could be fairly crude in design, like the rudimentary plate decked one across the Garth ironworks basin at Taffs Well (1856) and a similar one of the same date at the lower Ynysangharad works basin at Brown Lenox, Pontypridd. This one would have horrified the Health & Safety regulators of today, because it never had an outer rail or parapet! A well known private bridge at the Merthyr end of the canal was the cast iron towpath bridge over Anthony Hill's loading dock at Abercanaid, known more familiarly to the boatmen as the Plymouth Basin. Until demolished in the 1970s, its cast parapet was a memorial to the Plymouth works ironmaster, carrying the legend *A. Hill Plymouth 1849*. Nearby, at Graig colliery in 1843, L. & W. Thomas were permitted to make a drawbridge over the canal to convey their coal to the Hill's ironworks, on condition they sent no coal by the Taff Vale Railway.[7]

The 18th century was a period when engineers and builders seemed to be able to combine utility with beauty in the most functional of objects and nowhere is this more evident than on the British canals. Locks, warehouses, administrative buildings, lock cottages, cranes and bridges built at this time display a rightness of proportion and a pleasing use of materials. They are hardly ever pretentious. Looking in a little more detail at the bridges of the Glamorganshire Canal, built cheaply for a group of English and Welsh industrialists, we find the Pennant stone was the local building material. This rather sombre stone gave a visual unity to all the canal structures. Compared to the majority of the bridges on the Monmouthshire Canal (1796), those on the Glamorganshire were low and undersized. The masonry of the bridges lacks any form of refinement. It was roughly coursed, there were no string courses and no keystones, there were few subtle curves and many of the bridge arches tended to spring awkwardly from straight sides. Yet for the most part, Thomas Dadford's bridges were pleasant to look at and sat comfortably in the landscape.

It is only in two locations – both in North Road, Cardiff, that canal bridge design departed from the ordinary. Blackweir bridge was faced in carefully cut blocks of ashlar[8] and North Road Lock bridge was an attractive iron bridge, which incorporated some delicate wrought iron work and

The cast iron turnover bridge of 1849 at Melingriffith, which replaced an earlier swingbridge. A bridge here was made necessary when it was decided to transfer the towpath past the tinplate works to the opposite bank of the canal. The tight bend was the cause of horses slipping into the cut, resulting in several recorded deaths and claims on the company. The photograph is taken looking downstream and clearly shows the height that the towpath rose in order for the bridge to give adequate head-room for boats to pass below. The tops of the bridge side members were so badly worn by the rubbing action of tow ropes that the canal company installed a protective steel rail on each side. The depth of the grooves in the cast iron can be made out by the light shining through them. The narrowing of the canal to take the bridge span gave the company the opportunity to insert grooves in the masonry to take a set of stop planks. The photograph shows the steps and precariously narrow ledge leading from the towpath to beneath the bridge, where the canal labourers would insert the stop planks.

ILW collection

The decking of the Melingriffith turnover bridge, showing also the steel protecting rails and some of the tow-rope rubbing damage. The bridge has survived but has been removed to another display location nearby.
ILW photo April 1958, neg 1922

North Road Lock bridge, an attractive essay in cast iron with wrought iron detail, gave access to the Marques of Bute's grounds at Cardiff Castle. The delicacy of the design suggests the Regency and a date in the early 1820s. The architectural merits of this bridge remained unrecognised by Cardiff Corporation and in November 1949 workmen were sent to demolish it.
ILW photo 28 June 1949, neg 829

A Cardiff Corporation omnibus ducks beneath the trolley wires as it crosses Custom House Street bridge, at the south end of St. Mary Street, Cardiff, in 1951. The bridge was photographed here in its final form and by this date it marked the upper navigational limit of the canal. One of several Victorian era iron bridges crossing the canal in Cardiff, its girders were strengthened in 1903 to carry the rails of the city's electric tramways. The bridge detail was perfectly in tune with the romanticism of Lord Bute's medievalist architect William Burges. On the face of the arched girder are the twin arms of Lord Bute and the city of Cardiff.　ILW photo, neg 1088

a miniature heraldic shield of the Marquess of Bute with the words '*Nobilis Ira*'. Both these bridges gave access to Lord Bute's Cardiff parkland and their design was a conscious effort to enhance the view.

Three types of stone arched bridge could be found on the Glamorganshire Canal. The most numerous of these was the conventional bridge built with an arch wide enough to pass a boat and to include a paved way for the horses. In an agreement between the GCC and Thomas Dadford in 1790, it was enacted '*the Bridges to be 18 feet span with a Haling path under them.*'[9]

Whilst there must have been upwards of 60 of these standard bridges at the time of the opening of the canal in 1794, there were occasions when one or two were added later. In 1821 the canal company

'*Ordered that Mr Williams of Duffryn-frwd be allowed the sum of £15 and the tonnage of all materials on his erecting*

a Stone Bridge over the Canal in the Town Ditch instead of the present Wood one.'[10]

A second type of bridge was the 'turnover' bridge, which was designed to allow the towpath to change sides. Turnover bridges were built without a towpath and when a boat horse reached the bridge the towline had to be detached. The horse then crossed the bridge while the boat passed through and the line was re-attached on the other side.

A third type of bridge also involved interruption to the boatmen because of unhitching towlines. This was the locktail bridge, which were very common on the Glamorganshire because they were economical to build, since they crossed the canal at its narrowest place – a lock. Dadford also saved expense on his locktail bridges by not providing them with towpaths. A locktail bridge was always positioned below the bottom gates of a lock and so a descending boat could effectively 'drop' under its arch.

231

The James Street swing bridge, across the Sea Lock pond in Cardiff's dockland, formed part of a new road scheme linking the Bute docks with Grangetown. Opened throughout in 1890, the new road also crossed the River Taff by the much larger Clarence Road swing bridge. The canal bridge, built by Heavysides of Derby, weighed 360 tons and gave 42 feet of clearance to shipping when open. The tall cabin controlled working of the bridge, which was originally opened manually but converted to electrical operation in 1921. The bridge carried road traffic until it was dismantled in 1957 but was last swung for shipping about 1948.

ILW photo, 1 Aug 1957, neg 1847

Bridges carrying major public roads had usually been built to slightly larger dimensions than the rest but in general the stone crossings of the GCC were suitable only for light traffic, so had begun to be a hazard to the increasing motor traffic of the 1930s. The company did not place public notices of weight restrictions at its bridges but it must have been concerned at the problem. In the words of the last general foreman, '*they were mostly only 30 hundredweight cart bridges.*' That is, they had been designed to take maximum weights of $1^{1}/_{2}$ tons. Imagine the company's consternation every year at Tongwynlais Lock, when a showman's traction engine crossed the canal to the fair field in Ironbridge Road, trailing behind all the mobile accoutrements of the fairground and no doubt dislodging the parapets in the process.[11]

The rapid growth of mid 19th century Cardiff soon demanded new streets and improved communications, and the old pattern of stone bridges in central Cardiff was eventually swept away. Cardiff Corporation replaced them by larger Victorian designs in iron and these proved of considerable architectural interest.[12] Unfortunately, not one of them survives today. The Hayes canal bridge, which carried a public street horse tramway from 1872, had parapets of solid cast plate, with vigorous designs in Romanesque interlacing. There were Gothic designs at East Canal wharf and near the castle at Kingsway, where in the 1930s the decorative parapets saw the Saturday shopper's pennies thrown into the canal for the boy swimmers diving below. In the case of this Kingsway canal bridge, it is interesting to note that the original North Gate canal bridge of 1794 is still in place under the modern one and in daily use in present day Cardiff as a pedestrian subway. Elsewhere on the canal, urban development brought changes. At Pontypridd, alterations to four canal bridges were necessary for the opening of the electric tramways in 1905 and in Merthyr, where the canal had been disused since 1898, the local authority demolished Middle Lock bridge in the 1920s[13] to give better access for traffic between Canal Square and Dynevor Street.

In conclusion we may notice that the Glamorganshire Canal, $25^{1}/_{2}$ miles long, was crossed 17 times by the bridges of eight different competing railway companies, all of which, wholly or jointly, were to become merged with the Great Western Railway in 1922. Whilst most of these bridges were of iron or steel construction, the

Vale of Neath Railway bridge (1853) near Merthyr was of unusual interest, with its elliptical main stone arch over the canal and its two supporting openings. First of the modern railways to cross the canal was the Taff Vale Railway (1840). The last to cross were the lattice girders of the Cardiff Railway (1906), a line that was originally intended to be built in the bed of the canal itself.

The canal company's aqueduct at Abercynon, completed in 1792, is a single arched structure spanning a narrowing of the River Taff, sited a few hundred yards before the Taff joins its tributary the Cynon. The arch of the aqueduct springs from rock foundations on both banks and was built by Dadford so strongly that it has carried the traffic of a modern road to Aberdare since the 1920s, albeit with some necessary widenings over the original structure at road level.

Further information about the bridges – their official and their local names, for they were never identified by a number – are to be found in Appendices E and F.

Blackweir bridge where the towpath changed sides so as to protect the privacy of the Bute grounds at Cardiff. This charming snow scene is copied from a turn of the century lantern slide.
Courtesy Welsh Industrial & Maritime Museum, S.C. Fox collection, 73.731/35

An empty patent fuel boat passes under North Road bridge, Cardiff, as it approaches North Road Lock, circa 1910. In the foreground, the towpath winds around a horse slip. This decorative Victorian cast iron span, also known as Kingsway bridge, was constructed over the top of Thomas Dadford's original canal arch. Remarkably, this stone arch of 1794 survives to this day under Kingsway and serves as a pedestrian subway.

Courtesy Welsh Industrial & Maritime Museum, S.C. Fox collection 73.629/60

Gelli bridge, Llandaff North, looking towards Melingriffith. Ty Mawr can be seen above the cabin of the maintenance boat.

ILW photo, July 1943, neg 227

Ty Mawr bridge, Whitchurch. Note the paved horseway and contrast the superior cut stonework of this arch with that which was more typical at Gelli (above), only a few hundred yards downstream.
ILW photo Sept 1950, neg 1060

The lock tail bridge at Tongwynlais, with the village beyond. There was no towpath. Boats would pass out of the lock and through the bridge before being hitched onto the towrope. The building on the left is the Tongwynlais cornmill. This 1920s photograph is another by S.C. Fox.

Some road bridges survived in their original humped-back form until the end. This is College Road Lock bridge, Llandaff Yard, in 1943. Wartime anti-tank positions are in place across the road.
Courtesy Cardiff City Library

The first main line railway to cross the Glamorganshire Canal was the Taff Vale, by this bridge just north of Llandaff station. The canal towpath is on the left, whilst Ty Mawr Road climbs through the small arch on the right. Ty Mawr itself can be seen through the bridge girder frame. This GWR official photograph was taken on 31 May 1943. Neil Parkhouse collection

The Cardiff Railway bridge over the canal at Glan y Llyn. A coal train, hauled by ex- GWR 0-6-2T No. 41 (originally Rhymney Railway No. 45), is seen crossing the bridge bound for the National Coal Board's coking plant at Nantgarw. This was the Cardiff Railway's third crossing of the canal within two miles. ILW photo 3 Jan 1952, neg 1175

Llwynmellt Lock (Middle Lock), showing the Cardiff Railway bridge crossing the canal between Coryton and Tongwynlais.
ILW photo 27 March 1943, neg 215

GLAMORGANSHIRE CANAL – IRON BRIDGES

1. RHYDYCAR

2. PLYMOUTH BASIN, ABERCANAID 1849

3. GRAIG CHAPEL & HAFOD TANGLWS

4. MELINGRIFFITH 1849
Turnover bridge

5. SUNNY BANK WEIR 1851

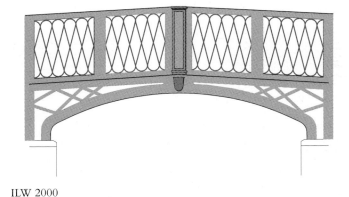

6. NORTH ROAD LOCK
Lord Bute's bridge c1820

Bridges 1-5 are one-piece cast iron designs. **1** *is preserved at Chapel row, Merthyr Tydfil.* **5** *is a towpath bridge, still in situ on a Nature Reserve near Melingriffith.* **6** *was something decorative for the Marquess of Bute's Lodge bridge, Cardiff Castle, c1820. It spanned the tail of North Road Lock and was demolished by Cardiff Corporation in 1949.*

ILW 2000

NOTES TO CHAPTER 12

1 Glamorganshire Canal Co. (GCC) Canal Co against Dadford, GRO QAW 2/118. Dadford Accounts for Extra work Cyfarthfa to Parl. Lock Items 9 and 20. Charles Hassall and William Pitt.
2 GCC Table of Distances from Cyfarthfa.
3 GCC minute book 25 Oct 1843.
4 GCC minute book 3 Sept 1806.
5 Ordnance Survey map, Merthyr, 25 inch 1st Ed. 1873-74.
6 GCC minute book 3 June 1818.
7 GCC minute book 25 Oct 1843.
8 Ashlar is a block of hewn and dressed stone with straight edges used in building.
9 GCC Agreement with Dadford 1790, GRO QAW 2/119.
10 GCC minute book 8 Jan 1821. Probably a site at Hills Street, between Queen Street and the Hayes Bridge in Cardiff.
11 Reminscences of T. Morgan in Rev'd R.L. Brown (ed.) *More About Ton*, Tongwynlais 1983, pp. 16 – 17.
12 J. Gloag *A History of Cast Iron in Architecture*, London 1948, pp. 328 - 9; 331.
13 F.J. Pedler *History of the Hamlet of Gellideg*, Merthyr 1930 p.44, 102.

The lock tail bridge at Forest Lock (Lock 43), here photographed in the 1920s by S.C. Fox, had a set of steps set into the upper parapet to allow the boatman quick access to the towpath. The lock house was planned to be built in 1827 but the resolution is repeated in the minute books in 1834.

Chapter 13

ARCHITECTURE – THE BUILDINGS

'My Canal commences at my Door down to the Sea Lock in Cardiff river and is now nearly finished. Our Boats carry about 25 Tons each and are attended by a little welch horse & 2 Men.'

So wrote Richard Crawshay in 1797, about the canal he had promoted with other Merthyr iron producers, between Cyfarthfa and the river port of Cardiff. The canal had been built cheaply, in accordance with Crawshay's business philosophy of utility with economy and his characteristic concern for the shareholders. There were no classical columns on Thomas Dadford's aqueduct at Abercynon, whilst the tunnel in Cardiff, built less than 11 feet wide, remained too narrow for boats to pass and was a bottleneck for more than 130 years. No boat horse taller than *'a little welch horse'* could comfortably walk under the bridges. These stringencies were operationally tiresome but they did not prevent the Glamorganshire Canal from achieving undreamed of prosperity for its proprietors.

Before the canal had been completed and opened to Cardiff in 1794, a number of buildings essential to the day to day running had been added to the architectural programme. The Navigation House at Abercynon was the most important of these administration centres, where the company's chief clerk and his assistants conducted canal business conveniently halfway between Cardiff and Merthyr. Navigation offices and toll houses were also built at Merthyr and at West Wharf in Cardiff, with attendant warehouses along the wharves. In 1797, the company built ten cottages for lock keepers and, at points along the line, further cottages were erected to house wharfingers, pond keepers, water tenders and other maintenance workers. Undoubtedly, the biggest architectural item on the GCC in its later years, and a vital one for operation of the canal, was the Pontyrhun engine house at Troedyrhiw, for which building stone was ordered to be provided in 1850. Three storeys tall and four bays long, with a hipped roof and tall stack, this very substantial building dominated the streets of Troedyrhiw like a Lancashire cotton mill, its steam engine raising water out of the River Taff from 1853 until the 1880s and pumping it 80 feet into the canal's Four Mile level. The Pontyrhun engine replaced an earlier Boulton & Watt type steam engine of 1809, which had its own engine house. At

the lower end of the architectural scale were the humbler buildings forming the carpenters' and smiths' shops at Navigation Yard, the Glamorganshire Canal Company's maintenance yard at Abercynon.

In the course of time groups of industrial workers' cottages were erected at wharves and basins along the canal line, often with associated public houses and stables. The development was gradual and piecemeal rather than planned, with the canal company often taking the initiative. The canal-bank cottages in Nantgarw village must have originated in this way and similarly the row of early industrial workers' cottages along the wharf at Trallwn (Pontypridd). At other times, private enterprise was allowed to build accommodation for workers and to erect stables, pubs and warehouses. A wholly private development around the Basin at Navigation (Abercynon) followed this pattern, as a result of the opening of the Dowlais, Penydarren and Plymouth companies' Merthyr Tramroad down to the exchange dock there in 1802.

Sadly very few of the buildings associated with life and work on the Glamorganshire Canal remain in existence today and those that have escaped destruction seem to have suffered heavily from insensitive alterations. We cannot bring back what has been lost but perhaps this is the right moment to examine more closely some of the canal buildings of the past and to comment briefly on their history, their form and their function, and their important associations with people. We shall start with the first building which seems to have concerned the canal company – the Navigation House at Abercynon.

The Navigation House

At one of the earliest GCC meetings, on 25 September 1790, it was minuted:

'It being deemed necessary that a House shall be built on Craig Evan Leyshon near to the Aqueduct for the use of the Proprietors, the Expense of which shall not exceed £100. Mr Cockshutt shall settle the plan and contract for the building such House as soon as possible.'

By the following January, the cost of the House was

Navigation House, purpose-built by Thomas Dadford and administrative headquarters of the canal company from 1792 to the early 1880s. It is now a public house. Since this photograph was taken the appearance of the building has been changed unsympathetically by the simple act of providing it with incongruous replacement windows.

ILW photo 1971, neg 2242

stated to be £270 and Dadford would build it and live as tenant there at a rental of £18 per annum.[1] It seems reasonable to suppose that the building was completed and in use by the early part of 1792, with Thomas Dadford using it as his base while he was constructing the canal, and running and administering the completed lengths of it on behalf of the canal company. Did Dadford believe his tenancy of Navigation House to be rent free? In December 1794, we learn that the GCC gave orders to distrain on his effects for the £36 owed them for two years unpaid rent at the House.[2]

The frontage of Navigation House overlooked the canal, with an uninterrupted view of what was going on between the aqueduct and the various exchange wharves and their tramroads. According to William Harrison's map of the canal (1830), the building had by then formed an inverted 'T' plan. There were three floors to the main house, providing offices for the clerks, a committee room, living accommodation for clerks and house servants, and there were rooms for visitors staying overnight on canal business. The usual stables and coach house completed the transport needs of the day. To protect the building from the weather the exterior wall, built of the local Pennant sandstone, had probably been rendered from an early date. The original roofing material is not known but in June 1831 the GCC

ordered the Navigation House and the Sea Lock house in Cardiff to be re-roofed in blue slates, which must have been brought into the canal through the Sea Lock after a sea passage from North Wales ports.[3] Over the years, the house appears to have been added to. In 1819, the roof of the office needed attention and an additional office was called for to accommodate the company's books and records.[4] One of the interesting amenities of Navigation House was the chief clerk's fishpond, across the road to the south, which provided for the official table. According to local tradition, the pond was still closely guarded as late as the 1880s by Thomas Shepherd, the canal company's last clerk at Abercynon.

Following the passing of the Glamorganshire Canal to Bute control in 1885, the canal company transferred its administration from Abercynon to Cardiff and the Navigation House was closed to canal business. It became a public house and is still licensed as a pub at the present day, happily retaining its name. Navigation House has stood for over 200 years, a well-mannered, sash windowed provincial Georgian house whose place in industrial history is still only poorly recognised. Today, the visitor will look with dismay at what has happened to its simple classic proportions, which have been destroyed by horizontal replacement windows.

The Duke of Bridgewater's Arms, Pentrebach.
P.G. Rattenbury photo

Duke of Bridgewater's Arms

The idea of an inn on the Merthyr to Cardiff turnpike road, on the line of the Glamorganshire Canal, seems to have been Richard Crawshay's. His letters to James Cockshutt and to a number of landowners between October 1790 and July 1791, indicate a keen interest in the project, if not an obsession. Crawshay was based at his London business house but periodically had to visit Cyfarthfa ironworks and, from 1790, to supervise Dadford's progress on the building of the canal. A new inn on the canal would, he thought, be a more suitable place to stay than the Angel (in Cardiff), his usual port of call. By April 1791, Crawshay was writing to Lady Dynevor (joint landowner, with John Richards, of the site to be taken for the Duke) and informing her that William Key, the land tenant, was willing to surrender the lease. He assured her ladyship that his plan '*is more calculated for a publick Good than my own personal interest.*' When the inn on the Dynevor land at Newbridge was built is not clear, nor is it certain

that Crawshay built it, but a conveyance exists to show that Thomas Dadford and his wife Ann owned the property in 1805, and that they sold the Duke's Arms that year to Richard Crawshay. The name 'Duke of Bridgewater's Arms' must have been given to the inn by Thomas Dadford, to show his admiration for the celebrated Canal Duke – Francis Egerton, 3rd Duke of Bridgewater.

The 'Duke' had an 'H' shaped ground plan, and faced the canal and the Pentrebach Road, a short distance to the north of Glyntaff church. Built in the local stone, with whitened exterior walls, the 'Duke' provided fairly substantial accommodation for travellers in a region not well endowed with hostelries. The building was indistinguishable in style from the larger Welsh farmhouse, with its roughly coursed walls, sashed windows and the builder's regard for Georgian symmetry. It seems to have been out of use as an inn by the 1880s, when O.S. plans of the period indicate that it was called 'Yr Hen Dy', (the Old House). The building was among many structures of transport interest swept away in Pontypridd, as a result of the construction of the A470 Cardiff-Merthyr trunk road.

The Canal Pubs

The Glamorganshire Canal with, it is said, over 200 boats at work in its heyday, had every reason to consider the boatman's need for rest and refreshment. Public houses were built at convenient points along the line, some where bridges crossed the navigation, others in towns and villages close to the canal towpath. On the Glamorganshire, the building of pubs seems to have been left to private enterprise, the canal company often granting permission to build on land adjoining the towpath. Some examples of canal inns will be briefly discussed beginning with a canal hotel in Cardiff with strong maritime connections, the Old Sea Lock on the bank of the Sea Lock basin.

The Newbridge Arms on the bank of the disused canal at Coedpenmaen in April 1971.
ILW photo, neg 2263

The Old Sea Lock Hotel, Sea Lock pound, Cardiff, photographed in the 1880s by G.H. Wills. Courtesy Cardiff City Library

Old Sea Lock hotel

In April 1812 the canal company allocated '*a piece of ground near the Waste Weir at the Sea Lock*' in Cardiff to James Walters, for building a hotel. Walters was a sea captain engaged in the Bristol trade, who in 1790 had acquired the coasting vessel *Cardiff Castle*. The Old Sea Lock hotel was useful to those in maritime trading on the canal, whose vessels could be seen moored literally outside the building's front door. James Walters's engagement with the GCC was for a term of 42 years, at a rent of £5 per annum. The Old Sea Lock hotel stood on the west bank of the canal, a pleasing example of Regency domestic architecture reduced to its simplest expression – a broad low frontage of two floors with central front door and fanlight, and with the characteristic low pitched roof with wide eaves. The building survived in a derelict condition until the 1970s.

New Sea Lock hotel

The terms 'Old' and 'New' Sea Lock refer to the building chronology of the pubs and not to the entrance lock on the canal after which they were named. The New Sea Lock hotel was part of the mid Victorian development of Cardiff docklands. It stood at the south end of Harrowby Street, near to the sand wharves of Sandridge & Co. It was a double fronted building with parapet, and its gable end faced the canal and the track of the GCC railway. The pub was swept away in the general clearances of canalside properties in the 1980s and 90s, which included Harrowby Street.

The Canal House, Merthyr Tydfil

Georgetown, once an important commercial centre because of the Glamorganshire Canal, could boast a

substantial number of Merthyr's public houses. Almost all of them were in streets but the Canal House stood on the towpath of the Penydarren pound, between Lock 1 at Jackson's bridge and Lock 2 at Penry Street. A genuine boatman's pub, it also incorporated a brewhouse. No photographs of the building seem to have survived and the canal in Georgetown was redeveloped by Merthyr Corporation in the 1920s.

The Llwynyreos, Abercanaid

The Llwynyreos, whose name means 'Nightingale Grove', is an uncompromising canal inn set on the Abercanaid towpath, with its back to the village and overlooking open country on a canal site that is still just recognisable. Standing two miles south of Merthyr, the Llwynyreos still has no proper public road to it but the

pub serves the village, and the needs of cyclists and walkers who follow the old towpath route of the Taff Valley Trail. Its survival as a working pub is remarkable when it is remembered that the last boats and boatmen passed its front door a century ago. The building is a simple double fronted house and, when photographed in 1947 (see page 92), its rather drab exterior suggested a plain mid Victorian style. The permanence of its name is assured in characterful relief across the front elevation.

The Custom House, Cardiff

Cardiff's original Customs House was based in High Street, near to the river quays. The Glamorganshire Canal created a new port with its mile long floating harbour and sea lock. A new Custom House was built at the head of the East Wharf on the canal, near the town's South gate,

The Custom House on East Canal Wharf in November 1974. The head of the canal's Sea Lock pound lay where the cars are parked. Now (2001) a new road from the city centre to old dockland (renamed Cardiff Bay) has been built on the bed of the re-excavated canal.   ILW photo Nov 1974, neg 2532

The company's offices and stables at Canal Place, Trallwn, Pontypridd in 1971 when they were occupied temporarily by Pontypridd Rugby Club.   Don Powell collection

1980s, the whole building was gutted and only the façade retained in a complete re-build when the Land Authority for Wales was established there. More recently, the Welsh Rugby Union have taken offices in the new building. It is to be hoped that its preservation is secure.

Company Houses and Cottages

Thomas Dadford may have built some of the first lock cottages before 1795. Roger Kinton, an early GCC boat checker and superintendent of locks, was allowed to live in '*the Co's cottage near Dyffryn frood [Nantgarw]*' in July 1795. Another minute book entry, on 7 July 1797, records abruptly '*Lock Keepers 10 Houses @ £34 .... £340.*' As the traffic on the canal became busier and congestion increased, more cottages were built for lock keepers. Portobello Lock cottage was the first authorised in 1815, Crockherbtown in 1818 (actually built on top of the Cardiff tunnel), Taffs Well in 1826, and Forest and Mynachdy in 1827.

Under still more pressure from the 1830s, the GCC ordered locks to be open around the clock, with a double set of keepers to cope with the traffic. Accommodation also had to be doubled and the minute book (29 September 1836) recorded '*a Cottage to be built adjoining the present one for the use of the second lock keeper at the Sea Lock.*' For the same reason an extra cottage was built on to the existing one at Mynachdy Lock.

All this activity, in harmony with Welsh rural building tradition, enhanced the landscape with whitened lock cottages and the appealing element of water. Today, with almost all of the Glamorganshire Canal now effectively destroyed, it is fortunate that a survey of one canal cottage was made, by J.B. Lowe and D.N. Anderson of the Welsh School of Architecture at UWIST, Cardiff. This was Coedpenmaen cottage at Tynygraig Lock (No 26), the survey being completed immediately before its demolition, as it stood in the path of contractors building the A470 Cardiff-Merthyr trunk road in June 1971. In *Iron Industry Housing Papers No. 2* (UWIST, 1972) the cottage is described as following the 'standard' double-fronted, four-room, two-storey layout, with extensive use of oak in the roof construction suggesting an early date of around 1811. External walls were of heavy roughly squared rubble, cement rendered and the roof had at some time been re-slated. Access to the upper rooms was by semicircular stone stairs. The authors also compare the Coedpenmaen cottage with Maes Llan cottage at Gelligaer, a similar example of rural housing of the same period. Both cottages were seen as being in continuity with an earlier 17th century tradition.

the building being leased to HM Customs for 99 years from 10 October 1821. This in turn was replaced on the East Wharf/Custom House Street site by the present building, dating from 1845. It has been described as a modest stuccoed building in Palladian dress and bearing a distinct resemblance to the Custom House at Bristol, erected eight years previously to designs by Sydney Smirke. Although not strictly a canal building, the Custom House, with its East Wharf doorway framed with paired pilasters supporting a segmental arch, does succeed in reflecting the importance of the canal to the commercial life of Cardiff in the 1840s. The impressive coat of arms facing the East Wharf was removed from the doorway during the 20th century, possibly to coincide with the transfer of business to HM Customs offices in Bute Street, now much nearer the Bute docks and centres of maritime trade. The 1845 Custom House still stands on its corner site, though no trace of the canal remains at East Wharf today. In the late

At the site of the 17th century Taff furnace in Tongwynlais, Ivy House (on the left), pre-dates the canal and is where the quarry owner William Price lived. On the right is Ivy Dene, a canal company cottage which housed the lengthsman who looked after the canal's weir and trunk. Today, the fine canal bridge has disappeared under the A470 but the houses remain.   ILW photo 3 Jan 1952, neg 1174

'From the quantity of lime made in this country most houses are whiten'd, which gives a gay appearance, as also the very roofs of the houses and churches: dazzling the eyes and appearing like undissolved snow.' [5]

The Welsh custom of whitewashing exterior and some interior wall surfaces was a regular procedure on the canal. Gilbert Randall, the canal foreman at Cilfynydd in 1949, commented that it was his father's job to limewash all the canal buildings between Pontypridd and Abercynon every year. The practice contributed to a cheerful appearance but its main purpose was to aid cleanliness and to weatherproof the buildings.

Two of the best preserved canal cottages surviving in 2000 were the lock house at the site of Taff's Well Lock (Glanyllyn) and the weir house Ivy Dene next to Ivy House (Tongwynlais).

The surviving Taff's Well Lock house of 1826.
ILW photo 31 May 1975, neg 2582

NOTES TO CHAPTER 13
1 GCC minute book 22 Jan 1791.
2 GCC minute book 16 Dec 1794.
3 GCC minute book 1 June 1831.
4 GCC minute book 16 June 1819.
5 John Byng, Viscount Torrington *Tour into S. Wales 1787,* Cardiff Central Library manuscript.

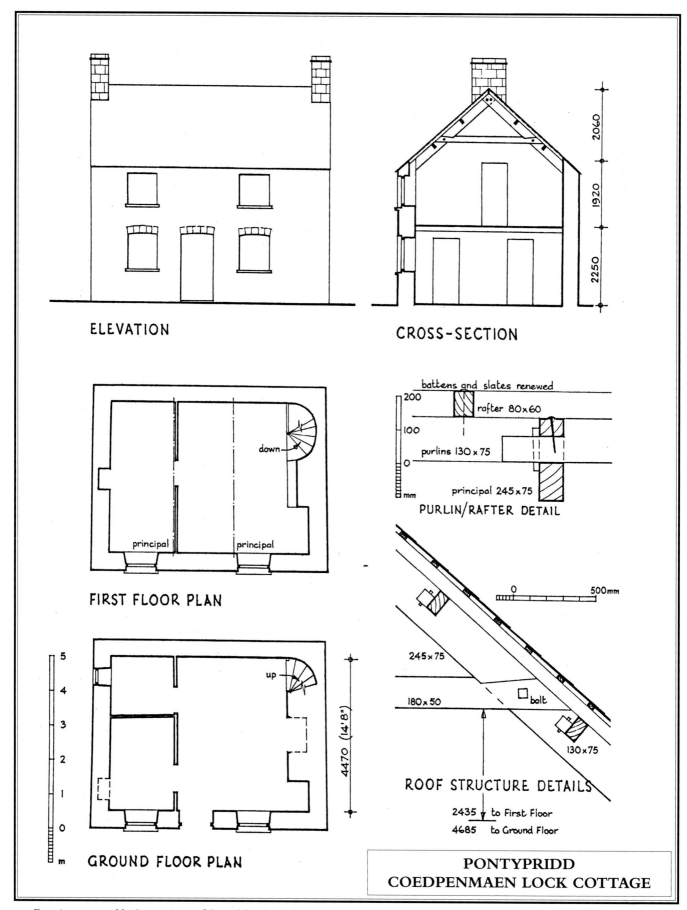

ELEVATION

CROSS-SECTION

2060

1920

2250

FIRST FLOOR PLAN

down

principal   principal

battens and slates renewed

200

100

0

mm

rafter 80×60

purlins 130×75

principal 245×75

PURLIN/RAFTER DETAIL

500mm

245×75

180×50   bolt

130×75

ROOF STRUCTURE DETAILS

GROUND FLOOR PLAN

5
4
3
2
1
0
m

up

4470 (14'8")

2435 to First Floor
4685 to Ground Floor

**PONTYPRIDD
COEDPENMAEN LOCK COTTAGE**

*Drawings prepared by Jeremy Lowe of the Welsh School of Architecture in 1972 from a survey made before the destruction of Coedpenmaen
Lock cottage which stood in the way of the A470 road scheme.*
Courtesy Jeremy Lowe

Appendix A

Two differing versions of the canal company's official Table of Distances have survived.

The first, printed by W. Williams of Merthyr Tydfil, is bound into Thomas Reece's copy of the canal Acts, which he has personally signed and dated 1809. Reece became Clerk in July 1808, on the death of Philip Williams. It is likely that he inherited the book from Williams's official papers, because there is evidence that the printed versions of the Acts in the book date from their enactment. The table certainly is no later than 1809 and there is a manuscript annotation 'Mr Griffith's Canal' at the entry for Deniah Lock – the Doctor's canal was built in 1810 and officially joined to the Glamorganshire in 1813.

Several copies of the second version of the Table of Distances survive. On some, Thomas Shepherd's name is printed at its foot. Shepherd was Clerk from June 1851 until the Marquess of Bute's committee took over in June 1885. Entries on the table suggest that it was produced in the early years of Shepherd's term, during the most prosperous period for the canal. In fact, a copy dated 1854, in Merthyr library, bears this out. The version seems to have remained in use at least until closure of the canal's upper section because one of the surviving copies was printed by Frost of Merthyr Tydfil and is dated 1895.

The obvious difference between the two versions is that the earlier gives the distances from the Sea Lock at Cardiff while the later gives the distances from Cyfarthfa. Many historical entries from the first have been inherited by the second since they had become commonplace landmarks for the boatmen to enter on their permits. A curious entry even on the early table is the 'Coed pen Main old Iron Yard'. This is possibly the site of the 1790s transshipment yard, when the southern section of the canal was still being built and iron was transferred from boat to road waggon to continue its journey to Cardiff.

The Table of Distances reproduced here, courtesy of Bill Hamlin, is a copy of the later version.

A TABLE OF DISTANCES

ON THE

GLAMORGANSHIRE CANAL,

FROM CYFARTHFA, VIZ.

TO

MILES. NAMES OF PLACES.
0¼...75 Yards above Canal Warehouse.
Cyfarthfa Ore Wharf and Basin, *Dowlais Penydarran* and Bute Yards, *Graig* Coal Yards and Pride's Storehouse, are situate between these Two ¼ Mile Marks.
0½...Lock No. 2.
Wainwillt Coal Yard and all the Storehouses, except the above named, are between these Two ¼ Mile Marks, and also the Timber Yards and Parliament Lock.
0¾...Site of old Brick Yard.
...*Rhydycar* Culvert.
1¼...Wooden Bridge at *Rhydycar*.
1½. 115 Yards above *Glyndyris* Locks, (No. 4 & 5.)
Mr. Crawshay's Pitwood Yard.
1¾. 280 Yards below *Glyndyris* Locks.
Wainwillt Colliery.
2 ...*Abercannaid* Barn.
Graig Colliery.
2¼...47 Yards below *Gethin* Upper Bridge.
2½...Opposite *Gethin* Farm House.
2¾...44 Yards below Pond Keeper's House.
3 ...115 Yards below *Penrhiw-yr-Onan Bridge*.
Evan Evans's *Pontyreen* Quarry.
3¼...17 Yards below *Squirrel's Castle*.
H. Allen's *Pontyreen* Quarry.
3½...Opposite Engineer's House at *Pontyreen*.
Cnwc Quarry.
3¾...Below *Cnwc* Bridge.
4 .. Upper end of Mr. Clive's Wood.
4¼... 92 Yards above *Nantmaen* Bridge.
4½...*Ynys ygorred* House.
4¾...Above *Hafod Tanglws*.
5 .. 80 Yards above *Perthyglyson* Upper Bridge.
5¼.. In *Perthyglyson* Wood.
5½...195 Yards above *Aberfan* Locks, (No. 6 & 7.)
5¾...28 Yards below *Aberfan* Wooden Bridge.
6 ...Lower end of Walling in *Aberfan* Rocks.
6¼...104 Yards above Weir.
6½...*Pontygwaith* Lock, (No 8.)
6¾...182 Yards below Highway Bridge.
7 ...57 Yards above *Pontcaedrwen*.
7¼...242 Yards below Upper Trunk.
7½...20 Yards above Powder Magazine.
7¾...327 Yards above *Cefnglas* Lock, (No. 9.)
8 ...40 Yards above Lock, (No. 10.)
8¼...40 Yards above *Goedrau'r* Coed House.
8½...65 Yards above Lock, (No. 14.)
Lock 17, and *Aberdare* Canal.
8¾...Opposite Mason's Shed.
Basin, and Powell and Co.'s Coal Tips.
9 ...Navigation House.
Lancaiach Coal Tip.
9¼...Trunk below Navigation House.
Wide Pool, T. Thomas's Limekiln and Railway Bridge.
9½...130 Yards below Old Stop Gate.
9¾...Opposite Park House.
10 ...North end of *Ynyscaedudwg*.
10¼...30 Yards above *Ynyscaedudwg* Lock, (No. 25.)
Ynyscaedudwg Limekiln.
10½...Waste Weir below Do.
10¾...30 Yards above *Bydwenarth* Wood.
11 ...120 Yards below *Bydwenarth* Culvert.
11¼...60 Yards below John Norton's Bridge.
11½...*Coedpenmain*, old Iron Yard.
11¾...40 Yards above Road Lock, (No. 27.)
Thomas Edward's Quarry.
12 ...Canal Warehouse, *Trallwn*.
Ynysyngharrad Upper Basin.
12¼...Upper Lock, (No. 31.)
Ynysyngharrad Lower Basin.
12½...Waste Weir, *Pentrebach*.
Pentrebach Quarries and Duke's Arms.
12¾...60 Yards below Arch under Turnpike Road.
13 ...Opposite River Row, *Treforest*.
Taff Vale and *Treforest* Works, and *Gwern-g-Gerwn*.

MILES. NAMES OF PLACES.
13¼...180 Yards below *Pwllywheiad* Bridge.
13½...*Duffryn* Lock, (No. 33.)
13¾...Lower end of *Duffryn* Farm.
14 ...Trunk above *Deniah* Lock, (No. 34.)
Rev. G. Thomas's Canal.
14¼...Waste Weir below *Deniah*.
Corrwg Foundry.
14½...30 Yards below Foundry Bridge.
14¾...140 Yards below Pentre Bridge.
15 ...15 Yards below Weaver's Bridge.
Maesmawr Coal Tip.
15¼...*Ty-yn-wern* Bridge.
15½...20 Yards below Culvert in College Land.
15¾...130 Yards above *Caerty du* Bridge.
16 ...Opposite *Caerty du*.
16¼...50 Yards above *Nantgarw*, Upper Waste Weir.
Nantgarw Storehouse.
16½...60 Yards above *Graig* Bridge.
Graigyrallt Colliery and Quarries.
16¾...110 Yards above *Bryncoch* Bridge.
17 ...70 Yards below Treble Locks, (No. 35, 36, & 37.)
17¼...60 Yards above *Taff's Well* Lock, (No. 38.)
17½...30 Yards above *Caeglas* Lock, (No. 39.)
John Morgan's Upper Limestone Quarry, (or No. 1.)
17¾...150 Yards below *Portobello* Lock, (No. 40.)
Evan Morgan's Limestone Quarry, (No. 2.) and John Morgan's lower Limestone Quarry, (No. 3.)
18 .. 40 Yards below Walnut Tree Bridge.
Thomas Thomas's Limestone Quarry, (No. 4.)
18¼...48 Yards above *Pentyrch* Bridge.
John Thomas's Limestone Quarry, (No. 5.)
18½...50 Yards below Old Stop Gate.
Tongwyrddlas Upper Coal Yard.
18¾...120 Yards below Ivy House.
Tongwyrddlas Lower Coal Yard.
19 ...120 Yards below Ton Lock, (No. 41.)
19¼...20 Yards above *Llwynmellt* Lock, (No. 42.)
19½...40 Yards above Forest Lock, (No. 43.)
19¾....Under the Hill at *Tyclyn*.
20 ...Opposite Sunny Bank.
Melin Griffith Basin.
20¼...4 Yards below *Melin Griffith* Works Bridge.
Melin Griffith lower landing Place.
20½ ..40 Yards above *Tymawr* Bridge.
20¾...Opposite *Gelly* House.
21 ...Opposite Hawthorn Cottage.
Coal Yards and *Llandaff* Upper Yard.
21¼...*Llandaff* Lock, (No. 45.)
Llandaff Lower Yard, Canal Co.'s Storehouses and W. Steel's Coal Yard.
21½ College Lock, (No. 46.)
21¾...80 Yards above *Gabalva* Lock, (No. 47.)
22 .. Opposite *Monachty* House.
22¼ ..Below *Monachty* Lock, (No. 48.)
22½ ..40 Yards above *Llystalybont* Boat Dock.
22¾...260 Yards below *Llystalybont* House.
23 ..300 Yards above Black Weir.
23¼...Black Weir Bridge.
23½...100 Yards above *Cathays*.
23¾...30 Yards above Turnpike Gate.
Town Coal Yards and North Gate.
24 ...50 Yards above Crockherbtown Lock, (No 50.)
Coffin & Co.'s Coal Yard, and Crockherbtown Lock.
24¼...Cock's Tower.
Robert Thomas's Coal Yard.
24½...South Gate.
Wharf, Bonded Warehouse, Timber Yards, and entrance cut to Bute Docks.
24¾...Limekiln on Moors.
Brick Yard.
25 ...Near the Bank.
Railway Dock.
25¼....
25½... Sea Lock.

Forty Feet of Oak, Elm, or Beech Timber, and Fifty Feet of Fir or Deal, Balk, Poplar, or Birch, not cut into Scantlings, shall be deemed, rated, and estimated as and for One Ton Weight.

THOMAS SHEPHERD,

Clerk to the Company of Proprietors of the Glamorganshire Canal Navigation.

Appendix B

A VIEW FROM THE BOAT

No boating guide book to the Glamorganshire and Aberdare canals has ever existed. Sadly, both the canals disappeared from the British inland waterway scene long before people were persuaded that conserving and restoring the waterways is better than destruction.

A View from the Boat is a reconstruction of a boat journey of just over a century ago. Although it has to be described as fiction, the whole of the writing is based on fact. Three boatmen born between 1863 and 1882 provided insights into what it was like to work on the boats to Merthyr and Aberdare, and in 1950 one of them with a phenomenal memory joined ILW to walk the nine miles of towpath from Cyfarthfa to Abercynon.

The Merthyr and Aberdare to Abercynon voyages are set in 1898. The rest of the way to Cardiff is described in 1914, a year before the canal was breached at Cilfynydd. Commentary and notes are set out in the form of a familiar modern canal touring guide.

Prothero & Clark, in *A New Oarsman's Guide* (1896), claimed to be the first to publish a guide to '*all such among the waterways of Great Britain and Ireland as it may be worth an oarsman's while to visit.*' Writing to inform the adventurous single-minded male members of the prestigious rowing clubs of the day, they praised the Welsh section of the Shropshire Union Canal and the Brecon & Abergavenny Canal – '*the 33 miles row from Pontymoile to Brecon is of a high order of beauty, such as not many of our natural rivers can surpass.*' Prothero & Clark were otherwise lukewarm about canals – '*Few canals are worth a visit for their own sake except as links in a through route*' – but they did give details of the multi-locked

Monmouthshire (Newport to Pontypool) and its equally steep Crumlin arm – '*from Newport to Crumlin and back is a good day's work for a light canoe, passing the locks on wheels.*'

A New Oarsman's Guide makes no mention of the Glamorganshire Canal and perhaps we need to be reminded that in 1896 there was no general interest in canals and no universal leisure. What is more, the rare prospective boating visitor would probably have been put off by the industrial nature of parts of the route and by the many locks. Local people of the valleys were not so concerned. They enjoyed the canals and knew their well-loved pockets of beauty, welcoming once a year the opportunity to get on the water with a social outing put on by one of the community church or chapel Sunday schools. Even the steam tug *Bute* is known to have taken pleasure boating trips from Cardiff to Tongwynlais, Castell Coch and Taff's Well.

A View from the Boat begins in Merthyr and presumes a hired boat, horse and boatman, with a permit for the trip obtained from the company's Cardiff office at West Wharf, where the appropriate toll would be paid. According to circumstances and the conventions of the period, a boat party might stay overnight in convenient hotels. The boatman would stay overnight on his boat – one of the type always readily available; the common cleaned-out Glamorganshire Canal 20-tonner in the charge of an owner-boatman like William Howells who, according to a surviving boat permit signed by the manager Lewis Llewelyn, took a picnic party from Coedpenmaen to Dynea in the summer of 1906.

Contemporary photographs of the canal show picnic parties in completely open boats and taking their chances with the weather!

Newbridge circa 1860
Mr and Mrs Hall's The Book of South Wales, the Wye and the Coast.

THE GLAMORGANSHIRE CANAL
CANAL HEAD to JACKSON'S BRIDGE,
MERTHYR TYDFIL
1898

Cyfarthfa

The canal begins in the Cyfarthfa iron and steel works property just below the Georgetown to Pandy Farm road, which connects the Pontstorehouse district of Merthyr with the Brecon road. Alongside the Canal Head, the Cyfarthfa works railway runs under the road and connects southwards with Georgetown and the Ynysfach works.

Water bubbles in through a pipe that lets in supplies from the works mill race. Looking north west from here, the valley is wide and open but the landscape is scarred by the heavy industry of the works and its attendant cinder tips. The River Taff is contained below high masonry walls and divides the works in two. Some of the older blast furnaces are built into the hill and seen from the road is a prominent engine house, and the casting sheds spreading towards the river. Distant to the north and set in hillside parkland is Cyfarthfa Castle, seat of ironmaster William Crawshay II, who commissioned this castellated mansion in 1824, from which he could view his iron-making empire.

The boat moves down the canal towards Georgetown. The river runs to the left, still hidden below its wall. Also on the left is the long building which houses the Crawshay rail finishing shop. Until recently the occasional independent trader came here to load light tramrails for Albion colliery at Cilfynydd but this pound is now deserted. On the west bank of the canal is the substantial graving dock of the Crawshays, which has been out of use since the company left the canal in 1885.

The canal narrows to pass through an opening bridge. Here, on the east bank, is the massive octagonal Crawshay chapel, which is followed by Chapel Row, a terrace of workmen's cottages. No. 4 Chapel Row is notable in the cultural life of Wales. It is the birthplace of Dr. Joseph Parry, Wales' most famous musician and composer. A wide basin follows where, on the west side, the Cyfarthfa boats unloaded the imported red ore, which was then taken in wagons to the Ynysfach furnaces through the street called Tramroadside.

The boat now reaches Lock No.1 and passes under the main road at Pont Storehouse. Next to the lock are the canal company's warehouses and yards. To the east is the river and the Bethesda Street river crossing at Jackson's bridge.

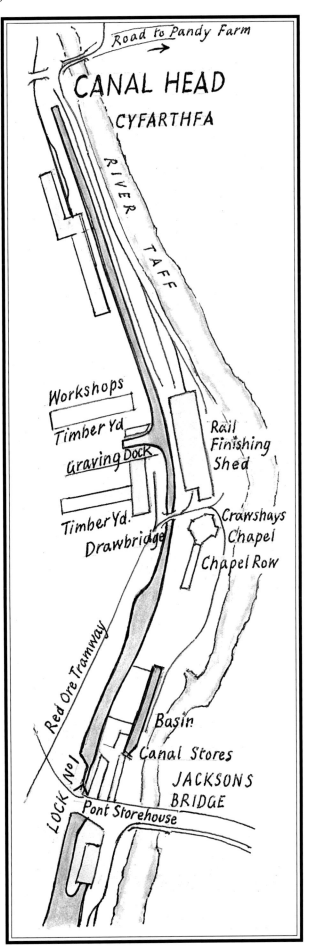

Cyfarthfa Castle built in the 1820s by William Crawshay II and surrounded by rolling parkland. This circa 1920 view is looking across part of the derelict remains of the Crawshay empire at Merthyr. SR collection

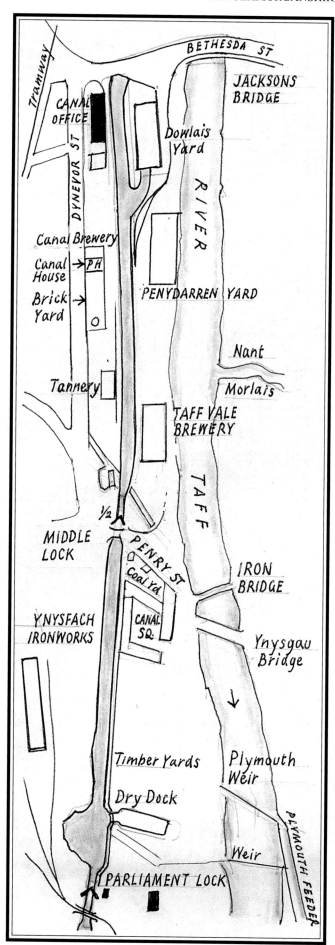

JACKSON'S BRIDGE
to PARLIAMENT LOCK

The canal runs its straight course southwards and is hemmed in between industrial buildings and yards. On the east side are the old Dowlais and Penydarren wharves and warehouses, and the tall Taff Vale brewery. On the west side, which carries the towpath, are the canal company's office, the Canal House public house and brewery, a former brickworks, and the skinyard and limepits. Although this part of Merthyr has declined in commercial importance, there is still a regular traffic on the waterway, worked by the Glamorganshire Canal Co's boats, which bring flour and general provisions from the Sea Lock in Cardiff to the Jackson's bridge warehouse. A diminishing number of canal traders bring house coal to Merthyr from the Abercanaid district but the neglected state of the cut is making the navigation of loaded boats very difficult.

At Penry Street the towpath changes sides and now will keep to the east side of the canal all the way to Abercynon. The road bridge at Penry Street is the locktail bridge of No.2 or Middle Lock and so there is no towpath under it. A boat crew can make a short stop here to walk down Penry Street, past the coal yard and Canal Square, to see Merthyr's iron bridge which crosses the River Taff. It was designed and built by Watkin George, chief engineer of Crawshay's Cyfarthfa ironworks, being completed in 1800.

From Penry Street, the canal continues its straight line through a rather derelict part of the town, with some timber yards on the east side and the gaunt engine houses and casting sheds of the Ynysfach ironworks on the west. From the boat these buildings present a picture of dilapidation and decay.

Parliament Lock is now reached. This is a permit lock, where loading bills are issued and examined by the lock keeper who works from a small toll office on the bank. Parliament Lock was prominent in the quarrelling and endless lawsuits over water rights that took place between the canal company and Richard Hill of Plymouth ironworks. The Plymouth weir on the Taff is close by the lock. It supplied water by a feeder to Hill's works.

Our journey down the canal would not have encountered the bridge seen here in this early 1920s view. Following closure of the canal at Merthyr, it was bridged by this flat span carrying a railway line into the old timber yard. On the right is Canal Square, whilst Penry Street bridge crosses the canal in the middle distance. SR collection

PARLIAMENT LOCK to UPPER ABERCANAID

Leaving Parliament Lock (No.3), the canal enters a man-made landscape reminiscent of the moon, a long trench between cinder tips which temporarily obscures contact with the outside world. Midway through these hills of cinder comes a high stone-arched bridge over the canal. A small arch in the bridge once accommodated a narrow gauge tramway from the Ynysfach works.

Rhydycar

A more open country is reached at Rhydycar bridge, where the canal passes a settlement of old industrial cottages, the homes of Crawshay's coal and ironstone miners. The remains of the engine house of the Rhydycar pumping pit, with its double acting Cornish beam engine, are close by.

The canal curves gently southwest towards Rhydycar iron bridge and Rhydycar farm, a remnant of the pre-industrial agricultural economy. It is now almost engulfed in the pit waste resulting from more than 100 years of coal and ironstone exploitation by Anthony Bacon and the Crawshays.

At Rhydycar iron bridge the boat turns to follow a generally southerly course again and passes under two railway bridges; the first carries the Brecon & Merthyr Railway (1868) and the second provides for the Vale of Neath Railway (1853), an interesting stone-built structure with an expansive elliptical arch over the canal, flanked by two supporting openings.

The boatman's view leaving Merthyr, of the bridges at Rhydycar, taken around the time this section closed in 1898. The lattice span of the B&M bridge is nearest, carrying the railway on its curve northwards towards Cefn Coed and, ultimately, Brecon. Beyond is the VNR arch. SR collection

Glyndyrus

The canal, now on a gentle curve, arrives at the two-rise Glyndyrus Locks, Nos 4 and 5, which lower the waterway 16ft 7ins on to the Four Mile Pond. This runs to Aberfan without a lock, the longest lockless stretch on the canal. The Glyndyrus lock keeper attends to the lock and is also responsible for the canal company's Glyndyrus Pond, the nearby reservoir constructed in 1806 on the recommendation of a survey by John Rennie.

Upper Abercanaid

Southwards from Glyndyrus, the canal reaches the small mining community of Upper Abercanaid. Here on the west bank stands the Cornish pumping engine of the Glyndyrus pit, which also worked a pump at nearby Pwll Tasker. A long range of miners' cottages is seen on the west bank, appropriately named Quay Row.

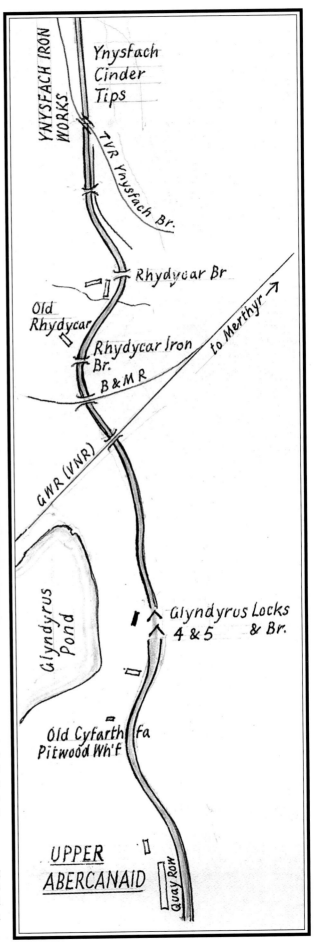

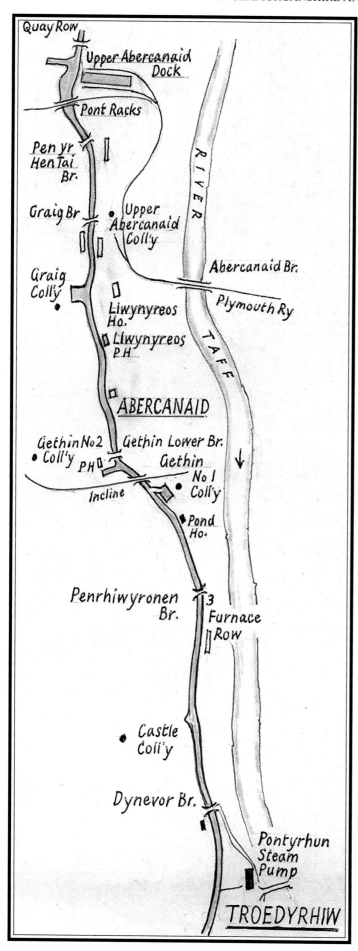

UPPER ABERCANAID to PONTYRHUN (TROEDYRHIW)

Upper Abercanaid

Passing under an iron bridge, the canal widens to assist boats to turn into the Hill's Plymouth private basin, a stone-lined dock lately used by the Plymouth company for shipping small coal. A smaller dock on the west side of the 'wide' may have been used by the famous Waun Wyllt steam coal pioneers, Robert and Lucy Thomas. The canal-side settlement of Upper Abercanaid continues in a south-easterly direction, the line of the canal dictating the alignment of Pond Row and Graig Row, small terraces built for colliers working at the Upper Abercanaid and Graig collieries. The Abercanaid pit stopped shipping out coal from the Plymouth basin about 1892 and the basin at Graig has not seen boats for many years.

Abercanaid

Abercanaid is a tidy stone-built village of terraced streets, laid out on a grid below the canal. The Llwynyreos public house faces the canal and is a welcome port of call for the boatmen. The view westwards is still surprisingly open and rural. Fields slope down to the water's edge and plenty of natural woodland survives.

Gethin

Gethin farm and the Gethin Arms pub now come into view on the west side of the canal, as the boat moves down the southern limits of Abercanaid. There is more colliery activity here. Gethin No. 1 pit (1849) is immediately alongside the towpath with a private canal basin. The striking architecture of the engine house – Pennant sandstone courses with bold limestone quoins and dressings – mark the property unmistakably as 'Crawshay Cyfarthfa'. An incline crosses the canal and carries a tramway to the No. 2 Pit, higher up the hill.

Building the canal from Merthyr to Gethin must have been comparatively simple for Thomas Dadford, its engineer. West of the Taff, the valley is wide and easy but south from Gethin to Quaker's Yard, it begins to narrow and deepen and mountain slopes crowd in. The canal now adopts its characteristic 'shelf formation' along the hillside, at first through woodland under Mynydd Gethin and later with views across the valley to Mynydd Cilfach yr Encil. Close to the river bank by Furnace Row is the site of an ancient iron furnace.

Castle Colliery

The canal hugs the hillside at Castle colliery, another Crawshay pit dating from 1869. Here is an outstandingly well-built engine house in the massive and decorative stone tradition of the Crawshays. The colliery is linked to Cyfarthfa by the Castle Pit & Gethin Railway, which now forms part of the Great Western & Rhymney Joint line (1886). The next bridge the boat passes through is Dynevor bridge, named after the nearby boatmen's and colliers' pub.

Troedyrhiw

The Four-Mile level looks down on the mining community of Troedyrhiw. A great engine house stands below the canal. This houses the canal company's Pontyrhun engine, a Maudslay steam pump erected 1850-53 to return water to the canal that had passed through the Plymouth works.

TROEDYRHIW to ABERFAN

Leaving Pontyrhun, (Troedyrhiw's old name on Ordnance maps), the canal swings round the parish church and crosses Nant Cwm Du. Here, a typical stone bridge of Dadford design conducts the Cwm Du lane over the canal and up a small side valley, leading to Mynydd Cnwc and its old quarries.

A lightly wooded reach of the canal now follows and human habitation is left behind. It is one of the surprises of the Glamorganshire Canal that its route in an industrialised valley can produce pockets of natural beauty like this. The towpath, too, is remarkably lonely. The water through 'Mr Clive's Wood' (as an old *Table of Distances* calls it) is notably shallower than the lengths through Castle colliery and Aberfan, and the few boatmen remaining at work on this Four Mile Pond say the going is very hard for a loaded horse boat. The explanation is that underground mining has not caused this part of the hillside to sink.

Aberfan

The canal emerges from woodland at Nant y Maen bridge and more open fields are a feature of the off bank as the navigation approaches Aberfan. Here the boat makes a wide turn past Ynysygored farm and its old lime kiln. A short distance ahead the GW & Rhymney Joint Railway crosses the canal on its way from Merthyr to Quaker's Yard. Aberfan, a none-too pretty mining village of long terraced streets, now comes into view.

As a settlement, Aberfan hardly existed before 1880. Looking below to the east, the boat crew will see John Nixon's Merthyr Vale colliery. Deep mining for steam coal started here in 1875. Damage to the canal has been considerable since then and the towpath, terraced high on the hillside, is continually sinking. So is the bottom of the canal. The water through Aberfan is now more than 12 feet deep.

On Aberfan's western hillside, the boat passes the fields and old hill farm of Hafod Tanglwys, which survives the urban development. Nearby there are relics of small scale coal mining, all pre-dating modern Aberfan and all served at one time by boats in the coal trade. Moving down the canal past milepost 5, we reach Perthigleision Upper bridge, Aberfan's road crossing of the canal for access to a street named Bryn Taf and to the cemetery. Perthigleision Upper is a flat decked bridge and the best place for reaching the village by road.

Station: Aberfan GW & RR Joint Railway, 300 yds.

The canal continues its progress southwards into open country and passes two ancient farms, Aberfan Fach and Aberfan Fawr, after which the mining village is named. The Four Mile Pond ends at Aberfan Locks, Nos 6 and 7.

Aberfan station, GW & RR Jt line, circa 1905. The view is looking towards Merthyr.
SR collection

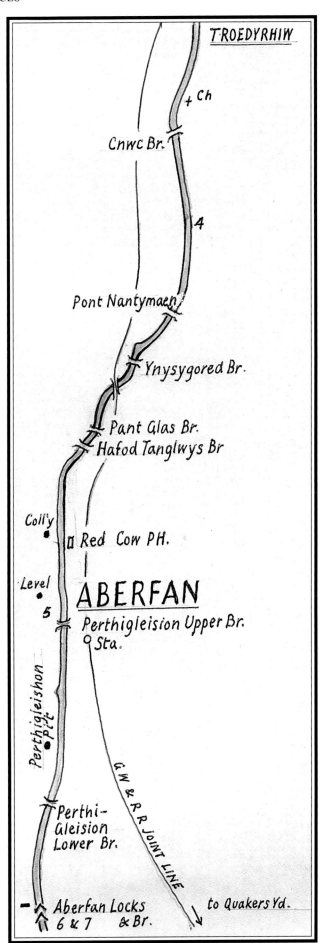

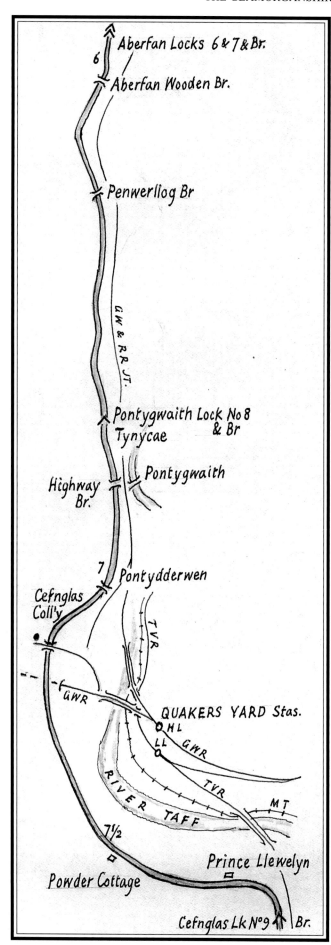

ABERFAN to CEFNGLAS

Aberfan Locks form a two-rise staircase and lower the canal 28ft. The upper lock, No. 6, is remarkably deep at 14ft 6 ins and claims to have the greatest fall on any narrow canal in Britain. The spring here is a useful fresh water source for the boatmen, whilst below the locks, the quiet sheltered bend on the navigation is a favourite overnight mooring for them. The tumbled rocks lying in the beechwoods above the canal are evidence of a landslip here in past geological time. Thomas Dadford had to cut through rock along these slopes and revetment walls were needed to support the towpath.

High to the west of the canal but invisible from the boat, the land rises to a rocky sandstone ridge on Cefn y Fan. The watershed of this mountain, which divides the Taff and Cynon Valleys, rises to over 1,300 feet on a featureless moorland summit called Twyn Brynbychan.

The canal, still lying at 500 feet above sea level, passes under Aberfan iron bridge in wooded surroundings and continues southwards on its hillside ledge past an old quarry, quite possibly one of those opened by Dadford for constructing the canal in 1790.

Pontygwaith

Light woodland contributes to a sylvan approach to Pontygwaith Lock, one of those without the attendance of a lock keeper. The canal bridge (Highway bridge) is at Tair Gefail and carries a lane linking Cefn Glas farm to the Merthyr-Cardiff turnpike road. The lane crosses the Taff over an attractive stone arch (Pont-y-gwaith), which is a reminder of the William Edwards bridge at Pontypridd. The little settlement of Pontygwaith is named after an ancient iron smelting site. The narrow valley brings the canal, River Taff, two railways and the Merthyr Tramroad close together here but in spite of this the traveller by canal boat on this hillside experiences a feeling of complete isolation.

Cefnglas

As the boat moves south towards Cefn Glas, the view to the east is remarkable for its natural beauty, a combination of a deep valley, quite extensive woodland and the River Taff rushing over rocks below. By contrast, on the canal's western side, the slopes of Cefn Glas are high, stone walled and covered in bracken. It is at this point, on a wide sweep of the Cefn Glas hillside, that Thomas Dadford's canal-building technique makes its clear mark against nearly a mile of moorland landscape. The scene is exactly as Dadford's navigators completed it in the 1790s. Only the workings of the little Cefnglas colliery are a new element.

There is more to see from the boat on this wide open, elevated pound but the steerer should be warned that the wind can sometimes be troublesome. In these conditions a boat can easily be driven into the bank as the water surface is whipped into waves. Across the valley is an extensive view. No less than three railway viaducts cross the river to and from the stations at Quakers Yard and the path of the Merthyr Tramroad emerges briefly from its tree lined course beside the Taff. As the boat proceeds around the loop there is much evidence of quarrying high to the west of Cefn Glas. A great gap in the skyline is locally called the Giant's Bite.

The valley of the Taff has meanwhile altered dramatically. The river has turned east and begins its deep canyon-like horseshoe around Quakers Yard, from which it finally emerges at Abercynon. For the moment a boat is facing east as it moves past Powder Cottage and reaches the Prince Llewelyn, a long whitened building which is both farm and welcome beer house. The long Cefnglas loop ends at Cefnglas Lock, the single lock at the head of the descent to Abercynon.

CEFNGLAS LOCK to THE BASIN (Abercynon)

Abercynon Sixteen locks

Cefnglas Lock (No. 9) is a single lock which begins the canal's remarkable descent down the hillside through 16 locks to Abercynon. Within one mile, a boat is lowered over 200 feet and a crew can reckon on 2 hours lock work to pass down to Lock Isaf (No. 24) at Abercynon. The locks are in a group of five at Goitre Coed and a concentration of 11 at Abercynon. All the locks, except Nos. 9 and 24, are grouped as staircase pairs.

At Cefnglas Lock, a lane from Goitre Coed farm crosses the canal and leads steeply down to the main road village of Quaker's Yard which lies in the valley bottom ($^1/_2$ mile.) The canal meanwhile by-passes the River Taff's loop, turns from east to south and passes over a low point in the Cefn Glas ridge, the towpath being heavily supported by stone walling as it rounds the much quarried hillside. Fifty feet below the canal, in a deep rock cutting, the Taff Vale Railway prepares to descend to Abercynon by its own incline (originally rope operated). This windswept hill slope of the Five Locks is still marked 'Incline Top' on OS maps of the district.

As the boat is lowered through Locks 12 and 13, a long narrow rectangle of land is seen to the east of the towpath. This strip, which continues well beyond the locks, is all that remains of Dadford's water-saving Cefnglas side ponds, mentioned in the engineer's 1791 report to the GCC. The navigation, now on a brief half mile level between locks, loops westwards and views unfold across the valley towards the parish of Llanfabon. A canal pub, the Royal Oak, soon appears along the towpath to provide a welcome break for boatmen about to face the rigours of the next 11 locks. Passing under Pont Haiarn (the 'Iron Bridge') where the canal side becomes more populous, the boat turns through the next bend and enters the top lock of the 11 lock flight.

Aberdare Canal Junction

At the exit from the tail of Lock 17, the canal enters a wide pool at the junction with the Aberdare Canal (right). A small canal community survives here, based on a dry dock, the lock cottage and a pub (now closed) called The Prince.

More hard work lies ahead as the boat begins to lock steeply down through the next three sets of staircase pairs. The average fall of each of them is around 26ft and the depth of their intermediate gate seems enormous, as the boat sinks down between the dark dripping walls. Crew members working with the windlass to raise the paddles, may have time to take in the view down the widening valley, where the new Dowlais colliery is prominent.

Note, on the way down the lock flight, the short arm of the canal going off to the left to the Mason's Yard, where stone is dressed for GCC repairs to locks and bridges. This was also the entry point of the short-lived 'new' or upper feeder conducted along the hillside from Quaker's Yard. The names of the locks here – Lock Odyn Galch and Lock Stackhouse – refer to a lime kiln and lime storehouse which stood by the mason's yard.

The canal reaches the bottom of the lock flight at Lock Isaf, Abercynon.

Abercynon

The Dowlais colliery went into production here in 1896 and is the reason for the phenomenal growth of this new mining settlement. Most of Abercynon lies to the west of the canal but new houses are being built on both sides of the lock flight. The GCC runs regular goods boats from Cardiff to Abercynon and unloading is done into a warehouse on Lock Isaf. A boat crew will find the main shopping street of Abercynon across the River Cynon from Lock Isaf.

Station: TVR with trains to Cardiff, Merthyr and Aberdare.

Owing to engineering problems, the Glamorganshire Canal between Merthyr and Abercynon was closed to all traffic on 6 December 1898. For similar reasons the Aberdare Canal was closed in 1900. Since 1900, the closing of these two sections of canal has caused Abercynon to be the new head of navigation.

The Basin

At the bottom of the 'Elevens', the canal turns sharply south-east to pass under the TVR incline and cross the aqueduct over the Taff, which it

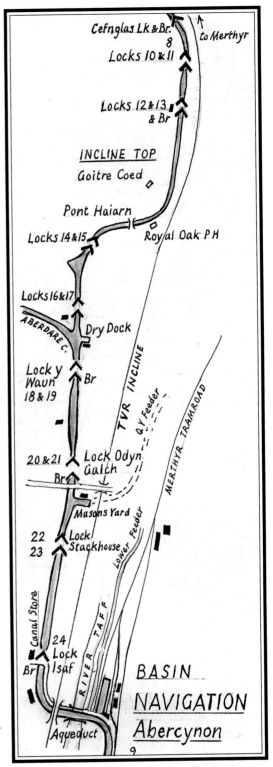

shares with the Aberdare turnpike road. On the east side of the river, the lower feeder enters the canal and immediately the old whitewashed cottages, stables and warehouses around the disused canal and tramroad Basin are briefly passed on the left. Only the base of a crane remains on the exchange wharf as a reminder of the Dowlais, Penydarren and Plymouth iron trade. Opposite the entrance to the Basin was Thomas Powell's wharf and coal tip, which was served by a branch of the Llanfabon Tramroad that once crossed the canal here, possibly by a drawbridge.

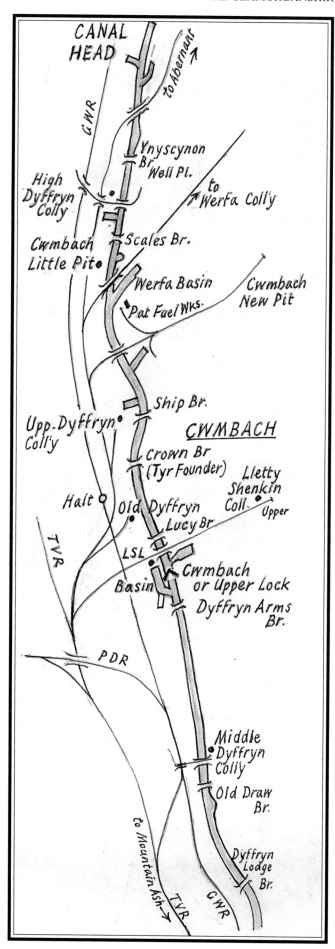

THE ABERDARE CANAL
ABERDARE to CWMBACH
1898

Canal Head

The Aberdare Canal begins alongside a series of wharves at Canal Head, where iron brought by tramroad from the furnaces of Hirwaun, Llwydcoed and Abernant was loaded into boats for shipment to Cardiff. Canal Head lies in a broad alluvial plain in the Cynon Valley, 1/2 mile below the town of Aberdare (pop. near to 45,000). The once busy yards present a general aspect of decay although the GCC goods boats still call at the Wharf regularly, carrying grain, flour and groceries up from Cardiff.

A feeder enters the canal here, conveying water off the River Cynon. For the whole of the 6 1/2 miles to the junction with the Glamorganshire Canal, the Aberdare towpath is on the outer slope of the hillside.

A boat crew starting from here will not find the going easy or entirely agreeable. The towpath is in some places under two feet of water due to underground mining and it would be difficult to find any canal more intensively exploited in the past by the coal industry – at least as far as Mountain Ash (3 1/2 miles). For this reason, cruising for pleasure on the Aberdare Canal is uncommon, except when local Sunday schools hire a boatman for an annual picnic outing in a canal boat.

As the boat moves from its moorings the first evidence of the Aberdare coal industry is seen on the south side of Canal Head. This is the private dock where, until recently, coal was brought across the valley by tramroad from Blaengwawr colliery, for loading into boats.

Cwmbach

At Cwmbach, where steam coal was first raised in 1837, a succession of canal, railway and tramway bridges cross the canal as it passes through a landscape of abandoned collieries, rows of colliers' cottages and banks of pit waste. One of the rows, Scale's Row, includes a canalside pub – the Scale's Arms.

Cwmbach Lock, called Upper Lock (1 mile) lowers the canal 9ft 3in. Nearby is the Lletty Shenkin colliery and the canal co's steam pump, which in recent years supplied water to the canal from the River Cynon. The village, still redolent of early mining, is left behind and the valley narrows.

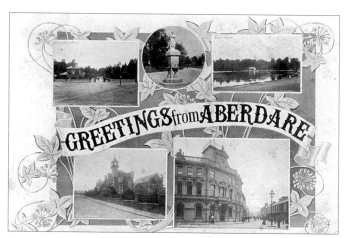

'Greetings from Aberdare' on an early 20th century picture postcard by Harris & Son of Merthyr, with views of the park, county school and Canon Street. Neil Parkhouse collection

DYFFRYN HOUSE to ABERCYNON

Mountain Ash

The canal approaches Mountain Ash around a wide curve, embracing the Dyffryn estate. Dyffryn House (left), prominent in parkland, was the country seat and birthplace of H.A. Bruce, barrister, MP for Merthyr, and better known as Home Secretary and later Baron Aberdare of Dyffryn.

A side valley, Cwm Pennar, opens to the north and the canal crosses its stream, Nant Pennar, over a minor aqueduct. Just ahead, Dyffryn Lock comes into view. It is quite shallow and lowers the boat a mere 3ft 10in to the canal's bottom level. The peace of this rural enclave is rudely shattered by the beat of Deep Dyffryn colliery's winding engines, which send alternate plumes of steam skywards. Now terraced on a right hand bend, the canal squeezes between railway, colliery and river, and soon reaches the stone-arched Ffrwd bridge, the central canal bridge in Mountain Ash (3½ miles). This Urban District is the largest intermediate mining settlement in the Cynon Valley and is divided into two halves by the river.
Stations: GWR to Pontypool Road and Neath. TVR to Abercynon and Cardiff.

Nixon's Navigation and Newtown

Leaving the canal wharf and warehouse (Ffrwd Crescent) the boat crew will see the River Cynon again as progress is made down the valley in a south-easterly direction, the river dropping rapidly towards Abercynon and leaving the canal on a high shelf on the hillside. Cresselly bridge, the next one below Mountain Ash, brings another colliery into view. This important pit, Nixon's Navigation, started production in 1860 and completely fills the valley floor. It was a canal freighter until a few years ago, with coal and pitwood wharves, a canal-served limekiln and a private dock.

Boatmen, or at least the boathorse, will need to take to the water again at Newtown, where the Collier's Arms bridge towpath has disappeared below the surface thanks to Nixon's activities. The watery experience has earned for the bridge the boatmen's name of 'Breeches and Leggins bridge'.

Penrhiwceiber

The traveller by canal will look with relief at the pretty half mile of wooded slope bordering the off side of the waterway on its way past Penrhiwceiber. By contrast, Cwmcynon colliery, passed on the towpath side, is the last major colliery to come into view. The boat now steers through the railway bridge of the GWR Vale of Neath line, which is turning eastwards to enter Cefn Glas tunnel on its way to Quaker's Yard. The canal meanwhile gently winds its quiet way into open country.

The high moorland shoulder of Cefn Glas now takes a hand in dictating the canal engineering and a long straight cut terraces the waterway along its final mile, with the off side rising steeply to quarries above the 700ft contour at Daren y Celyn.

When the wind is from the south-west, steering a boat away from the bank on such an elevated and exposed position can be a tricky experience.

Aberdare Canal Junction

The canal narrows past the site of the Aberdare Canal's stop lock and joins the Glamorganshire Canal (6½ miles) at a wide pool at the tail of Lock 17. A pub, the Prince, on the Aberdare towpath, presides over the small canal community, which includes a lock cottage and a dry dock.

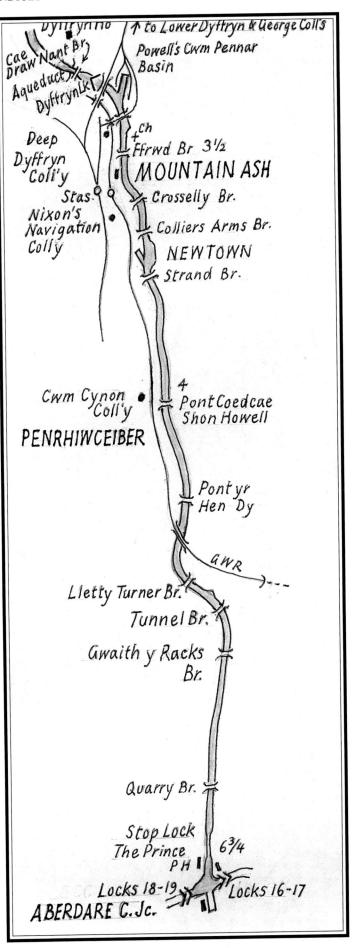

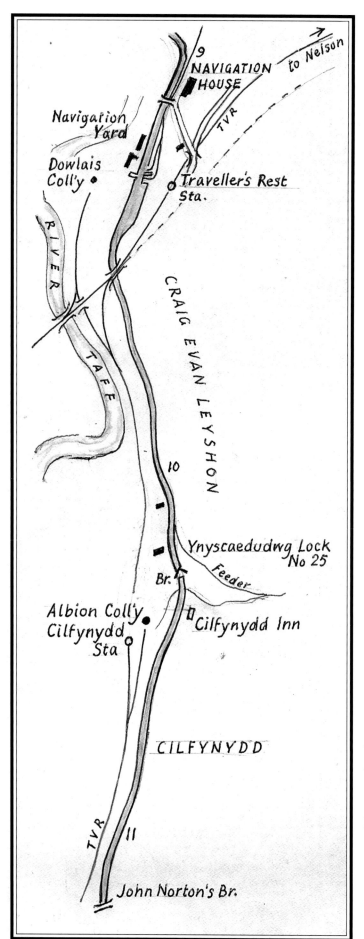

THE GLAMORGANSHIRE CANAL NAVIGATION HOUSE to CILFYNYDD 1914

The boat passage to Ynysangharad and then on to Cardiff (see Volume 2) now continues with a description of how the canal looked to a boat crew in 1914.

Continuing its straight course southwestwards, the canal passes the remains of more tramroad-connected wharves and a basin, all overlooked from the east by the huge mass of moorland called Craig Evan Leyshon. The wharves are followed by a flat area of marshland, once a wide basin or reservoir, which boatmen called the Llyn.

The old canal workshops at Navigation Yard, now out of use, are seen on the towpath side. They adjoin the pitwood yards of the extensive Dowlais Cardiff colliery (1896), whose steam engine houses dominate the view to the west.

Straightness is not a characteristic of the Glamorganshire Canal and as the boat turns under the Llancaiach branch railway bridge at Ynysydwr, a gently winding contour course is resumed. The canal now follows the rather barren and featureless lower slopes of Cilfynydd Common, with only the occasional sheep for company. The Taff has meanwhile emerged from its shallow canyon at Abercynon into a broad flood plain, until it is confined again at Craig yr Esg. The scenery across the valley to the west is attractively wooded especially where the rocky Nant Clydach, tumbling down from Ynysybwl, leaves its valley to join the Taff.

Turnpike road and canal now keep close company as the crew steer for the entrance to the single lock at Cilfynydd.

Cilfynydd

The lock is called Ynyscaedudwg, after a farm in the fields below the canal which was lost in the 1880s, when it became the site of Albion colliery, a development that caused the mushroom growth of Cilfynydd in the rush for Welsh steam coal. The boat crew sees little of this long linear village, which is higher on the hillside behind stone walls but from time to time the Pontypridd UDC trams make themselves heard. The canal is conducted along a precipitous hill slope and is here at its most gravity-defying. This does not ease until the navigation reaches John Norton's bridge (Pont Shon Norton), 11 miles.

As proof of the rural nature of much of the route of the canal, this was the boatman's view across the Taff Valley, taken from where it ran along the lower slope of Craig Evan Leyshon. SR collection

COEDPENMAEN to YNYSANGHARAD

Coedpenmaen

Intermittent terraces of houses, linear street patterns and pockets of quarrying are the hallmarks of the Pontypridd canal scene, as the urban way ahead runs through Coedpenmaen, a northern suburb. Early 19th century artists and writers hurried here to celebrate the beauty of the nearby Berw waterfalls on the Taff. Across to the west of the canal, the rocky woodland hill of Craig yr Esg still dominates.

Pontypridd

The Newbridge Arms pub looks on to a 'wide' in the canal as it begins its descent through a deep staircase pair of locks to Trallwn wharf. (12miles) The Queen's Hotel is nearby.

The upper wharf serves a cornstores (1850) and a branch canal runs to the East Street bakery of Hopkin Morgan, the mainstay of the GCC's carrying trade.

The single lock at Trallwn (No. 30) leads down to the GCC's wharf, stores and yard, where their horse drays deliver to all parts of the town.

Pontypridd, a busy market town, lies across the Taff to the west, at the confluence of the Rivers Taff and Rhondda. Its industries are coal mining and engineering. In the past, access to the town was over the beautiful stone bridge built (too steep for vehicles) by William Edwards in 1755. Its effect is marred by the modern flat bridge built alongside it in 1856. To view the Old Bridge, arrange to leave the boat at the wharf and walk down Llanover Street (right). The main shopping street of Pontypridd – Taff Street – lies on the other side of the bridge.

Ynysangharad

Beyond Trallwn wharf the navigation curves away to the south and east, running parallel with the Berw feeder. The deep staircase locks at Ynysangharad lower the canal 20ft 5in and stand alongside the famous Newbridge Chain & Anchor works established by Samuel Brown in 1818. One or two boats can usually be seen in the lower basin, loading chain and shackles for carriage to Cardiff.

William Edwards' graceful arch, Pont-y-ty-pridd, circa 1860.
From Mr and Mrs Hall's
The Book of South Wales, the Wye and the Coast.

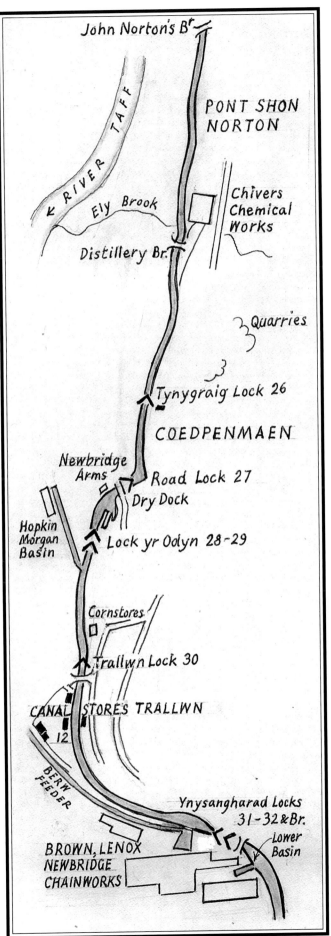

John Norton's Br

PONT SHON NORTON

RIVER TAFF

Ely Brook

Chivers Chemical Works

Distillery Br.

Quarries

Tynygraig Lock 26

COEDPENMAEN

Newbridge Arms

Road Lock 27

Dry Dock

Hopkin Morgan Basin

Lock yr Odyn 28-29

Cornstores

Trallwn Lock 30

CANAL STORES TRALLWN

12

BERW FEEDER

Ynysangharad Locks 31-32 & Br.

Lower Basin

BROWN, LENOX NEWBRIDGE CHAINWORKS

Appendix C
LOCKS AND LEVELS

Glamorganshire Canal Lock Dimensions from Board of Trade Returns 1888

NO.	NAME	LENGTH	WIDTH	DEPTH ON CILL	FALL	TOTAL FALL (from Cyfarthfa)
1	Lock 1	67ft 0in	9ft 3in	3ft 6in	12ft 0in	12ft 0in
2	Middle	65ft 0in	9ft 6in	4ft 6in	6ft 10in	18ft 10in
3	Parliament	65ft 3in	9ft 8in	4ft 6in	7ft 10in	26ft 8in
4-5	Glyndyrus	66ft 2in	10ft 0in	3ft 9in	8ft 9in	35ft 5in
		66ft 6in	9ft 10in	3ft 10in	7ft 10in	43ft 3in
6-7	Aberfan	65ft 6in	9ft 10in	3ft 6in	14ft 6in	57ft 9in
		65ft 6in	10ft 2in	4ft 0in	13ft 6in	71ft 3in
8	Pontygwaith	65ft 3in	9ft 10in	4ft 0in	12ft 0in	83ft 3in
9	Cefn Glas	65ft 4in	9ft 7in	3ft 9in	13ft 3in	96ft 6in
10-11		67ft 0in	9ft 9in	3ft 8in	13ft 2in	109ft 8in
		65ft 0in	9ft 9in	3ft 8in	12ft 9in	122ft 5in
12-13		66ft 0in	9ft 9in	3ft 4in	13ft 0in	135ft 5in
		65ft 6in	9ft 9in	3ft 8in	12ft 9in	148ft 2in
14-15		66ft 0in	9ft 6in	3ft 8in	13ft 6in	161ft 8in
		66ft 0in	9ft 4in	4ft 2in	12ft 8in	174ft 4in
16-17		66ft 6in	9ft 8in	4ft 3in	13ft 2in	187ft 6in
		65ft 3in	10ft 0in	4ft 6in	11ft 9in	199ft 3in
18-19	Lock y Waun	66ft 3in	9ft 6in	4ft 4in	13ft 9in	213ft 0in
		66ft 0in	9ft 8in	4ft 4in	13ft 6in	226ft 6in
20-21	Lock Odyn galch	65ft 0in	10ft 5in	4ft 6in	12ft 2in	238ft 8in
		66ft 0in	10ft 8in	3ft 6in	12ft 10in	251ft 6in
22-23	Lock Stackhouse	66ft 10in	9ft 9in	4ft 6in	12ft 6in	264ft 0in
		65ft 0in	9ft 9in	3ft 8in	13ft 6in	277ft 6in
24	Lock Isaf	66ft 6in	9ft 9in	4ft 4in	12ft 8in	290ft 2in
25	Ynyscaedudwg	66ft 0in	9ft 9in	4ft 0in	12ft 0in	302ft 2in
26	Tynygraig	67ft 0in	9ft 9in	4ft 0in	11ft 9in	313ft 11in
27	Road	66ft 0in	9ft 10in	4ft 0in	12ft 0in	325ft 11in
28-29	Lock yr Odyn	65ft 9in	9ft 6in	3ft 6in	12ft 6in	338ft 5in
		65ft 9in	10ft 2in	3ft 9in	11ft 6in	349ft 11in
30	Trallwn	66ft 9in	9ft 9in	3ft 2in	11ft 9in	361ft 8in
31-32	Ynysangharad	66ft 0in	10ft 0in	3ft 4in	10ft 11in	372ft 7in
		66ft 0in	10ft 0in	3ft 3in	9ft 6in	382ft 1in
33	Dyffryn	65ft 0in	9ft 9in	3ft 8in	10ft 4in	392ft 5in
34	Dynea	65ft 9in	9ft 9in	4ft 3in	10ft 0in	402ft 5in
35-37	Treble	66ft 0in	10ft 0in	6ft 0in	9ft 6in	411ft 11in
		66ft 0in	10ft 0in	4ft 0in	12ft 2in	424ft 1in
		66ft 0in	10ft 0in	5ft 0in	12ft 0in	436ft 1in
38	Taffs Well	66ft 0in	9ft 8in	4ft 0in	8ft 11in	445ft 0in
39	Cae Glas	65ft 0in	9ft 9in	4ft 0in	9ft 0in	454ft 0in
40	Portobello	65ft 0in	9ft 10in	4ft 0in	8ft 11in	462ft 11in
41	Ton	65ft 6in	9ft 7in	3ft 9in	9ft 0in	471ft 11in
42	Llwynmallt	65ft 6in	9ft 6in	4ft 10in	9ft 2in	481ft 1in
43	Forest	67ft 0in	9ft 0in	4ft 0in	10ft 8in	491ft 9in
44	Melingriffith	66ft 5in	9ft 10in	4ft 0in	9ft 2in	500ft 11in
45	Llandaff	66ft 0in	9ft 8in	4ft 0in	7ft 0in	507ft 11in
46	College	66ft 0in	9ft 8in	4ft 2in	6ft 6in	514ft 5in
47	Gabalfa	66ft 0in	9ft 8in	4ft 6in	7ft 6in	521ft 11in
48	Mynachdy	66ft 0in	9ft 8in	4ft 1in	6ft 10in	528ft 9in
49	North Road	66ft 0in	9ft 5in	4ft 0in	5ft 0in	533ft 9in
50	Crockherbtown	66ft 9in	9ft 3in	5ft 0in	9ft 8in	543ft 5in

Note: The bottom level of the Glamorganshire Canal was the mile-long Sea Lock pound. The Sea Lock pound was held to a height of about 25 feet above OS mean sea level. A new lock (no 51), not included in the BoT 1888 returns, was added during the period of Bute control. It slightly raised the water level between Crockherbtown Lock, the Junction Canal and the West and East Bute docks, so that all were on the same level. The authors have added lock names and the total fall calculation to this table. Linked lock numbers refer to locks built in staircase pairs or (in the case of Locks 35-37) a staircase treble.

Appendix D
LOCKS AND LEVELS
Aberdare Canal Lock Dimensions from Board of Trade Returns 1888

NO.	NAME	LENGTH	WIDTH	DEPTH ON CILL	FALL	TOTAL FALL (from Canal Head)
1	Cwmbach	67ft 0in	9ft 8in	4ft 6in	9ft 3in	9ft 3in
2	Duffryn	67ft 0in	10ft 3in	6ft 6in	3ft 10in	13ft 1in

Note: The depth on cill at Duffryn was altered in red ink from 6ft 6in to 6ft 10in.

Appendix E
GLAMORGANSHIRE CANAL BRIDGES
Cyfarthfa to Ynysangharad

DIST.	NO.	BRIDGE NAME	NOTES
1/4	161B	Cyfarthfa Draw Bridge	c1801 wooden bridge at Cyfarthfa chapel, taking tramroad from Ynysfach casting houses to Cyfarthfa rolling mills and from the Red Ore wharf to Ynysfach.
	161A	Pont Storehouse: Bethesda Street Bridge	1792 stone bridge below Lock 1 carrying towpath from left to right bank and taking main parish road from Swansea to Jackson's bridge across river.
1/2	163	Middle Lock Bridge	1792 stone bridge below Lock 2, Penry Street, carrying towpath from right to left bank and taking road to Ynysgau iron bridge across river.
			Timber planking towpath bridge across dock at Parliament Lock.
	300	Parliament Lock Bridge	1792 stone locktail bridge at Lock 3. Adapted c1801 as cinder tramroad bridge.
	294	TVR Ynysfach Branch Railway Bridge	Built under TVR Act 1882.
			Pre 1814 accommodation bridge to Ynysfach cinder tramroad and tips .
	295	Ynysfach Bridge	Pre 1811 stone accommodation bridge to Ynysfach cinder tips, crossing tramroad by a second smaller arch.
			Pre 1814 accommodation bridge to Ynysfach cinder tramroad and tips .
	254	Rhydycar Foot Bridge	Pre 1814 wooden bridge for track leading from Lower Wern farm to river ford and stepping stones. The track between canal and river was later diverted by tipping from Ynysfach.
1 1/4	250	Rhydycar Iron Bridge	Iron bridge at Rhydycar farm taking parish road to the river ford. The bridge is now preserved and re-erected at Chapel Row, Cyfarthfa. It replaced a pre-1809 scaffold bridge.
	251	Brecon & Merthyr Railway Bridge	1866 B&MR lattice girder bridge.
	252	Vale of Neath Railway Bridge	1851 elliptical stone arch. Extant.
1 1/2	135	Glyndyrus Lock Bridge	1792 stone lock-tail bridge at Locks 4 and 5. It once had a second arch leading to a private boat house or store.
	282	Quay Row Iron Bridge	c1850 iron bridge leading from Upper Abercanaid to the Plymouth Dock.
2	283		1849 iron towpath bridge across entrance to the Plymouth Dock.
	284	Pont Racks	1841 wooden tramroad bridge from Waunwyllt colliery.
	285	Pen yr Hen Tai Bridge	1792 accommodation bridge to Abercanaid Farm.
	12	Graig Bridge; Capel yr Graig Bridge	1792 wooden bridge from Thomas Key's coal level. Perpetuated to take road to Graig farm and Waunwyllt farm and later Graig Chapel. Renewed as an iron bridge c1850.
2 1/4	11	Gethin Upper Bridge; Llwyn yr Eos Bridge	Pre 1814 accommodation bridge. Later gave access to the Graig Pit from Abercanaid and the Llwyn yr Eos public house.
2 1/2	9	Gethin Lower Bridge; Gethin Farm Bridge	1792 wooden bridge giving access to Gethin farm and later from Newton Street, Abercanaid to the Gethin Arms.
	8	Gethin Incline Bridge	1849 tramway bridge to connect Gethin No 2 Pit with the Gethin No 1 and its basin on the canal. Said to have incorporated tipping mechanism to allow boats to be loaded directly from the bridge.
2 3/4			Footbridge near pond keeper's house.
3	273	Ashroad Bridge; Penrhiw yr Onen Bridge	1792 stone bridge taking road from Ashroad to the old Troedyrhiw furnace on the river bank.
	272	Dynevor Arms Bridge	1792 stone bridge taking parish road from farms on the hillside to the river bridge at Pontyrhun.
3 3/4	271	Cnwc Bridge; Cwm Du Bridge; Owen's Bridge	1792 stone bridge to take the Cwmdu valley road to the river. Just downstream from Cwm Du limekiln.
4 1/4	21	Nantmaen Bridge	1792 stone accommodation bridge from Nant y Maen farm.
4 1/2	22	Ynysygored Bridge	1792 stone bridge at Ynysygored farm, just downstream from the winding hole for boats delivering limestone to the kiln there.
	23	Ynysygored Railway Bridge	1884 GW&RR girder bridge.

DIST.	NO.	BRIDGE NAME	NOTES
	17	White Bridge	[*This bridge actually post-dates the canal's closure*] 1914 Warren girder bridge to take tramway from Nixon's Navigation colliery at Merthyr Vale to waste tips above Aberfan.
	24	Pantglas Bridge	Pre 1814 wooden footbridge.
	25	Hafod Tanglwys Bridge	1792 wooden accommodation bridge to Hafod Tanglwys Uchaf farm and Hafod Tanglwys Isaf farm, renewed as a cast iron bridge c1850.
5	20	Perthigleision Upper Bridge	Pre 1814 wooden bridge providing access to Perthygleision farm from limekiln on towpath. Also taking road from Perthygleision colliery (pre 1830). Located at the southern entrance to the later Aberfan Cemetery.
	26	Perthigleision Lower Bridge	1792 stone road bridge taking road from Perthigleision farm.
	27	Aberfan Lock Bridge	1792 stone lock-tail bridge at Locks 6 and 7, to take track from lock house to Aberfan Fawr farm.
5¾	28	Aberfan Wooden Bridge	1792 wooden accommodation bridge, later giving access to the quarries south. Swivel bridge 1809. Described as iron bridge 1890s.
		Penwerllog Bridge	1792 accommodation bridge.
6½	234	Tyn y Cae Lock Bridge	1792 stone lock-tail bridge at Lock 8.
	232	Highway Bridge; Tair Gefail Bridge	1792 stone road bridge taking parish road to the river bridge, Pontygwaith.
7	233	Pont y Dderwen; Pontcaederwyn Bridge	1792 stone accommodation bridge from Cefn Glas. Extant.
		Cefn Glas Colliery Bridge	Post 1836 tramway bridge from colliery.
		Cefn Glas Lock Bridge	1792 bridge below Lock 9, providing access from Cefn Glas and Goitre Coed to Quaker's Yard.
		Lock 13 Bridge	1792 bridge below Locks 12 and 13 providing access from lock house and Goitre Coed to Abermafon (Fiddler's Elbow).
		Pont Haiarn	Pre 1814 iron bridge providing access from Goitre Coed to towpath and later Royal Oak public house.
			Towpath bridge across entrance to boat dock at Aberdare Canal Junction (below lock 17).
		Lock y Waun Bridge	1812 stone bridge below Lock 19 carrying the Aberdare Canal towpath to join the Glamorganshire Canal towpath.
8¾		Lock y Odyn Bridge	1792 stone bridge below Lock 21 taking the original route of the parish road from Aberdare to the Cardiff-Merthyr road. From 1798 it also carried the towpath from the left bank to the right bank of the canal. This became necessary when the upper feeder was built to enter the canal at this point.
		Lock Stackhouse Bridge	1798 stone bridge below Lock 23 carrying the towpath from the right bank to the left bank of the canal.
		Lock Isaf Bridge	Stone road bridge below Lock 24 taking the Aberdare turnpike road across the canal to join the towpath prior to sharing the river crossing on the aqueduct.
		Taff Vale Railway Bridge	1840 TVR bridge
		The Aqueduct	1792 taking the canal, towpath and (from 1809) the Aberdare turnpike across the River Taff.
			1792 towpath bridge across entry of feeder at the Basin. From 1809 it also carried the Aberdare turnpike.
			1802 towpath bridge across entrance to Merthyr Tramroad Company's Basin at Navigation. From 1809 it also carried the Aberdare turnpike.
		Llanfabon Tramroad Bridge	1819 wooden tramroad bridge to take Sir William Smith's Llanfabon tramroad to its terminus at the tipping wharves on the opposite bank to the towpath. This is likely to have been a drawbridge – as was the crossing over the Merthyr Tramroad.
9		Navigation Yard Bridge; Navigation House Bridge; Shepherd's Bridge	1792 stone turnover bridge to take the towpath from left to right bank of the canal. The bridge was extended c1809 to incorporate a second arch across the Merthyr Tramroad extension to its coal shipping basin where the Llanfabon tramroad also originally ran.
9¼			Towpath bridge across boat dock at Navigation Yard next to the trunk.
		Taff Vale Railway Llancaiach Branch Bridge	1841 timber railway viaduct.
		Ynyscaedudwg Lock Bridge	1792 stone bridge below Lock 25, taking the road from Ynyscaedudwg farm to the Merthyr-Cardiff turnpike.
			1792 aqueduct across the Caedudwg brook.
11¼		Pont-shon-norton; John Norton's Bridge	1792 stone road bridge taking the original Cardiff road across the canal to Coedpenmaen.
		Glan Ely Bridge; Chemical Works Bridge; Distillery Bridge	1810 bridge from towpath to Glanely house and, later, the Royal Oak public house on the turnpike, near the later Pontypridd chemical works.
		Tynygraig Lock Bridge	c1900 footbridge below Lock 26.
11¾		Road Lock Bridge	1792 stone road bridge below Lock 27 taking the original turnpike back across the towpath and canal from right to left bank, near the Newbridge Arms.
			c1825 towpath bridge across entrance to Coedpenmaen foundry basin, later Hopkin Morgan bakery basin.
12		Trallwn Bridge; Cornstores Bridge	1792 stone road bridge below Lock 30 at foot of Cornstores Hill, Trallwn.
			1806 towpath bridge across entrance to upper basin at Brown Lenox chainworks.
12¼		Ynysangharad Bridge	1792 stone bridge below Locks 31 and 32, connecting lock house with towpath. Also carried the connecting road from the old turnpike to the chainworks entrance.
			1806 towpath bridge across entrance to lower basin at Brown Lenox chainworks.

Note: No. column is as numbered in W.L. Davies *The Bridges of Merthyr Tydfil*, Cardiff 1992. The GCC did not number their bridges.

Scales bridge, at Cwmbach on the abandoned Aberdare Canal, circa 1925.
Courtesy Aberdare Library

Appendix F
ABERDARE CANAL BRIDGES
Canal Head to Junction with Glamorganshire Canal

NO.	BRIDGE NAME	NOTES
		1844 towpath bridge over entrance to Blaengwawr colliery's dock at Canal Head.
		1851 Abernant Rly (Aberdare Iron Co) skew bridge. Cast and wrought iron encased in concrete. Extant.
1	Ynyscynon Bridge	1812 footbridge from towpath to turnpike and Ynyscynon farm (Well Place).
		Tramway from David Williams' High Dyffryn colliery (1844) (S) to tipping area on N bank.
		Towpath bridge over entrance to High Duffryn colliery's dock at pit head.
2	Scales Bridge	1812 stone road bridge. Located between High Dyffryn colliery (S) and Cwmbach Little Pit (S), from later Scales Row and public house (S) to Timothy Row (N) and the Aberdare to Cwmbach road.
		1851 tramway from John Nixon's Wyrfa colliery (1844) (N) to TVR.
		Towpath bridge across entrance to Aberdare Coal Co dock.
		Canal aqueduct/culvert.
3		1812 (improved 1841) road bridge below Aberdare Coal Co culvert, from towpath to Thomas Morgan David's farm and site of later Collier's Arms.
		1851 tramway from Aberdare Coal Company's Cwmbach New colliery, Thomas Wayne's Abernant y Groes colliery (1837) (N) to TVR.
		Towpath bridge over entrance to basin at Upper Duffryn colliery (1843).
4	Cwmbach Bridge	1812 road bridge from towpath to turnpike and Abernant y Groes (Cwmbach) at later site of Upper Duffryn colliery and near Ship and Castle Inn.
5	Tir y Founder Bridge; Crown Bridge	1812 stone road bridge from towpath between T. Powell's Upper Dyffryn colliery (1843) (S) and T. Powell's Old Dyffryn colliery (1840) (S) to turnpike at Tir y Founder, near Crown Inn.
		Towpath bridge across dock at Old Dyffryn colliery.
		Towpath bridge across second dock at Old Dyffryn colliery.
		Road bridge from towpath between canal company's pumping engine and Lletty Shenkin Lower colliery (S) to Lucy Row and Tir Founder Road.
		1851 tramway from W. Thomas' Lletty Shenkin Upper colliery (1843) (N) to tipping wharf with TVR at Lletty Shenkin Lower colliery.
6	Duffryn Tir y Founder Bridge	1812 accommodation bridge just below Upper Lock, from W. Thomas' Lletty Shenkin Lower colliery (1843) basin (S) and towpath, later leading to the Duffryn Arms public house and Tir Founder Road.
		1843 towpath bridge over entrance to Lletty Shenkin Lower colliery basin.
		Tramway from T. Powell's Middle Dyffryn colliery (1850) (N) to both TVR and West Midland Railway.
	Old Draw Bridge	1837 tramway wooden drawbridge from towpath to Bruce's Duffryn colliery (N).
		Towpath bridge over weir to River Cynon above Duffryn Bridge. This major overflow was necessary to release the waters from the slopes of Craig y Dyffryn.
7	Duffryn Bridge	1812 road from Abercwmboy (and Bont Ddu across the River Cynon) to the Duffryn estate (N) and Cwmpennar.
		Canal aqueduct/culvert for Nant Pennar.
8	Cae Draw Nant Bridge	1812 accommodation bridge from Abercwmboy Isha to Duffryn estate at point where Nant Pennar was crossed by the canal.
		Towpath bridge across entrance to Thomas Powell's coal dock.
		Just below Dyffryn Lock. 1853 tramway from T. Powell's Lower Dyffryn (George), or Cwm Pennar, colliery (1850) (N) to TVR.
		c1855 tramway from David Williams' Deep Dyffryn colliery (1850) (S) to waste tip and quarry.

NO.	BRIDGE NAME	NOTES
9	Ffrwd Bridge	1812 stone road bridge, Mountain Ash. The primary road, past St Margaret's church (N), connecting Aberffrwd with Aberdare turnpike.
10	Troed y Rhiw Forest Bridge; Creselly Arms Bridge	From turnpike to Navigation Villa (N), Troed y Rhiw House, and Fforest Lodge.
		Tramway from Navigation colliery (S) to quarry (N). Post-dates the canal.
11	Collier's Arms Bridge; Cat Bridge; 'Breeches and Leggins' Bridge	1812 stone bridge. From turnpike to Fforest Level and Colliers Arms (N).
		Towpath bridge over entrance to dock near limekiln above Strand bridge.
12	David John Rees's Bridge; Strand Bridge; Newtown Bridge	1812 stone bridge, Newtown. Road from limekiln on towpath (S) to Newtown.
13	Pont Coed Cae Shon Howell	1812 bridge opposite Penrhiwceiber. From turnpike and towpath to Coed Fforest Uchaf. Adjacent to Nixon's later Cwmcynon colliery (other side of railway).
		Canal aqueduct/culvert for Nant Dafad.
14	Pont yr Hen Dy; Old House Bridge	1812 bridge from turnpike and towpath to stone wharf and tramway from quarry. Adjacent to later GWR Penrhiwceiber station.
		1858-64 West Midland Rly.
15		1812 road bridge, from turnpike at Lletty Turner (S) across River Cynon to canal and farm between Fforest Uchaf and Fforest Isaf.
16	Tunnel Bridge	1812 farm track bridge, from turnpike to a farm (N) in Coed Fforest Uchaf, later covered by West Midland Railway and West Tunnel Cottages (N).
17	Gwaith y Racks iron bridge	1812 road bridge from turnpike to Old Coal Level and smithy (1885 map) on N canal bank (Cefn Glâs).
18		1812 iron foot bridge from turnpike to mountain road to Goetre Coed.

Notes:

1. Towpath was on south (right) bank of canal throughout.

2. (S) and (N) indicate which side of canal the colliery, for example, was situated.

3. The numbers listed in the first column are the sequence numbers of the bridges from the Aberdare end as at building of canal, shown on the unpublished 1814 OS 2in survey. The Aberdare Canal Company did not number their bridges.

Appendix E
CLERKS OF THE GLAMORGANSHIRE CANAL
Until its sale to the Marquess of Bute

Date	Name
1790 – June 1799	John Wood (Cardiff Town Clerk and banker)
June 1799 – June 1801	Patrick Copeland
June 1801 – July 1808 (died in office)	Philip Williams
July 1808 – June 1830	Thomas Reece
June 1830 – Feb 1848 (died in office)	George Forrest (Cyfartha's cashier)
Feb 1848 – June 1851	John Forrest (George's nephew)
June 1851 – June 1885	Thomas Shepherd

INDEX – GENERAL

INDEX – PEOPLE

A visit of industrial archaeologists to the site of the canal at Gethin in the late 1960s was rewarded by the appearance on the towpath of the ghosts of a canal boatman and his horse.
Bob Marrows photo

This book is dedicated with affection to:

Bill Gomer, Boatman and Warehouseman, Rhydyfelin
Harry Watts, Boatman and Lock keeper, Cardiff
Thomas Jones, Boatman, Llandaff
John Close, General Foreman, Gabalfa

who served the Glamorganshire Canal.